TAKING SIDES

Clashing Views on Controversial

Issues in Classroom Management

TAKING SIDES

Clashing Views on Controversial

Issues in Classroom Management

Selected, Edited, and with Introductions by

Tish Holub, Ph.D.
School psychologist, USD 497 Lawrence public schools and adjunct professor, University of Missouri–Kansas City

and

Robert G. Harrington, Ph.D.
Professor, department of psychology and research in education, University of Kansas

McGraw-Hill/Dushkin
A Division of The McGraw-Hill Companies

To my four wonderful children Laura, Anna, Kelly, and Casey, who showed me what great kids are all about; and to my loving wife, Beth, who supports me in everything.
—Bob Harrington

To my loving and humorous husband, John, as well as my father, mother, and sister, who have always been at my side.
—Tish Holub

Photo Acknowledgment
Cover image: Geostock

Cover Acknowledgment
Maggie Lytle

Printed on Recycled Paper

Preface

Classroom management is one of the most controversial areas in education and the main source of stress among educators. The wide array of viewpoints about classroom management is evidenced by its many theories. What is sure is that no classroom-management theory will work all the time with all student misbehavior; a theory will work only when an educator fully understands the intricacies of classroom-management approaches.

There is no better way to tease out these important issues than to frame them in the form of controversial perspectives. Healthy debate forces readers to examine the critical issues and to form their own opinions. Unlike other texts that present one side of an issue, *Taking Sides: Clashing Views on Controversial Issues in Classroom Management* presents two very cogent but very different viewpoints on the same issue in classroom management. It is our hope that after reading and discussing the issues in this volume, you will come away with a better understanding and insight about what it takes to prevent misbehavior, select an appropriate intervention when disruption does occur, and teach new replacement behaviors to students who lack classroom skills.

Taking Sides: Clashing Views on Controversial Issues in Classroom Management is a new edition to the Taking Sides series. We hope that you find our approach to be hopeful and positive. The ultimate goal of good classroom management is to help students become successful learners—not to discipline them. That is why the cover image depicts students positively participating in class. That is our goal. There are many roads to that goal, and the purpose of this text is to investigate the terrain of each of those pathways. We have carefully selected controversies. Some are enduring. Some are current. All are taken from concerns voiced by educators to us. Our goal was to include articles that met the following criteria:

- Articles must address the controversy clearly.
- Articles must clearly take a pro or con position.
- Articles must be recent, preferably after the year 2000.
- Articles must be from reputable journals or other sources.
- Articles must be written by reputable authors.

Educators, you have taught us what is important about classroom management. We hope you find that essential relevance to your work as a classroom manager evidenced in our selections that follow.

Plan of the Book This book includes 21 issues that address areas of active debate in the policy and practice of classroom management. We have grouped the issues into four parts. Each issue is framed as a question and begins with an Introduction, which sets the stage for discussion. Two readings that present YES and NO contrasting points of view come next. Each issue closes with a Postscript, which summarizes the expressed points of view, suggests other points of view, and provides additional readings on the topic at hand. The Introductions and Postscripts also feature a series of questions to stimulate your thinking as you weigh the topic and its relationship to classroom management.

To expand your thinking, refer to the On the Internet pages that precede each part. These contain a sampling of Internet site addresses (URLs) that present varied points of view as well as links to related sites and bibliographies for further study. The YES and NO positions on every issue express strongly held opinions. You may agree or disagree with the authors, or you may find that your own view lies somewhere in between. You will likely identify additional perspectives as you study the issues more thoroughly. You will certainly find connections between issues. Perhaps class discussion will lead you to formulate a new and completely different response to issue questions. Doubtless, as you continue in your professional and personal life, your ideas will change and develop. What is critical as you read this book is to reflect on positions, options, and emotions, so that you can decide what you think and use your opinion to guide your actions and decisions.

In Part 1, the thematic question concerns whether good classroom management is compatible with good classroom instruction. We believe that this is a major theme in classroom management today. Teachers are concerned that they do not have the necessary time to be good teachers and manage all of the emotional and behavioral needs of their students. They feel pressured to meet the demands of No Child Left Behind legislation and spend class time on traditional teaching rather than dealing with student problems. Some educators believe that the range and severity of student problems have increased. Others believe that families should manage their student's mental health problems at home so that they can get back to teaching.

Teaching has become one of the most stressful professions, and much of that stress is attributed to student misbehavior. Teachers question how to motivate some students and whether they can be taught the academic habits of students who are successful in the current high-stakes testing environment. Students with special needs are included in regular education classrooms by law. What behavior challenges do these students represent? Are educators prepared? One of the biggest problems of student behavior is AD/HD. There are many misconceptions about the origins of AD/HD and how to manage it, including sugar in the diet as a contributing factor. Teachers need to have a better understanding of what causes AD/HD and what instructional and behavioral interventions work in controlling the symptoms.

What are the rights of regular education students? Do students in special education have special rights? Is it fair that students with special needs receive so much of the teacher's attention? These are compelling questions that teachers want answered. As a result of these learning challenges and demands on the teacher's time, some educators, parents, and classmates are becoming increasingly intolerant and feel that spending too much class time with disruptive students and students included with a range of disabilities is not fair to the rest of the class. Should classrooms be more tolerant despite the pressures for student achievement?

In Part 2, we discuss whether teacher management of student misbehavior can be effective. Every teacher wants to know what works and what doesn't work. A perennial problem that all educators seem to face is student disrespect and talking back. Is this learned behavior? Can it be controlled? Is it the teacher's fault for mismanaging the situation by using authoritarian management techniques? Can a teacher help a child learn a replacement skill, like problem solving? Teacher disrespect is a very controversial topic and quite upsetting to most educators.

Positive reinforcement is one of the most often-used strategies to change student behavior. Some authors suggest that positive reinforcement is overused and that it can teach students to over-rely on the teacher. Others state that positive reinforcement must be used to improve student self-concepts as learners. Another strategy that teachers rely on is time-out. Some new schools build time-out areas as part of their architecture. Does time-out work? How should it be used? Are there negative outcomes to guard against?

Many teachers and parents would like to return to the old axiom, "spare the rod and spoil the child," but there are many forms of punishment that have been applied in public schools. To what extent do these techniques work? What are the unintended side effects? Should punishment be banned outright in schools? What harm does it do to student morale and self-concept? Does punishment infringe on a student's right to be treated with dignity?

One theme that emerges consistently is whether classroom-management problems are attributable to a lack of character and virtues that must be taught by parents and schools. One side of the controversy says that character must be taught, and the other side says that schools should stay away from teaching "values"—that this is the domain of parents.

Clearly, teachers are faced with a plethora of classroom-management strategies, each with its own strengths and weaknesses. The basis of good classroom management is problem solving—knowing which technique to apply to each classroom-management problem. There is no simple answer, but Part 2 should assist you in sorting out the issues.

Educators regularly ask whether student problems are due to genetics or home environment. This is the topic of Part 3, where we take a look at the systemic and school-wide factors that can contribute to classroom behavior problems and how to deal with them. Are students disruptive because of school-based bullying, parenting styles, or in-born temperament? If children are "born that way," then teachers wonder if temperament can be managed. If the problem is in the home, teachers question the role of parents in their own child's behavior management. If the problem is bullying, then there is a school-wide problem that needs to be managed. In each instance, systemic intervention and not classroom intervention alone may be needed.

One systemic problem that challenges teachers' management skills is bullying. Bullying takes on many forms, including physical bullying, teasing, sexual bullying, and shunning. Is bullying a natural part of child development? Do students need to get tough? Does some bullying make children more resilient? Is it a normal part of growing up? On the other hand, is bullying hurtful to children and adolescents, and how should it be handled?

Because U.S. public schools educate students from all over the world, there are many cultural differences in behavior and relationships in the classroom. To what extent should teachers have respect for student cultural differences, and to what extent must they insist on everyone following a common code of conduct? Can insensitivity to cultural norms contribute to classroom disruption?

Parents need help with disruptive children and adolescents as much as teachers do. They are not sure how to manage their children's talking back, defiance, and ultimate noncompliance. Many parents are at wit's end. They will report that they have "tried everything, but nothing works." When schools offer parent education programs, many times the very parents who need the most help do not show up for the training. What factors contribute to the success of school-based parent education programs? Is it the role of the schools to provide parent education to needy families?

Some law enforcement officers and school administrators have considered "profiling" students who are apt to commit the most severe classroom misbehaviors. What are the ethical problems associated with identifying the characteristics of "problem" students before they commit an infraction? Are there any benefits to knowing the profile of students who are most apt to be problem students?

Given that schools are getting tough on student misbehavior, what are students' rights? Should there be a balance between the rights of teachers and the rights of students? Students will claim that they have First Amendment rights to wear what they want, to say what they want and to do what they want. Do they? What are the boundaries of student and teacher rights in the classroom? Teachers ask this question frequently and are often confronted by irate parents who say, "You can't treat my child that way." Can they, or can't they? How far can a school go to make a classroom safe?

Most schools today—regardless of whether it is rural or urban—must face the thematic question in Part 4: How should schools respond to severe behavior management challenges? Zero tolerance is one of the controversial approaches to deal with severe behavior management problems. Can zero-tolerance rules be applied fairly? Are they open to interpretation, or should they be applied to all students without regard to circumstances? Should there be a range of consequences depending on the circumstances of the zero-tolerance violation?

Students with oppositional defiant disorder often move to conduct disorders if they have not been managed successfully in the earlier grades. This means that they are now more than just disrespectful and offensive;

they are getting in trouble with the law. High school teachers especially will report that they do not have the time or the training to work with these very challenging students. They will say that if the previous elementary and middle school teachers have not been successful in managing the problem, what are they to do at this late point? What is the role and responsibility of teachers working with students with severe behavior problems? Is it too late to help these students once they get into serious trouble with the law, or do teachers play an integral role in helping these students with conduct disorders stay in school and in reaping the benefits of an education?

There is an increasingly large group of students with mental health problems who come to school and have a right to a public education. In previous years many of these students would have been educated in residential institutions or would have received private mental health services. Some of these students are formally diagnosed, but many are undiagnosed or experience only some of the symptoms necessary for a diagnosis. How can teachers help these students to overcome their mental health challenges to learning? What types of instructional modifications should teachers be expected to make? How can therapeutic teaching be used to support these students on the road to recovery?

Many students are taking prescription medications to help them with their learning difficulties and their mental challenges, including AD/HD, depression, bipolar disorder, and anxiety disorders. What is the role of medication in behavior management? Do educators rely too much on drugs to manage a problem? What is the role of educators in working with doctors and in reporting the effects of medications?

When behaviors rise to the level that class cannot continue, then teachers and administrators may consider suspension or expulsion as an option. Are these effective strategies? When should they be used? Are these strategies used to get rid of tough students? Who ends up in suspension or expulsion? Is the process biased?

Sometimes student disruption escalates to violence, whereby the safety of other students and the teacher is in question; perhaps the student is even threatening to hurt him/herself. When should a teacher restrain an aggressive student? What are the legal pitfalls and the psychological fallout from such action?

A word to the instructor An *Instructor's Manual with Test Questions* (both multiple-choice and essay) is available through the publisher for the instructor using this volume of Taking Sides. A general guidebook, *Using Taking Sides in the Classroom*, which discusses the methods and techniques for integrating the pro-con approach into any classroom setting, is also available. An online version of Using Taking Sides in the Classroom and a correspondence service for Taking Sides adopters can be found at http://www.dushkin.com/usingts/.

Taking Sides: Clashing Views on Controversial Issues in Classroom Management is only one title in the Taking Sides series. If you are interested in seeing the table of contents for any of the other titles, please visit the Taking Sides Web site at http://www.dushkin.com/takingsides/.

Acknowledgments   We would like to extend our sincere appreciation for all the support, suggestions, and encouragement in the development and writing process offered by Jill Peter, Senior Developmental Editor, and Larry Loeppke, Managing Editor of the Taking Sides series at McGraw-Hill/ Dushkin. They saw the need and the benefit of this edition and cheered us on throughout.

We also want to thank our spouses, Beth Harrington and John Taylor, for supporting us, for reminding us of deadlines, and for fielding questions about almost every aspect of book writing. Bob Harrington wishes to thank his four daughters, Laura, Anna, Kelly, and Casey, for providing insights from the students' perspective about how to do classroom management "right" so that students continue to want to learn.

Additional thanks go to all of the students with whom we had the privilege of working with over the years, for showing us the range of challenges they face in learning, and to all of the educators with whom we have consulted who have showed us what the "real" controversies are in classroom management.

We look forward to receiving feedback and comments about this new edition on *Taking Sides: Clashing Views on Controversial Issues in Classroom Management* from faculty, students, regular and special education classroom teachers, as well as their paraprofessionals and teacher aides, and all of the support staff such as school psychologists, school counselors, school social workers, speech language clinicians, OTs and PTs, and school administrators. It is our sincere hope that you will find this book innovative and applicable to your daily work in classrooms all across America. We can be reached via the internet (rgharrin@ku.edu), or you can write to us in care of the Taking Sides series at McGraw-Hill/Dushkin.

Robert "Bob" G. Harrington, Ph.D.
University of Kansas

Leticia "Tish" Holub, Ph.D.
Lawrence Public Schools
University of Missouri–Kansas City

Contents In Brief

Contents

George W. Bush, our forty-third president of the United States of America,
proposes that the essential work of democracy is to educate future Americans to govern in the twenty-first century and that the No Child Left Behind
Act reflects a belief that every child can learn through greater teacher and
student accountability. Susan Black, an *American School Board Journal*
contributing editor and education research consultant from Hammondsport,
New York, contends that teachers are stressed out since the passage of
No Child Left Behind due to the mounting needs of troubled students,
accountability demands to accomodate a widening range of student behaviors, and preparing students for the relentless series of standardized
assessments.

Ross W. Greene is director of cognitive-behavioral psychology at the Clinical
and Research Program in Pediatric Psychopharmacology at Massachusetts
General Hospital and an associate professor of psychology in the department of psychiatry at Harvard Medical School. Professor Green and his
research associates contend that students with AD/HD are significantly more
stressful to teach than their classmates without AD/HD. Tawnya Kumarakulasingam is coordinator of school psychological services in the Scottsdale,
Arizona, schools, and Robert G. Harrington is a professor in the department
of psychology and research in education at the University of Kansas. They
found that teacher stress and teachers' levels of hope are predictive of emotional exhaustion and depersonalization. Hope serves as a moderator of
teacher stress.

Elizabeth A. Linnenbrink is an assistant professor of educational psychology in foundations of education at the University of Toledo, and Paul R. Pintrich was a professor of education and psychology and chair of the combined program in education and psychology at the University of Michigan. These authors conclude that it is not appropriate to label students as "motivated" or "unmotivated" since they believe that motivation is a skill that can be taught to all learners. Kathryn R. Wentzel is a professor at the University of Maryland in the department of human development, and Deborah Watkins is an assistant professor at York College of Pennsylvania in special education. They argue that levels of peer support and acceptance in the classroom are important social factors in improving student motivation and behavior; without them, students may not be able to improve motivation.

Eric Carbone is a professor in the department of teaching and learning at New York University. He describes how classroom teachers can improve the learning enviroments of students with AD/HD in their inclusionary classrooms in ways that support the strengths of these students. Regina Bussing is an associate professor and chief of the division of child and adolescent psychiatry, department of psychiatry, pediatrics, and health policy and epidemiology at the University of Florida. Professor Bussing et al. contend that large class sizes, time requirements, and a lack of teacher training combine to make teachers unprepared to teach students with AD/HD in the regular classroom.

James M. Kauffman is the Charles S. Robb Professor of Education, University of Virginia, Charlottesville; and Kathleen McGee and Michele Brigham are high school special education teachers. They believe that sometimes there is too much tolerance and accommodation for a wide range of student misbehaviors in classrooms. Teachers need to raise their learning expectations for students with special needs. Jennifer Holladay is a program coordinator for the journal *Teaching Tolerance*. She participated in this survey project that found that teachers think that teaching tolerance to their students and other teachers should be a top educational priority.

Alfie Kohn is an author and lecturer. Kohn postulates that traditional classroom-management strategies often used in schools today do not promote a mutually caring and respectful classroom environment and results in increased student disrespect. Jeremy Swinson is a senior educational psychologist and honorary lecturer at Liverpool John Moores University, and Mike Cording is an educational consultant in Southport, England. They support the use of assertive discipline (a traditional classroom-management strategy), even for those students who are disaffected, discouraged, and disrespectful. They maintain that corrective procedures change behavior and do not contribute to student disrespect.

Alfie Kohn, the author of eight books on education and human behavior, believes that positive reinforcement is overused and that, contrary to common belief, may have potentially negative effects on students. K. Angeleque Akin-Little and Steven G. Little are professors at the University of the Pacific. They debate that the benefits of positive reinforcement far outweigh the detriments to students and offer suggestions for the appropriate use of reinforcement programs in educational settings.

Christine A. Readdick and Paula L. Chapman are professors at Florida State
University whose child interviews have shown that preschoolers perceive
time-out as a punishment, and they are unable to explain why they were
placed in time-out, thus reducing its effectiveness. Robert G. Harrington is a
professor in the department of psychology and research in education at the
University of Kansas who argues that time-out has been used effectively with
preschoolers and elementary students to reduce noncompliance, and he
provides guidelines for the effective use of the time-out strategy.

Issue 9.   Is Punishment an Effective Technique to Control Behavior?   138

Shannon R. Brinker, Sara E. Goldstein, and Marie E. Tisak are professors in
the department of psychology at Bowling Green State University. They contend that children think that conventional punishment works best for conventional classroom transgressions, but removal punishment (e.g., grounding)
works best for moral violations. In either case, children believe that punishment works. John W. Maag is a professor in the department of special education and communication disorders at the University of Nebraska-Lincoln.
He contests that while conventional punishments may make a classroom
safer for the moment, they fail to teach socially appropriate behaviors.

Issue 10.   Should Character Count?   156

Maurice J. Elias is a professor at Rutgers University and vice-chair of the
leadership team of the Collaborative for Academic, Social and Emotional
Learning (CASEL). Elias and his colleagues believe student success
depends on more than just test scores and that teachers should pay as much
attention to student behavior and character as they do to student grades.
David Elkind, professor emeritus at Tufts University and a prolific writer,
researcher, and lecturer, believes that character education is a luxury that a
public school cannot afford. He contends that there is no research to support
the practice and that it detracts from valuable teaching time.

PART 3   SCHOOL-WIDE MANAGEMENT STRATEGIES   171

Christopher H. Skinner and Christine E. Neddenriep are professors at the University of Tennessee. They suggest that perhaps a more effective strategy to change school climate and social relationships through bully-proofing is to teach peers to report the incidental positive behaviors of bullies rather than tattle on their misbehaviors. Charles Go is a youth development advisor in Alameda, California, and Shelley Murdock is a community and youth development advisor in Pleasant Hill, California. They contend that students can be both bullies and victims as part of a continual cycle and that bully-proofing programs that label youths as either victims or bullies will not "fix" the bullies.

Laurel M. Garrick Duhaney is an assistant professor in the department of educational studies at the State University of New York at New Paltz. Garrick Duhaney suggests that when culturally sensitive behavior-management strategies are employed, school violence can be reduced. Judy Groulx and Cornell Thomas are associate professors in the department of educational foundations and administration in the School of Education at Texas Christian University. They contend that teachers working in urban schools enter the field of teaching with misconceptions about students of color and consequently feel uncomfortable in their behavior management because their university coursework did not adequately prepare them.

Kathleen Vail is an associate editor of *American School Board Journal.* Vail believes that perhaps the best way to help students with their classroom misbehaviors is to first help their parents learn better ways to raise their children at home. Amy E. Assemany is a professor at the State University of New York at Albany, and David E. McIntosh is a professor at Ball State University. They argue that parent education programs are likely to fail, citing premature parental dropouts, parental failure to engage and participate, and failure to maintain gains when parent educators do not consider the contextual factors of socioeconomic disadvantage of the family, family dysfunction, and severity of the child's externalizing behaviors.

Gale M. Morrison is a professor at the University of California at Santa Barbara, and Russell Skiba is a professor at Indiana University. They share the perspective that students who are involved in various types of school-based offenses and subsequent disciplinary actions are at increased risk for later violence and other unsafe behaviors that threaten the overall safety of school campuses. They argue that the propensity for violence may be mitigated depending upon the response of individual school disciplinarians. Kirk A. Bailey, who is a professor at the Hamilton Fish Institute on School and Community Violence at George Washington University, raises suspicions about how profiling for violence might violate the constitutional rights of students, including protections against discrimination, unlawful search and seizure, and privacy.

Sam Chaltain is the coordinator of the Freedom Forum's First Amendment Schools Project in Arlington, Virginia. Chaltain offers data that suggest that many teachers do not know the five freedoms protected under the First Amendment to the Constitution, and if they do not know the freedoms, they cannot be expected to protect student rights. Chaltain believes that in fostering student rights and related responsibilities, schools foster safer schools. Benjamin Dowling-Sendor is an authority on school law and is an assistant appellate defender of North Carolina in Durham. Dowling-Sendor contests that schools are being placed in the middle between defending the rights of students who want an education and those who would disrupt the school climate. Through case law, Dowling-Sendor demonstrates the levels of incivility that have crept into our schools and how schools must walk a tightrope to show that whatever student misbehaviors are encountered, schools may restrict student speech only if they have a well-founded fear of classroom disruption.

PART 4 SEVERE BEHAVIOR CHALLENGES 273

W. Michael Martin, supervisor of the office of elementary education for the Loudon County (VA) public schools, suggests that zero-tolerance policies are necessary to keep public schools safe for all children but claims that zero tolerance does not necessarily mean that an offending student must be suspended or expelled. He offers alternative remedies. Jeanette Willert, an assistant professor and coordinator of secondary education at Canisius College in Buffalo, New York, and Richard Willert, a child and family therapist at Condrell Counseling Center in Orchard Park, New York, counter that zero tolerance does not work since it blames the child as being traumatized and incapable of reform. These authors believe that schools should begin to teach students tolerance for others, coping skills, cooperative learning strategies, and pro-social communications skills as ways for violent students to manage their own anger.

Issue 17. Can Schools Provide Effective Intervention for Adolescents with Conduct Disorders?   289

YES: **Monica M. Garcia, Daniel S. Shaw, Emily B. Winslow, and Kirsten E. Yaggi,** from "Destructive Sibling Conflict and the Development of Conduct Problems in Young Boys," *Developmental Psychology* (vol. 36, no. 1, 2000)   *291*

NO: **Leihua Van Schoiack-Edstrom, Karin S. Frey, and Kathy Beland,** from "Changing Adolescents' Attitudes About Relational and Physical Aggression: An Early Evaluation of a School-Based Intervention," *School Psychology Review* (Spring 2002)   *301*

Monica M. Garcia et al. are professors in the department of psychology at the University of Pittsburgh. These colleagues present research to show that early destructive sibling conflicts and rejecting parenting are predictive of later aggressive behavior problems, thus suggesting that adolescence may be too late to change this aggressive pattern of social interactions. Leihua Van Schoiack-Edstrom is a research scientist at the Committee for Children. Van Schoiack-Edstrom and colleagues have shown that adolescent students enrolled in their second year in the Second Step Program decreased in their overall endorsement of aggression and perceived difficulty of performing social skills, thus discounting the contention that adolescence is too late for students to improve conduct disorders.

Issue 18. Should Schools Treat the Mental Health Needs of Students?   311

YES: **Marc S. Atkins, Patricia A. Graczyk, Stacy L. Frazier, and Jaleel Abdul-Adil,** from "Toward a New Model for Promoting Urban Children's Mental Health: Accessible, Effective, and Sustainable School-Based Mental Health Services," *School Psychology Review* (Spring 2003)   *313*

NO: **Heather Ringeisen, Kelly Henderson, and Kimberly Hoagwood,** from "Context Matters: Schools and the 'Research to Practice Gap' in Children's Mental Health," *School Psychology Review* (Spring 2003)   *324*

Marc S. Atkins, Patricia A. Graczyk, Stacy L. Frazier, and Jaleel Abdul-Adil are professors at the University of Illinois at Chicago. They take the position that schools should take the lead in providing mental health services to needy students by encouraging greater involvement of families in children's mental health services, by creating teacher key opinion leaders as on-site experts on topics related to children's mental health, and by implementing the PALS (Positive Attitude toward Learning in School) program to foster and maintain parents and children in treatment. Heather Ringeisen is chief of the child and adolescent services research program at the National Institute of Mental Health. Researchers Ringeisen, Henderson, and Hoagwood contest that while students and their families might well benefit from mental health services in other contexts, current research has paid insufficient attention to the school context and has not offered means by which school organizations and the behaviors of professionals within those schools might need to be modified to support school-based mental health programs.

David A. Brent is a professor of psychiatry at the University of Pittsburgh School of Medicine. Professor Brent discusses the historical concern of child and adolescent suicide as well as the factors that have contributed to the drop in suicide rates in recent years. He concludes that specific antidepressants (SSRIs) are a viable treatment for pediatric depression, and discontinuing their usage would put treatment for depression back 25 years. Jennifer Couzin is a contributing author to *Science*. Couzin offers evidence that when school-age children use SSRIs to treat anxiety and depressive disorders, they are at increased risk of suicidal ideations and suicide. The medications may prove to have little value in treating their depression.

Douglas C. Breunlin is a research professor at the Family Institute at Northwestern University along with researchers Rocco A. Cimmarusti, Tara L. Bryant-Edwards, and Joshua S. Hetherington. These researchers think that schools over-rely on suspensions and expulsions and alternatively should consider utilizing a conflict-resolution training program as a means to prevent and manage violent behaviors in schools. Perry Zirkel is Iacocca Professor of Education at Lehigh University. Zirkel insists that schools have the right to keep their schools safe through suspensions and expulsions even if it means limiting the rights of students to say whatever they might like to of an offensive, derogatory, salacious, or threatening nature on the Internet.

Joseph B. Ryan and Reece L. Peterson, professors at the University of Nebraska-Lincoln, support the use of physical restraint in the public schools with the proviso that schools ensure that teachers receive training in physical restraint, that they create standards for the use of restraint procedures, that they maintain records about who is restrained, and that they require notifying parents and administrators. Sandy K. Magee and Janet Ellis, professors at the University of North Texas, oppose the use of physical restraint in schools due to its detrimental effects, including the escalation of the very behavior it was designed to reduce.

Introduction

Chicken Little, The Sky Is Falling!

> Chicken Little stood around underneath a tree.
> Something fell and hit her head. She said, "Goodness me?"
>
> "Oh, my goodness!" she did screech. "The sky is falling!"
> She ran around, yelling out, "We must tell the king."

So goes "Chicken Little," the well-know children's tale. We all know the sky wasn't really falling, but it made no difference to Chicken Little. The same is true in classroom management. When falsehoods, half-truths, or misrepresentations are repeated enough times, they become reality for some less-informed individuals. Statistics can be intimidating and can make people myopic with regard to the whole picture and the whole truth. For example, many classroom-management texts begin with a chapter on violence and aggression in schools today. These texts typically provide plenty of statistics about how schools are unsafe and how students and their property are the subjects of attacks with great regularity (Conoley & Goldstein, eds., *School Violence Intervention: A Practical Handbook*, 2nd ed, The Guilford Press, 2004). Newspapers and magazines take these statistics and make them into headlines for popular consumption. For example, Walker, Ramsey, and Gresham (*Antisocial Behavior: Evidence-Based Practices*, Wadsworth/Thompson Learning, 2004) report that between 2 percent and 6 percent of U.S. children and youths manifest some form of conduct disorder. (Conduct disorder is a condition involving aggression, property destruction, and deceitful behavior that persists over one year.) Walker, Ramsey, and Gresham note that half of these youths will maintain the disorder through adulthood, and the remaining half will undergo significant adult adjustment problems. Such statistics are worrisome. Educators are induced to believe that classroom-management problems are inevitable, are intractable, and perhaps, are even their own fault because they are not educating these students correctly. What they miss is the fact that, even under the most dire interpretations of these statistics, 94 percent of school-age students are not conduct-disordered at all—they are "normal."

Indeed, only a small subset of school-age students are aggressive in schools today. This is not to minimize the adverse effects that these aggressive students have on school climate. The range of behaviors that these students display includes lying, cheating, stealing, bullying, sexually acting out, bringing weapons to school, running away, being truant, setting fires, displaying offensive behaviors (such as swearing), refusing to comply, and arguing and complaining about school. The fact of the matter is, however, that most students are behaving just fine and are achieving at a very high level of performance in school. In a well-documented book called *The Manu-factured Crisis: Myths, Fraud and the Attack on America's Public Schools* (Addison-Wesley, 1995), Berliner and Biddle refute the claims that "the sky is falling" when it comes to public education in the United States. In fact, they retort that most students are safer in school than anywhere else. Most students comply when asked, are attentive, have set enviable and lofty goals for themselves, want to please their teachers, get along reasonably well with their peers, and are good citizens in their communities. Teachers and parents can be rightfully proud of the jobs that they have done in teaching and raising these children and adolescents.

In *Taking Sides: Clashing Views on Controversial Issues in Classroom Management*, why do we choose to present a balanced view of the status of student behavior in public education rather than predictions of inevitable catastrophe? Don't poignant statistics motivate educators to do some-thing about the problem by reading the book on classroom management they clutch in their hands? Why don't we jump on the bandwagon and focus on the small minority of students who create the majority of class-room-management problems? We don't because we want educators to know the facts and to understand that they are already doing a great job much of the time. With some extra help, hopefully from this text, educa-tors can reach that small minority of students who seem unreachable. We want educators to have hope and optimism and to know that most stu-dents want to do better—even the ones who cause huge disruptions in their classrooms. In many cases, the students just don't know how.

Educators must have a "can-do" attitude, and this is not obtained through intimidation and misinformation. Classroom management is a crucial and positive part of educators' professions. It is important that teachers see classroom management as part of good instruction and not just about getting students to desist and to comply. Classroom manage-ment can also be about teaching students important new skills that will help them throughout their lives. Teaching students to have greater emo-tional intelligence is part of good teaching, and teaching them to have a wider range of social skills helps them become better students, especially when they work in groups with other students. Teaching parents how they can be a helpful part of their children's positive adjustment is part of the home-school collaborative. Teaching students to have more positive attributions about their abilities is an attitude that will build them up for life. No, the sky is not falling, even though it seems like it somedays.

What most teachers need in the area of classroom management is information. They need to know the facts on both sides about behavioral issues that they struggle with everyday. That is the purpose of this volume, *Taking Sides: Clashing Views on Controversial Issues in Classroom Management*. Armed with these facts, educators are quite capable of engaging in the prob-lem-solving process and in making decisions that are in the best interests of their students and their entire classroom. Educators are empowered when they understand the principles of good classroom management and the idiosyncracies of their applications to unique circumstances.

Behavior Management That Works

What is good behavior management? How can educators know when they have done a good job in applying a management principle to a particular classroom-management situation? Most books on classroom management expect teachers to get children to desist, obey, and comply with demands made by the teacher, and to choose a classroom-management technique that "fits" with their management style, personality, or teaching philosophy. Nothing could be further from the truth. It struck us that perhaps it would be helpful for educators to know the principles of behavior management that "work." When educators know what the goals of good behavior management are, they may be in the best possible position to use the information in this volume to their greatest advantage.

Simplicity

There is an overwhelming multitude of classroom-management strategies available to the educational practitioner. One guiding principle that can help cut through the quagmire of theory is "simplicity." Educators are less likely to implement behavior-management schemes that are elaborate and require much materials development. For example, when proximity control is all that is needed to get a student back on-task, time-out is unnecessary and in fact runs the risk of escalating the situation.

Efficiency

Some classroom-management techniques work for the moment, but teachers find themselves revisiting the same classroom behavior problems over and over again. Other techniques momentarily suppress the inappropriate behavior, but it will inevitably flare up again, sometimes with even greater frequency and intensity. This is often the case with punishment—it may quickly suppress misbehaviors in children and adolescents, but other misbehaviors often take the place of the original misbehavior. Classroom-management interventions that work should be efficient in that once they are applied, the child's questionable misbehavior should be modified relatively permanently.

Practical

Not all classroom-management interventions that change behavior can be practically applied in the classroom. For example, according to some high school teachers, classroom-management techniques that might work in the elementary classroom may not work in their secondary-level classroom. An example is classroom meetings—they are wonderful means of developing a sense of classroom community, belongingness, ownership of rules, classroom-wide self-evaluation, self-reinforcement, and goal-setting skills. However, high school educators rightfully claim that they do not always have the time to hold regular classroom meetings since they have their students for such limited lengths of time, compared to elementary school teachers.

Effective

Because there are so many theories of classroom management, knowing which management strategies to apply with which type of problems is difficult for educators. Also, not all behavior-management techniques work equally well with all behavior problems, and behavioral symptoms can be confusing and belie the underlying causes for misbehavior. Take, for example, passive-aggressive behavior. It might be possible to apply assertive discipline to students who "resist" getting started on their seatwork by warning them and then by following up with various punishments. On the other hand, if the problem is lack of goal-setting ability, perhaps the students might best be managed using Glasser's Choice Theory, where they are guided by a series of well-phrased questions, such as, What are you doing? What is your goal? How is your behavior helping you reach your goal? If the student with AD/HD is not starting the seatwork because the task is too difficult or too long, perhaps an instructional modification would be more effective. What management technique will work best is often dictated by what the problem is—it should match the problem, rather than simply address the symptomatic behaviors alone.

Positive

Many classroom-management texts wrongly suggest that the goal of behavior management is to get students to desist and to correct them. When educators correct students, they are generally using compliance-managing skills; they are manipulating consequences. The problem with focusing on negative behaviors is that a student may be successfully managed to "stop hitting his neighbor," but he may still not be working at the instructional task at hand. Classroom management that works generally focuses on positive replacement behaviors, rather than negative behaviors. This means that teachers are encouraged to develop positive rules and procedures—to "catch 'em doing something right"—and to develop positive short- and long-term goals for students. Classroom management that works also teaches new skills and reinforces students on a regular basis for demonstrating those skills. In this case, the student might best be directed to "keep your hand to yourself; turn to page 32, and begin the first five problems."

Improves Learning

It is not enough for students to be seated, quiet, attentive, and social in class; if the students aren't learning, then all of these efforts at classroom management have missed their mark. A classroom-management technique that works has instruction and subsequent student learning as its primary goals. This does not mean that students are not instructed in emotional intelligence, empathy training, or tolerance building. All of these skills can be directly related to skills that students can use to become better students and better learners. Our goal is not for students to become unthinking automatons who bow to every comment from an omniscient educator. As a matter of fact, in her compelling book *The Edison Trait:*

Saving the Spirit of Your Nonconforming Child (Times Books, 1997), Palladino makes the case that too much misdirected behavior management can make for an unthinking, uncritical student who has lost the capacity to think for him/herself. Palladino urges behavior managers to "save the spirit of your nonconforming students." Good behavior management does not stifle independence, creativity, divergent thinking, originality, or giftedness in the name of compliance; instead, it teaches students that there is nothing wrong with holding an independent viewpoint—but that there is a socially appropriate way of respectfully disagreeing. Behavior management that works is respectful to the needs of the student and the teacher.

Systemic

Unfortunately, most behavior management focuses on the misbehaving student and not the system, regardless of how dysfunctional the system is. For example, a student with fetal alcohol syndrome may need frequent reminders of the requirements of an instructional task and may require frequent re-teaching. When behavior managers are uninformed about the dynamics of fetal alcohol syndrome, they may think that the student isn't complying and may start a regimen of compliance management; in fact, curricular and instructional modifications may be in order. Behavior management that works considers the interaction of dynamic variables that can affect behavior, including genetics, home life, aptitude, prior academic history, classmates, classroom rules, curriculum, instruction, physical environment of the classroom, and temperament. Good behavior management involves a problem-solving approach in which the final decision about intervention is made only after all reasons for the behavior are carefully considered.

Developmentally Appropriate

Many behavior-management theories fail to discuss how to choose an appropriate goal for intervention. In this way, these theories are not based in a value. In other words, whatever behavior is irksome to the teacher is a behavior that may need to be changed. But, what happens when the teacher has a low tolerance level for behavior, even behavior that is developmentally appropriate? For example, it would be unreasonable to try to "manage" a preschooler to sit in his/her seat for half an hour. Preschoolers want to explore, to be active, to interact, and to play; it is not in their nature to sit for so long. Behavior management that works is developmentally appropriate for the student. Educators who are good behavior managers have a good knowledge of child development and developmental milestones.

Value for Child and Classroom

Every good behavior management has a foundation in value; it is important to value the goals of the child and his/her place in the classroom. For example, it may be possible to apply a behavioral intervention that insists on compliance without any sensitivity to the child, his/her culture, or his/her sense of self-worth. When children are publicly disciplined, they often feel like a spectacle and belittled. Their place in the classroom may be even more precarious because now they are seen as a "class clown"—someone to be avoided, perhaps. All classroom management should be conducted with special attention to the dignity and respect for students from all diverse cultural and racial backgrounds. Behavior management that works improves a student's standing in class and does not diminish the student.

"Can't Do" Versus "Won't Do"

One of the most primary distinctions to make when it comes to classroom management that works is to understand the difference between "can't do" and "won't do" problems. "Can't do" problems are skill deficits; "won't do" problems are compliance problems. An educator knows whether a student has a "can't do" or a "won't do" problem by checking the behavioral history of the child and asking the most basic question: Has this child ever been able to perform the behavior that I am asking for? If the answer is no, then the child most likely has a "can't do" problem, and the educator needs to make instructional or curricular modifications to accommodate the student. If the answer is yes, then the student likely has a "won't do" problem, and the student needs to be managed to use the skills he/she possesses. When "can't do" problems are compliance-managed, the student becomes frustrated; when "won't do" problems are managed through over-accommodation, then students are taught that it is not necessary to put forth their own best effort, that it is not important for them to work independently, and that they can rely on someone else even when they are perfectly capable of solving the problem themselves. Such management makes students weaker. Behavior management that works clearly distinguishes between these two major problem domains, and behavioral interventions are designed accordingly.

Back-Up System

Educators are often given the impression that all good classroom management takes place solely in the classroom and is provided solely by the classroom teacher. This is not true. All teachers will eventually need the support of a school psychologist, social worker, school resource officer, crisis team, or a principal. For example, a student may be so disruptive that he/she needs to be removed from the classroom, and the teacher needs some assistance. The purpose of a back-up system is to provide systematic support to the classroom teacher when a severe disruption arises. When a back-up plan is in place, the teacher knows who will provide support to his/her classroom management, what form that support will take, and how to get assistance right away.

Building Plan

All good classroom management is embedded in the context of a school-wide building plan that contains school-based policies that support the rules and procedures of the classroom. All teachers provide their classroom rules, procedures, and management plan to the principal so that there are no surprises and so that the school administration can support the teaching staff wholeheartedly. For example, schools commonly have policies about in-school suspension; unfortunately, these policies are not always appropriately applied. Some students are sent to in-school suspension for being tardy for class. Now, they not only missed the 5 minutes for which they were tardy, but they missed the entire class. It would have been far better for the building plan to state that missed class work due to tardiness will be completed during the student's own free time, not during in-school suspension. In this way, the student sees the logical consequence of missing class. This is a building plan that supports the on-time goal of the teacher.

Acquisition Phase

Behavior change is sometimes a gradual, stressful, and sometimes even anxiety-arousing process that occurs after days or weeks of shaping and gradual goal-attainment. Reasonably, teachers would like to see misbehavior changed as soon as possible, if not immediately. The problem is that students with a long behavioral history may resist and test the teacher, claiming the teacher is picking on them. They may make fun of the new strategy that the teacher is trying to apply, or they may threaten, intimidate, or warn the teacher that they could get violent. All of these tests are designed to get the teacher to become inconsistent and to ultimately maintain the inappropriate behavior. When unwilling students learn new complex behaviors, they may defy and resist for 2 to 3 weeks. In approximately the third week, the behavior will often plateau and decline, and then the appropriate behavior will increase. Behavior management that works takes into consideration this period of time, which is called the acquisition phase. Teachers need to be the most consistent during the acquisition phase, despite resistance from the student.

Coaching and Cheerleading

During the acquisition phase, teachers may be prone to becoming upset, frustrated, and even angry with the offending student. In order to make it through the acquisition phase, teachers may need more than the usual support, including coaching and cheerleading. Coaches need to remind the teachers to stay calm and teach strategies to do so. Furthermore, coaches need to make sure that the behavior manager is applying the agreed-upon behavior management—interventions fail because they are not applied consistently. In addition, teachers need to be motivated to keep up the good work. It is not uncommon in the moment to lose sight of the small amounts of good behavior change that have been achieved. Behavior management that works is sensitive to even small changes in behavior and rewards the teacher for consistency and for a positive attitude.

Implementable

Classroom consultants may make recommendations that cannot be carried out. For example, a behavior management consultant may suggest that a student be placed in detention over the lunch period to make up the work that he/she refused to do during the morning class periods. The classroom teacher may then ask, "Will I have to miss my lunch period every day to monitor the detention?" If the answer is yes, then the intervention is not implementable. Alternatively, if the responsibility for overseeing the detention area over the lunch period were to be shared among a group of teachers, then the likelihood that the intervention will be applied consistently is increased. Behavior management plans that work are implementable.

Generalizability

Most classroom misbehavior is very situation-specific, meaning that misbehavior may occur in some classroom environments but not in others. If teachers want behavior changes in their classrooms, they need to plan for change and not expect generalized behavioral changes just because another teacher is conducting an intervention in his/her classroom. If the student has similar problems in multiple classrooms, then specific interventions may need to be developed for each classroom. There may be unique stimuli within each classroom that are controlling the problematic behavior. Behavior management that works does not assume generalizability from one classroom to the next, but makes plans to ensure generalizability.

Maintenance

Sometimes, educators are surprised, disappointed, and frustrated when behaviors that they thought were under control escalate again for no apparent reason. There are two reasons why behavior changes are not maintained over time. The students may not have learned long-term adaptive skills to replace inappropriate behaviors with more appropriate behaviors. Furthermore, when students are not reinforced for their continued demonstration of good behavior, the frequency with which they show that behavior may actually decline. Behavior management that works begins with continuous reinforcement for compliance to positive classroom rules followed by "fading," or intermittent reinforcement for rules compliance. Eventually students are "encouraged" for their own self-statements about their own behaviors. In this manner, students move from extrinsic reinforcement for new behaviors to intrinsic reinforcement for behaviors that are in their own best interests. Intrinsic motivation is more likely to be maintained over time.

Ethical

Behavior-management procedures should be ethical when changing behavior; they shouldn't cause more harm than good, and they should take into consideration any unintended side effects of the intervention.

For example, isolating students for hours in time-out rooms that are unventilated, unlit, and unmonitored may "work" in that these children may not want to revisit the isolation rooms, but such a procedure violates "Protection of Child Welfare" principles as specified by all professional Codes of Professional Conduct in education. All educators have an ethical obligation to "first, do no harm." In other words, the primary obligation of a behavior manager is to ensure the emotional and physical well-being of the student. Behavior management that works ensures that the self-worth of the student remains intact even during the intervention and even after it is completed.

Legal

Students have rights in schools, including the right to free expression, as long as it does not interfere with the education of others in the classroom. What this means is that teachers cannot disapprove and manage a behavior that is protected under the First Amendment. For example, a student may wear a political statement on a shirt that displeases the teacher. Students have the right to political dissent. On the other hand, if a sexually explicit shirt is so offensive and distracting that other students cannot pay attention in class, the educator may have the right under school behavioral and zero-tolerance policies to request the student to change the shirt. Behavior management that works employs zero-tolerance policies that are made clear in advance and that provide for a range of offenses depending on the circumstances, such as frequency of prior offenses, intention to offend, and age and knowledge of the student.

Teacher Acceptability

All teachers have preferences for various styles of classroom intervention. Some teachers prefer interventions that are more instructional in nature; others prefer behavioral or assertive discipline approaches; and still others prefer approaches based in counseling practice, such as Glasser's Choice Theory. Classroom teachers will only apply a management approach that they know and approve of. Teachers will not apply a classroom-management approach that flies in the face of their philosophy of education. Otherwise, such an approach will be met with resistance and will not be implemented. Behavior management that works has passed muster with the teacher.

Based on Recommended Practices in Classroom Management

Best practices in classroom management are based in research and have been shown to be effective when applied to various types of problems. Best practices are the gold standard in behavioral intervention. Unfortunately, research in the area of classroom management is a "work in progress" and is incomplete. Consequently, behavior managers must rely on recommended practices that are based in sound theory and practice but perhaps not always in research. This can create some confusing situations. For example, "new" approaches crop up weekly for dealing with classroom behaviors. Then again, some "old" disproven approaches still remain and have become urban legends. As for "new" approaches, there are many recommendations for untested herbal therapies that are said to help students with AD/HD. On the other hand, many educators still believe the myth that excess sugar causes hyperactivity, despite consistent research evidence to the contrary. Behavior management that works is informed by recent research and by reference to recommended practices by recognized authors on the topic. Fly-by-night therapies, unvalidated Internet recommendations, and pop culture op-ed pieces appearing in magazines should be avoided as reputable sources of information about recommended practices.

Humor in Classroom Management

As you read this volume of readings, you will find repeatedly that there is no substitute for a good attitude when it comes to classroom management. Hope, optimism, and perseverance are hallmarks of successful classroom behavior managers. They don't take themselves too seriously, they have a sense of humor, and they are democratic in their management style, not authoritarian. A successful classroom manager must strive to maintain a good relationship with the offending student, no matter what. Two authors who tout the benefits of humor in the classroom are Loomans and Kolberg, who co-authored *The Laughing Classroom: Everyone's Guide to Teaching with Humor and Play* (H J Kramer, 1993).

Perhaps the best way to illustrate the benefits of humor applied to classroom management is through a case example. There was an elementary school principal who prided himself on using humor to defuse potentially explosive situations with students. One day, the principal found it necessary to discipline a student for a minor infraction. As the male student walked away, he muttered to himself, "Jerk, big jerk." The principal called the student back and asked him, "What did you say?" The student repeated the offensive words for the principal to hear. The principal would have been well within his rights to discipline the student, but chose to do otherwise. Instead, he asked the boy to return in 45 minutes at the end of the school day and be prepared to answer the question, What is a jerk? The boy looked perplexed but took the principal's instruction and pondered the question. The intervening 45-minute time period gave the boy time to think and to recover. When he returned to the principal's office, the principal once again asked, "Now I want to know what you think a jerk really is." The boy hesitated and then responded, "A jerk is someone who is kind, and understanding, and most of all forgiving." Not being one to miss an opportunity for exaggeration, the principal responded, "Well then, a jerk is a good thing in your mind; that must be why you called me a 'big jerk' because I think that I am very kind, and understanding, and most of all forgiving." The wise principal then continued to seal the deal with the young boy. He asked him, "I could tell that you were upset when you walked away; what were you upset about?" The boy responded that he was upset that the principal had disciplined him publicly in front of the other students. The principal struck a compromise. He said, "I promise to never discipline you again in front of the other students if you promise to never again call me a big jerk, because unlike you I find being called a jerk to be hurtful and offensive." The principal had obtained his goal: he maintained a good relationship with the student, he engaged the student in problem solving, and he got the student to apologize. They both had a good laugh because both of them knew what *really* just happened.

Humor in classroom management is best when it occurs naturally and is not contrived. It can even happen inadvertently. For example, a statement on a recent classroom-management exam at once captured the sentiments of many classroom managers but also showed the perils of over-reliance on spell-check in word-processing programs. The result is humorous. In response to a case study question, a student responded: "If this does not work, this student should have their desk far removed from the rest of their classmates until they re-write a new behavior plan. Hopefully, no further intervention will be necessary, but if so, then in-school suspension would be appropriate. The next consequence would be out-of-school suspension and finally permanent EXPLOSION." We think the student intended to say "expulsion."

Classroom management can actually be a fun part of teaching when approached with knowledge and enthusiasm. Hopefully, the pages that follow in this book will provide the knowledge about the intricacies of classroom management so that you will find within yourself the enthusiasm to work with the many students who rely on you to work with them and never give up on them.

On the Internet . . .

ERIC Digest on Teacher Stress and Burnout

This 2002 ERIC publication on understanding and preventing teacher burnout discusses the nature of the stress response, the construct of burnout, and burnout prevention at various levels, including primary, secondary, and tertiary prevention.

http://www.ericdigests.org/2004-1/burnout.htm

Illinois State University

Professor Kathleen McKinney provides information for teachers related to student motivation. She focuses on common sense and hands-on approaches that when provided together will increase intrinsic motivation in students.

http://www.cat.ilstu.edu/conf/intrinsicmot.shtml

Children's Development Institute

The Children's Development Institute provides ideas related to various classroom strategies and interventions for teachers, such as cognitive impulsivity and task completion. There is specific information regarding teaching and managing students with AD/HD in the classroom. Also, references for pertinent books and materials on the topic are listed.

http://cdipage.com/teacher.htm

Diversity Activities on the Diversity Council Web Site

The Diversity Council Web site includes resources on the home page regarding educational opportunities for teaching tolerance and reducing prejudice. This specific site hosts various activities for elementary-age students to engage in learning about various cultures and peoples.

http://diversitycouncil.org/elActivities.shtml

PART 1

Behavior Management and Classroom Instruction

*H*ow well are teachers prepared to manage the everyday challenges in their classrooms? Elementary, middle, and high school teachers are required to meet the No Child Left Behind mandate, but can they do so when faced with such daunting behavioral challenges from their students? Behavior management takes precious instructional time. Classroom management is one of the major sources of teacher stress too, especially when managing students with special needs. Do some teachers experience less stress because of their own positive attitudes and the unique ways that they manage their classrooms? If so, perhaps theses skills can be shared. Some students just don't seem to care. They are unmotivated. Lack of student motivation is a perennial problem, but how should it be handled? Can students be taught how to think like more successful students, or is poor motivation due to lack of support from the classroom community? Most teachers today have at least one student with a disability in their classrooms. How prepared are teachers to manage the special instructional and behavioral needs of these students? Do they have the training, resources, and support personnel to get the job done? Inclusion has presented a whole new set of management challenges to the classroom teacher. Finally, with all of the diversity within a single classroom, sometimes intolerance can be a source of classroom management problems in itself. Could education in tolerance, empathy, and cooperation help? In Part 1, we explore the factors that contribute to preventing classroom-management problems.

- Can Teachers Manage the No Child Left Behind Mandate and Student Misbehaviors Too?

- Is There a Relationship Between Teacher Stress and Student Misbehavior?

- Is Teaching the Habits of Highly Successful Students the Best Approach to Improve Student Motivation?

- Students with AD/HD in the Regular Classroom: Are Teachers Prepared to Manage Inclusion?

- Can There Be Too Much Tolerance and Accommodation for Diversity of Student Behavior in the Classroom?

ISSUE 1

Can Teachers Manage the No Child Left Behind Mandate and Student Misbehaviors Too?

YES: George W. Bush, from "The Essential Work of Democracy,"
Phi Delta Kappan (October 2004)

NO: Susan Black, from "Stressed Out in the Classroom," *American School Board Journal* (October 2003)

ISSUE SUMMARY

YES: George W. Bush, our forty-third president of the United States of America, proposes that the essential work of democracy is to educate future Americans to govern in the twenty-first century and that the No Child Left Behind Act reflects a belief that every child can learn through greater teacher and student accountability.

NO: Susan Black, an *American School Board Journal* contributing editor and education research consultant from Hammondsport, New York, contends that teachers are stressed out since the passage of No Child Left Behind due to the mounting needs of troubled students, accountability demands to accommodate a widening range of student behaviors, and preparing students for the relentless series of standardized assessments.

There is no doubt that the expectations placed upon teachers are ever increasing; no matter what the grade level, teaching is a tremendous responsibility. Teachers are expected to ensure that all students are achieving up to their highest ability levels and that their lesson plans are interesting and motivating to all students. Teachers are the first professionals that students contact when they seek counseling for personal problems, and they must work supportively with all parents no matter how much cooperation they may receive in return. Teachers are expected to make appropriate individualized instructional modifications for students with special needs and to provide supportive assistance to them when necessary, while at the same time being sensitive to the differences of students from diverse cultural, racial, ethnic, geographic, and linguistic backgrounds. Teachers are responsible for a tremendous amount of paperwork in their daily schedules, including individualized educational plans, records of staff meetings, notes home, and grading student homework. Amidst all of these role demands, according to the No Child Left Behind Act (NCLB), teachers need to ensure that all children are reading and doing math at grade level, regardless of the children's prior learning experiences and motivation. All of this must be accomplished while managing the instructional and behavioral classroom environment of 25, and sometimes over 30, students.

The demands on teachers' time and personal emotional resources can result in a tremendous sense of personal stress. The question that must be asked is whether it is feasible for most teachers to address both the demands of the NCLB mandate and the wide range of classroom-management challenges. Time is limited. What should be the priority in the classroom—academics or behavior? Is it possible to be accountable for the academic improvement of such a wide range of students without dealing with their emotional and behavioral needs first? Is good classroom management prerequisite to good learning, or can a teacher focus on academic achievement alone? Is it possible to get all students achieving at grade level when there are so many demands on students and teachers today?

In a recent article in *Phi Delta Kappan*, President George W. Bush stated, "Nothing is more important to America's future than teaching our children the skills they need to be successful." The president claims that the education of all students at grade level in reading and mathematics is the "essential work of democracy" and that every child can learn. When educational expectations are high, America's children will rise to meet them. He believes that the achievement gap between minority students and white students is caused by the "soft bigotry" of low expectations. Bush postulates that students will only believe in themselves if their adult parents and teachers believe in their capability for academic success too, and that low-achieving students have been hidden in classroom test score averages, grade retentions, and alternative programs. He believes that the quality of teaching is the single most important indicator of how well students learn. President Bush demands NCLB.

While President Bush suggests that NCLB is not intended to place teachers in untenable situations where failure is inevitable, the job-related stress that many teachers experience today may suggest otherwise. Susan Black sees stress as a way of life for teachers. They are overwhelmed by the demands to get all students to grade-level performance in reading and math, simultaneously manage troubled students in their classrooms, respond to ever-increasing workloads and the curricular demands of NCLB and the never-ending tests for the students, and deal with endless demands on their time. Black maintains that the signs of teacher stress are self-defeating beliefs, cynicism, apathy, and rigidity. When teachers are stressed, student learning suffers, and achievement goes down. Black contends that when the delicate balance between the demands of classroom management, personal stress management, and high-stakes achievement testing is met, teachers are able to perform at their best. In order for this balance to be restored, teachers must be empowered. Schools must recognize that teachers are overwhelmingly stressed because good classroom management is prerequisite to good instructional management, and this perspective is not taken into consideration in the NCLB mandate. Teachers need to be given the time it takes to manage and instruct their classrooms well. One goal cannot be met without the other.

George W. Bush  **YES**

The Essential Work of Democracy

Nothing is more important to America's future than teaching our children the skills they need to be successful. Every child must receive a quality education if America is to be a prosperous and hopeful country. Our rapidly changing global economy is creating new industries that compete for highly skilled workers from around the world, and young people in America must be able to compete for every job in the new economy. The success of every industry depends on the availability of an educated work force. Our national security is increasingly dependent upon attracting more students into technology and engineering careers. Improving our quality of life through medical breakthroughs and alternative fuel technologies requires cultivating the next generation of innovators and scientists. And our schools face the challenge of preparing the next generation of American citizens to govern in the 21st century. The challenge to educate future Americans can be called the essential work of democracy. Making America safer, stronger, and better demands a world-class education system.

Education has been, and continues to be, a top domestic priority of mine and of my Administration. On my second day in office, I sent to Congress the boldest plan in a generation to improve our public schools—a plan to raise educational standards for every child and to require accountability from every school. These reforms were entitled No Child Left Behind (NCLB) to reflect my belief that every child can learn. When expectations are high, America's children will rise to meet them. I signed NCLB into law less than one year later, thanks to unprecedented bipartisan support from members of Congress.

This year, we celebrate the 50th anniversary of the historic Brown v. Board of Education decision, which declared the doctrine of "separate but equal" unconstitutional. Brown gave children equal access to school buildings, but many students today still suffer inequality in the education they receive. Some students are taught well, while the rest—mostly African American, Hispanic, special-needs, limited-English-proficient, and low-income students—fall behind or drop out.

By the time they reach 12th grade, only one in six African Americans and one in five Hispanics can read at grade level. Only 3% of African Americans and 4% of Hispanics are testing at the proficient level in mathematics. The achievement gap between African American students and white students in the fourth grade who are reading at or above the proficient level is 28 percentage points. This educational divide is caused by the soft bigotry of low expectations. Many excuses have been offered, but the result is still the same. Students are more likely to stop believing in themselves if they think adults have stopped believing in them. This is unacceptable.

Our government must speak for disadvantaged children who have been unheard and overlooked. They are the children who were hidden behind the averages and shuffled from class to class, grade to grade, without receiving the attention they needed and deserved. We need No Child Left Behind.

We are meeting the challenge and fulfilling my promise to improve education with the resources necessary to improve the achievement of all our children. I have provided the largest increase in federal education funding in our nation's history and the highest percentage gain since President Johnson left office. Since I took office:

- Elementary and secondary education funding has increased $12.1 billion (49%), from $24.8 billion in 2001 to a proposed $36.9 billion in 2005.
- Title I funding for low-income schools has increased $4.6 billion (52%), from $8.8 billion in 2001 to a proposed $13.3 billion in 2005.
- Special education funding has increased $4.7 billion (75%), from $6.3 billion in 2001 to a proposed $11 billion in 2005.
- Funding for reading programs has quadrupled.

With these increased resources, we are asking states and schools to set higher standards so that we can make sure that every student is learning. NCLB requires states to develop accountability plans to ensure that all students become proficient in reading and math and that achievement gaps between students of different socioeconomic backgrounds are closed. States develop their own plans to measure student achievement, report student and school progress to parents, identify areas for improvement, and provide support for struggling schools and options—including public school choice and tutoring—for children in underperforming schools.

Accountability must include measuring results, which is why NCLB requires annual assessments in reading and math. Contrary to the charges of some, these assessments are not intended to punish schools or highlight "failure." Rather, assessments are a diagnostic tool, to identify problems early, when our chances of correcting them and helping students get back on track for success are highest.

Poor performance will no longer be hidden. Results will no longer be kept from parents. We will continue to work with schools that are performing poorly. Assessment results will be used to guide decisions, target resources, and reward success. When we find struggling schools, we will give them time, incentives, and resources to correct their problems. Such schools will be able to try other methodologies, perhaps other leadership, to make sure that they are teaching children. And through the Reading First program, we are giving schools the tools to ensure that every child can read on grade level by the end of the third grade.

When we demand more from our schools, we should provide them with the flexibility they need to improve. Education reform is a national priority, but implementing reform is a state and local responsibility. Although NCLB establishes broad parameters and goals for improving student achievement, essential decisions about how to reach those goals are left to state and local officials. States have the flexibility to make dozens of crucial decisions, such as determining the academic standards that express what students should know and determining the accommodations that will be made and alternative assessments that will be available for students with limited proficiency in English and for students with disabilities. Instead of a one-size-fits-all solution, NCLB allows states to define the standards used to measure adequate yearly progress (AYP), including using nonacademic indicators, such as student attendance, in addition to assessment results.

States and school districts also have unprecedented flexibility in how they use federal education funds. It is now possible for school districts to transfer up to 50% of the federal formula grant funds they receive under certain programs to other federal programs, including Title I. School districts can allocate funds to meet their particular needs, such as hiring new teachers, increasing teacher pay, purchasing more technology, or purchasing new instructional materials.

Parents also have more options available to them under NCLB, because government should trust parents to make the right decisions for their children. In schools that do not meet state standards for at least two consecutive years, parents may transfer their children to a better-performing public school or a charter school. Students in schools that do not meet state standards for at least three consecutive years are eligible for federal-paid tutoring, after-school services, and summer school. More than 1,600 schools, universities, churches, synagogues, and companies have been approved by states to provide children with the extra help they need to catch up.

NCLB also takes into account the vital role of teachers in the intellectual and moral education of children. Teachers inspire students, encourage them to imagine and explore the possibilities of life, and nurture their natural abilities. And, most important, they teach children how to read and write.

We know that giving students the skills they need early in elementary school prepares them to succeed in the later grades. That is why I have quadrupled reading funding through the Reading First program to teach all students to read on grade level by the end of the third grade. Already, $2.5 billion in Reading First grants have been provided to over 3,800 schools to implement research-based reading programs in the classroom. Reading First is improving reading instruction and raising student achievement for more than 1.2 million students in kindergarten through third grade. Effective early reading instruction can prevent the difficulties that too many American students, especially disadvantaged students, now face.

Recent studies confirm what parents have always known—the quality of teaching is the single most important indicator of how well students learn. I believe that every child in America deserves a high-quality teacher, and that every teacher deserves the respect and support worthy of a profession that is so important to America's future.

My budget makes available nearly $5.1 billion in annual support for teachers through professional development, salary incentives, loan forgiveness, and tax relief. We are investing $2.9 billion to help schools recruit teachers for high-need areas, offering signing bonuses and other financial incentives to teachers in high-need subject areas, providing mentoring opportunities for teachers and principals, establishing pay-for-performance programs, and reducing class size. Many of NCLB's programs go so far as to require that a portion of funds be directly used to support teachers in areas such as professional development. I have proposed expanding loan forgiveness from $5,000 to $17,500 for math, science, and special education teachers who teach in low-income schools. Teachers also benefit from the current $250 above-the-line tax deduction for classroom expenses teachers pay for themselves, and I have proposed increasing the deduction to $400. Eligible expenses include books, supplies, computers, software, and other materials that a teacher uses daily as part of his or her job.

◦◦◦

We already see considerable evidence that No Child Left Behind is working for teachers and students. When I entered office in January 2001, only 11 states were in full compliance with federal education accountability standards. By 10 June 2003, all 50 states had developed accountability plans that push schools and students to perform to their full potential. The most recent results on the National Assessment of Educational Progress, the nation's report card, indicate that mathematics scores for fourth- and eighth-graders jumped significantly between 2000 and 2003. African American, Hispanic American, and low-income students accounted for some of the most significant improvements. And the achievement gap between white students and black students is closing for both fourth- and eighth-graders.

The most recent reporting of state assessment results from the 2003–04 school year also demonstrates that schools are improving and students are meeting high expectations:

- In Maryland, the percentage of African American third-graders who are reading proficiently increased 16 percentage points in one year. The percentage of Hispanic fifth-graders achieving proficiency in math increased nearly 10 percentage points. And 25 schools exited school improvement status this year after meeting their performance objectives.
- The number of schools identified as needing improvement in Wisconsin decreased to just 54 this year. Twenty-eight schools left the list because they met annual performance objectives for two straight years.
- Georgia has narrowed the achievement gap between African American and white students from 13 percentage points down to 8. In addition, Hispanic students narrowed the gap with their white classmates by four percentage points.

Further evidence is provided by a recent report by the Council of the Great City Schools, which reviewed test scores from 61 urban school districts in 37 states and found significant improvement in reading and math in the first year under NCLB. Fourth-grade reading scores jumped five percentage points, and math scores jumped by nearly seven percentage points to 51%.

In the face of this exciting progress, opponents of reform fall back on old arguments to undermine support for No Child Left Behind. One of the most common complaints is that the law constitutes an unfunded mandate. But such claims rely on accounting gimmicks that distort the truth. Independent, nonpartisan research underscores the fact that states have access to enough funding to accomplish the goals of NCLB. The Government Accountability Office recently concluded that the law is not an "unfunded mandate." In another study, Massachusetts State School Board Chairman James Peyser and economist Robert Costrell determined that there is enough funding to success-fully implement NCLB. Yet another study, conducted by Accountability Works, determined that federal funding exceeds the state and local "hard costs" resulting from specific NCLB requirements. The fact is, as a nation, we spent $488 billion last year on K-12 education—more than on national defense and more per pupil than any other nation in the world except Switzerland. Given this level of investment, it should not be too much to ask that every stu-dent be able to read at grade level. And thanks to the success of No Child Left Behind, more children today can be proud of their reading and math skills.

Now we must extend to high schools the success we are achieving in elementary schools. My 2005 budget includes new initiatives to improve the quality of education at our nation's high schools and better prepare students for success in higher education and the job market. These efforts include $100 million to help striving readers, $120 million to improve math educa-tion, $40 million to bring professionals with subject-matter knowledge into the classroom, an additional $28 million to expand Advanced Placement courses, and $12 million to expand the State Scholars program to all 50 states to encourage high school students to take a rigorous curriculum that will pre-pare them for college.

As No Child Left Behind and our new high school reforms help to ensure that every child graduates from high school prepared for college, I have also taken steps to make college affordable for all students, particularly those from low-income families. My 2005 budget includes a record $73 billion for financial aid that will help 10 million students attend college. Students and their families are eligible for nearly $9 billion in tax credits and deductions, including $2.6 billion for an above-the-line deduction of up to $4,000 annu-ally in higher education expenses. My 2005 budget requests $12.9 billion in Pell Grant funding to make college affordable for low-income students—an increase of $4.1 billion (47%) since 2001. In addition, the number of Pell Grant recipients has risen by approximately one million since 2001, while the maximum grant has increased from $3,750 in 2001 to $4,050 in 2005. Stu-dents completing a rigorous high school curriculum are eligible for a $1,000 Enhanced Pell Grant, bringing the total maximum Pell Grant award a student could receive up to $5,050.

To make certain America remains the most innovative economy in the world, I propose to provide thousands of students with up to $5,000 in assistance to pursue their studies in math and science. Students graduating from college with good math and science skills will be prepared to compete for the best jobs of the 21st century and lead the next generation of innovation.

The debate about education reform is a debate about our nation's future. It is about jobs, opportunities, economic and national security, and the prosperity of our families. It is also about personal growth, intellectual development, and the joy of learning. A caring, compassionate nation must not leave even one child behind.

We have made tremendous progress over the last four years, but we have more work to do. We have a solemn obligation to our children to see that every child has a quality education. It is not enough for us to hope that things will improve. We must commit ourselves to staying the course and make the changes necessary to reach every child.

Susan Black

 **NO**

Stressed Out in the Classroom

"I don't know how much more I can take," a math teacher told me recently. "The pressure goes up every day, and so does my stress level."

That same day, a fifth-grade teacher took me aside and confessed, "I'm so stressed. Today a student who speaks limited English was added to my class, and tonight I have to mark report cards. On top of that I have an early breakfast meeting with parents."

Stress seems to be a way of life for teachers. Many teachers I work with describe themselves as overwhelmed. They admit to feeling anxious and apprehensive—especially about meeting the mounting needs of troubled students, doing justice to an all-consuming curriculum, and getting kids ready for a relentless series of tests.

And they complain about tension throughout their schools. As the math teacher put it, "Some days my school feels like a powder keg that's about to explode."

Or, as a high school English teacher told me after a particularly hectic week, "With so much stress, something has to give. I'm afraid it will be me."

Wear and Tear

She could be right. Stress, researchers say, is biological in nature. And work-related stress can be physically harmful, according to the American Federation of Teachers' online Healthfile—especially when it triggers certain chemical reactions.

When the brain senses stress, the hypothalamus alerts the pituitary, which, in turn, signals the adrenal glands to secrete the hormone cortisol and other substances. In the right amount, cortisol helps regulate blood pressure, insulin, metabolism, and cardiovascular functions. But chronic stress or extreme stress can trigger the release of too much cortisol, and that can spell trouble. Excessive cortisol destroys brain cells in the hippocampus, resulting in short-term memory impairment, rapid weight gain, irritability and other mood problems, high blood pressure, and fatigue.

Work-related pressures can create considerable wear and tear. Physical effects can include headaches, fatigue, ulcers, upset stomach, and insomnia, as well as more serious nerve disorders, increased heart rates, and cardiovascular disease.

Psychological effects often include outbursts of anger, bouts of depression, unremitting tension and anxiety, confusion, indecisiveness, and constant worry. In some cases, say researchers who've studied stress in teachers, serious stress can lead to panic attacks and lingering feelings of inadequacy.

Stress also takes its toll on teachers outside the classroom, according to a study of Midwestern teachers by Minnesota-based Optum Research. Approximately 40 percent of respondents reported high levels of job stress and said it mostly affected their personal and family life. Job stress also affected the teachers' physical health, job performance, and mental health and their students' academic achievement, researcher Mark Attridge found. Only 12 percent of the teachers in the study reported low or very low levels of stress.

Sources of Stress

What causes teachers to feel stress? The source can be a personal problem . . ., an inability to live up to lofty ideals, or difficult working conditions.

A study by Isaac Friedman, published in a 2000 issue of the *Journal of Clinical Psychology*, found that beginning teachers who impose impossibly high standards on themselves often fail to live up to their ideals and end up emotionally and physically exhausted. In many cases, he found, these teachers packed up their shattered dreams and left the profession.

A veteran teacher who participated in one of Friedman's clinical workshops described being "haunted by a feeling of dissatisfaction" and "a sense of failure." She blamed herself for never having enough time to devote to her students. Many teachers who succumb to stress hold similar self-defeating beliefs, Friedman says. Teachers who feel inadequate and view their jobs as "excessively burdensome" often grumble about being on overload. Trying to cope, they may become cynical, apathetic, and overly rigid.

Other sources of teacher stress can be traced to administrators. For example, a 1999 study conducted by C.A. Harris describes the relationship between principals' leadership styles and teacher stress in three U.S. elementary schools. In the school with the lowest teacher stress, the principal communicated a clear vision for the school and had a close, personal relationship with the staff.

The International Stress Management Association, based in Waltham Cross, England, reports similar conclusions in its publication *Stress News*. Studies in the United States, England, Germany, and Canada indicate that principals are a key factor in heightening or lowering teacher stress. Principals who offer their staff strong social support provide a buffer that helps reduce teachers' job-related tension.

A 1997 study of teacher stress in Mid-western public high schools conducted by Medica, a health plan provider, found teacher stress was highest among those who reported having little social support from colleagues, friends, and family. The high-stress teachers suffered from depression and fatigue and said they had little control over administrative issues and little time to perform their jobs and routine tasks such as paperwork.

What Schools Can Do

Taking steps to reduce occupational stress can be good for students and teachers alike. Stressed-out teachers often succumb to emotional and physical exhaustion, develop negative attitudes toward students and colleagues, and perform below par in the classroom. In turn, students' learning suffers, and achievement goes down.

Alleviating teacher stress can be a cost-saving measure as well. Job stress can lead to increased absenteeism, sending substitute teacher costs skyrocketing. (Some researchers report a ripple effect, noting that students whose teachers fail to show up tend to have higher-than-average absenteeism.) Schools also face costs associated with recruiting and replacing burned-out teachers who opt to leave the profession altogether.

The key to dealing with teacher stress, researchers say, is to tackle it on two fronts: cause and effect.

Writing in the *Journal of Instructional Psychology*, Carolyn Wiley of Dublin's University College says it's important to zero in on root causes of stress, which means accurately assessing a school's culture and climate. She also proposes some tried-and-true methods for reducing teacher stress, such as designing clear administrative guidelines and responsibilities, providing teachers with mentors and other forms of social support, and involving teachers in such decisions as hiring and goal setting.

Wiley suggests using a well-known business strategy that avoids mismatches between newly hired employees and their job assignments. In education, that might mean thinking twice before placing a teacher who's accustomed to working by the book on a team with other teachers who favor projects and activities.

She also recommends that principals provide realistic job previews during recruitment and interviews to inform prospective teachers of working conditions, students, and school expectations. For teachers who have already been hired, Wiley encourages principals to provide the freedom to experiment with new workplace designs, such as teaming or nongraded classrooms.

No one can alleviate all the causes of teacher stress, of course, but schools can provide training for teachers in stress-reduction strategies. Optum researchers developed a stress-management program for teachers that involved group activities and the use of exercise rooms. Follow-up assessments showed that 34 percent of the teachers who participated in the program reduced their stress levels. In the control group, only 6 percent of teachers managed to lower their stress.

Such strategies might give stressed-out teachers a respite from their daily grind, but they won't remedy underlying problems that keep teachers off balance, and they won't change the self-perceptions that contribute to stress.

The National Mental Health Association says reducing and controlling stress takes determination, persistence, and time. No doubt your board and staff will face some stressful moments as you tackle teacher stress in your district. For the sake of your teachers and your students, it's worth the effort.

Selected References

Attridge, Mark, and others. "Trouble at the Head of the Class: Teachers Say Job Stress Impacts Their Students' Academic Performance, But It's a Condition That Can Be Reversed." *EAP Digest*, Fall 2000, pp. 30–32.

Friedman, Isaac. "Burnout in Teachers: Shattered Dreams of Impeccable Professional Performance." *Journal of Clinical Psychology*, 2000, pp. 595–606.

Harris, C.A. "The Relationship Between Principal Leadership Styles and Teacher Stress in Low Socioeconomic Urban Elementary Schools." *Dissertation Abstracts International*, 1999.

"Is Stress on the Job Making You Sick?" Washington, D.C.: American Federation of Teachers, Healthfile, 2000. `www.aft.org/publications/psrp_reporter/fall2000/stress.html`.

Jarvis, Matt. "Teacher Stress: A Critical Review of Recent Findings and Suggestions for Future Research Directions." *Stress News*, January 2002. `www.isma.org.uk/stressnw/teachstress1.htm`.

"Stress: Coping With Everyday Problems." Alexandria, Va.: National Mental Health Association, Factsheet, 2003. `www.nmha.org/infoctr/factsheets/41.cfm`.

Wiley, Carolyn. "A Synthesis of Research on the Causes, Effects, and Reduction Strategies of Teacher Stress." *Journal of Instructional Psychology*, June 2000.

POSTSCRIPT

Can Teachers Manage the No Child Left Behind Mandate and Student Misbehaviors Too?

Accountability is the buzzword that teachers live by today. High-stakes competency tests dictate what teachers will teach, what instructional goals they will set for their students, and how much time they have to spend on matters other than instruction. There is pressure to spend as much time as possible on direct instruction. The mantra is, "Time on task gets translated into better reading and math scores." Nevertheless, many students come to class with competing emotional and behavioral needs that must be addressed. These needs take time too. Should the teacher "gloss over" these needs and move forward nevertheless? Should the teacher spend precious classroom time teaching social skills, character education, personal responsibility training, and bully-proofing, among other topics to be discussed in this edition of Taking Sides? What happens to students when their emotional and mental health needs are not being met?

This first issue, *Can Teachers Manage the No Child Left Behind Mandate and Student Misbehaviors Too?,* is an important one. It forces teachers to ask the hard question about what teaching really is. Do teachers teach to the whole child, both intellect and emotions? Can a child learn if he or she is not emotionally ready to? Are the goals of No Child Left Behind legitimate and attainable given what we know about the normal distribution of human abilities? Does the competency testing movement increase pressure on students to the point where it is self-defeating because it takes time and creates stress? Should high-stakes testing drive education and what is taught? Can teachers juggle all of these demands on their skills to be master teachers and to be "one-minute" behavior managers as well? Time is of the essence. Teachers feel the pressure. How should they respond to the demands of NCLB? Should the emotional needs of children come first, or do the politics of the NCLB pressure them to abandon Maslow's hierarchy of needs and the basic emotional needs of children in favor of higher-order needs for high achievement in reading and math? These are tough ethical questions facing the entire profession. The answers will change the face of teaching and perhaps its future, at least as it is practiced in public education.

For more detail on the No Child Left Behind mandate, refer to *No Child Left Behind* (The White House, 2001) or http://www.nochildleftbehind.gov. For a look at what quality education could and should be, consider reading, W. Glasser, *The Quality School*, 3rd ed. (Harper Perennial, 1998). For the response of educators to NCLB, you should check the following sites: National Education Association (http://www.nea.org); Association for Supervision and Curriculum

14

Development (www.ascd.org); National Parent Teacher Association (http://www.pta.org); National Association of Elementary School Principals (http://www.naesp.org); National Association of Secondary School Principals (http://www.nassp.org); National School Boards Association (http://www.nsba.org); National Parent Teacher Association (http://www.pta.org); National Association of School Psychologists (http://www.naspweb.org); and American School Counselor Association (http://www.schoolcounselor.org).

ISSUE 2

Is There a Relationship Between Teacher Stress and Student Misbehavior?

YES: Ross W. Greene, et al., from "Are Students with ADHD More Stressful To Teach? Patterns of Teacher Stress in an Elementary School Sample," *Journal of Emotional and Behavioral Disorders* (Summer 2002)

NO: Tawnya Kumarakulasingam and Robert G. Harrington, from "Relationships Between Classroom Management, Teacher Stress, Burnout, and Levels of Hope," *Dissertation Abstracts International* (2002)

ISSUE SUMMARY

YES: Ross W. Greene is director of cognitive-behavioral psychology at the Clinical and Research Program in Pediatric Psychopharmacology at Massachusetts General Hospital and an associate professor of psychology in the department of psychiatry at Harvard Medical School. Professor Greene and his research associates contend that students with AD/HD are significantly more stressful to teach than their classmates without AD/HD.

NO: Tawnya Kumarakulasingam is coordinator of school psychological services in the Scottsdale, Arizona, schools, and Robert G. Harrington is a professor in the department of psychology and research in education at the University of Kansas. Drs. Kumarakulasingam and Harrington found that teacher stress and teachers' levels of hope are predictive of emotional exhaustion and depersonalization. Hope serves as a moderator of teacher stress.

Attention-deficit/hyperactivity disorder (AD/HD) is the largest single area of childhood psychopathology, affecting an estimated 2–5% of school-age children (perhaps one student in every other classroom). Symptoms include having difficulty paying attention in class and sitting quietly, and being impulsive and acting out before thinking. All of these skill deficits associated with AD/HD can create considerable management challenges for teachers. After all, it is well known that the parent-child relationship may suffer when a student is diagnosed with AD/HD, in part because of oppositional defiant behavior often associated with this syndrome. Some teachers may be more suited to contend with the behaviors of a student with AD/HD than others.

A recent study by Greene, et al. suggests that students with behavior problems associated with AD/HD are significantly more stressful to teach than students without AD/HD; however, individual teachers showed a low-to-moderate relationship between levels of teacher stress in response to the frequency and severity of a student's behavior. Teachers' stress response to students with AD/HD may vary due to the "fit" between characteristics of both the student and teacher, known as "student-teacher compatibility." In turn, the response of both the teacher and the student may vary depending upon the classroom environment in which the teacher must teach and the student must learn. Only students with associated oppositional/aggressive behaviors were consistently identified by teachers as making them feel more stressed. Furthermore, Greene contends that teachers may engage in significantly higher rates of negative interactions with students with AD/HD as compared to other students. Finally, students with AD/HD tend to take more of the teacher's attention in general, whether that attention is positive, neutral, or helpful. Greene and his associates explain these findings in that inattentive/overactive behaviors tend to be viewed as involuntary, whereas oppositional student behaviors are viewed by teachers as voluntary and coercive. When teachers believe that student misbehaviors are deliberate, they may be less willing to make appropriate classroom adaptations for these students, thus frustrating the student with AD/HD who may need to learn replacement skills such as problem solving and frustration tolerance.

In a contrasting study, Kumarakulasingam and Harrington found that teacher self-efficacy in classroom management did not make a significant contribution to the prediction of emotional exhaustion or depersonalization, two features of teacher burnout. In other words, whether or not teachers saw themselves as good classroom managers was not predictive of feeling emotionally stressed, underappreciated, and frustrated. Teacher self-efficacy in classroom management did make a significant contribution to the prediction of personal accomplishment, meaning that teachers who felt good about their classroom-management skills also felt good about their ability to reach personal goals in teaching and classroom management. On the other hand, teacher stress associated with classroom management and teacher's personal levels of hope made a significant contribution to the prediction of emotional exhaustion and depersonalization associated with teacher burnout. Those teachers with more hope were able to see themselves as having more personal accomplishments and consequently less personal stress. Kumarakulasingam and Harrington contend that it is not the oppositionality of the student that makes the difference in the teacher's ability to cope and manage a student; instead, the teacher's own personal self-perceptions about his/her ability to manage that classroom and the hope that he/she will be successful and will meet his/her own self-stated goals is important.

Ross W. Greene, et al.

Are Students with ADHD More Stressful to Teach? Patterns of Teacher Stress in an Elementary School Sample

The inattentive and hyperactive-impulsive behaviors characteristic of children with attention-deficit/hyperactivity disorder (ADHD) are known to have adverse effects on the quality of parent-child interactions and to significantly increase levels of parenting stress. Very little is known, however, about the effects that children with ADHD have on their teachers. This is a surprising circumstance, as students with ADHD exhibit a variety of behaviors in the classroom that may seriously disrupt the teaching process and impede their own learning, including off-task behavior, motoric restlessness, and intrusive verbalizations....

In practical terms, quantifying teacher stress may provide clinically relevant information about the teacher-student relationship and identify specific areas of stress associated with teaching a particular child. This information may be useful in identifying at-risk teachers (i.e., teachers most vulnerable when dealing with a challenging child) so that interventions may be applied to facilitate development of appropriate coping skills.

In this initial examination of stress in teachers of students with ADHD, several basic research questions were studied. We hypothesized that . . . (a) students with ADHD would be rated as more stressful to teach compared with students without ADHD, (b) the stress reported by teachers in response to students with ADHD would be highly individualized, (c) those students with ADHD also evidencing oppositional/aggressive behavior or social impairment would be rated as more stressful to teach than students who had ADHD but not these associated difficulties, and (d) teachers' ratings of stress would be correlated, but only moderately so, with ratings of students' actual behavior.

Method

Participants

A total of 64 general education elementary school teachers (62 women) participated in this study. Student participants included 64 children with ADHD

From *Journal of Emotional and Behavioral Disorders* by Ross W. Greene, Sara K. Beszterczey, Tai Katzenstein, Kenneth Park, and Jennifer Goring. Copyright © 2002 by Pro-Ed, Inc. Reprinted by permission. References omitted.

placed for the majority of the school day in a general education classroom. Of the 64 children, 50 were boys. The mean age was 8.4 years, with an age range of 5 years to 11 years and a grade range of kindergarten to fifth grade. Because the purpose of this study was to examine stress in teachers of students with ADHD in general education classrooms, students spending the majority of the school day in a special education classroom were excluded. Student participants (one per class) were enrolled in the classrooms of the participating teachers for the full school year during which data were gathered. An additional 38 non-ADHD comparison children also participated. Of this group, 29 were boys. The mean age was 8.4 years, with an age range of 6 years to 10 years and a grade range of kindergarten to fifth grade. These students were selected from the same classrooms as the teachers and the students with ADHD. The teacher and student participants were drawn from 27 schools in 23 different school systems in the Boston suburban area. Although all socioeconomic levels (SES) were represented in the sample, approximately 75% of children were from middle and upper middle class backgrounds. There were no significant differences in SES between the two groups of students.

All participants with ADHD had been previously diagnosed with the disorder by a physician or mental health professional. Parents of each student with ADHD completed a semistructured diagnostic interview by telephone prior to the student's entry into the study to confirm the diagnosis of ADHD and screen for other disruptive behavior disorders. The instrument used covered verbatim criteria for ADHD, conduct disorder, and oppositional-defiant disorder from the Diagnostic and Statistical Manual of Mental Disorders, Fourth Edition (DSM-IV). The reliability and validity of this instrument has been demonstrated in prior studies of children with ADHD. Because all of the students with ADHD undergoing screening had been previously diagnosed with the disorder, many were already taking medication to reduce ADHD-related symptoms. Thus, parents were asked to respond to interview questions based on their child's behavior when the child was not taking the medication.

Among students with ADHD, 16 (25%) satisfied DSM-IV criteria for ADHD/Predominantly Inattentive Type, 0% for ADHD/Predominantly Hyperactive-Impulsive Type, 46 (72%) for ADHD/Combined Type, and 2 (3%) for ADHD Not Otherwise Specified. Children designated in the last category met criteria for at least 10 symptoms of ADHD but did not fully satisfy criteria for any of the three established ADHD categories. Forty-eight (75%) of the students with ADHD met the diagnostic criteria for oppositional—defiant disorder, and 15 (23%) met the criteria for conduct disorder. These rates are consistent with rates found in other studies of boys with ADHD (e.g., Biederman et al., 1996). Parents of students in the control group also completed the telephone diagnostic interview. Among control students, two (5%) satisfied diagnostic criteria for oppositional—defiant disorder; none qualified for a diagnosis of ADHD or conduct disorder.

Because of the sequence and logistics of recruitment procedures described next (i.e., identifying and screening students with ADHD first and classmates without ADHD subsequently), it was not possible to keep telephone interviewers blind to a child's status (i.e., ADHD or non-ADHD). To ensure diagnostic accuracy, diagnostic interviews were audiotaped and reliability estimates were obtained by having 22 (20%) of the interviews reviewed by a licensed clinical child psychologist who was blind to each child's status. Kappas between interviewer and psychologist were 1.0 for ADHD, 1.0 for oppositional-defiant disorder, and .91 for conduct disorder. . . .

Measures

The teachers completed various instruments related to teacher characteristics prior to the beginning of the school year. Additional instruments related to teacher stress and student functioning were completed by the teachers at two points (late fall and early spring) during the school year. Direct observations of students' behavior and student-teacher interactions were conducted at two similar points during the school year by research staff members. Parents provided information about each child's medication status and family SES at two similar points during the school year.

Teacher Ratings of Tension and Frustration   Prior to the beginning of the school year, teachers completed the Student-Teacher Tension Checklist (STTC). This instrument, designed specifically for use in this study, lists verbatim DSM-IV behaviors for ADHD and ODD; teachers are asked to indicate the degree to which each behavior causes them tension or frustration on a scale of 1 (the behavior causes no tension or frustration) to 5 (the behavior causes extreme tension or frustration). . . .

Teacher Ratings of Stress   At two points during the school year (late fall and early spring) teachers completed the Index of Teaching Stress (ITS). The ITS quantifies teachers' subjective level of stress in response to a specific student. . . . Teachers are instructed to rate each item for the degree to which the behavior is stressful or frustrating in their interactions with a specified student, rather than how often the behavior occurs, on a scale of 1 (never stressful or frustrating) to 5 (very often stressful or frustrating). . . .

The ITS consists of two global scales: Student Characteristics (Part A) and Teacher Characteristics (Part B). The two global scales can be combined to create a Total Stress Score. The Student Characteristics section is composed of five subscales: ADHD (e.g., "Often cannot stay occupied more than 10 minutes"), Emotional Lability/Low Adaptability (e.g., "Reacts very strongly when something happens"), Anxiety/Withdrawal (e.g., "Seems very worded and nervous"), Low Ability/Learning Disabled (e.g., "Does not seem to learn as quickly as most others"), and Aggressive/Conduct Disorder (e.g., "Seems to have no guilt after misbehaving"). The Teacher Characteristics section is composed of four subscales: Self-Doubt/Needs Support (e.g., "For this student I feel I am not being a very good teacher"), Loss of Satisfaction From Teaching (e.g., "This student adversely affects my ability to enjoy teaching"), Disrupts Teaching Process (e.g., "This student takes my attention away from other children"), and Frustration Working with Parents (e.g., "Unable to agree with parents re: handling child"). . . .

Teacher Ratings of Students' Classroom Behavior   At two similar points during the school year, teachers completed the Teacher Report Form (TRF). The TRF assesses a variety of child behavior problems, as well as the degree to which a child's behavior deviates from age and gender norms, and yields six subscales

(Aggression/Noncompliance, Anxiety/Depression, Social Withdrawal, Attention Problems, Social Problems, and Delinquent Behavior). . . .

Direct Classroom Observation   At two points during the school year (late fall and early spring), trained observers conducted classroom observations, using a modified version of the Teacher Interaction Code (TIC), a coding system used to examine student-teacher interactions. Observers coded teacher responses toward a designated student with ADHD or a nondisabled peer as neutral, negative, positive, or providing help. Prompted via a "bug in the ear" device, coders observed behavior for 10 seconds and coded for the subsequent 5 seconds during 20 minutes of full class discussion/instruction and 20 minutes of independent seatwork (observations were conducted at prearranged times during which teachers indicated such activities would be taking place). Observers were blind to the child's status (i.e., with ADHD or without ADHD). Observers were trained to use the observational system by first reviewing the codes with the principal investigator and then practicing in classrooms until satisfactory familiarity, proficiency, and reliability were achieved. No significant differences were found for the four categories of observed behavior across the observations; thus, total scores for each class of teacher behavior were computed for the combined 40 minutes of observation across both observation sessions (80 minutes total). For 20% of the observations, two observers coded the same teacher to obtain reliability estimates; reliability (kappa) for these observations was .80.

At the same two points during the school year, observers also completed the Child Behavior Checklist-Direct Observation Form (CBC-DOF), a checklist consisting of 96 problem items, each rated on a scale of 0 (behavior not observed) to 3 (definite occurrence with severe intensity or greater than 3 minutes duration) after 10 minutes of observation. The CBC-DOF consists of six syndrome subscales (Withdrawn/Inattentive, Nervous/Obsessive, Depressed, Hyperactive, Attention Demanding, and Aggressive) and has been shown to have satisfactory psychometric properties. . . .

Results

Differences in Teacher Stress and Observed Behavior Between Students With and Without ADHD

For all analyses, significance was defined at the .01 level to protect against Type II errors. Teachers reported significantly greater stress in their interactions with students with ADHD as compared to controls. . . . This was true for the Total Stress Score, the Student Characteristics global scale (Part A) and its five subscales (ADHD, Emotional Lability/Low Adaptability, Anxiety/Withdrawal, Low Ability/ Learning Disabled, and Aggressive/Conduct Disorder), and the Teacher Characteristics global scale (Part B) and all four of its subscales (Self-Doubt/Needs Support, Loss of Satisfaction From Teaching, Disrupts Teaching Process, Frustration Working with Parents). . . . No significant association was found between teacher age or years of teaching experience and levels of teacher stress.

Association Between Student Behavior and Teacher Stress

As noted previously, we hypothesized that there would be low to modest overlap between teachers' ratings of students' behavior (i.e., ratings on the TRF) and teachers' ratings of stress in response to the same behaviors (i.e., ratings on Part A of the ITS). This hypothesis was generally confirmed by correlation analyses (only ratings for students with ADHD were included in these analyses). The correlation between the Attention Problems subscale of the TRF and the ADHD subscale of the ITS was .57; the correlation between the Aggressive/Noncompliance subscale of the TRF and the Aggressive/Conduct Disorder subscale of the ITS was .43; and correlations between the Anxiety/Depression and Social Withdrawal subscales from the TRF and the Anxiety/Withdrawal subscale of the ITS were .45 and .64, respectively. . . .

Association Between Subjective Response to ODD and ADHD Behaviors and Subsequent Stress Level

We next examined the degree to which teacher ratings (on the STTC, which was completed prior to the school year) of the tension and frustration caused by behaviors diagnostic of ADHD and ODD were associated with subsequent stress ratings in response to individual students with ADHD (only ratings for students with ADHD were included in these analyses). We identified as "high stress" teachers whose ITS Total Stress scores were one standard deviation above the mean. In this manner, we identified 15 teachers with very high levels of stress. Although we found that the teachers varied widely in the degree to which ADHD and ODD behaviors caused them tension or frustration, these ratings were not associated with the subsequent degree of stress a teacher experienced in response to an individual student with ADHD.

Effect of Oppositional/Aggressive Behavior and Social Impairment on Teacher Stress

Finally, we examined the degree to which the level of social impairment and oppositional/aggressive behavior for students with ADHD was associated with heightened levels of teacher stress and differences in student-teacher interactions. Using methodology similar to that employed in previous studies of social impairment in children with ADHD, we identified as "socially impaired" any student with ADHD whose score on the Social Problems subscale from the TRF was one standard deviation above the mean for all ADHD students. In this manner, we identified 10 students with ADHD who were scored as having social impairments. . . . On the Total Stress score and the Student Characteristics global scale (Part A) from the ITS these students were rated as significantly more stressful to teach when compared to students with ADHD who were not rated as socially impaired. . . .

For oppositional/aggressive behavior, similar methodology was used. We identified as "highly oppositional/aggressive" any student with ADHD whose score on the Aggressive/Noncompliance subscale from the TRF was one standard deviation above the mean for all students with ADHD. Using this methodology, we identified 11 students with ADHD as oppositional/aggressive. . . . On the Total Stress score, Parts A (Student Characteristics) and B (Teacher Characteristics), and on numerous ITS subscales, these students were rated as significantly more stressful to teach. . . .

Discussion

The above findings clarify our understanding of several issues related to the stress teachers experience in teaching students with ADHD. We found, as hypothesized, that students with ADHD are rated as significantly more stressful to teach (across multiple domains) as compared to their classmates without ADHD; however, teacher stress appeared to be highly individualized (i.e., large ranges for each global scale and subscale of the ITS were found). Correlational data showed a low to modest degree of overlap between the frequency and severity of a child's behavior and the severity of a teacher's stress. Finally, teachers reported significantly greater stress in teaching students with ADHD who displayed oppositional/aggressive behavior or social impairment as compared to students with ADHD who did not have these associated difficulties. . . .

Data obtained through direct observation of student-teacher interactions indicated that teachers engaged in significantly higher rates of negative interactions with students with ADHD as compared to students in the control group. However, our findings also indicated that teachers engaged in significantly higher rates of other behaviors (positive, neutral, providing help) with students with ADHD. Therefore, although students with ADHD appear to consume a significantly higher percentage of teacher attention, it seems clear that such attention is not solely composed of negative interactions.

Our findings further suggested that teacher stress occurs only partially as a function of a student's actual behavior (there was a low to moderate correlation between teacher stress and observer ratings of a child's actual behavior). Combined with the finding that teacher stress scores varied widely, there is the strong suggestion that teacher stress is a highly individualized phenomenon, with the implication that interactions between teachers and students with ADHD-like interactions between such children and their parents—are best conceived as a reciprocal process incorporating characteristics of both interaction partners. As noted earlier, such a perspective is consistent with theories emphasizing the transactional nature of adult and child outcomes.

Not surprisingly, students with ADHD who evidenced a high level of oppositional/aggressive behavior or social impairment were rated as more stressful to teach than their counterparts with ADHD who did not display these associated features. . . .

One finding regarding oppositional/aggressive behavior requires further clarification. We found that when students with ADHD were identified as highly oppositional/aggressive based on parental report, significant differences in teacher-reported stress did not emerge for those students as compared to students who were not. When oppositional/aggressive behavior was based on teacher report, significant differences in teacher stress between the two groups of students with ADHD did emerge. This finding presumably underscores the situational specificity of oppositional behavior; that is, many children who exhibit oppositional behavior at home do not do so at school. Those who do evidence oppositional behavior at school are, as one might expect, experienced by teachers as being more stressful. . . .

Conclusions

. . . These findings . . . have important ramifications for teacher training. The ITS may be viewed not merely as an indicator of a specific teacher's stress response to a given student but also as a gauge of the "fit" between characteristics of both individuals, or what has been referred to as "student-teacher compatibility." Counterproductive interactions between student and teacher may therefore best be understood as evidence of incompatibility rather than as a problem residing in either student or teacher. From such a perspective, the goal of intervention is to improve compatibility rather than to "fix the problem student" or "fix the problem teacher." . . .

Along these lines, researchers have shown that teachers' attributions and responses differ dramatically for inattentive/overactive behaviors versus aggressive behaviors. In other words, whereas inattentive/overactive behaviors tend to be viewed as involuntary, oppositional behavior is more typically viewed as volitional, goal-oriented, and coercive. This view of oppositional behavior has been increasingly called into question. For example, it has been argued that oppositional behavior may be more accurately understood as the byproduct of cognitive skill deficits in the domains of flexibility, problem-solving, and frustration tolerance. Intervention programs aimed at helping adults understand oppositional behavior as a deficit in cognitive skills and at remediating such skills deficits have been developed as an alternative to the coercion model and contingency management procedures flowing from this model commonly implemented in schools. Such programs may serve to enhance student-teacher compatibility.

It has also been argued that the classroom environment can either exacerbate or moderate the difficulties in self-regulation, social functioning, and rule-governed behavior of students with ADHD. Less traditional classroom management models emphasizing the importance of a social curriculum have been proposed. In such models, students are helped to understand individual differences, taught strategies for helping each other, and encouraged to view the classroom as a community of learners in which all students have strengths and limitations. Such models may provide a viable option for pursuing greater student-setting, student-teacher, and teacher-setting compatibility and may represent an essential component of teacher training in the future.

NO ↵

**Tawnya Kumarakulasingam
and Robert G. Harrington**

Relationships Between Classroom Management, Teacher Stress, Burnout, and Levels of Hope

T oday's schools continue to confront serious student misbehaviors often necessitating involvement of police and crisis intervention teams. Schools currently concern themselves with such student problems as drug and alcohol abuse, pregnancy, suicide, rape, robbery, burglary, arson, bombings, murder, absenteeism, vandalism, extortion, gang warfare, abortion, and venereal disease. The top three problems facing our public schools today include drug abuse, violence such as gangs and fighting, and lack of discipline.

Although most teachers in the United States in 2000 indicated that they believed that they were well prepared in classroom management, 29% indicated that they were not well prepared to maintain order and discipline in their classrooms. Amongst teachers with three or fewer years of teaching in the United States in 2000, approximately half of these teachers indicated that they were not at all well prepared to manage their classrooms. In addition, twenty general education teachers in a study conducted by Wilson, Gutkin, Hagen & Oats demonstrated difficulties brainstorming interventions to use with students who were labeled difficult-to-teach. Approximately two-thirds of teachers of students with emotional and behavioral disorders in a study by George, Gersten, and Grosenick, stated that their university education did not adequately prepare them to teach students with emotional and behavioral disorders. In another study by Nichols, 77 special education teachers expressed their frustrations and dissatisfaction with their university preparation and professional development opportunities in classroom management. Ninety-five percent of the teachers in another study said that they learned their classroom management skills on the job rather than from their university education. Some researchers suggest that teachers often select intervention strategies that are not empirically valid and that many of the empirically valid strategies are not well-implemented by teachers. Teachers consistently complain about being underprepared in the area of classroom management.

The evidence from the literature indicates that the frequency and severity of student misbehaviors continue to be a concern and that our teachers

From University of Kansas, 2002. Copyright © 2002 by Tawyna Kumarakulasingam, Ph.D., NCSP. Reprinted by permission. Dr. Kumarakulasingam is the School Psychologist and Psychology Department Chairperson in the Tempe Elementary School District #3, Tempe, Arizona. References omitted.

repeatedly report inadequate classroom management skills. Therefore, it is not surprising that teachers's difficulties managing student misbehaviors constitute a major source of stress for today's teachers. Researchers in one study found that pupil recalcitrance accounted for the highest source of stress for teachers. Pupil recalcitrance referred to misbehaving students, impolite and disruptive students, and class discipline problems. Forth-nine percent of teachers surveyed in a study by Salo cited lack of student motivation and poor student conduct as extremely stressful. Borg in a review of research studies concluded that student misbehaviors, discipline problems, disobedience, poor student motivation and poor student attitudes contributed significantly to teachers' stress. Borg, Riding, and Falzon surveyed 1,074 teachers in 81 state-run elementary schools in the Maltese Islands and found that pupil misbehaviors were the most stressful to teachers. Pupil misbehaviors included disruptive behaviors, classroom management difficulties, discipline problems, and students' poor attitudes. Sixty-percent of 5,000 American and Canadian teachers reported student discipline problems as the most stressful aspect of their jobs. Remy found a significant correlation between student discipline and teachers' stress in a survey of 585 teachers in 28 elementary schools in San Diego, California. Boyle, Biorg Falzon, and Baglioni rechecked the validity of an earlier study and found that student misbehaviors accounted for most of the variance when predicting teachers' stress. These studies appear to indicate a strong relationship between classroom management difficulties, particularly with student misbehaviors, and teacher stress.

When discussing teachers stress, the term burnout is often used interchangeably. However, teachers' stress is not synonymous with burnout. Cherniss stated that when professionals were unable to effectively cope with stress, and at the same time, were unable to avoid stress, they became physically and emotionally exhausted. In other words, these professionals became burned out.

In research on Cherniss' model of burnout, Burke and Greenglass found that for teachers certain work settings and stress antecedents correlated with six aspects of burnout. Burnout involved reduced work goals, lower personal responsibility, poor student outcomes, less idealism, emotional detachment, alienation from work, and greater self-interest. More recently, Farber differentiated between two types of teachers who both appear to be burned out. Farber described the "worn-out teacher" as a person who loses hope and eventually gives up trying when exposed to too much stress. The classically "burned out teacher" as proposed by Farber is a person who diligently works to the point of exhaustion, ". . . . in pursuit of sufficient gratification or accomplishment to match the extent of stress experienced" until this person also gives up trying.

Rudow wrote. "Teachers subject to burnout are those who are involved, devoted, and conscientious." Teachers who entered the teaching profession with idealistic helper motives and goals set on making a positive difference with students tended to be more susceptible to the negative effects of stress and more likely to burnout. Examples of teachers' helper motives might include, "love for children," "all students can achieve," "helping all weak students," and "never being absent." Some of these helper motives might be viewed as irrational beliefs about the teaching profession. Forman explained that teachers who held irrational beliefs about the teaching profession were more likely to negatively perceive stressors. When confronted with stressors such as student misbehaviors, Forman stated that teachers who held these rigid beliefs were more likely to be affected negatively by teacher stress.

One of the most widely accepted and researched definitions of burnout comes from Maslach, Jackson and Leiter. Burnout pertains to the psychological symptoms of Emotional Exhaustion, Depersonalization, and reduced Personal Accomplishment that can happen to professionals who work directly with other people in a helping type of relationship. Maslach and Jackson defined Emotional Exhaustion, Depersonalization and Personal Accomplishment as:

> Emotional exhaustion refers to feelings of being emotionally overextended and depleted of one's emotional resources; Depersonalization refers to a negative, callous, or excessively detached response to other people (often the recipients of one's service or care); and reduced Personal Accomplishment refers to a decline in one's feelings of competence and successful achievement in one's work.

Remarkably, some teachers seem to manage to cope with the demands and stress of teaching, despite limited classroom management skills and an increasingly high prevalence of student misbehaviors in their classrooms. These teachers might be hypothesized as possessing a high level of hope, which might help these teachers cope effectively with the demands and stresses of teaching. Teachers who enter the teaching profession with high hope could be described as professionals who successfully set meaningful and realistic work goals, easily problem-solve multiple pathways to reach their goals, and who are motivated to pursue their goals.

Work goals that teachers set may be long-term or daily goals. "Goals may be short or long term, but they need to be of sufficient value to occupy conscious thought. All goals must be attainable, yet contain some uncertainty." Being motivated to reach these personally set work goals involves more than teachers imagining themselves reaching their goals. Teachers must be able to physically and mentally activate themselves to reach their work goals despite any obstacles such as classroom management difficulties, especially with students who misbehave.

The self-motivation towards personally set work is referred to as "Agency thoughts" or "Will Power." Snyder, Feldman, Taylor, Schroeder, and Adams wrote that persons with high hope say positive affirming statements to themselves. Positive self-talk helps people to maintain their motivation to achieve their goals. Problem-solving multiple pathways to reach these goals is referred to a "Pathway Thoughts" or "Waypower." Pathway thought also involves the use of positive self-talk messages that help people keep their focus on the development of new strategies for achieving their goals. The obstacles that prevent teachers from reaching their goals are referred to as "barriers" or "goal blockages."

Most noticeably, Snyder, and Snyder McDermott, Cook and Rapoff wrote about hope and professions of teaching in their two books, *Psychology of Hope* and *Hope for the Journey*. In Snyder's 1994 book, he described a burned out teacher in the context of lost hope. Snyder uses Christina Maslach's definition of burnout.

He applied Ayala Pines' work with burned out teachers to his concept of hope by writing. "One of the primary researchers on the topic of burnout, Ayala Pines, has suggested that burnout can be understood as an instance in which one's important work-related goals are frustrated by blocking circumstances." Barriers to teachers's goals might be construed as student discipline problems or classroom management difficulties, Hypothetically, the death or loss of hope may be a precursor to burnout in teachers. Certainly, Snyder hypothesized that the death or loss of hope, which involved continued goal blockages, can eventually lead to negative emotions. Moreover, Snyder, McDermott, Cook, and Rapoff in their 1997 book, once again related the loss of hope to teacher burnout, In fact, Rodriguez-Hanley and Snyder suggested that the process of losing hope leads to burnout.

In summary, high hope teachers might be more likely to help their students be more disciplined and academically engaged than low hope teachers. However, this idea that high hope teachers might be better classroom managers than low hope teachers has not been investigated. Classroom management problems could be construed as significant stressors for teachers. Perhaps, teachers, with high hope are better able to tolerate these stressors than teachers with low hope. Moreover, persons with high hope may be able to more easily activate their pathways and agency thinking than do persons with low hope. Snyder, Mcdermott, Cook and Rapoff imply that a relationship exists between teacher stress, burnout, and teacher's level of hope. In fact, based on these two books one might believe that high hope teachers probably are less bothered by student discipline problems, less stressed and burned out and are perhaps more successful as classroom managers than low hope teachers. The arguments sound plausible and yet, there is no significant scientific research to support or to negate these specific hypothetical relationships with the population of teachers. Based upon a review of the literature, it appears evident that further examination of the relationships between classroom management with students who misbehavior, teacher, stress, teacher burnout, and hope is warranted. Consequently, this research offers the two following research questions as a way of providing a validation for the start of this line of research.

Research Questions

Research Question 1

What are the relationships between teacher self-efficacy in classroom management, teacher stress, teachers burnout, (Emotional Exhaustion, Depersonalization, and Personal Accomplishment) and teachers' levels of hope?

Research Question 2

Do teacher self-efficacy in classroom management, teachers' levels of hope, and teachers' stress predict teacher burnout (Emotional Exhaustion, Depersonalization, and Personal Accomplishment)?

Sample

This study was intended to be representative of the northeast Kansas population of female, general education, elementary school teachers. A minimum of 100 female, general education, elementary school teachers was originally proposed for this study. To reach this goal of 100 teachers, given that return rates of 40% or lower were not uncommon, 329 female, general education, elementary school teachers from five northeast Kansas school districts were solicited for participation. . . .

Instruments

Four instruments were selected for this study. The Classroom Management—Discipline subscale of the Teacher Efficacy in Classroom Management and Discipline Scale measures teacher self-efficacy in classroom management. The Stress Scale from the Quality of Teacher Work Life (QTWL) measures teacher stress. The Maslach Burnout Inventory—Educators Survey (MBI-ES), measures teacher burnout. Finally, the Hope Scale measures teachers' levels of hope. . . . The order of the instruments in the teachers' packets was counterbalanced to control for any order effects. . . .

Procedure

Data were collected employing two approaches. The first approach involved an onsite data collection. Data were collected onsite for efficiency. Schools were randomly selected from a list of schools in each district. Five schools within three school districts gave permission for the onsite administration. . . .

The second approach used a mail survey to collect data. Dillman's (2000) recommendations for mail surveys using the total design method were followed in the mail survey approach. Schools were randomly selected from a list of schools in each district. Ten schools did not give permission for onsite administration of the questionnaire. . . . In the ten schools, all female, general education teachers were mailed a questionnaire packet. . . .

Additionally, each teacher received a self-addressed, stamped envelope to facilitate prompt return of the questionnaires. The cover letter instructed teachers to return their completed questionnaires in the self-addressed, stamped envelope included in their packet by a specific data that was two weeks later.

Each packet, however, was coded with a number to help the researcher follow-up with a reminder postcard in two weeks after the initial mailing of the questionnaire packet. The postcard functioned both as a thank-you and as a reminder to teachers to complete and return their questionnaires (Dillman, 2000). See appendix I for a copy of the follow-up postcard.

Four weeks after the initial mailing of the questionnaires, a replacement packet of questionnaires was mailed to teachers who had not yet sent back their completed questionnaires. . . .

Sample

Participants

A total of 227 usable teacher questionnaire packets were obtained from 32 schools in these five northeast Kansas school districts [for an overall participation rate of 69%]. . . .

Years of teaching experience Teacher participants reported an average of 13.308 years of teaching experience. . . .

Grade level of students Teacher participants were divided logically into four categories based upon the grade level of students taught. A total of 71 teachers taught students in pre-kindergarten, kindergarten, and first grade. A total of 71 teachers taught students in second and third grades. A total of 57 teachers taught students in fourth and fifth grades. A total of 28 teachers taught students across all elementary school grades. These teachers taught classes such as art, physical education, and music.

Further Discussion of the Results

This part of the discussion of the results focuses on how the overall results compare with results obtained in the research literature. Particular attention is paid to discussion of the results of the research questions and how the results fit within the framework of the hope model.

The National Education Goals Panel stated that by the year 2000, that all schools in the United States of America would be free of violence and that all students would be educated in an environment free of class disruptions. In this study, teachers answered the open-ended question, "List the top three student behaviors in your classroom that you consider to be the most difficult to manage." . . . The most frequently reported student behaviors that teachers considered to be the most difficult to manage involved defiance, passive-aggressive behaviors toward academic tasks, class disruptions, poor social skills, and Attention Deficit Hyperactivity Disorder. Only three teachers stated that they had no behavioral concerns. Within the poor social skills category, a total of 43 teacher responses were noted for disrespect toward peers and/or adults. Although there were only about 8 percent of the teacher responses noted for category 6, "Physically and/or verbally aggressive behaviors toward peers," many of the behaviors reported by teachers were quite violent such as stabbing, throwing chairs, fighting, sexual misconduct, bullying, and destroying property.

Many of the teachers who participated in this study perceived themselves as at least adequate in their abilities to prevent and intervene when students misbehave and/or disrupt their classrooms. Eight teachers earned the top score of 84 on the Teacher Efficacy in Classroom Management and Discipline Scale. A total of 65 teachers earned scores equal to or higher than 78.

Scores on the Teacher Efficacy in Classroom Management and Discipline Scale, in this study, ranged from a low of 27 to a high of 84, meaning that a few teachers did not view themselves as adequate classroom managers. The lowest score obtained on the Teacher Efficacy in Classroom Management and Discipline Scale in this sample of elementary school teachers was 27, which was significantly below the mean score of 71.63 for this sample. The United States Department of Education reported that 29% of all teachers in the United States of America in 2000 stated that they were not well prepared to maintain order and discipline in their classrooms. When early career teachers were considered, almost 50% stated that they were poorly prepared to manage their classrooms.

Teachers who experienced frequent student misbehaviors and class disruptions in their classrooms tended to report higher levels of stress than did other teachers. In the research literature, teachers considered student motivation, student misconduct, poor student attitudes, and disobedience as the most stressful student misbehaviors. In this study, the top five student behaviors most frequently cited by teachers as being the most difficult to manage included defiance, passive-aggressive behaviors toward academic tasks, class disruptions, poor social skills, and Attention Deficit Hyperactivity Disorder. A positive and moderate correlation of .34 was noted between teacher self-efficacy in classroom management and teacher stress. Teachers, who believed that they could prevent and intervene when students misbehave and/or disrupt their classes, tended to report lower levels of teacher stress.

Teachers who continue to be confronted with the stress of teaching, particularly with goal blockages that are viewed as being outside the control of teachers, tend to become burned out. In this study, teachers who reported higher levels of teacher stress than did other teachers also reported higher levels of Emotional Exhaustion and Depersonalization and lower levels of Personal Accomplishment than did other teachers. Researchers consistently reported that poor classroom climate (student discipline problems, student apathy, verbal and physical abuse by students, low student achievement), continue to be related to teacher burnout. In this study, teacher stress accounted for a significant proportion of the variance in Emotional Exhaustion and Depersonalization . . . when the hypothesis that teacher burnout could be predicted by teacher stress, teacher self-efficacy in classroom management, and teachers' levels of hope was tested. In this study, teachers who found themselves unable to cope with the stress of teaching tended to report higher levels of Emotional Exhaustion and Depersonalization and lower levels of Personal Accomplishment.

Teachers, in this study, who perceived themselves as being able to prevent and intervene when students misbehaved reported higher levels of hope and felt more Personally Accomplished than did other teachers. Despite teachers' report of challenging behavior problems, teachers in this study perceived themselves as adequate classroom managers. Perhaps teachers who perceived themselves as adequate classroom managers were actually more successful in preventing and intervening when students misbehaved and/or disrupted their classrooms. Maybe teachers, who perceived themselves as better classroom managers, were actually better classroom managers. Furthermore, perhaps teachers were better classroom managers because of hope, which helped them overcome goal blockages such as classroom management problems. Teachers, who were able to overcome goal blockages (stressors such as classroom management problems) and ultimately reach their goals, may be less stressed and less burned out than other teachers. . . .

Interestingly, in this study, teachers' perceptions of their abilities to prevent and intervene when students misbehave did not predict Emotional Exhaustion and Depersonalization. This same sample of teachers, however, reported significantly challenging student behaviors that would be difficult for them to manage in their classrooms. Yet, higher levels of teacher self-efficacy in classroom management were related to higher levels of hope, greater feelings of Personal

Accomplishment, and less teacher stress. Teachers who view themselves positively as classroom managers may still be at risk for Emotional Exhaustion and Depersonalization. . . .

Freudenberger and Rudow stated that helping professionals, such as teachers, who start their careers as idealistic, hopeful, and naïve were more likely to become stressed and burned out. In fact, Rudow noted that teachers who tended to be idealistically motivated to help students succeed were more prone to be burned out. The helper motive examples that were noted by Rudow were similar to the rigid beliefs that were reported by teachers in this study. Some of the rigid beliefs espoused by teachers in this study included, "All students follow the rules." "Refuse to be interrupted or deterred." "Give 100% to work with students." Future researchers may want to examine whether differences in teacher stress, teacher burnout, self-efficacy in classroom management, and teachers' levels of hope exist between teachers who have rigid beliefs and teachers who do not have any rigid beliefs about students and the teaching profession.

Freudenberger and Rudow suggested that hopeful teachers might be more likely to be affected negatively by stress and therefore be more likely to become burned out. Snyder, McDermott, Cook, and Rapoff wrote that burnout might occur instead when professionals experience a loss of hope, particularly when faced with a serious obstacle to an important teacher directed goal. In particular, professionals who lose hope and experience continued blocked goals tend to develop negative emotions. These low hope teachers might possibly feel defeated when they encounter barriers to their work goals. On the other hand, high hope teachers might continue to perceive themselves as reasonably good classroom managers despite some continued student misbehaviors. High hope teachers probably view these classroom disruptions as challenges that can eventually be overcome. Snyder, McDermott, Cook, and Rapoff presented the hypothesis that teachers with high levels of hope, compared to teachers with low levels of hope, coped better with stress and did not easily reach burnout.

Teachers, in this study, perceived themselves as moderately Emotionally Exhausted, only slightly Depersonalized, and highly Personally Accomplished. Teachers may indeed the Emotionally Exhausted despite being hopeful and perceiving themselves as effective classroom managers despite the continuation of stressors (goal blockages), particularly if these stressors tended to be viewed as being outside the realm of control of teachers. . . .

In this study, teachers' levels of hope were moderately and positively related to teacher self-efficacy in classroom management and Personal Accomplishment and moderately and negatively related to Emotional Exhaustion and Depersonalization. Teachers' level of hope were positively and only weakly correlated with teacher stress. As teachers' levels of hope increased, teacher self-efficacy in classroom management increased, teachers' feelings of Personal Accomplishment increased, and teachers experienced less burnout and slightly less stress. . . .

POSTSCRIPT

Is There a Relationship Between Teacher Stress and Student Misbehavior?

All students can present considerable classroom management challenges to new and experienced teachers alike. Nevertheless, students with AD/HD can provide special challenges. I am reminded of a brand new teacher who was attending a workshop training session I was presenting on the topic of managing students with AD/DH in the regular classroom. She was accompanied by her superintendent. As usual, I spiced up my presentation with lots of real case studies of students with AD/HD who were having difficulty behaving. I assumed that most teachers were familiar with the special challenges that students with AD/HD could present and that I would provide them with a range of strategies that they could use to help improve academic and behavioral performance. As the presentation proceeded it became obvious to me and the rest of the audience that there was some considerable distress up front where this young woman was seated with her superintendent: Every time I gave a description of a particular behavior that a student with AD/HD might emit, this young woman in the front row would respond with a sigh, a groan, and rock in her chair. I continued the workshop until the first break where the superintendent approached me and asked whether we could speak. I agreed.

The superintendent explained that what I was saying was interesting, but that everything I was saying was making her young colleague frustrated and stressed. My examples and commentary reminded her of the students she was trying to teach. I started to apologize but was interrupted by the superintendent. I was told that there was no need to apologize and that I had done a good job of describing the problem behaviors associated with AD/HD and in providing ideas about how to treat these problems in the classroom. At this point, I was perplexed about why then this novice teacher was so obviously exasperated and stressed during the presentation. If I was providing useful information, why wasn't the teacher responding positively to the new information?

The three of us sat down and discussed the situation. It appeared that the teacher had the idea that teaching was all about instruction. She thought that classroom management would be a minimal part of her job. She did not feel prepared to teach a student with AD/HD in her classroom, making her feel extremely stressed, incompetent, and hopeless. She was expressing sentiments that she had made a mistake in choosing teaching as a career. As we talked further it became clear that despite the fact that the teacher agreed that the strategies we were discussing might actually help her teach and manage students with AD/HD, she did not know whether she had the emotional energy and personal motivation to get the job done. There was a distinct disconnect between what she thought teaching was and the emotional skills that she was able to bring to the task. She sounded hopeless. What concerned the superintendent the most was that here was a very bright person whom she wanted to retain, but she was afraid that she might not be able to do so. She wanted to know two things. In the short run, how can we get this new teacher motivated to use the information being presented? In the long run, will this teacher quit the profession?

I referred to the concepts expressed in this issue. I explained that there can be a relationship between the level of teacher stress and the level of student misbehavior, but there does not have to be if the teacher holds some important beliefs. I explained that stress can be moderated if a teacher is hopeful about the possibilities of a successful outcome with a difficult student, if the teacher is able to handle personal stress along the way to reaching that goal, and if the teacher believes that she has the classroom-management skills to reach the goals she has set for the student. I think that this case study exemplifies how despite the fact that students with AD/HD can be challenging, they do not necessarily have to be overwhelming to the individual. It all depends upon whether the teacher is hopeful, goal-directed, and feels good about his or her own skills in classroom management. I will leave it up to you to assess whether you think this young teacher stayed in the profession of teaching or not.

For more information about how to handle personal stress, refer to the following: L. Gorman, *52 Relaxing Rituals* (Hallmark Cards, 1996) and P. Wilson, *Instant Calm* (Penguin Books, 1999). A great book for dealing with the oppositional behavior associated with 60 percent of the cases of AD/HD is E. Verdick and M. Lisovskis, *How to Take the GRR out of Anger* (Free Spirit, 2003). If you want to understand your teaching-related stress from a humorous point of view, see E. Verdick, *Stress Can Really Get You Nervous* (Free Spirit, 2003). To interject a bit of therapeutic humor into your classroom to reduce your stress and that of your students, try reading D. Loomans and K. Kolberg, *The Laughing Classroom* (KJ Kramer, 1993). For a personal dose of humor that will help you see that others have to cope with stress, read T. Mico, *Life Stinks* (Ariel Books, 1995). To power up your optimism for the task ahead of you, read A.L. McGinis, *The Power of Optimism* (Harper Paperbacks, 1993).

ISSUE 3

Is Teaching the Habits of Highly Successful Students the Best Approach to Improve Student Motivation?

YES: Elizabeth A. Linnenbrink and Paul R. Pintrich, from "Motivation as an Enabler for Academic Success," *School Psychology Review* (Summer 2002)

NO: Kathryn R. Wentzel and Deborah E. Watkins, from "Peer Relationships and Collaborative Learning as Contexts for Academic Enablers," *School Psychology Review* (Summer 2002)

ISSUE SUMMARY

YES: Elizabeth A. Linnenbrink is an assistant professor of educational psychology in foundations of education at the University of Toledo, and Paul R. Pintrich was a professor of education and psychology and chair of the combined program in education and psychology at the University of Michigan. These authors conclude that it is not appropriate to label students as "motivated" or "unmotivated" since they believe that motivation is a skill that can be taught to all learners.

NO: Kathryn R. Wentzel is a professor at the University of Maryland in the department of human development, and Deborah Watkins is an assistant professor at York College of Pennsylvania in special education. They argue that levels of peer support and acceptance in the classroom are important social factors in improving student motivation and behavior; without them, students may not be able to improve motivation.

Is an age-old question. Can student motivation be taught or is it a personality trait that is inborn and immutable? Or perhaps it is a student characteristic that is dependent upon the social climate and sense of community support engendered by the classroom teacher and student peers. Can unmotivated students be taught the habits of highly successful students? If it were possible to teach unmotivated students to think and act like successful students, it would be a tremendous assist for classroom teachers. In that case, teaching student motivation to learn could become part of the classroom curriculum. On the other hand, if student motivation could be engendered by managing the classroom climate, the teacher would be able to skillfully employ peers to model good classroom motivation skills. In either case, teachers would have a strategy to improve the interest and motivation of students who complain that they don't care, want to quit school, aren't interested, and are bored. The controversy that we address in this issue is how best to get students to become more motivated as a strategy to improve student behavior in the classroom. Are there internal skills that the student must learn, or is student motivation more dependent upon the classroom context in which learning takes place?

Linnenbrink and Pintrich contend that motivation is an enabler for academic success and that it is best thought of as a skill that is taught using cognitive behavior therapy. They contend that students should not be thought of as "motivated" or "unmotivated" but that students should be viewed as missing specific skills in areas such as self-efficacy, positive attributions, intrinsic motivation and goal orientation all of which are central cognitive skills that enable a student to be successful at school. Furthermore, these authors believe that motivation is not a stable personality trait but that it can be influenced and improved directly through instruction. They also believe that students need to be taught to think like other classmates who are more successful in academics. In this way, students are being taught the habits of other highly successful students. This perspective should give hope to classroom teachers, school psychologists and counselors that there is something that they can do to improve the attitudes of students who don't seem to care about school.

In sharp contrast to the view that student motivation is shaped by teaching new cognitive skills, Wentzel and Watkins contend that classroom peers have the capacity to motivate and encourage unmotivated students both academically and behaviorally in the ways they provide social support, encourage a sense of belongingness in the class, and tolerate and empathize with students who may be struggling in the class. The authors suggest that when students perceive that they are accepted by peers in a classroom they are more likely to express sentiments of positive satisfaction with school, feelings of academic self-efficacy, and an orientation toward meeting positive goals both academically and behaviorally. On the other hand, when students themselves are shunned by others, they are more likely to be uninterested in school and often disengage by dropping out of school entirely.

Thus, the controversy is struck. Should teachers work on developing an individual sense of motivation in students? Is it the job of teachers to instill motivation in their students? Alternatively, does motivation of students spring from the foundation of a positive classroom atmosphere. This is an interesting controversy because it raises the question about whether the teacher is responsible for all motivation and consequent learning that takes place in the class or whether the individual student and classroom peers share some of that responsibility.

YES ↩

**Elizabeth A. Linnenbrink
and Paul R. Pintrich**

Motivation as an Enabler
for Academic Success

Psychologists and educators have long considered the role of motivation in student achievement and learning. Much of the early research on student achievement and learning separated cognitive and motivational factors and pursued very distinct lines of research that did not integrate cognition and motivation. However, since at least the 1980s there has been a sustained research focus on how motivational and cognitive factors interact and jointly influence student learning and achievement. In more colloquial terms, there is a recognition that students need both the cognitive skill and the motivational will to do well in school. . . .

The integration of motivational and cognitive factors was facilitated by the shift in motivational theories from traditional achievement motivation models to social cognitive models of motivation. One of the most important assumptions of social cognitive models of motivation is that motivation is a dynamic, multifaceted phenomenon that contrasts with the quantitative view taken by traditional models of motivation. In other words, these newer social cognitive models do not assume that students are either "motivated" or "not motivated" or that student motivation can be characterized in some quantitative manner between two endpoints on a single continuum. Rather, social cognitive models stress that students can be motivated in multiple ways and the important issue is understanding how and why students are motivated for school achievement. This change in focus implies that teachers or school psychologists should not label students as "motivated" or "not motivated" in some global fashion. Furthermore, assessment instruments that generate a single global "motivation" score for students may be misleading in terms of a more multifaceted understanding of student motivation. Accordingly, in the discussion of motivation as an academic enabler, many aspects of student motivation including self-efficacy, attributions, intrinsic motivation, and goals are considered.

A second important assumption of social cognitive models of motivation is that motivation is not a stable trait of an individual, but is more situated, contextual, and domain-specific. In other words, not only are students motivated in multiple ways, but their motivation can vary depending on the situation or

From *School Psychology Review*, vol. 31, issue 13, Summer 2002, pp. excerpts from 313–327. Copyright © 2002 by National Association of School Psychologists. Reprinted by permission. References omitted.

context in the classroom or school. Although this assumption makes it more difficult for research and assessment efforts, it means that student motivation is conceived as being inherently changeable and sensitive to the context. This provides hope for teachers and school psychologists and suggests that instructional efforts and the design of classrooms and schools can make a difference in motivating students for academic achievement.

This situated assumption means that student motivation probably varies as a function of subject matter domains and classrooms. For example, within social cognitive models, motivation is usually assessed for a specific subject area such as math, reading, science, or social studies and in reference to a specific classroom or teacher. In some ways, this also fits with teachers' and parents' own perceptions and experiences as they find that some children are quite motivated for mathematics, whereas others hate it, and also observe these motivational differences with other subject areas as well. . . .

A third assumption concerns the central role of cognition in social cognitive models of motivation. That is, it is not just the individual's cultural, demographic, or personality characteristics that influence motivation and achievement directly, or just the contextual characteristics of the classroom environment that shape motivation and achievement, but rather the individual's active regulation of his or her motivation, thinking, and behavior that mediates the relationships between the person, context, and eventual achievement. That is, students' own thoughts about their motivation and learning play a key role in mediating their engagement and subsequent achievement. . . .

Rather than discussing all the different motivational constructs that may be enablers of student achievement and learning, this article will focus on four key families of motivational beliefs (self-efficacy, attributions, intrinsic motivation, and goal orientations). These four families represent the currently accepted major social cognitive motivational theories and, therefore, seem most relevant when thinking about how motivation relates to achievement and other academic enablers. For each of the four general components, the components are defined, a summarization is given for how the motivational component is related to student achievement and learning as well as the other academic enablers discussed in this special issue, and some implications for instruction and assessment are suggested. . . .

Adaptive Self-Efficacy Beliefs as Enablers of Success

A common layperson's definition of motivation is that it involves a strong personal interest in a particular subject or activity. Students who are interested are motivated and they learn and achieve because of this strong interest. Although interest as a component of student motivation will be discussed later, one of the more important motivational beliefs for student achievement is self-efficacy, which concerns beliefs about capabilities to do a task or activity. More specifically, self-efficacy has been defined as individuals' beliefs about their performance capabilities in a particular context or a specific task or domain. Self-efficacy is assumed to be situated and contextualized, not a general belief about self-concept or self-esteem. For example, a student might have high self-efficacy for doing algebra problems, but a lower self-efficacy for geometry problems or other subject areas, depending on past successes and failures. These self-efficacy beliefs are distinct from general self-concept beliefs or self-esteem. . . .

Self-efficacy has been positively related to higher levels of achievement and learning as well as a wide variety of adaptive academic outcomes such as higher levels of effort and increased persistence on difficult tasks in both experimental and correlational studies involving students from a variety of age groups. Students who have more positive self-efficacy beliefs (i.e., they believe they can do the task) are more likely to work harder, persist, and eventually achieve at higher levels. In addition, there is evidence that students who have positive self-efficacy beliefs are more likely to choose to continue to take more difficult courses (e.g., advanced math courses) over the course of schooling. In our own correlational research with junior high students in Michigan, we have consistently found that self-efficacy beliefs are positively related to student cognitive engagement and their use of self-regulatory strategies (similar in some ways to study skills) as well as general achievement as indexed by grades. . . .

In summary, having generally positive self-efficacy is adaptive for school learning and achievement as well as other academic enablers, suggesting that schools should seek to develop positive self-efficacy beliefs in their students.

At the same time, two important caveats need to be stressed about attempts to facilitate positive self-efficacy beliefs in students. First, as noted earlier, self-efficacy is not self-esteem and the two constructs should not be confused. Self-efficacy is a judgment of task-specific capabilities and is based on actual accomplishments and success and failures, whereas self-esteem is a much more general affective evaluation of the self. The second caveat relates to the issue of inaccuracy in self-efficacy beliefs. The generalization about the positive link between self-efficacy and achievement may suggest that self-efficacy should always be as high as possible. However, it seems that it is more adaptive to have self-efficacy beliefs that are relatively accurate or calibrated to actual accomplishments. . . . Students should not overestimate or underestimate their capabilities for schoolwork, rather they should have fairly accurate, but optimistic, beliefs about their efficacy to accomplish school work. This implies that teachers and other school personnel should attempt to foster positive, but accurate, self-efficacy beliefs.

In terms of instructional implications, self-efficacy is best facilitated by providing opportunities for students to succeed on tasks within their range of competence and through these experiences actually develop new capabilities and skills. Self-efficacy is not fostered by providing inaccurate or effusive praise to students in the absence of specific task accomplishments. This type of praise is meaningless and invalid and may foster inaccurate beliefs in students who think they are capable of some task, such as reading, when in fact they are not very good readers. Therefore, it is important that educators calibrate tasks and assessments so that success is attainable. By having a variety of tasks in the classroom and multiple forms of assessments such as portfolios, essays, and project-based assessments, classroom teachers may be able to provide all students with opportunities to be successful, thus fostering self-efficacy among all students. . . .

Adaptive Attributions as Enablers of Success

Attribution theory, which focuses on attempts to understand why events occur, is another important line of research on achievement motivation. Similar to other motivational theories, research on attributions did not focus initially on academic achievement. However, Weiner's research relating attributions to students' behaviors and success in academic settings has done much to further an understanding of how attributions relate to learning in school. Although much of Weiner's research was conducted with college undergraduates, others such as Borkowski have applied attribution theory to elementary and secondary students.

Attribution theory suggests that when a failure or success occurs, such as failing a math exam or doing particularly well on an assignment, individuals will analyze the situation to determine the perceived causes for the failure or success. These causes may be environmental factors, such as a distracting testing environment or bias on the part of the teacher, or personal factors, such as lack of knowledge, ability, or failure to prepare adequately for the exam. These perceived causes can be categorized into three causal dimensions: stability (how stable the perceived cause is), locus (whether the cause is internal or external), and controllability (whether or not the perceived cause can be controlled). Using these three causal dimensions, a specific cause can be categorized into one of eight cells. For instance, a student who fails an exam may say it is due to instructor bias (external, stable, controllable) or lack of ability (internal, stable, uncontrollable). According to attribution theory, it is the individual's focus on why success or failure occurred that explains specific psychological outcomes such as future expectancies, self-efficacy, and affect. These psychological outcomes have been further linked to behavioral outcomes such as engagement and achievement.

In general, research on attributions suggests that for success it is adaptive to attribute the success to stable, internal factors such as ability, skill, or talent as these factors should also be present for future tasks. Attributions to unstable but controllable internal factors such as effort are especially adaptive in that effort can be modified based on the demands of the situation. On the other hand, for failure, attributions to factors that are unstable are more adaptive. For instance, attributing failure to lack of effort (unstable, controllable, internal) not only allows the student to protect his or her self-worth, it also helps the student to see a way to avoid failure in the future (by exerting more effort). Attributing failure to bad luck (unstable, uncontrollable, external) can also be adaptive because it means that the circumstances perceived to cause the failure may not be present in future situations.

Researchers who focus on children with learning disabilities or under-achieving children find similar patterns of adaptive and maladaptive attributions; however, they further suggest that effort attributions be associated with strategy use. That is, rather than attributing success to effort, success should be attributed to effortful strategy use. This maybe especially important for children with learning disabilities in that effort may not always lead to success. Furthermore, rather than attributing failure to lack of effort alone, attributing failure to the lack of strategy use or use of inappropriate strategies helps dispel the inappropriate belief that effort always leads to success, but still helps to convey the idea that success is possible.

Although attribution theory does not suggest a direct link of adaptive attributions to academic achievement and other academic enablers, some indirect links can be made via other psychological processes. For instance, adaptive attributions are associated with higher expectancies for success, enhanced academic self-efficacy, and positive affect such as pride or hopefulness. These psychological outcomes are in turn associated with engagement (persistence and choice) and study skills (via self-efficacy), as well as actual achievement. Carr et al. also suggested that attributions to external factors hinders the acquisition of strategies because external attributions provide little reason for children to learn strategies—suggesting that attributions are important for learning strategies.

Attribution theory is useful for school psychologists and practitioners in that individuals' beliefs about the causes of events can be changed through feedback and other environmental manipulations. In particular, teachers' reactions following success or failure can influence students' attributions suggesting that the teacher plays an important role in the types of attributions students make. For example, a teacher's expression of pity following failure makes it more likely that a student will attribute the failure to low ability (internal, stable, uncontrollable).

In addition to teachers' reactions, teachers can influence students' attributions by providing feedback to students following success or failure. In doing so, it is first important for teachers to assess whether success or failure has occurred for a particular student based on the student's judgments of success or failure. Following this, the teacher should consider the situation and help the student make adaptive but accurate attributions. For failure settings, it is useful for students to attribute the failure to unstable causes as this helps to ensure that there is a possibility for success in the future. For instance, it is often adaptive to attribute failure to lack of effort or inappropriate strategy use. If the failure was due to lack of appropriate strategy use, it is not useful to tell the student to try hard. Rather, the teacher may need to work with the student to help them develop the strategies and skills necessary to succeed in the future. For success, attributions to effort are also adaptive, especially if the student did indeed try hard. It is also adaptive to attribute success to appropriate strategy use as this helps to encourage the use of strategies in the future and is internal. However, success is also possible without great effort, so when appropriate, it is also adaptive to attribute success to talent or skill. . . .

Intrinsic Motivation as Enabler of Success

The concept of intrinsic versus extrinsic motivation is certainly prevalent within social-cognitive models of motivation and is thus included in this review of motivation as an academic enabler. Intrinsic motivation is defined as motivation to engage in an activity for its own sake, whereas extrinsic motivation refers to motivation to engage in an activity as a means to an end. . . .

Whereas interest in general is defined as the interaction between the individual and his or her environment, interest theorists have distinguished between personal or individual interest and situational interest.

Personal interest reflects an individual's interest in a particular topic or domain. It is often measured by students' reports of how much they like or enjoy a particular activity or domain. Personal interest is thought to be somewhat stable over time and is partially a function of individuals' preferences as well as aspects of the task. In contrast, situational interest is based entirely on the features of the learning context and may be short term or long lasting. . . .

Mitchell suggested that situational interest could be broken into two factors: catch and hold. Catch factors are thought to stimulate students (i.e., "catch" their attention). They include innovative or novel instructional techniques such as using an exciting computer program, having students learn course material by playing a game, or allowing students to work on a group project together. In contrast, hold factors are thought to empower students by making the content meaningful so students view the content as useful, or by encouraging students' involvement in the task. For instance, emphasizing how a particular mathematics lesson is useful for bookkeeping or planning a budget may help to make the material more meaningful to students. Providing activities that encourage active student involvement such as small group work or discussions rather than lectures is also useful for promoting the hold factor of situational interest. Interest researchers have given increased attention to the hold factor as it seems to be a better predictor of continuing interest than the catch factor. . . .

For teachers and school psychologists, these results suggest that academic achievement, study skills, and engagement can he increased by tapping into students' interests. This can be done by building upon personal interest or creating situational interest. That is, allowing students to work on topics they find personally interesting may help them to engage in such a way that they use better strategies for learning and ultimately achieve at higher levels. One way to capitalize on personal interest is to allow students to pick topics for class projects or reports. Admittedly, it is difficult to design classroom activities that capitalize on the personal interest of all students in the classroom; therefore, educators should also consider ways to enhance situational interest.

Teachers trying to enhance situational interest should think about how to promote both catch and hold factors. For instance, when designing classroom activities, having an exciting experiment in science or using an innovative computer program in social studies may spark situational interest and engage students at that particular moment. This is useful for engaging students in a specific activity, but may not translate into interest in future activities. Therefore, teachers should also consider how to promote the hold factor of situational interest, such as trying to make the topic meaningful to students. This may be done by capitalizing on the utility of what is being learned (e.g., for things outside of school or fortune goals). . . .

Adaptive Goal Orientations as Enablers of Success

The final perspective for motivation discussed in this article is achievement goal theory. Achievement goal theory is one of the most prominent theories within motivational research today. Goal theory proposes that there are two general goal orientations that concern the purposes individuals are pursuing when approaching and engaging in a task. Achievement goal theorists have used a variety of labels to refer to these two goals including learning and performance goals, task and ability goals, task-involved and ego-involved, and mastery and performance goals. Although there are slight variations in the interpretation of these goals under these various labels, they will be referred to here as mastery and performance goals for simplicity. Mastery goals orient learners to "developing new skills, trying to understand their work, improving their level of competence, or achieving a sense of mastery based on self-referenced standards." In contrast, performance goals orient learners to focus on their ability and self-worth, to determine their ability by outperforming others in competitions, surpassing others in achievements or grades, and receiving public recognition for their superior performance.

In the literature on mastery and performance goals, the general theoretical assumption has been that mastery goals foster a host of adaptive motivational, cognitive, and achievement outcomes, whereas performance goals generate less adaptive or even maladaptive outcomes. Moreover, this assumption, particularly the adaptive mastery goal assumption, has been supported in a large number of empirical studies on goals and achievement processes. The logic of the argument is that when students are focused on trying to learn and understand the material and trying to improve their performance relative to their own past performance, this orientation will help them maintain their self-efficacy in the face of failure, ward off negative affect such as anxiety, lessen the probability that they will have distracting thoughts, and free up cognitive capacity, thus allowing for more cognitive engagement and achievement. In contrast, when students are concerned about trying to be the best, get higher grades than others, and do well compared to others under a performance goal, there is the possibility that this orientation will result in more negative affect or anxiety, increase the possibility of distracting and irrelevant thoughts (e.g., worrying about how others are doing rather than focusing on the task), and that this will diminish cognitive capacity, task engagement, and performance. . . .

In summary, empirical evidence suggests that the adoption of mastery goals relates positively to school learning as well as other academic enablers such as study skills and engagement. . . .

The types of tasks used in the classroom can convey very different messages to students regarding the general goal structure of the classroom. To encourage mastery goal adoption, Ames recommends using tasks that are meaningful and appropriately challenging. For instance, rather than having students complete a series of worksheets, having students engage in hands-on, applied activities in math and science can help to challenge students and help them see how what they are learning in school relates to things outside of school. Furthermore, using a variety of tasks not only allows students to choose among tasks they find personally interesting but also helps to decrease the opportunity for social comparison. The authority structure of the classroom also sends important messages regarding the achievement goal-orientation of the classroom. By allowing students to have autonomy in the classroom and reducing the authority of the teacher, mastery goals can be promoted. For instance, giving students a set of assignments and allowing them to choose the order in which they will complete them helps to grant autonomy to the students and thus encourage mastery. Evaluation and recognition are often quite salient to students and play a large role in setting the "tone" of the classroom as emphasizing mastery or performance. To foster mastery goal adoption, evaluation should focus on individual improvement as well as mastery of ideas. For instance, evaluating students on their improvement over several drafts of a written assignment can help to focus students on learning rather than on performing better than others. In addition, private rather than public recognition of students' efforts and improvement helps to promote a mastery-oriented learning environment. . . .

Conclusion

This article has focused on four keys components of student motivation. Based on research on these four components, suggestions have been offered regarding what teachers and school psychologists can do to promote students' motivation. . . . These suggestions are based on the multidimensional view of motivation as well as the idea that motivation is not a stable trait but reflects an interaction between the context and what the student brings to the context. Accordingly, it is inappropriate to label students as "motivated" or "unmotivated"; rather, school psychologists and other educators are urged to consider ways in which the learning environment can be altered to enhance all students' motivation based on a variety of motivational constructs including academic self-efficacy, attributions, intrinsic motivation, and achievement goals. Although there is certainly a need for additional research on how specific changes to the classroom context influence multiple aspects of students' motivation in school, it is clear from what is known that the context shapes students' motivation, engagement, strategy use, and achievement. Therefore, teachers and school psychologists are urged to focus on changes that can be made to the school or classroom environments to help all students, rather than citing lack of motivation for a particular student as a reason for lower than expected academic performance.

Peer Relationships and Collaborative Learning as Contexts for Academic Enablers

Numerous studies have documented positive relations between children's relationships with peers and a range of social and intellectual enablers, including motivational orientations reflected in goals and values, and skills related to self-regulation, social interaction, and problem solving. These findings illustrate how learning is inextricably linked to the social contexts within which children learn, and highlight the notion that the development and use of academic enablers is highly dependent on the characteristics of and opportunities provided by learning contexts. This article focuses on the development of students' academic enablers within two types of peer contexts. First discussed are ways in which peer relationships can motivate students to engage in learning activities as well as socially appropriate behavior. Second, ways are described in which peer collaborative contexts can promote academic engagement as well as provide a supportive structure for the development of specific problem-solving skills. . . .

Peer Relationships as Motivational Contexts

Despite the extensive literature linking peer acceptance to academic outcomes, little is known about the underlying processes that can explain these relations. Several researchers have demonstrated that associations between peer acceptance, rejection, and academic outcomes can be explained in part by behavioral styles that contribute to peer competence as well as academic functioning. In particular, prosocial displays of behavior such as helping, cooperating, and sharing have been linked to peer acceptance and popularity as well as to academic achievement, whereas aggression and antisocial displays of behavior have been related to peer rejection and academic problems.

To the extent that behavioral styles account for positive associations between peer relationships and academic outcomes, the quality of peer relationships perse is likely to play a relatively small role in promoting social and academic competence in the classroom. A growing body of research, however,

From *School Psychology Review*, vol. 31, issue 13, Summer 2002, pp. 366–377. Copyright © 2002 by National Association of School Psychologists. Reprinted by permission. References omitted.

also provides evidence that the nature of a student's relationships with peers might contribute to their academic performance indirectly by way of motivational outcomes. For instance, being accepted by peers has been related positively to satisfaction with school, perceived academic competence, and pursuit of goals to learn and to behave in socially appropriate ways, whereas being rejected by peers has been related to low levels of interest in school and disengaging altogether by dropping out. In turn, ample evidence documents significant and positive links between these motivational enablers and students' behavioral and academic competencies at school.

Assuming that these associations between peer relationships and motivation reflect some level of peer influence, what is it about peer relationships that might contribute to students' motivation to learn and to behave appropriately? One explanation is that students' perceptions of their relationships with peers rather than actual levels of acceptance are the most proximal predictor of motivation. Indeed, perceiving positive relationships with peers is likely to promote a student's sense of emotional well-being and social relatedness; in turn, this positive sense of self and relatedness is likely to support positive engagement in classroom activities. In contrast, perceiving negative relationships or rejection is likely to lead to emotional distress and subsequent disaffection with and alienation from classroom activities.

As articulated by Connell and Wellborn, this perspective has roots in attachment theory and is based on the notion that if students' needs for social relatedness are met at school (i.e., if they feel securely attached to others and consequently experience a positive sense of self and emotional well-being), they also will be motivated to engage in positive social and cognitive interactions within the school setting. A slightly different explanation is that students who feel securely attached also are likely to have a history of successful socialization experiences that have taught them to regulate emotions effectively when faced with new challenges and experiences. In contrast, children who have not experienced secure relationships tend to enter situations with detachment or high levels of emotional distress. Each perspective proposes a slightly different set of processes whereby attachments with others lead to positive engagement with the environment. Both suggest, however, that students who perceive low levels of peer social support are likely to experience psychological distress and, as a consequence, disengage from classroom learning and social interactions. . . .

Researchers have clearly documented significant relations between students' peer relationships, perceived support from peers, and their motivation to achieve academically. How might this information be used to promote positive motivational orientations in the classroom? One promising strategy for research is to focus on gaining a better understanding of the underlying belief systems that are reflected in a general perception of social support. In this regard, Ford has described a set of context beliefs about social relationships and settings that have the potential to link generalized perceptions of social support and belongingness to classroom functioning. Specifically, Ford argues that within specific situations, individuals formulate beliefs concerning the correspondence between their personal goals and those of others, the degree to which others will provide access to information and resources necessary to achieve one's goals, and the extent to which social relationships will provide an emotionally supportive environment. This implies that students will engage in positive social and academic activities when they perceive the classroom as a (a) place that provides opportunities to achieve social and academic goals; (b) safe and responsive environment; (c) place that facilitates the achievement of goals by providing help, advice, and instruction; and (d) place that is emotionally supportive and nurturing. . . .

Assuming that students' perceptions of peer support are at least moderately related to the actual quality of their peer relationships, facilitating the development of positive peer relationships in the classroom can help teachers promote students' adoption of classroom goals. For example, the larger peer group can be the source for behavioral standards, especially when students as a group are held accountable for the behavior of the group's members or when teachers use peer group leaders to monitor the class when they must leave their classrooms. Cooperative learning activities can also provide contexts in which peers hold each other accountable to certain standards of conduct; socially responsible behavior in the form of helping and sharing knowledge and expertise is an integral part of the cooperative learning process. Improving the quality of peer relationships should be of special concern for teachers and administrators who work with students during the transition years of middle school. Many young adolescents enter new middle school structures that necessitate interacting with larger numbers of peers on a daily basis. In contrast to the greater predictability of self-contained classroom environments in elementary school, the relative uncertainty and ambiguity of multiple classroom environments, new instructional styles, and more complex class schedules often result in middle school students turning to each other for information, social support, and ways to cope. Students who have access to positive peer supports are likely to adapt to the demands of middle school transition in more positive ways than those without such supports.

Finally, one of the more interesting questions with respect to the motivational impact of peer relationships is the strength of influence when compared to that of parents and other adults. Studies that include perceptions of both parents and peers provide evidence that perceived support from parents predicts children's outcomes to a much greater extent than perceived support from peers. Similar findings for teachers suggest that being liked by teachers also might offset whatever the negative effects of peer rejection might be on children's adjustment at school. Specifically, Wentzel and Asher report that being liked by teachers is related more strongly to the adoption of school-related goals than a high level of peer acceptance. Moreover, children who have few friends and are neither well liked or disliked by their peers appeared to be the most highly motivated students and most well liked by their teachers. Therefore, it appears that the existence or quality of peer relationships are not destined to influence motivation negatively or positively if supportive relationships with parents or teachers exist.

In summary, peer relationships can facilitate the development of motivational enablers to the extent that they are perceived by the student as positive and supportive. The significance of these perceptions is borne out in students' pursuit of positive social and academic goals, which in turn, predict positive classroom behavior and academic grades. The implications of this work are especially clear for creating developmentally appropriate classrooms for young adolescents. Although children are interested in and even emotionally attached to their peers at all ages, they exhibit increased interest in their peers and a growing psychological and emotional dependence on them for support and guidance as they make the transition into adolescence.

Peer Collaboration and Social Interactions as Facilitators of Learning

In addition to establishing links between peer relationships and academic outcomes, researchers also have demonstrated that within the context of collaborative learning activities, peer interactions can facilitate engagement as well as the development of specific intellectual skills. Collaborative learning involves the joint structuring of an activity with shared participation of two students in which outcomes for each individual are typically documented. This is in contrast to cooperative learning, which involves activities within four-to six-member groups and in which gains are most often gauged by group-level performance rather than by the development of individual skills.

Of interest for discussion in this article is that specific academic enablers have been associated with peer collaborative learning. These include intellectual enablers such as positive engagement in learning activities, improved problem-solving skills, and increases in recall and comprehension of material, as well as positive social communication and negotiation skills. The development of these intellectual and social enablers has been documented most often when less competent students have peer partners who are competent in the task, have good social communication skills, provide ability-related positive feedback, and who clearly articulate problem-solving strategies.

As noted earlier, collaborative peer dyads are most often composed of children who are probably acquaintances but not good friends. Therefore, the processes whereby peers promote the development of academic enablers are likely to be quite different from those that function within the context of students' interpersonal relationships with peers. How do peer interactions in collaborative dyads promote the intellectual and social functioning of less competent students? Research on peer social interaction and cognitive development is typically framed within the theoretical framework of Vygotsky, with researchers proposing that development is likely to occur when a cooperative exchange of ideas takes place within a zone of proximal development. Vygotsky refers to the zone of proximal development as that range spanning from where a child can function independently in a cognitive sense, to a more advanced level where he or she has the potential to develop when in collaboration with a more capable peer. The cognitive outcomes are a result of an active process of negotiation and shared decision making.

Vygotsky makes it clear that the role of a child's social partner is critical to the learning process. Indeed, he proposes that not only is a difference in the level of expertise between partners necessary, but also an understanding by the more advanced partner of the abilities of the less advanced child so that information can be presented at a developmentally appropriate level. Therefore, the challenge for the advanced partner is to find a technique that will facilitate as well as motivate positive social interactions and communication with the less advanced partner. This process of "scaffolding" extends the range of the less advanced child by bridging the gap between current skill and desired skill, thereby allowing him or her to accomplish a task not otherwise possible.

Research on collaborative peer learning has confirmed that children do not naturally develop constructive interaction patterns without specific training. Without explicit preparation, more competent children collaborating with less competent peers tend to offer help in the form of lectures and demonstrations, rarely elaborate their explanations or allow their partner to apply new information on their own, and often ignore their less competent partners altogether. Collaborative interaction skills, however, can be enhanced by training higher achieving peers to interact constructively, develop conceptually rich explanations, and engage their less competent peers in strategic behavior. When this takes place, less competent peers demonstrate increases in verbal communication skills, more collaborative social interactions, and more positive learning outcomes. . . .

Conclusions

In this article it has been argued that peers have the potential to provide contexts that can have a profound effect on the development of students' academic enablers. Although motivation and interpersonal skills have been presented as somewhat independent from cognitive enablers, it is clear that these social and intellectual processes can work in integrated fashion to promote positive academic outcomes at school. . . . Social skills reflecting positive feedback and encouragement can motivate task engagement within collaborative learning contexts. In addition, perceptions of positive interpersonal relationships with peers can be powerful motivators of active engagement in the academic activities of the classroom. . . .

POSTSCRIPT

Is Teaching the Habits of Highly Successful Students the Best Approach to Improve Student Motivation?

Can unmotivated students be taught the habits of highly successful students? There are some habits of thought in which highly successful students engage. All of these cognitive skills can be encouraged and improved with the skillful assistance of teachers. In this sense, Linnenbrink and Pintrich believe that the habits of highly successful students can be taught.

Among the cognitive skills that successful students need to learn is to believe in themselves or to have a sense of self-efficacy. Students with high self-efficacy believe that they have the capability to perform an instructional task. Students who believe in their skills have more persistence on a task and work harder at a task. A second set of cognitive skills that might enable student motivation includes adaptive attributions. Attributions are the student's attempts to understand the causes for their successes and failures. Was this success or failure due to my own efforts or lack thereof? Is this a situation that I think I can change? Who is responsible for change to occur—the student or the teacher? Linnenbrink and Pintrich suggest that successful students have beliefs that they are in control, that with effort instructional outcomes can change, and that they are mostly responsible for reaching personal instructional goals.

A third academic enabler is intrinsic motivation. What makes a topic interesting? Why should a student care? How is it relevant to their life? How can teachers catch and hold the interest of their students such that the instructional topic is meaningful to their students? A fourth and final set of cognitive skills that successful students use in learning is adaptive goal orientation. Successful students view school as a set of skills that they must achieve and that is their personal goal that they must try to master. Mastery goal achievement is taught when teachers focus on individual improvement rather than focusing on comparisons to others.

Because Wentzel and Watkins believe that much of student motivation is in the hands of peers, they would side with the position that the habits of highly successful student cannot be taught. Essentially, the theory suggests that when classroom climates are positive and accepting and supporting, students learn better and behave better. This theory of positive peer support as an enabler of student motivation has its base in attachment theory whereby students' needs for social relatedness are met at school, allowing them to feel like they fit in with others. Similarly, students who have been securely socialized at home are more likely to be able to regulate their own emotions and feel ready to meet the social and academic challenges at school. The implication for classroom teachers is that students are more likely to be motivated to work toward academic goals and get along well with others if they see the classroom as a setting that supports them, if they feel safe, if the classroom is empathetic to their needs, if the students feel like they can receive help and advice with problem solving, and if they see the classroom climate as emotionally supportive and nurturing.

What can classroom managers do to take advantage of both points of view in motivating students? They can bridge the gap by not only teaching the cognitive habits of highly successful students to all students but they can work to develop a classroom community whereby all students feel willing and ready to take the chance to practice these cognitive skills in an accepting environment whereby students can learn equally from their successes as well as their failures and whereby students can learn to take risks with the full support of the classroom community.

For more valuable information on motivating unmotivated students read D. Bloch, *Positive Self-Talk for Children* (Bantam, 1993) and M. Seligman, *The Optimistic Child* (Harper Perennial, 1995). For more on the needs for social support by children look for B. James, *Handbook for Treatment of Attachment: Trauma Problems in Children* (The Free Press, 1994).

ISSUE 4

Students with AD/HD in the Regular Classroom: Are Teachers Prepared to Manage Inclusion?

YES: Eric Carbone, from "Arranging the Classroom with an Eye (and Ear) to Students with ADHD," *Teaching Exceptional Children* (November/December 2001)

NO: Regina Bussing, Faye A. Gary, Christina E. Leon, Cynthia Wilson Garvan, and Robert Reid, from "General Classroom Teachers' Information and Perceptions of Attention Deficit Hyperactivity Disorder," *Behavioral Disorders* (August 2002)

ISSUE SUMMARY

YES: Eric Carbone is a professor in the department of teaching and learning at New York University. He describes how classroom teachers can improve the learning environments of students with AD/HD in their inclusionary classrooms in ways that support the strengths of these students.

NO: Regina Bussing is an associate professor and chief of the division of child and adolescent psychiatry, department of psychiatry, pediatrics, and health policy and epidemiology at the University of Florida. Professor Bussing et al. contend that large class sizes, time requirements, and a lack of teacher training combine to make teachers unprepared to teach students with AD/HD in the regular classroom.

When students with disabilities are placed in alternative settings like special education, they can be perceived as somehow different or impaired. Inclusionary educational practices have the effect of normalizing these students: They respond appropriately to the positive expectations that their regular education peers have for them, they can achieve at a higher level, their behavior improves, and they can develop positive social relationships and thus broaden their base of social support. Finally, inclusionary practices allow students with special needs to remain in the regular education curriculum, which is important if they are to remain at grade-level achievement.

While Eric Carbone concedes that many teachers are minimally quali-fied and may feel burdened, overwhelmed, and lack confidence to work with students with AD/HD, he believes that teachers can arrange their classrooms and use general instructional strategies so that the three major learning and behavior problems of AD/HD may be prevented. For example, for the child with hyperactivity, teachers should incorporate movement into their teaching activities and frequently monitor the student. They might modify the physical environment by providing positive peer models. For the student impulsivity, he recommends occasional time away for the student to contemplate his or behavior and its consequences. Finally, for the inattentive student, he suggests using color (e.g., a higlighter) to emphasize important task features, such as highlighting the operations on a math fact sheet.

In the end, Carbone claims that instructional adaptations alone will not be a cure-all for students with AD/HD who are included in the regular class-room environment. Instead, he contends that a multimodal approach that includes not only instructional and physical accommodations but also medi-cation, positive home-school partnerships, and behavioral interventions, is needed.

Carbone has suggested that regular education teachers can take advan-tage of the many materials that are in the marketplace to educate themselves about accommodations for students with AD/HD. Nevertheless, the question arises whether regular education teachers think they have been prepared for-mally in their university courses to work effectively with these students.

In direct contrast to Carbone's sentiments, Bussing and colleagues offer a different viewpoint on the ease with which students with special needs can be included in the regular classroom. Bussing et al. applied survey methods to examine five sources of AD/HD information: (1) exposure to students with AD/HD, (2) self-study about AD/HD, (3) formal AD/HD training, (4) perceived teacher confidence in instructional tasks for successful inclusion of students with AD/HD, and (5) perceived barriers to such instruction.

Despite the facts that virtually all teachers under study had read at least one article on AD/HD, that 60 percent had read a book about AD/HD, that half of the teachers had received some preservice AD/HD training during their educations, and that three-fourths had received in-service training after gradu-ation, these teachers still felt inadequate regarding theinclusionary teaching of students with AD/HD. Almost all teachers (94 percent) wanted more training in AD/HD instruction and behavior management. Interestingly, teachers expressed lowest confidence in their abilities to manage personal stress related to these students. Large class sizes and time requirements of special interven-tions were described as the greatest barriers to instruction of students with AD/HD. Bussing and her colleagues recommend that regular education teach-ers need more preservice and in-service training in instruction and behavior management of AD/HD that would include specific skills-based training and stress management.

Eric Carbone

 **YES**

Arranging the Classroom with an Eye (and Ear) to Students with ADHD

The child in your classroom who regularly squirms in his seat, who stares at walls, and whose desk is an avalanche of crumpled papers may not be a day-dreamer or an idle, unmotivated student, but rather a prime candidate for an attention deficit/hyperactivity disorder (ADHD) classification. The National Information Center for Children and Youth with Disabilities (www.nichcy.org) has characterized ADHD as developmentally inappropriate levels of inattention, impulsivity, and hyperactivity.

Although no one knows exactly what causes the condition, the genetic nature of ADHD suggests a neurobiological explanation. Though its characteristics were identified in students as early as 1902, the condition now known as ADHD has suffered through years of ambiguity and inaccurate labels, such as moral deficit and minimal brain dysfunction. With the establishment of specific diagnostic procedures in the DSM-IV, however, as well as federal legislation (Individuals with Disabilities Education Act, IDEA) that provides special education services to children with ADHD under the categories of "other health impaired," "emotionally disturbed," or "learning disabled," public and professional awareness of the disorder has improved. Presently, it is estimated that ADHD affects 3% to 5% of school-age children.

Inclusive Environments and ADHD

Because just half of these children qualify for special education and because of the trend toward more inclusive classrooms, general classroom teachers are being faced with increasing responsibilities for students with ADHD. These teachers, many of whom have minimal training in working with students with special needs, are likely to feel burdened, overwhelmed, and unconfident in tackling ADHD. Fortunately, the abundance of literature discussing this condition can do much to assist in effective, pedagogical decision making.

This article describes how educators can *physically alter* a general education classroom in ways that support the strengths of children with ADHD, not exacerbate their problems. . . . Too often, teachers make changes in the classroom *after* a child's inattention has caused him or her to fall significantly behind.

From *Exceptional Children*, vol. 34, no. 2, 2001, pp. 72–81. Copyright © 2001 by Council for Exceptional Children. Reprinted by permission. References omitted.

Here, I emphasize *antecedent* interventions, that is, classroom changes directed toward proactive change, before a problem becomes overwhelming. Through discussing the four major "difficulties" of students with ADHD, this article presents general strategies for accommodating the instruction of children with attention problems. Then, for each difficulty, the article presents "structural responses"—to the *physical* environmental conditions—for children who generally fit the description. . . .

By no means do these suggestions call for a complete renovation of every inclusive classroom, but rather are designed as simple, easy-to-implement interventions to diminish the emergence of characteristic problems of children with ADHD.

Difficulty #1—Hyperactivity

The student often fidgets with hands or feet or squirms in seat; often leaves seat in classroom when expected to remain seated.

Characteristics

The two problematic symptoms of hyperactivity—fidgeting and out-of-seat behavior—are not found in all children with attention disorders, but are cited by parents and teachers as major challenges of ADHD. While some identified children are only slightly active and restless in specific contexts (i.e., boring lecture, math), others constantly exhibit a high activity level that not only prevents them from completing their own work, but that is also distracting to the performance of peers. These students appear to be driven by a motor, unable to hit the brakes when necessary.

Children who exhibit hyperactivity are also more prone to sleep problems, bedwetting, and temper tantrums and are often described as intrusive, bossy, show-offs, defiant, and unable to maintain friendships (Turnbull et al., 1999). This is manifested in their preference for less structured activities like climbing and cycling, rather than drawing and other fine-motor tasks. The strong emphasis on fine-motor skills observed in almost all schools is perceived by the child with ADHD as a constraint on his movement and inevitably sets up a scenario of frustration, aggression, and poor achievement.

Hyperactivity is closely related to theories of stimulation because, as Sydney Zentall noted (1983), gross-motor movements characterize low arousal, whereas repetitive fidgeting reflects overstimulation. If this is true, it is possible to conclude that subtle classroom changes to assigned tasks and the physical environment can regulate stimulation levels to the appropriate degree for the child with ADHD.

General Strategies

Educators and researchers have identified three general strategies for dealing with students' excessive activity:

- *Incorporating movement* into classroom life, in the form of role play and other active curricular responses, is effective.

- *Positive peer attention* can directly influence the behavior of students with ADHD.
- *Frequent teacher monitoring* is a well-documented strategy.

How can a classroom physically accommodate students' needs for gross-motor exercise, active curriculums, peer attention, and consistent teacher feed-back and supervision—which have been proven to increase the on-task behavior of students with ADHD? Whereas early management models emphasized confined settings (e.g., private cubicles, study carrels), today, "open classrooms," loosely-structured arrangements offering multiple simultaneous instruction (e.g., centers), dominate. Because critics have labeled these more open models as psychologically damaging or noisy and visually distracting, it appears that we need alternative structural responses to manage students with hyperactive symptoms.

Structural Response

First, keep in mind the characteristic behaviors of these individuals (fidgeting, inability to sit, preferences for gross-motor activity), as well as the suggested general interventions (channel activity, peer role models, positive teacher rein-forcement). It takes considerable thought and planning to select the child's location in the classroom, as well as introduce supportive classroom features. Here are some suggestions. . . . :

- Arrange the classroom in a *traditional row-seating pattern*, because this is the most structured and predictable option. Placing the child at a table with five other classmates detracts from the child's attentiveness.
- Simply placing the child in a desk is not enough; his *placement* in the room is crucial. That desk should be positioned in the front row, where he or she is less likely to be disturbed by a neighbor's new hairstyle or flashy sweater.
- Remove the child from *potentially distracting areas,* such as near windows or pencil sharpeners.
- To provide for *immediate feedback and close monitoring,* place the child directly next to your desk. Close proximity to the instructor may also alleviate an additional dilemma of the child with ADHD—reluctance to ask for help when experiencing difficulty.
- Surround the child with ADHD with well-behaved, attentive classmates as desk neighbors. This placement will automatically *encourage positive peer interactions.* Additional opportunities for peer interaction can be arranged by placing tables in the back of the classroom for occasional cooperative learning activities.
- For children who seem to be *overstimulated,* designate a stimuli-reduced area of the room, where a child who is fidgety and overly aroused can complete his or her assigned task. One way of achieving this is by creat-ing an *isolated peninsula* in the back of the room, a square-shaped area surrounded on three sides by bookcases (books facing outward to pre-vent distractions) or other "obstacles." Clear this area of any overly-stimulating visual information so as to prevent overload. You could include some plush chairs and pillows to provide the child a safe,

comfortable place in which to focus. If the area is large enough, you could even use it as a whole-group meeting/presentation area.

- For children who seem to be *underaroused,* allow them to use this getaway place to jump around and let off some steam. Another structural accommodation for the child would be a seating placement on the far right or far left rows, where he or she can stretch out while interrupting as few neighbors as possible.
- You may consider providing *additional desks* for students to move to if they need to. Explain that when they feel restless or need physical movement, they can quietly pick up their materials and temporarily move to a new, "free" desk. This serves to provide an outlet for physical stimulation while still maintaining the child on task.
- To address the hyperactive child's reluctance to tackle fine-motor activities, small *interactive centers* requiring fine muscle control (art center, computers, map skills area) should dot the classroom to provide plentiful practice opportunities.
- Because children with ADHD are often self-conscious about their need to take daily medication, provide children with a secure place to keep and take pills.

Of course, these structural suggestions assume that a traditional row seating pattern is both feasible and supported by teachers, administrators, and students. However, current trends toward cooperative learning and "open classrooms" have reduced the practicality and popularity of this arrangement.

Even though parallel row seating remains the ideal layout for students with ADHD, teachers in more modernly arranged classrooms can still find ways to make room for the suggested strategies. You can create quiet, stimulireduced areas in almost any environment; and you can still provide the child with ADHD or other attentional difficulties with a "second seat," albeit at an alternate table. Similarly, creative teachers can still persuade "positive" peer role models to surround the child with ADHD at a designated table or center.

The structural classroom changes described here are not designed to be definitive or inflexible. Rather, they are suggested as starting points, which you can creatively tailor to your needs and those of your students.

Difficulty #2—Impulsivity

The student often blurts out answers before questions have been completed; often has difficulty waiting his or her turn; often interrupts or intrudes on others.

Characteristics

The second detrimental dimension of ADHD is impulsivity. The child who presents impulsive behavior requires immediate gratification, and so appears to act before thinking. This disregard for the consequences of an action often leads the child with ADHD to break classroom rules and social norms without a specific intention or plan to do so. Consequently, whereas the impulsive child experiences frequent teacher reprimands early in his school years, his or her adolescence is characterized by social rejection and isolation and peer labels of "immature" and "weird."

In addition to social consequences, impulsive responding produces academic errors because the person with ADHD fails to wait long enough to consider alternative information and consequences. Inability to delay responding often manifests itself in:

- Poor test-taking performance, specifically on multiple-choice formats.
- Poor planning skills.
- Failure to carefully read directions, because this requires waiting.

These academic consequences indicate a desperate need for classroom interventions.

General Strategies

The general impression that impulsiveness is an issue "internal" to the child has led to a wealth of research examining the effect of various behavioral strategies on the child's internalization of social norms. These strategies typically take the form of three behavior modification approaches—cognitive-behavior therapy; timeouts; and positive reinforcement.

- *Cognitive-behavior therapy* and its emphasis on self-assessment and metacognition have proven inadequate for children with ADHD.
- Timeouts, or *reflective cooling periods,* have also been criticized as psychologically damaging and have the potential to backfire if the child misinterprets the removal from an uninteresting classroom as a reinforcer.
- *Positive reinforcement* is an excellent tool for reducing impulsive activity and improving on-task behavior and academic performance.

Plan carefully when you establish a schedule of positive reinforcement for the child with impulsivity. First, children with ADHD respond better to *secondary reinforcers,* that is, material rewards like food and small toys, rather than "natural" reinforcers like verbal praise.

Second, *response cost*—a system of *removing* tangible reinforcers for inappropriate actions—has proven more effective than reward-only programs in maintaining desired behaviors. Because response cost only reduces inappropriate behavior (it does not directly teach expected behavior), a combination of positive reinforcement and a penalty system appears like a most effective behavioral strategy. How then can the impulsive child's unusual sensitivity to rewards and fines be applied to the *structural* organization of a classroom?

Structural Response

The implementation of a *token economy* is a first step. Token systems reward appropriate behavior with points or other items that are valueless by themselves. At designated periods (i.e., weekly, monthly), those accumulated tokens are "cashed in" for rewards with previously ascribed point values. The token economy can be of great value to the impulsive child because it offers a tangible reason to act appropriately and avoid a "fine."

The implementation of a response cost program is a five-fold process between teacher and student:

- Discuss the problem behavior with the child.
- Mutually agree on a reinforcer.
- Establish the amount of the fine.
- Establish the means to communicate the fine.
- Ensure that reinforcement outweighs "fines."

It is the fourth step, the "means," that can directly involve the physical environment. Children with ADHD must know that they have been fined so that they can begin to internalize those behaviors that are expected. If you write a check-minus in your grade book, will the child with ADHD learn that his or her impulsive actions need to be self-regulated?

The classroom should make room for an area devoted exclusively to a progress chart of token accumulation. This chart should clearly label all students' names and use Velcro icons to indicate points and should be placed in direct view of the students on the chart[.] . . . All students, classified or not, should participate in the proposed token economy, as this lends itself nicely to the use of group contingency models and positive peer pressure from typical students onto those identified with ADHD. The child's proximity to the token area is important because it increases the likelihood of *self-monitoring,* because the child is continually aware of potential consequences—negative and positive—of his or her behavior. To ensure the child's awareness of these consequences, post lists of "fineable" behaviors and "redeemable" reinforcers with their corresponding point values. . . .

To address the previously noted negative social repercussions experienced by impulsive children, try constructing a *group-reward chart* that reinforces the entire class on a monthly basis for their collective cooperation. In this way, group-contingency reward systems may encourage classmates to support and assist impulsive or disruptive peers. For the child with ADHD, positive social interaction may be a greater benefit than any material reward. Addressing the impulsivity of children in a structured way is especially difficult considering the neurological nature of the disability. An environment that surrounds the child with physical, observable warnings to think before acting, however, is a step in the right direction.

Difficulty #3—Inattention and Distractibility

The student is easily distracted by extraneous stimuli; often does not seem to listen when spoken to directly; often fails to give close attention to details or makes careless mistakes.

Characteristics

Attention is a multitask process, requiring us to focus, select something to attend to, sustain focus for a necessary period, resist distractions, and finally shift our attention elsewhere. ADHD affects a child at one or more of these processing steps, as reflected in often-used adjectives of inattentive students as "lost in a fog," internally preoccupied, confused, and apathetic.

Some people have argued that children with ADHD struggle to filter out irrelevant sensory information. See Zentall for a discussion of the *optimal stimulation* theory. This argument has generated support for classrooms devoid of environmental stimulation (e.g., removal of colorful bulletin boards or brightly hued paints; use of Venetian blinds instead of clear windows).

The literature indicates, however, that this blank physical arrangement fails to improve the attention and academic performance of children with ADHD. Why? Perhaps because it emphasizes the *quantity* of external stimuli rather than its *quality*. Children with attention disorders, like all others, are attracted to environmental conditions that are novel, that is, unfamiliar or unexpected. An unusual cloud pattern, or a teacher's new pin may be novel and, therefore, more distracting than the continuous hum of a fan.

General Strategies

Strategies for improving student attention have emphasized the use of interesting and varied tasks, such as games, role-play, and educational videos, to place novelty on instruction rather than the extraneous environment. The hope is that the pull of the creative task will be stronger than any potential distractor in the physical classroom. Though researchers have applauded the addition of visual stimulation to classroom tasks, be wary of how you integrate novel qualities (color, size) into instruction. In one study, experimenters applied novel changes (color) to unimportant features of a task (e.g., random use of colored chalk) and found that it interfered with the task performance of students with ADHD more than a control group. Further research indicated, however, that color (and presumably other novel qualities) can improve the performance of children with ADHD only when it is added to *increase important task features*.

In addition to being sensitive to visual novelty, the child who appears inattentive is also especially sensitive to changes in sound. Classroom noise produces negative effects on the performance of children with ADHD because auditory processing cannot be shut out as easily as visual stimuli.

Further research, though, revealed that, like visual stimuli, not *all* noise is detrimental. Only during complex, multiple-step or unfamiliar/newly introduced tasks does added noise produce inattention and increased errors. When students work on familiar tasks with structured responses, the addition of moderate levels of classroom noise yields better results and attention to task than quiet conditions. Apparently, silence can be just as much of a distraction as high noise levels.

The use of novel sounds during simple tasks is supported through the research of Thomas J. Scott. Scott documented the enhanced productivity of four hyperactive-inattentive boys on arithmetic problems in musical classroom settings, where background sound was provided by Beatles albums. The complete removal of sensory stimuli from the physical environment of children with ADHD is unwarranted. What is needed, though, is careful planning and creativity on teachers' parts to develop instruction that is more attractive than factors in the external world.

Structural Response

How can an altered physical environment help children who are easily distracted?

- Pay attention to removing *potentially distracting features* from the room (e.g., flashy bulletin boards). But direct most of your effort at making the classroom conducive to novel/varied tasks that compete against the external characteristics of the area for the child's attention.
- Make sure that *furniture and classroom structures* are designed to provide for an easy transition to a variety of instructional approaches. Administrators should remove any chairs bolted to the floor so desks can be manipulated for activities requiring greater amounts of space. The classroom . . . is a good model because it enables small groups to work at tables, allows for teacher-centered whole-class instruction, and provides for student-directed work at centers.
- Use *color and other novel qualities* to highlight important task features as you modify instruction.
- Place an *overhead projector* in the classroom. This provides a strong visual impact to draw students' attention. The overhead also allows you to face the students and monitor who is attentive and who is not. . . .

⋅⋅⊙⋅⋅

- To address a child's aversion to classroom noise during unfamiliar and difficult tasks, set up a *listening center* as an important structural accommodation. This center would consist of earphones connected to a listening device.
- When the center is not being used for instructional purposes, you might recommend that a child with ADHD complete a *new, complex* task while "tethered" to the center. In addition to restraining the child, these earphones can help filter out distracting levels of classroom conversation for the inattentive student.
- The listening center has another advantage in its capacity to hold prerecorded instructions or verbal homework assignments on tape, which would be at the easy disposal of the child with attentional problems. The literature indicates the positive contribution of background noise on attentive behavior during the completion of *familiar* and *simple* tasks; thus, the listening center should be stocked with stereo equipment.
- While the class is in a transition or is doing a daily free-writing activity, play some music or run a fan.

It is unrealistic to try to remove all visual stimuli from a classroom and construct soundproof walls, as a way of providing structural adaptations for a class with an ADHD population. The overhead projector and listening center, though, are must-haves in any classroom so teachers can monitor environmental stimuli accordingly for those students with attention problems.

Difficulty #4—Disorganization

The student often has difficulty organizing tasks and activities; often loses things.

Characteristics

Though the DSM-IV classified ADHD characteristics into categories of hyperactivity, impulsivity, and inattention, two symptoms—difficulty organizing tasks and losing things—reflect the ADHD child's problems with organization. Children with attentional problems often have difficulties with three areas of organization—tidiness of school materials, time management, and handwriting.

- Children with ADHD often *misplace or lose their belongings and school-work* and have problems handling materials that have multiple pieces. They are easily identified in the general education classroom by the messy, haphazard appearance of their desks and even acknowledge their own organizational deficiencies. It is not difficult to understand how these problems can affect the classroom performance of students with ADHD.
- Children with ADHD struggle in *planning activities* within a time framework. These time-estimation skills are needed in the classroom to arrive on time, complete tasks within defined limits, and monitor test taking. Research indicates serious deficiencies in these abilities for ADHD populations. In particular, individuals with attention disorders tend to overestimate the length of time intervals, posing serious implications for classroom performance, including procrastination and failure to complete tests and assignments.
- Children with ADHD often have *poor handwriting*—often, haphazard and illegible. Although studies looking at potential differences in manual dexterity and coordination between populations with and without attention disorders have been inconclusive, most experts agree that the ADHD child's slower motor-response speed is the result of visual-motor deficits. Their disorganized penmanship has also been interpreted as a failure to sustain attention to the repetitive nature of writing.

Structural Response

Although you can directly teach organization skills to your students with ADHD, you can also manipulate the physical classroom to aid all children's tidiness of materials, time-estimation skills, and handwriting.

- Set up and use *individual student mailboxes,* similar in construction to those for teachers found in most school offices. . . . To ensure that the child with ADHD remembers homework assignments and other school notices, the teacher can easily drop off those items in the child's mailbox.
- Add a routine *end-of-the day check* of the mailboxes into your classroom procedures so that students do not forget these notices.
- Rather than having the students solely responsible for maintaining their notebooks and materials in their desks, you may want to *allocate*

classroom space for bins that can house those objects. When they need something, students can easily retrieve their books and notebooks without wasting time rummaging through disheveled desks for a particular text or notepad.

- These shelves can also hold student folders and work so that papers are kept neatly and *organized by content area*. You can code (e.g., with paint) the folders and bins that hold student work of the same subject area, using a matching color scheme.

Each of these structural interventions—mailboxes, bins, and color-coded materials—serve to decrease the child's tendency to lose or forget those items needed to successfully complete in-class and homework assignments. Consider designing additional or alternative organizational structures that are suitable to your instructional goals and classrooms' physical limitations.

Two more organizational problems that you can address through structural adaptations are poor time management and handwriting.

Place a small clock that counts *down* time on the child's desk. This is an easy method of increasing children's awareness of remaining time and spurring on the development of an appropriate plan of action.

Although the clock may initially be a source of distraction, attention can be restored after repeated exposure and practice using the timing device.

Remedy poor penmanship by *reducing the need for handwriting*. This can be accomplished by making room in the class for several computers or word processors. These devices prevent children from becoming overly frustrated with the chore of handwriting, while simultaneously assisting them in the fine-motor control many children need to develop.

Computers, time clocks, and colorcoded bins and mailboxes are simple physical adaptations to make in any classroom to improve student organization, and consequently, attention.

Final Thoughts

The structural suggestions provided here are just that—suggestions and ideas, not definitive guarantees of success in reducing the problematic characteristics of children with ADHD . . . for a summary of ideas presented here). In fact, most authors of behavior-modification strategies caution against the appearance of a "honeymoon effect," that is, a brief period of student compliance followed by an inevitable return to negative original behaviors.

This novelty effect may be especially true of children with ADHD, who, as already documented, are particularly receptive to new sensory changes in their environment and equally quick to tire after repeated exposure. If teachers are to adopt the strategies mentioned here, they must do so cautiously, without unrealistic expectations. Teachers should probably regularly update the suggested structural responses (e.g., return to brief period of student self-seating; use of blackboard instead of overhead) when signs of waning interest and diminished novelty begin to surface. No single recipe of structural changes can be applied to all students with attention disorders.

The far-ranging success of the child with attentional problems in the general education setting depends on a multimodal approach to intervention, using instructional and physical accommodations, as well as medication, positive home-school partnerships, and proven behavioral strategies. Only then will the apparent "fog" surrounding the child with ADHD begin to evaporate.

NO ↵

Regina Bussing, et al.

General Classroom Teachers' Information and Perceptions of Attention Deficit Hyperactivity Disorder

Attention deficit/hyperactivity disorder (ADHD) is one of the most commonly diagnosed and studied childhood psychiatric disorders (Barkley & Murphy, 1998). . . .

ADHD is not presently recognized as a category of disability under the Individuals with Disabilities Education Act (IDEA), although advocates and professional groups have argued that ADHD should be included. Students with ADHD currently are eligible for special education services under existing categories of disability. In addition, because ADHD would likely result in an impairment in a major life activity (i.e., learning), students with ADHD will often be eligible for services under Section 504 and are thus entitled to due process and related services. Estimates suggest that around 25% to 50% of students with ADHD qualify for special education services, with the majority of those students being served under the Behavior Disorders and Learning Disabilities categories. Students also may be served under the Other Health Impaired category.

It is, however, a mistake to view ADHD as solely a special education problem. Most children with ADHD spend the majority of their time in general education classrooms, and almost all children with ADHD spend at least a portion of their day in general education classrooms. Because students with ADHD are served, at least to some extent, in inclusive classroom settings, both special education and general education classroom teachers are required to work effectively with these students. . . .

While there is agreement that teachers need more training in ADHD, little research has addressed how teachers perceive their ability to work successfully with students with ADHD (i.e., their confidence or self-efficacy) and what problems teachers perceive as major barriers to the effective education of these students. This information is relevant for two reasons. First, an individual's self-efficacy beliefs concerning an activity may be a determining factor in the

From *Behavioral Disorders*, vol. 27, no. 4, August 2002, pp. 327–338. Copyright © 2002 by CCBD Publications. Reprinted by permission. References omitted.

decision to engage in the activity; may affect performance, since self-efficacy has been shown to correlate positively with performance; and can affect teaching performance when difficulty is encountered. Thus, teachers' confidence in their ability and training may be an important determinant of performance. Working successfully in the classroom with children with ADHD poses a challenge to any teacher. If teachers do not have sufficient knowledge of what to expect when working with children with ADHD or lack training in practical, effective techniques to help these children succeed, they are unlikely to respond effectively.

Second, knowledge of what aspects of working with children with ADHD are likely to be perceived as most (or least) difficult and what the major perceived barriers to success are should serve as a guide for teacher training programs and texts. ADHD is a complex disorder that encompasses multiple disciplines (e.g., psychology, pharmacology, medicine, education), and it is impossible to cover every possible aspect of ADHD in preservice training. Therefore, training for teachers should center on the problems they are most likely to encounter and the most effective and efficient means of dealing with those problems. This knowledge may also be of value for those working in a collaborative or consultative situation for pinpointing possible areas of immediate concern. . . .

The present study had three goals:

1. To investigate three sources of general education teachers' ADHD information (i.e., experience teaching students with ADHD, self-study, formal training).
2. To assess teacher confidence in being able to complete instructional tasks for successful inclusion of students with ADHD and to identify predictors of confidence.
3. To examine perceived barriers to effective programming for students with ADHD and identify whether barriers vary across school districts.

We hypothesized that teachers' ADHD training experiences vary by total years of teaching experience and that teachers' confidence in their ability to complete ADHD-relevant instructional tasks is influenced by their ADHD instruction and training, exposure to students with ADHD in the classroom, self-study about ADHD, and total years of teaching experience.

Method

Participants

The study population consisted of general classroom elementary teachers from five school districts in North Florida. Information about school district characteristics was derived from administrative data sets contained in the *Florida School Indicators Report* published by the Florida Department of Education. . . . To be eligible for participation, a teacher needed to teach elementary school students in general education classes and not have a special education certification. After obtaining school district administrative permission for the study, we constructed a master list of eligible teachers with the help of each district's personnel office. From this list we selected a random sample proportional to the number of eligible teachers in each district to invite to participate in the study, for a total of 600 invited teachers.

Of the 419 teachers who completed surveys (70% response rate), 54 did not meet full eligibility criteria and were excluded from the analysis, resulting in a participation rate of 61%. Exclusion was mostly (71%) due to teachers' indicating that they had special education certification. The response rate is in the normal range for mail surveys, and is considered adequate for analysis.

Procedure

Informed consent was obtained from each participant, with procedures approved by the institutional review committee of the University of Florida. Using the school truck mail systems, we mailed the teachers the survey, the informed consent form, and a $5 gift certificate and provided a return envelope for the materials. A follow-up letter was sent to teachers who had not returned the survey within 6 weeks, followed by a second letter with another copy of the survey 1 month later.

Measures

Teacher Characteristics

Permission was obtained from Jerome, Gordon, and Hustler to use questions from the Teachers' Knowledge and Attitudes about ADHD survey to obtain demographic information about individual teachers. Teachers indicated their gender, age range, educational achievement, total years of teaching experience, and grade taught. They also rated their level of agreement that ADHD is a legitimate educational problem, whether they thought ADHD should be grounds for exceptional designation in the IDEA process, and whether they felt they could benefit from additional training surrounding the evaluation and treatment of ADHD (all rated as absolutely yes, maybe yes, maybe no, absolutely no, don't know).

ADHD Information Sources

Questions from the same survey were used to assess how many students diagnosed with ADHD teachers had taught in the past 2 years (rated as none, 1–2, 3–5, 6 or more). Teachers indicated how many books and articles about ADHD they had ever read (each rated as none, 1–2, 3–5, 6 or more). They also reported how much formal ADHD training they had received, including the extent of preservice ADHD instruction received during their teacher education and the extent of postgraduate inservice ADHD training (both rated as none, brief, or intensive).

Confidence in Implementing Accommodations and Barriers to Effective Programming

A survey developed by Reid and colleagues was used to assess teachers' confidence in their ability to implement classroom accommodations for students with ADHD and their perceptions of barriers to effective programming for these students.

This survey contains 10 items addressing teachers' confidence in their ability to accomplish instructional tasks for the successful inclusion of students with ADHD. These items reflect activities that would be encountered in classroom practice and were derived from a set of competencies necessary to work with children with disabilities in inclusive classrooms. Respondents rate their confidence in their ability to perform tasks on a scale of 1 (no confidence) to 5 (strong confidence). Confidence ratings were summed across the 10 items for a total confidence score with a range from 10 (lowest confidence) to 50 (highest confidence). Reid and colleagues reported a Crohnbach's alpha of .82 for the confidence items in their previous study. In the current study, Crohnbach's alpha for the 10 confidence items was .89, indicating good reliability.

An additional 13 items address potential barriers to effective programming, rated on a scale of 1 (not important) to 5 (extremely important). Barriers were selected to reflect practical difficulties that could be encountered by classroom teachers based on previous research examining behavioral demands of less restrictive settings. Reid and colleagues reported a Crohnbach's alpha of .70 for the 13 barrier items among a sample of 449 third-grade general education teachers. In the current study Crohnbach's alpha was .79, indicating good internal consistency.

Statistical Analysis

Bivariate analyses of ordinal variables were conducted using the Kruskal Wallis test. Otherwise, bivariate analyses were conducted using chi-square tests of proportions for discrete variables and analysis-of-variance procedures for continuous variables. Scheffe's test was used to conduct multiple comparisons because it remains valid under a wide variety of conditions. For ease of interpretation and analysis, the variable Years Teaching Experience was converted from an ordinal format (1–2 years, 3–8 years, 9–15 years, 16–25 years, 26 or more years) to midpoint means in years (e.g., 3–8 years was coded as 5.5 years). An Intensive Reader summary variable was created that distinguished between teachers who had read at least one book and three articles about ADHD and those who had read fewer. We examined district differences for all teacher characteristics and information sources, finding only minimal variations that are not reported in the results section. The relationship between district and confidence and barrier ratings was assessed; findings are reported in the text and tables. Multiple regression analysis was used to assess the relationship between overall teacher confidence and its hypothesized predictors. Regression coefficients indicating the nature of the relationship between predictors and outcome variables were estimated. Each coefficient shows the change in outcome for a unit change in the predictor variable. Data analysis was conducted using STATA version 5.

Results

Teacher Characteristics

We analyzed 365 teacher surveys. . . . Briefly, most of the teachers were female, were more than 41 years old, had taught for 9 years or more and had earned a bachelor's degree. They were evenly spread over grades K through 5. Virtually all thought ADHD was a legitimate education problem, and about half thought it should be grounds for exceptional designation in the IDEA process.

Teachers' Sources of ADHD Information

. . . Almost all teachers ($N = 339$, 93%) reported having taught at least one or two children and 63% ($N = 229$) reported teaching at least three children with a diagnosis of ADHD during the previous 2 school years. Virtually all teachers reported some self-study about ADHD. About half of the teachers had read one or two books about ADHD, and almost all had read at least one article. In addition, 47% were intensive readers, having read a book and at least three articles. The proportion of intensive readers rose as the number of students with ADHD taught increased, from 25% among teachers without exposure to students with ADHD, to 41% for those who had taught 1 or 2 students, 48% for those having taught 3 to 5 students, and 58% for those having taught 6 or more, $F (3,359) = 3.73, p < .02$.

Half of the participants had not received formal ADHD training during the course of their teacher education ($n = 181$, 50%), about one third had received brief training ($n = 110$, 30%), and one fifth had received extensive training ($n = 72$, 20%). Undergraduate-level ADHD training varied with years of teaching experience (Kruskal Wallis χ^2 [2] $= 72.5, p < .0001$), such that teachers with ADHD training had taught fewer years (brief training $M = 9.6$ years, $SD = 7.1$; extensive training $M = 10.3$ years, $SD = 7.9$) than their colleagues without such training ($M = 17.9$ years, $SD = 8.4$).

The majority of teachers ($n = 236$, 65%) had received brief ADHD training since graduation. About a quarter of the sample had received no postgraduate ADHD training ($n = 88$, 24%), and only a small proportion had received intensive training ($n = 41$, 11%). Postgraduate ADHD education varied with years of teaching experience (Kruskal Wallis χ^2 [2] $= 45.3, p < .0001$), but in the opposite direction of undergraduate training. Teachers without any postgraduate ADHD education had taught for fewer years ($M = 8.8$ years, $SD = 8.2$) than teachers who reported brief ($M = 15.5$ years, $SD = 8.5$) or extensive training ($M = 16.1$ years, $SD = 9.1$). More than 90% of the teachers indicated that they would benefit from further training.

Teacher Confidence in Implementing ADHD Accommodations

Teachers' average confidence score was 38 ($SD = 6.9$; 77% of maximum confidence level), with a range from 13 to 50 and a mode of 38 ($n = 28$; 7.7%). Teachers identified the same three areas of least confidence across all five districts. Lowest confidence was expressed in their ability to manage the stress caused by students with ADHD in the classroom, with 64% of the teachers ($n = 233$) reporting no, a little, or only some confidence. The second area of low confidence was adjusting lessons or materials for students with ADHD, with 46% of the teachers ($n = 167$) reporting low confidence levels. Finally, 41% of the teachers ($n = 145$) indicated that they had no, a little, or only some confidence in their ability to set up an effective behavior contract with students with ADHD. . . .

The relationships between teacher confidence and experience teaching students with ADHD, books and articles read, ADHD training, total years of teaching experience, and district were examined in a multivariate regression model, $F_{(9,354)} = 4.4$, $p < .0001$, $R^2 = .08$). Confidence scores were independently predicted by having instructed three or more students with ADHD (coefficient = 2.9, $p < .05$), and by having read at least one book and more than 3 articles (coefficient = 2.4, $p < .001$). Teachers in districts A (coefficient = 4.4, $p < .01$) and E (coefficient = 5.3, $p < .001$) had higher confidence scores than those in district C after controlling for other model variables.

Barriers to Effective Instruction of Students with ADHD

The following were rated as the four greatest barriers in all five districts: class size, time needed for interventions, severity of child's problem, and lack of training. No district differences were found for the proportion of teachers rating individual barriers as extremely important, or for mean importance ratings across all 13 barriers. . . .

Discussion

Results indicate that, as hypothesized, teacher ADHD training was related to years of teaching experience. Teachers who had been in the field longer were less likely to have had pre-service ADHD training but more likely to have participated in inservice training than their colleagues with fewer years of teaching experience. This suggests that the rate of ADHD preservice training during regular teacher education has increased. This conclusion is further supported by the fact that over 90% of the teachers surveyed in the current study reported having had any ADHD training, a rate considerably higher than the 56% described by Reid and colleagues 1994. This is an encouraging finding, because lack of training had been rated among the top three barriers to successful teaching of students with ADHD and because overwhelming numbers of teachers in this and other studies expressed a strong interest in further ADHD training.

The high levels of interest in ADHD training found in this study may be a reflection of the high rates of teacher exposure to students with ADHD in general classroom settings. Virtually all participating teachers had taught at least one or two students with diagnosed ADHD in their general education classroom over the previous 2 years. Higher rates of exposure to students with ADHD were related to higher rates of self-study, suggesting that teachers who experienced the challenges of teaching these pupils sought out their own training resources. Fortunately, a number of excellent texts and trade books featuring extensive sections detailing practical techniques for working with children with ADHD have become available in recent years to meet such teacher needs.

Higher rates of exposure to students with ADHD and more intensive self-study independently predicted higher rates of teachers' confidence in their ability to accommodate students with ADHD. Contrary to our hypothesis, however, receipt of ADHD preservice instruction or of inservice training did not relate to the confidence score. This may reflect differences in the immediate relevance of material covered through these different information sources. Self-study likely focuses on urgent information needs the teacher has identified, whereas a formal ADHD training curriculum may cover more generic topics of less immediate relevance to an individual participant.

Without question, curriculum development for ADHD training for general classroom teachers should be based on needs assessments. The teachers in this study identified several ADHD training needs, most notably how to manage the stress caused by students with ADHD in the general classroom, how to adjust lesson plans to the needs of students with ADHD, and how to develop behavior contracts. . . . Our findings suggest that inservice training on ADHD for general classroom teachers should specifically include stress management techniques to reduce stress and the risk of burnout.

The other two areas of least confidence (i.e., adjusting lesson plans, setting up behavior contracts) require specific training experiences for teachers to increase their competency and comfort level with these tasks. Such training efforts seem worthwhile, since a variety of classroom-based behavioral interventions have been shown to be effective with students with ADHD, such as response cost, token economies, positive reinforcement, and contingency contracting. Unfortunately, few general education undergraduate programs offer systematic training in these techniques, and this lack of preparation may contribute to the concern over stress.

The absence of a district effect on perceived barriers is surprising, given that the districts varied greatly in characteristics likely to affect barriers, such as district size, level of administrative sophistication, proportion of families in poverty, and availability of mental health professionals. Teachers in all districts identified the same four items as teachers surveyed by Reid and colleagues in 1994 as the most serious barriers to effective programming for students with ADHD: large class size, time needed to administer specialized interventions, severity of students' problems, and lack of training.

The first two barriers, class size and time requirements for specialized interventions, speak to teachers' concerns about having insufficient time to appropriately address the needs of students with ADHD served in the general classroom setting. It is possible that teachers may overestimate the time required to actually implement interventions with proven effectiveness due to unfamiliarity with the technique. In that case, this barrier would be amenable to strategic training efforts. However, the barriers caused by large class sizes cannot be expected to respond to training and will likely require administrative interventions, such as reducing class size or increasing the teaching support personnel allocated to inclusive classrooms as the number of students with special needs increases. . . .

Conclusion

Training in ADHD should be included in preservice and inservice education for general education teachers. The need for such training is well demonstrated by the results of this study and others. The training should include techniques with demonstrated effectiveness for students with ADHD, such as eliminating distractions, incorporating physical activity, using shortened assignments, incorporating choice, and matching assignment difficulty to students' skill level. It should also include specific techniques that have demonstrated effectiveness, such as school-home notes, token economies, time out, response cost, peer tutoring, and self-regulation methods.

One aspect of ADHD training that has not been addressed previously in the literature is stress management. The results of this and the previous study both point to this as an important component for teacher training. . . .

POSTSCRIPT

Students with AD/HD in the Regular Classroom: Are Teachers Prepared to Manage Inclusion?

One of the largest areas of disability for students across all age ranges is attention deficit/hyperactivity disorder (AD/HD), which affects 2–5% of school-age children. These children often have difficulty sitting in their seats by fidgeting, squirming, or being hyperactive. They may also be inattentive, easily distracted by the extraneous sights and sounds around them so that they are not focusing on the teacher and instruction. A third feature of students with AD/HD is that they are often impulsive: They act before they think things through, shout out answers in class, grab class materials from other students, or say things to other students that they later regret.

These features of AD/HD are often referred to as "can't do" problems. They are skill deficits that require adaptations in the regular classroom. For example, students with attention problems sometimes need to work in quieter spaces, be seated up front by the teacher, or have the number of problems on their worksheets reduced. Simple strategies like these may help the student to focus. Students who are hyperactive may be asked to work for short periods of time followed by brief physical outlets so they can expend some of their excess energy. When they are impulsive, they may be taught to "think out loud" about what might happen if they took a particular course of action, like borrowing another student's calculator without asking first. Many books have been written about how classroom teachers can make classroom accommodations for students with AD/HD.

Given all of the presumed benefits of inclusionary educational practices, one would assume that regular education teachers know how to integrate students with AD/HD into regular classrooms, that they know how to adapt the curriculum so that these students can be successful, that they know how to assist these students in coping with the challenges of social skills development, which may be part of their disability, and that they know the features of the disability so that they can report to parents regarding progress in important developmental areas. In addition to specific skills and experiences in working with students with disabilities, one might also assume that these teachers have enough time and support to meet the educational challenges that a student with disability could present in the regular education classroom. After all, inclusionary practice is not just a good idea, it is one of the goals of the Individuals with Disabilties Education Act (IDEA). While students with AD/HD are not identified as a categorical area for service delivery under IDEA, they are still eligible for services for at least part of the school day under existing categories of disability such as behavior disorders, learning disability, or other health impairment. In addition, there are many students with AD/HD who are never formally identified and will be educated in the regular classroom totally.

This question has arisen, however: Are we correct in assuming that teachers are well trained and are comfortable in making instructional accommodations for students with AD/HD? Furthermore, if they are not comfortable in making instructional accommodations with students who are included in one of the most prevalent disability areas, then what should we expect when teachers are asked to work with students with mental, emotional, and physical disabilities that are even less prevalent than AD/HD? If recent graduates are not educated about the treatment of students with AD/HD in the regular classroom, can one hope more senior teachers who graduated years earlier have any greater level of training and experience? Bussing and colleagues say, no, teachers do not feel ready to meet the inclusionary needs of students with AD/HD. Furthermore, she concludes that time and personal stress are the biggest obstacles to educating these students.

There is so much that a general education teacher needs to know. Should schools of education be more responsible for providing preservice and in-service educational opportunities on AD/HD management and personal stress management, or is it the responsibility of the individual teacher to "bone up" on the subject of AD/HD by simply reading about it in the many books and articles that are readily available? If neither approach is feasible, then should students with severe symptoms of AD/HD be included in the regular classroom nevertheless and be taught by teachers who do not feel prepared to teach and manage them? There may be serious ethical and legal issues that arise when the implications of the answers to these questions are considered.

For one of the best current resources on how to manage the antisocial behaviors associated with students with disabilities, consider reading: Hill M. Walker, E. Ramsey, and F. M. Gresham, *Antisocial Behavior in School: Evidence-Based Practices,* 2nd ed. (Wadsworth/Thompson Learning, 2004). Excellent resources with practical ideas for instructional and behavioral management of students with AD/HD in the regular classroom include G.L. Flick, *ADD/ADHD Behavior Change Resource Kit* (Center for Research in Education, 1998); S.F. Reif, *How to Reach and Teach ADD/ADHD Children* (Center for Applied Research in Education, 1999); and A.F. Reif and J.A. Heimburge, *How to Reach and Teach All Students in the Inclusive Classroom* (Center for Research in Education, 1996).

ISSUE 5

Can There Be Too Much Tolerance and Accommodation for Diversity of Student Behavior in the Classroom?

YES: James M. Kauffman, Kathleen McGee, and Michele Brigham, from "Enabling or Disabling? Observation on Changes in Special Education," *Phi Delta Kappan* (April 2004)

NO: Jennifer R. Holladay, from "Survey Says? *Teaching Tolerance* Asks Educators about the Social Climate of Their Classrooms," *Teaching Tolerance* (Spring 2000)

ISSUE SUMMARY

YES: James M. Kauffman is the Charles S. Robb Professor of Education, University of Virginia, Charlottesville; and Kathleen McGee and Michele Brigham are high school special education teachers. They believe that sometimes there is too much tolerance and accommodation for a wide range of student misbehaviors in classrooms, and teachers need to raise their learning expectations for students with special needs.

NO: Jennifer Holladay is a program coordinator for the journal *Teaching Tolerance.* She participated in this survey project that found that teachers think that teaching tolerance to their students and other teachers should be a top educational priority.

Often the initiator of classroom disruptions is an individual student. It is true that sometimes a student will misbehave of his or her own volition, but there are situations when it is the classroom peers who provoke misbehavior in a particular student. Peers may stimulate a response from students in a multitude of ways. Some students shun others and don't let them into their clique. Some students may deliberately be bullies, aggravating others into a verbal or physical confrontation. Some students tease and diminish other students' feelings of self-worth. Some students may belittle other students with their remarks about disabilities such as AD/HD, Tourette syndrome (tics), or Asperger's syndrome. Some may say hurtful comments about a different race or religion, make sexist remarks or sexually harass others at the school lockers between classes, or mock other students who are gay or lesbian. All of these behaviors are hurtful and may provoke a response from the student they target. Minimally, the classroom climate is eroded, and it is difficult for the teacher to develop a positive sense of classroom community.

What all of these scenarios have in common is student intolerance for diversity in the classroom. When these situations go unnoticed or unchecked by teachers, then students may receive the false impression that this intolerant behavior is permitted or accepted. Worse yet, when teachers are intolerant and fail to recognize the special circumstances of students with disabilities and make the necessary instructional accommodations, they may compound an already difficult situation for a student.

In a compelling article, Jennifer Holladay wrote that her research discovered that acceptance and tolerance are not evident in many schools today. For example, students made sexist and homophobic remarks and used sexual epithets and slurs toward certain religious groups. More surprisingly, she found even higher levels of intolerance among teachers—twice the frequency heard from students. The teachers' intolerance was reflected in their remarks, attitudes, or permissiveness of intolerant comments. Most often it is subtle, but the message is very clear to other teachers and to their students. While many teachers report that they try to infuse their classrooms with anti-bias messages, they state that there are few classroom materials that stress classroom tolerance for a wide range of forms of student diversity, and that other forms of resources for teaching tolerance must be developed, including video, CDs, CD-ROMs, posters, and music. Some teachers think that teaching tolerance to build classroom community is not part of their job. Another reason why some teachers have resisted teaching tolerance is because they want to resist alienating parents who may not share their sense of tolerance. Some teachers report that it is not fair when tolerance is displayed for the socially inappropriate behaviors of students but there is intolerance for those same behaviors from other students without disabilities.

An alternative to this point of view is expressed by James Kauffman and colleagues. In the general sense, Kauffman and his co-writers are not against teachers instructing students in tolerance for their fellow classmates, but there is a more subtle issue that they raise. They contend that in the specific case of teachers instructing students with disabilities, too much tolerance can be just as destructive as not enough tolerance. They certainly recognize situations where little or no instructional or behavioral accommodations have been made for students with disabilities with the results that these students remain disabled without the assistance they need to reach their full range of academic and social skills. On the other hand, these authors state when teachers and other students make too many classroom accommodations, the students with disabilities may become enabled. They insist that both extreme examples of under- and over-accommodation for students with disabilities do not permit these students to meet their behavioral and educational goals.

YES ◀ James M. Kauffman, Kathleen McGee, and Michele Brigham

Enabling or Disabling?
Observations on Changes
in Special Education

Conceptions of how best to educate students with disabilities have shifted toward one of two extremes: denying that disabilities exist or accommodating them to the extent that there is no expectation of student progress toward realistic goals. The authors contend that both attitudes defeat the primary educational aim of helping all students achieve their highest potential.

SCHOOLS need demanding and distinctive special education that is clearly focused on instruction and habilitation. Abandoning such a conception of special education is a prescription for disaster. But special education has increasingly been losing its way in the single-minded pursuit of full inclusion.

Once, special education's purpose was to bring the performance of students with disabilities closer to that of their nondisabled peers in regular classrooms, to move as many students as possible into the mainstream with appropriate support. For students not in regular education, the goal was to move them toward a more typical setting in a cascade of placement options. But as any good thing can be overdone and ruined by the pursuit of extremes, we see special education suffering from the extremes of inclusion and accommodation.

Aiming for as much normalization as possible gave special education a clear purpose. Some disabilities were seen as easier to remediate than others. Most speech and language disorders, for example, were considered eminently remediable. Other disabilities, such as mental retardation and many physical disabilities, were assumed to be permanent or long-term and so less remediable, but movement toward the mainstream and increasing independence from special educators were clear goals.

The emphasis in special education has shifted away from normalization, independence, and competence. The result has been students' dependence on whatever special programs, modifications, and accommodations are possible, particularly in general education settings. The goal seems to have become the appearance of normalization without the expectation of competence.

Many parents and students seem to want more services as they learn what is available. Some have lost sight of the goal of limiting accommodations in order to challenge students to achieve more independence. At the same time, many special education advocates want all services to be available in mainstream settings, with little or no acknowledgment that the services are atypical. Although teachers, administrators, and guidance counselors are often willing and able to make accommodations, doing so is not always in students' best long-term interests. It gives students with disabilities what anthropologist Robert Edgerton called a cloak—a pretense, a cover, which actually fools no one—rather than actual competence.

In this article, we discuss how changes in attitudes toward disability and special education, placement, and accommodations can perpetuate disability. We also explore the problems of ignoring or perpetuating disability rather than helping students lead fuller, more independent lives. Two examples illustrate how we believe good intentions can go awry—how attempts to accommodate students with disabilities can undermine achievement.

"But he needs resource. . . . " Thomas, a high school sophomore identified as emotionally disturbed, was assigned to a resource class created to help students who had problems with organization or needed extra help with academic skills. One of the requirements in the class was for students to keep a daily planner in which they entered all assignments; they shared their planner with the resource teacher at the beginning of class and discussed what academic subjects would be worked on during that period.

Thomas consistently refused to keep a planner or do any work in resource (he slept instead). So a meeting was set up with the assistant principal, the guidance counselor, Thomas, and the resource teacher. As the meeting was about to begin, the principal announced that he would not stay because Thomas felt intimidated by so many adults. After listening to Thomas' complaints, the guidance counselor decided that Thomas would not have to keep a planner or show it to the resource teacher and that the resource teacher should not talk to him unless Thomas addressed her first. In short, Thomas would not be required to do any work in the class! When the resource teacher suggested that, under those circumstances, Thomas should perhaps be placed in a study hall, because telling the parents that he was in a resource class would be a misrepresentation, the counselor replied, "But he needs the resource class."

"He's too bright. . . ." Bob, a high school freshman with Asperger's Syndrome, was scheduled for three honors classes and two Advanced Placement classes. Bob's IEP (individualized education program) included a two-page list of accommodations. In spite of his having achieved A's and B's, with just a single C in math, his mother did not feel that his teachers were accommodating him appropriately. Almost every evening, she e-mailed his teachers and his case manager to request more information or more help for Bob, and she angrily phoned his guidance counselor if she didn't receive a reply by the end of the first hour of the next school day.

A meeting was scheduled with the IEP team, including five of Bob's seven teachers, the county special education supervisor, the guidance counselor, the case manager, the principal, and the county autism specialist. When the accommodations were reviewed, Bob's mother agreed that all of them were being made. However, she explained that Bob had been removed from all outside social activities because he spent all night, every night, working on homework. The accommodation she demanded was that Bob have no homework assignments. The autism specialist agreed that this was a reasonable accommodation for a child with Asperger's Syndrome.

The teachers of the honors classes explained that the homework in their classes, which involved elaboration and extension of concepts, was even more essential than the homework assigned in AP classes. In AP classes, by contrast, homework consisted primarily of practice of concepts learned in class. The honors teachers explained that they had carefully broken their long assignments into segments, each having a separate due date before the final project, and they gave illustrations of their expectations. The director of special education explained the legal definition of accommodations (the mother said she'd never before heard that accommodations could not change the nature of the curriculum). The director also suggested that, instead of Bob's sacrificing his social life, perhaps it would be more appropriate for him to take standard classes. What Bob's mother was asking, he concluded, was not legal. She grew angry, but she did agree to give the team a "little more time" to serve Bob appropriately. She said she would "be back with her claws and broomstick" if anyone ever suggested that he be moved from honors classes without being given the no-homework accommodation. "He's too bright to take anything less than honors classes, and if you people would provide this simple accommodation, he would do just fine," she argued. In the end, she got her way.

Attitudes Toward Disability and Special Education

Not that many decades ago, a disability was considered a misfortune—not something to be ashamed of but a generally undesirable, unwelcome condition to be overcome to the greatest extent possible. Ability was considered more desirable than disability, and anything—whether a device or a service—that helped people with disabilities to do what those without disabilities could do was considered generally valuable, desirable, and worth the effort, cost, and possible stigma associated with using it.

The disability rights movement arose in response to the widespread negative attitudes toward disabilities, and it had a number of desirable outcomes. It helped overcome some of the discrimination against people with disabilities. And overcoming such bias and unfairness in everyday life is a great accomplishment. But the movement has also had some unintended negative consequences. One of these is the outright denial of disability in some cases, illustrated by the contention that disability exists only in attitudes or as a function of the social power to coerce.

The argument that disability is merely a "social construction" is particularly vicious in its effects on social justice. Even if we assume that disabilities are socially constructed, what should that mean? Should we assume that socially constructed phenomena are not "real," are not important, or should be discredited? If so, then consider that dignity, civil rights, childhood, social justice, and nearly every other phenomenon that we hold dear are social constructions.

Many social constructions are not merely near and dear to us, they are real and useful in benevolent societies. The important question is whether the idea of disability is useful in helping people attain dignity or whether it is more useful to assume that disabilities are not real (i.e., that, like social justice, civil rights, and other social constructions, they are fabrications that can be ignored when convenient). The denial of disability is sometimes expressed as an aversion to labels, so that we are cautioned not to communicate openly and clearly about disabilities but to rely on euphemisms. But this approach is counterproductive. When we are able only to whisper or mime the undesirable difference called disability, then we inadvertently increase its stigma and thwart prevention efforts.

The specious argument that "normal" does not exist—because abilities of every kind are varied and because the point at which normal becomes abnormal is arbitrary—leads to the conclusion that no one actually has a disability or, alternatively, that everyone has a disability. Then, some argue, either no one or everyone is due an accommodation so that no one or everyone is identified as disabled. This unwillingness to draw a line defining something (such as disability, poverty, or childhood) is based either on ignorance regarding the nature of continuous distributions or on a rejection of the unavoidably arbitrary decisions necessary to provide special services to those who need them and, in so doing, to foster social justice.

Another unintended negative consequence of the disability rights movement is that, for some people, disability has become either something that does not matter or something to love, to take pride in, to flaunt, to adopt as a positive aspect of one's identity, or to cherish as something desirable or as a badge of honor. When disability makes no difference to us one way or the other, then we are not going to work to attenuate it, much less prevent it. At best, we will try to accommodate it. When we view disability as a desirable difference, then we are very likely to try to make it more pronounced, not to ameliorate it.

Several decades ago, special education was seen as a good thing—a helpful way of responding to disability, not something everyone needed or should have, but a useful and necessary response to the atypical needs of students with disabilities. This is why the Education for All Handicapped Children Act (now the Individuals with Disabilities Education Act) was written. But in the minds of many people, special education has been transformed from something helpful to something awful.

The full-inclusion movement did have some desirable outcomes. It helped overcome some of the unnecessary removal of students with disabilities from general education. However, the movement also has had some unintended negative consequences. One of these is that special education has come to be viewed in very negative terms, to be seen as a second-class and discriminatory system that does more harm than good. Rather than being seen as helpful, as a way of creating opportunity, special education is often portrayed as a means of shunting students into dead-end programs and killing opportunity.

Another unintended negative consequence of full inclusion is that general education is now seen by many as the only place where fair and equitable treatment is possible and where the opportunity to learn is extended to all equally. The argument has become that special education is good only as long as it is invisible (or nearly so), an indistinguishable part of a general education system that accommodates all students, regardless of their abilities or disabilities. Usually, this is described as a "unified" (as opposed to "separate") system of education. Special education is thus something to be avoided altogether or attenuated to the greatest extent possible, regardless of a student's inability to perform in a general setting. When special education is seen as discriminatory, unfair, an opportunity-killing system, or, as one writer put it, "the gold-plated garbage can of American schooling," then it is understandable that people will loathe it. But this way of looking at special education is like seeing the recognition and treatment of cancer as the cause of the problem.

The reversal in attitudes toward disability and special education—disability from undesirable to inconsequential, special education from desirable to awful—has clouded the picture of what special education is and what it should do for students with disabilities. Little wonder that special education stands accused of failure, that calls for its demise have become vociferous, and that contemporary practices are often more disabling than enabling. An unfortunate outcome of the changing attitudes toward disability and special education is that the benefit of special education is now sometimes seen as freedom from expectations of performance. It is as if we believed that, if a student has to endure the stigma of special education, then the compensation should include an exemption from work.

Placement Issues

Placing all students, regardless of their abilities, in regular classes has exacerbated the tendency to see disability as something existing only in people's minds. It fosters the impression that students are fitting in when they are not able to perform at anywhere near the normal level. It perpetuates disabilities; it does not compensate for them.

Administrators and guidance counselors sometimes place students in programs for which they do not qualify, even as graduation requirements are increasing and tests are mandated. Often, these students' testing is modified although their curriculum is not. The students may then feel that they have beaten the system. They are taught that the system is unfair and that the only way to win is by gaming it. Hard work and individual responsibility for one's education are often overlooked—or at least undervalued.

Students who consistently fail in a particular curriculum must be given the opportunity to deal with the natural consequences of that fact as a means of learning individual responsibility. For example, social promotion in elementary and middle school teaches students that they really don't have to be able to do the work to pass. Students who have been conditioned to rely on social promotion do not believe that the cycle will end until it does so—usually very abruptly in high school. Suddenly, no one passes them on, and no one gives them undeserved credit. Many of these students do not graduate in four years. Some never recover, while others find themselves forced to deal with a very distasteful situation.

No one wants to see a student fail, but to alter any standard without good reason is to set that same student up for failure later in life. Passing along a student with disabilities in regular classes, pretending that he or she is performing at the same level as most of the class or that it doesn't really matter (arguing that the student has a legal "right" to be in the class) is another prescription for disappointment and failure in later life. Indeed, this failure often comes in college or on the job.

Some people with disabilities do need assistance. Others do not. Consider Deborah Groeber, who struggled through degenerative deafness and blindness. The Office of Affirmative Action at the University of Pennsylvania offered to intercede at the Wharton School, but Groeber knew that she had more influence if she spoke for herself. Today, she is a lawyer with three Ivy League degrees. But not every student with disabilities can do or should be expected to do what Groeber did. Our concern is that too many students with disabilities are given encouragement based on pretense when they could do much more with appropriate special education.

Types of Accommodations

Two popular modifications in IEPs are allowing for the use of calculators and granting extended time on tests and assignments. Calculators can be a great asset, but they should be used when calculating complex problems or when doing word problems. Indiscriminate use of a calculator renders many math tests invalid, as they become a contest to see if buttons can be pushed successfully and in the correct order, rather than an evaluation of ability to do arithmetic or use mathematical knowledge.

Extended time on assignments and tests can also be a useful modification, but it can easily be misused or abused. Extended time on tests should mean continuous time so that a test is not studied for first and taken later. Sometimes a test must be broken into smaller segments that can be completed independently. However, this could put students with disabilities at a disadvantage, as one part of a test might help with remembering another part. Extensions on assignments need to be evaluated each time they are given, not simply handed out automatically because they are written into an IEP. If a student is clearly working hard, then extensions may be appropriate. If a student has not even been attempting assignments, then more time might be an avoidance tactic. Sometimes extended time means that assignments pile up and the student gets further and further behind. The result can then be overwhelming stress and the inability to comprehend discussions because many concepts must be acquired in sequence (e.g., in math, science, history, and foreign languages).

Reading tests and quizzes aloud to students can be beneficial for many, but great caution is required. Some students and teachers want to do more than simply read a test. Reading a test aloud means simply reading the printed words on the page without inflections that can reveal correct answers and without explaining vocabulary. Changing a test to open-notes or open-book, without the knowledge and consent of the classroom teacher, breaches good-faith test proctoring. It also teaches students dependence rather than independence and accomplishment. Similarly, scribing for a student can be beneficial for those who truly need it, but the teacher must be careful not to add details and to write only what the student dictates, including any run-on sentences or fragments. After scribing, if the assignment is not a test, the teacher should edit and correct the paper with the student, as she might do with any written work. But this must take place after the scribing.

How Misguided Accommodations Can Be Disabling

"Saving" a child from his or her own negative behavior reinforces that behavior and makes it a self-fulfilling prophecy. Well-intentioned guidance counselors often feel more responsibility for their students' success or failure than the students themselves feel. Sometimes students are not held accountable for their effort or work. They seem not to understand that true independence comes from what you know, not whom you know. Students who are consistently enabled and not challenged are never given the opportunity to become independent. Ann Bancroft, the polar explorer and dyslexic, claims that, although school was a torment, it was disability that forged her iron will. Stephen Cannell's fear for other dyslexics is that they will quit trying rather than struggle and learn to compensate for their disability.

Most parents want to help their children. However, some parents confuse making life easier with making life better for their children. Too often, parents feel that protecting their child from the rigors of academic demands is in his or her best interest. They may protect their child by insisting on curricular modifications and accommodations in assignments, time, and testing. But children learn by doing, and not allowing them to do something because they might fail is denying them the opportunity to succeed. These students eventually believe that they are not capable of doing what typical students can do, even if they are. Sometimes it is difficult for teachers to discern what a student actually can do and what a parent has done until an in-class assignment is given or a test is taken. At that point, it is often too late for the teacher to do much remediation. The teacher may erroneously conclude that the student is simply a poor test-taker.

In reality, the student may have been "protected" from learning, which will eventually catch up with him or her. Unfortunately, students may not face reality until they take a college entrance exam, go away to college, or apply for a job. Students who "get through" high school in programs of this type often go on to flunk out of college. Unfortunately, the parents of these students frequently blame the college for the student's failure, criticizing the postsecondary institution for not doing enough to help. Instead, they should be upset both with the secondary institution for not preparing the child adequately for the tasks to come and with themselves for their own overprotection.

The Benefits of Demands

Many successful adults with disabilities sound common themes when asked about their ability to succeed in the face of a disability. Tom Gray, a Rhodes Scholar who has a severe learning disability, claims that having to deal with the hardest experiences gave him the greatest strength. Stephen Cannell believes that, if he had known there was a reason beyond his control to explain his low achievement, he might not have worked as hard as he did. Today, he knows he has a learning disability, but he is also an Emmy Award-winning television writer and producer. Paul Orlalea, the dyslexic founder of Kinko's, believes God gave him an advantage in the challenge presented by his disability and that others should work with their strengths. Charles Schwab, the learning-disabled founder of Charles Schwab, Inc., cites his ability to think differently and to make creative leaps that more sequential thinkers don't make as chief reasons for his success. Fannie Flagg, the learning-disabled author, concurs and insists that learning disabilities become a blessing only if you can overcome them. Not every student with a disability can be a star performer, of course, but all should be expected to achieve all that they can.

Two decades ago, special educators thought it was their job to assess a student's achievement, to understand what the student wanted to do and what an average peer could do, and then to develop plans to bridge the gap, if possible. Most special educators wanted to see that each student had the tools and knowledge to succeed as independently as possible. Helping students enter the typical world was the mark of success for special educators.

The full-inclusion movement now insists that every student will benefit from placement in the mainstream. However, some of the modifications and accommodations now being demanded are so radical that we are doing an injustice to the entire education system. Special education must not be associated in any way with "dumbing down" the curriculum for students presumed to be at a given grade level, whether disabled or not.

Counselors and administrators who want to enable students must focus the discussion on realistic goals and plans for each student. An objective, in-depth discussion and evaluation must take place to determine how far along the continuum of successfully completing these goals the student has moved. If the student is making adequate progress independently, or with minimal help, special education services might not be necessary. If assistance is required to make adequate progress on realistic goals, then special education may be needed. Every modification and every accommodation should be held to the same standard: whether it will help the student attain these goals—not whether it will make life easier for the student. Knowing where a student is aiming can help a team guide that student toward success.

And the student must be part of this planning. A student who claims to want to be a brain surgeon but refuses to take science courses needs a reality check. If a student is unwilling to attempt to reach intermediate goals or does not succeed in meeting them, then special education cannot "save" that student. At that point, the team must help the student revisit his or her goals. Goals should be explained in terms of the amount of work required to complete them, not whether or not the teacher or parent feels they are attainable. When goals are presented in this way, students can often make informed decisions regarding their attainability and desirability. Troy Brown, a university dean and politician who has both a doctorate and a learning disability, studied at home with his mother. He estimates that it took him more than twice as long as the average person to complete assignments. Every night, he would go to bed with stacks of books and read until he fell asleep, because he had a dream of attending college.

General educators and special educators need to encourage all students to be responsible and independent and to set realistic expectations for themselves. Then teachers must help students to meet these expectations in a more and more independent manner. Special educators do not serve students well when they enable students with disabilities to become increasingly dependent on their parents, counselors, administrators, or teachers—or even when they fail to increase students' independence and competence.

Where We Stand

We want to make it clear that we think disabilities are real and that they make doing certain things either impossible or very difficult for the people who have them. We cannot expect people with disabilities to be "just like everyone else" in what they can do. The views of other writers differ:

The human service practices that cause providers to believe that clients [students] have inadequacies, shortcomings, failures, or faults that must be corrected or controlled by specially trained professionals must be replaced by conceptions that people with disabilities are capable of setting their own goals and achieving or not. Watered-down curricula, alternative grading practices, special competency standards, and other "treat them differently" practices used with "special" students must be replaced with school experiences exactly like those used with "regular" students.

We disagree. In our view, students with disabilities do have specific shortcomings and do need the services of specially trained professionals to achieve their potential. They do sometimes need altered curricula or adaptations to make their learning possible. If students with disabilities were just like "regular" students, then there would be no need whatever for special education. But the school experiences of students with disabilities obviously will not be—cannot be—just like those of students without disabilities. We sell students with disabilities short when we pretend that they are no different from typical students. We make the same error when we pretend that they must not be expected to put forth extra effort if they are to learn to do some things—or learn to do something in a different way. We sell them short when we pretend that they have competencies that they do not have or pretend that the competencies we expect of most students are not important for them.

Like general education, special education must push students to become all they can be. Special education must countenance neither the pretense of learning nor the avoidance of reasonable demands.

Jennifer R. Holladay

 **NO**

Survey Says? Teaching Tolerance Asks Educators About the Social Climate of Their Classrooms

"Envision the year 2020. What issues do you think will present the greatest challenges to our schools then?" the moderator asked. For the teachers gathered together on a rainy spring day in Minneapolis, the answers came swiftly: "diversity," "differences," "racism," "violence."

"We've made great strides in the last two decades," said one educator. "But it's frustrating to see all the hate out there. And then you think 'Wow, that's not a teeny, tiny problem. That's a lot of people—a lot of children.'"

As a member of one of three focus groups assembled in Minneapolis and Houston, this educator, along with 26 of her peers, engaged in honest and, at times, difficult discussions about the realities of classroom teaching. Their insights laid the groundwork for Teaching Tolerance's first nationwide survey of attitudes about the state of U.S. schools and the usefulness of available anti-bias classroom materials, including its own products.

Administered by Lake, Snell, Perry and Associates, an opinion research firm based in Washington, D.C., the 1999 survey polled 600 randomly selected subscribers to *Teaching Tolerance* magazine and, to provide for a comparative analysis, also asked questions of 500 classroom teachers who do not use the program's materials.

The State of U.S. Schools

Although a vast majority of participants described race relations in their schools as good, the educators polled believe that bias is an issue on their campuses, in their classrooms and in teachers' lounges.

"We don't have a lot of problems with active racism, like hate crimes, among our students," said Margaret, a high school English teacher. (*All names have been changed.*) "But I'm not sure that there is a whole lot of actual acceptance [of differences] either. The barriers between groups aren't really being broken down."

When respondents were asked specific questions about racist, sexist, homophobic and other biased behaviors, a clearer picture of school intolerance emerged. According to the teachers polled nationwide, students make sexist and homophobic comments often and use racial epithets and slurs toward particular religious groups somewhat frequently. By the same measure, respondents reported dramatically high levels of intolerance among their teaching peers. Comments suggesting racial and religious intolerance, for example, were heard almost twice as frequently from colleagues as from students. . . .

"I have heard colleagues say things like 'I don't shop in [certain neighborhoods] anymore; it's just too *dark* over there,'" said Tim, a 3rd grade teacher. "That attitude and others like it translate into the classroom setting, and the way that some kids of color are treated is just frightening."

Tools for Tolerance

Where do teachers turn to combat prejudice among peers and students? Most educators surveyed integrate articles from the popular media or multicultural textbooks, literature and videos as a first line of defense. Some also choose to engage in active dialogue with bigoted colleagues or students.

Although a majority of teachers polled believe that there are an adequate number of anti-bias resources available, many feel that those materials are not relevant to their classrooms. "A lot of teachers tend to think, 'Well, I teach math.' Or 'I'm teaching biology. What does tolerance have to do with that?'" remarked Abigail, who teaches algebra.

As a tool for rectifying this problem, 77 percent of the subscribers surveyed rated Teaching Tolerance materials the best available or better than average. Respondents cited the broadness of the topics covered as a major strength.

"*Teaching Tolerance* is 'one-stop shopping,'" Jeanne, a media specialist, commented. "It talks about boys. It deals with gay and lesbian issues. It covers a wide array of Native American topics and other race and ethnic issues. There once was even an article on body size. Other materials often just talk about color and avoid comparable hot topics."

Room for Improvement

Teaching Tolerance and other multicultural programs may well have overlooked an important player in the struggle for tolerance, however. When asked who or what posed the greatest challenge to anti-bias initiatives, a large portion of survey respondents said "parents." . . . In order to maximize effectiveness, these educators say, multicultural materials need to include a parental component.

"Like it or not, teachers are in a position in which we have to educate families, too," Thomas, an 8th grade history instructor, said. "If a teacher goes out on a limb with a topic, he or she runs the risk that a child will go home and say something to a parent. If you can't get support from parents [or guardians], your lesson will fail."

Educators subscribing to *Teaching Tolerance* also identified several "improvement areas" specific to the program's magazine and curriculum kits. "The articles don't need to be quite so long," one teacher lamented, while another said, "I would like to see more lessons, because it is really nice when you have something you can use right away."

The main complaint from subscribers, however, concerned infrequency of publication. Sixty-four percent of those polled echoed the sentiments of Mandy, an ESL instructor, who said simply: "I would like to see the magazine more often." . . .

Resources of all kinds—magazines, books, videos, posters, music CDs, CD-ROMS and others—are needed, these educators argued, not just for students but for practitioners. "Teaching Tolerance materials and other tools for change expose me to different perspectives, different cultures and different languages," said Lanita, who teaches psychology. "They encourage self-growth, so that I, in turn, can model acceptance and understanding for students. Differences are hard for grown-ups, too, you know."

POSTSCRIPT

Can There Be Too Much Tolerance and Accommodation for Diversity of Student Behavior in the Classroom?

Tolerance is a virtue that we all could use more of. Just read the newspaper and many instances of intolerance in our daily adult lives stand out: road rage, police reports of family disturbances, nasty election campaign slogans, name-calling by nations engaged in border disputes, suicide car bombers, and horrific human rights violations by military personnel. At the student level, intolerance takes many forms, from racial slurs, Pope jokes, sexual innuendos, mimicking a stutter, nicknaming someone "Fatso," laughing at the antics of a child with hyperactivity, and prodding a rageful response from a child with autism.

Those who believe in a systemic approach to classroom management make claims that the only way to develop caring classrooms is to teach all students about tolerance and empathy for others. In this manner, the incidence of classroom misbehaviors may be reduced because all students feel a sense of belonging and acceptance. Furthermore, when students are taught tolerance, the classroom climate is changed from a competitive, individualistic climate to a cooperative, group-oriented climate. "All for one and one for all."

When tolerance is the goal then group contingencies for good behavior by the entire class makes sense. When tolerance is understood, then students complain less that special attention to students with special needs is unfair. They realize that the special attention that those students need is equitable since those students need that attention. When tolerance is one measure of virtue, students learn that their understanding of disability, their acceptance of race, their sharing of friendships, their empathy for the misfortunes of others, their sense of fairness, and their sense of inclusion makes them better classroom citizens as well.

Despite all of these presumed benefits of teaching tolerance, Kauffman offers another point of view that tolerance, acceptance, and accommodation in the extreme may not be such a good thing. There are many forms of classroom accommodations, including using calculators in math tests, shortening assignments, extending deadlines for completion of assignments, reading tests aloud, open-book testing, and scribing for a student who has difficulty writing. All of these accommodations under some circumstances can hold merit and allow the student to show the skills that may be hidden by disability, but when these accommodations are unwarranted, then the student may learn to become manipulative, coercive, and more dependent on others.

Kauffman expresses the strong belief that students with disabilities must be given the same option to succeed or not succeed just like every other student. Teachers should not "save" students. Kauffman believes that teachers must skillfully discern what the student with disabilities can and cannot do, carefully craft lesson plans, and make challenging behavioral expectations. Kauffman and colleagues insist that teachers, students, and parents should frequently reassess the goals of any special education accommodations and question whether they are necessary. All students need to be taught to be responsible for themselves and independent and to set their own realistic goals as much as possible. This is the essence of independence, which is a goal of most special education interventions. The role of the teacher should be to assist that student to meet his or her own academic and behavioral goals with less and less assistance. Kauffman maintains that the best way to empower students with disabilities is to insist that they put forth effort to learn and that they behave in the classroom. When too much accommodation and too much tolerance are shown, these students learn that they do not have to put forth effort to meet their own goals, and such enablement will only make these students less successful in academic and social domains alike.

It has been said that teaching is an art. To be a good teacher, an individual must have a sixth sense. Kounin (*Discipline and Group Management in Classrooms,* Holt, Rinehart and Winston, 1970) has referred to this sixth sense as "withitness." In the area of tolerance, teachers must use this sixth sense to understand when intolerance is getting in the way of a positive classroom climate and when too much tolerance is aiding and abetting students whose primary motive is to avoid work and avoid responsibility for misbehavior. A delicate balance is what is needed.

For more information on the theory of a cooperative approach to discipline, read L. Albert, *Cooperative Discipline* (American Guidance Service, 1996, 2003). For specific strategies for implementing a cooperative discipline approach, consider reading L. Albert, *Cooperative Discipline Implementation Guide: Resources for Staff Development* (American Guidance Service, 2003). For useful child-centered bibliotherapy to assist in teaching tolerance, discuss the following materials with students: A. Dobrin, *Love Your Neighbor: Stories of Values and Virtues* (Scholastic, 1999) and J.L. Wycoff, *20 Teachable Virtues* (Berkley, 1995). Two bibliotherapy sources on the topic of acceptance of differences are K. Cave and C. Ridell, *Something Else* (MONDO, 1994) and T. Parr, *It's Okay to Be Different* (Little Brown, 2001). Recommended reading if you are interested in learning how to teach empathy to children is L. Eyre and R. Eyre, *Teaching Your Children Sensitivity* (Fireside, 1995). Finally, I highly recommend a wonderful little book of bibliotherapy for young children related to tolerance in the classroom: J. Garrison and A. Tubesing, *A Million Visions of Peace* (Pfeiffer-Hamilton, 1996).

Teachnet.com

Teachnet.com was created in 1995 to provide information to teachers by teachers. This site provides numerous ideas on classroom and behavior management. The range of strategies and interventions is large and includes activities such as classroom jobs for students.

http://teachnet.com/how-to/manage/

Temple University's Collaboration for Excellence in Teacher Preparation

This is a project-sponsored site by the National Science Foundation. The link below addresses classroom management in a comprehensive manner, including managing the physical space of the classroom, creating classroom routines, establishing standards of conduct, learning and knowing students, and setting up instruction for positive student behavior.

http://www.temple.edu/CETP/temple_teach/
cm-intro.html

Intervention Central

Intervention Central was created by an expert in the field of behavior management— a New York special education administrator, program developer, and school district trainer on behavior management. The document associated with this site provides helpful information related to punishment and how it should be used most effectively within a school and/or classroom setting.

http://www.interventioncentral.org/htmdocs/
interventions/behavior/punishguidelines.shtml

Character Counts

Character Counts is a nonprofit, nonpartisan, nonsectarian character education framework. It teaches six pillars of character, which include trustworthiness, respect, responsibility, fairness, caring, and citizenship. Information for implementation within communities is provided, as well as specific information about the program.

http://charactercounts.org

PART 2

Teacher Management of Student Misbehavior

*E*ven though every educator has had at least one course in classroom management, educators are frustrated that students still show disrespect toward them. They want control over their classrooms and respect from students. Some educators demand it and employ traditional classroom-management techniques to get it. Can controlling management procedures backfire and result in the very disrespect educators are trying to avoid? Contingency management through rewards and punishments is usually at the top of the list of corrective procedures. What are the side effects of applying a positive reinforcement technique? When positive reinforcement does not "work," what may be some of the reasons? Time-out has been used for years to manage a wide range of student misbehaviors, from being off-task to committing a violent act. Is time-out overused? How can it be used more judiciously? Students need to learn the consequences of their choices, but if punishment is so effective, then why do educators seem to use it more and more and with the same offending students? Is there something missing from the punishment paradigm? Finally, there is a resurgence of interest in character education as a means of teaching values, virtues, and moral responsibility toward the rest of the class and the school. Is there a place for character education in public schools? Should development of students of character be considered just as important an instructional goal as students of intelligence? In Part 2, we debate the pros and cons of the many strategies that teachers regularly employ in classroom management.

- Does the Authoritarianism of Traditional Classroom Management Contribute to Student Disrespect?

- Is Positive Reinforcement Overused?

- Should Time-Out Be Timed Out?

- Is Punishment an Effective Technique to Control Behavior?

- Should Character Count?

ISSUE 6

Does the Authoritarianism of Traditional Classroom Management Contribute to Student Disrespect?

YES: Alfie Kohn, from "Almost There, But Not Quite," *Educational Leadership* (March 2003)

NO: Jeremy Swinson and Mike Cording, from "Assertive Discipline in a School for Pupils with Emotional and Behavioural Difficulties," *British Journal of Special Education* (June 2002)

ISSUE SUMMARY

YES: Alfie Kohn is an author and lecturer. Kohn postulates that traditional classroom-management strategies often used in schools today do not promote a mutually caring and respectful classroom environment and results in increased student disrespect.

NO: Jeremy Swinson is a senior educational psychologist and honorary lecturer at Liverpool John Moores University, and Mike Cording is an educational consultant in Southport, England. They support the use of assertive discipline (a traditional classroom-management strategy), even for those students who are disaffected, discouraged, and disrespectful. They maintain that corrective procedures change behavior and do not contribute to student disrespect.

One of the most common and traditional forms of classroom management is corrective discipline, in which the classroom teacher deals with problems once they occur. There is little or no attempt at prevention. Often corrective discipline involves some form of mild punishment such as time-out, response cost, or social disapproval. Corrective discipline is very popular among classroom teachers because it allows the teachers to wait to manage the offending student until the behavior becomes a major disruption in the classroom. One of the major complaints by teachers about corrective discipline, however, is that by the time the student misbehavior escalates to the level that it must be dealt with, the student may be talking back to the teacher, showing a bad attitude, shouting, getting physical, or running out of the classroom.

Teachers also complain that students are disrespectful. The question arises whether traditional classroom management contributes to that level of disrespect by the mere fact that it is a reactive management approach rather than a proactive one.

Alfie Kohn begins the debate by offering the point of view that traditional classroom management as epitomized by assertive discipline impedes the creation of caring classrooms and thus may actually increase the incidence of student-teacher disrespect. Kohn says that there are specific persistent features of traditional classroom management that are incompatible with the development of caring, respectful classrooms.

Overall, Kohn believes that teachers are well-intentioned, but he wants to challenge them to think about what are the goals, both intended and unintended, of their choice of classroom-management approach. Could it be possible that we are treating our students with disrespect in the way that we manage them and that in return teachers reap what we have sewn?

In sharp contrast to Kohn's view of classroom management where caring and respect are highly prized goals, Swinson and Cording seem to operationalize good classroom management as "on-task" behavior and reduction in the number of disruptive incidents. These authors contend that assertive discipline can be applied successfully to reach these goals. Assertive discipline is a management procedure that is often applied school-wide in which teachers publish their rules and consequences for good and bad behavior, provide continuous feedback whether students are meeting expected behavioral goals, and if not, they are sanctioned with mild punishment in escalating order as these students' behavior becomes more intense.

What is most interesting about this article is that these authors provide research evidence that shows that assertive discipline can be used effectively even with students with behavior disorders who are disaffected and very discouraged. Furthermore, teachers using assertive discipline were observed to use fewer verbal admonishments and negative written statements than had been observed prior to the utilization of assertive discipline. The authors conclude that traditional behavioral management as epitomized in assertive discipline that employs the carrot-and-stick approach can instill a positive atmosphere in a classroom not only for younger students but for older students as well. This finding is in direct contrast to Kohn's view. Is it possible that students who are taught through reward and punishment learn how to behave and consequently feel better about themselves, their teachers, and other students? Is it possible that perhaps teachers really do know what is best for their students and that mutual respect is best shown when teachers lead and earn respect and when students obey the rules that their teachers set out for them?

Almost There, But Not Quite

T he late education researcher John Nicholls once remarked to me that he had met a lot of administrators who "don't want to hear a buzz of excitement in classrooms—they want to hear nothing." His implication was that some teachers strive to keep tight control over students, less because of their principles than because of their principals. After all, their evaluations may depend not on whether their students are engaged and happy, or curious and caring, but whether they are silent and orderly.

Schools can still purchase standardized discipline programs—or, for that matter, develop home-grown strategies—that rely on heavy-handed, old-school techniques intended to break down students' resistance and coerce them into conformity. These days, though, programs more commonly use progressive rhetoric and palatable-sounding strategies. These strategies may invoke such notions as dignity, cooperation, responsibility, love, and logic. They may rely on positive reinforcement rather than punishment. In fact, they may appear so reassuringly humanistic that we have to remind ourselves that their basic objective—compliance—is unchanged.

Rudolf Dreikurs, for example, is an author I liked a lot—until I finally sat down and read him. The "logical consequences" programs that he inspired, as well as other attempts to use pleasant-sounding means to achieve authoritarian ends, prompted me to write a book on the subject a few years back. More recently, a group of researchers confirmed in a study of 64 elementary classrooms that although most teachers try to maintain "control with a light touch," their goal typically remains to control students. Almost all of the teachers interviewed by the researchers endorsed the need to teach "good citizenship," but it turned out that most of them defined that quality in terms of "maintaining order and work effort . . . following rules [or] respecting authority."

Asking the Right Questions

What matters, then, are the fundamental questions that drive educational practice, even if they are not posed explicitly. Some teachers and administrators want to know, How can we get these kids to obey? What practical techniques can you offer that will make students show up, sit down, and do what they're told? Other educators begin from an entirely different point of departure. They ask, What do these kids need—and how can we meet those needs?

The more I visit classrooms, talk with teachers, and read the literature, the more convinced I become that you can predict how a school will look and feel just from knowing which set of questions the adults care about more. You don't even need to know their answers (which tactics they will use to secure compliance, in the first case; what they believe students need, in the second). The questions are what matter.

Even educators who try to focus on students' needs, however, may feel themselves caught in an undertow, pulled back to traditional assumptions and practices that result in their doing things to students rather than working with them. Some aren't even aware that this is happening. I have long been intrigued by our tendency to assume that we have arrived when, in fact, we still have a lot farther to go. Consultants will tell you that few barriers to change are as intractable as the belief that one doesn't need to change. When you tell some teachers about a new approach, they instantly respond, "Oh, I'm already doing that." And sometimes they are—sort of, but not entirely.

In a classic essay, David K. Cohen described a math teacher who firmly believed that she taught for understanding. Indeed, she used many innovative activities and materials—for example, having her students do number sentences and calendar activities—yet she had adopted them without questioning her traditional assumptions about pedagogy, such as the idea that the goal is to produce right answers rather than to understand mathematical principles from the inside out. The result was a classroom that subtly discouraged students from exploring ideas, even as the teacher prided herself on how effectively she encouraged such exploration.

Going Part of the Way

Exactly the same partial success, often accompanied by a gap between perception and reality, shows up in the ways that many classrooms are structured, how they feel to students, and how people are treated within them. A half-dozen examples follow. You may find yourself adding more.

Blaming the Students

Some teachers consciously try to create a "working with" classroom, yet automatically assume that when students act inappropriately, they have a behavior problem that must be fixed. It is the students who must change, and the teacher stands by to help them do so.

Norman Kunc, who conducts workshops on inclusive education and non-coercive practices, points out that "what we call 'behavior problems' are often situations of legitimate conflict; we just get to call them behavior problems because we have more power" than the students do. (You're not allowed to say that your spouse has a behavior problem.) Some teachers respond with fury when they have a conflict with a student, and some respond with understanding, but few teachers have the courage to reflect on how they may need to reconsider their own decisions. A San Diego educator, Donna Marriott, stands out for having done just that:

> If a child starts to act up, I have learned to ask myself: "How have I failed this child? What is it about this lesson that is leaving her outside the learning? How can I adapt my plan to engage this child?" I stopped blaming my children.

Unsettling as it may be to acknowledge, an awful lot of smart, warm, empathetic teachers continue to blame their students when things go wrong. They may not even be aware that they are doing this.

Keeping Control of the Classroom

A teacher may allow students to make decisions in the classroom—even boast about how they are empowered—while limiting the number, significance, or impact of these choices to ensure that he or she remains comfortably in control. The teacher may hold class meetings, for example, but unilaterally determine what will be discussed, who will speak and when, how long the meeting will last, and so on. Consider a teacher in Washington state who boldly hung a sign at the front of her classroom that read, "Think for yourself; the teacher might be wrong!" Gradually, though, she realized that her classroom remained in important ways teacher-centered rather than learner-centered. Her practices were still "authoritarian," as she later realized:

> I wanted [students] to think for themselves, but only so long as their thinking didn't slow down my predetermined lesson plan or get in the way of my teacher-led activity or argue against my classroom policies.

Missing the Systemic Factors

Some educators work hard to cultivate a caring relationship with each student—to earn his or her respect and trust. They understand how traditional management techniques erode those relationships. However, problems persist in their classrooms, at least partly because the teachers lack a wider perspective that illuminates what happens among the individuals involved. As Sylwester writes,

> Misbehavior is to a classroom what pain is to a body—a useful status report that something isn't working as it should.

The underlying problem—of which that misbehavior is but a symptom—may not be limited to the needs of a given student. Just as some therapists move beyond the "identified patient" to consider the dynamics of the family as a whole, the teacher may need to address at the systemic level his or her own role and the way in which all the students in the classroom interact.

Many teachers believe that everything would be perfect if only they could get rid of a particular student who is always causing trouble. But if that student is finally removed, another student may pop up, like the next tissue in the box, to fill the role previously played by his or her classmate. In other words, educators can only make so much progress if they understand individuals but overlook roles and systems.

Ignoring Problems with the Curriculum

Teachers who work with students to create a caring community—and who respond constructively to setbacks that develop—sometimes pay insufficient attention to deficiencies in the academic curriculum. As a result, they are forever struggling to get students to pay attention to tasks that, frankly, don't deserve the students' attention. Misbehavior may continue primarily because students resist instruction that emphasizes decontextualized skills or requires rote recall; activities intended to raise test scores rather than to answer authentic questions; lessons that they find neither relevant nor engaging—and that they had little or no role in designing. Truly, the question of how a classroom is "managed" is inextricably linked to the theory of learning that informs curriculum content and instruction. This is why I have talked in the past, only half in jest, about a modest attempt to overthrow the entire field of classroom management. No matter how much progress is made in that field, it can never accomplish meaningful goals if it is divorced from pedagogical matters.

Settling for Self-Discipline

Some educators reject rewards and punishments, believing, as I do, that a child may act in the desired way only in order to receive the former or avoid the latter. These educators want students to be self-disciplined, to internalize good values so that they no longer need outside inducements.

But even this goal is not ambitious enough. The self-disciplined student may not be an autonomous decision maker if the values have been established and imposed from outside, by the adult. Accepting someone else's expectations is very different from developing one's own (and fashioning reasons for them). Creating a classroom whose objective is for students to internalize good behavior or good values begs the question of what we mean by "good." Moreover, it may amount to trying to direct students by remote control.

Manipulating with "Positive Reinforcement"

Finally, educators who resist the usual carrot-and-stick approach to discipline may fail to understand that praise is just another carrot—an extrinsic inducement—analogous to a sticker, an A, a pizza, or a dollar. Even classrooms that otherwise seem inviting are often marred by eruptions of evaluation from the teacher, as students are told they've done a "good job." In these classrooms, support and approval are made contingent on doing what pleases or impresses the teacher—precisely the opposite of the unconditional acceptance and empowerment that students need.

Considerable evidence demonstrates that positive reinforcement tends to make children more dependent on adult approval and less interested in whatever they had to do to get that approval—for example, learning or helping. Joan Grusec, a developmental psychologist, found that young children who received frequent praise for displays of generosity tended to act slightly less generous on an everyday basis than other children did. Every time they heard "Good sharing!" or "I'm so proud of you for helping," they became a little less interested in sharing or helping. They came to see each action not as something valuable in its own right, but rather as something they had to do to get a good reaction from a grown-up.

This problem is not limited to excessive, effusive, or transparently manipulative praise. Offering any verbal reward to encourage a particular behavior is an example of "doing to" rather than "working with." Because many wonderful teachers have never been invited to consider this idea, they may be taking away with one hand what they work so hard to offer with the other.

Going Farther

None of these six problems is necessarily fatal. Teachers who feel a twinge of guilty recognition while reading about them may well have classrooms that, in most respects, provide successful and even inspiring learning environments. One hopes that the people who created these successful classrooms are willing to challenge not only the conventional wisdom (for example, about the nature of children or the need for discipline) but also their own practices and premises. We ought to be pleased with how far we've come—but not so pleased that we can't see how much farther we have to go.

Jeremy Swinson and
Mike Cording

Assertive Discipline in a School for Pupils with Emotional and Behavioural Difficulties

Introduction

Assertive Discipline is a behaviourist in-service training package designed to help teachers improve classroom behaviour and hence reduce the amount of teaching time lost due to disruptive and uncooperative behaviour. The Assertive Discipline training programme consists of a series of six video presentations together with a text book and workbooks designed to be used by teachers of different age groups of children. The training is lead by a trained leader. The essential message of Assertive Discipline is very simple. The advice has three components:

- Make your requirements clear—that is, publish clear and unambiguous rules and ensure all directions given to the class, groups or individuals are concise, unambiguous and easily understood.
- Give continuous positive feedback when pupils are successfully meeting your requirements.
- Publish a hierarchy of mild but irksome sanctions, which are applied consistently, for any rule breaking.

Generally teachers are advised to give very clear instructions to their pupils; to look for pupils who are doing as they have been told; and to acknowledge this in a positive manner. Advice is also given on how to engage pupils who are off-task. Finally, for those who do not do as they are told or refuse to comply, the use of the sanctions hierarchy is explained.

Although the programme was originally designed for schools in the USA, it has nevertheless received generally positive reviews in the UK.

However, there have been some dissenting voices. Robinson and Mains raised ethical and philosophical issues which were responded to elsewhere. Rigoni and Walford complained about the lack of evidence used to support Assertive Discipline, a claim refuted by Melling and Swinson. A more fundamental criticism was raised by Hanko, who suggested that praise-based strategies such as Assertive Discipline are ineffective with the 'very discouraged', 'disaffected' children

From *British Journal of Special Education*, vol. 29, no. 2, June 2002, pp. 72–75. Copyright © 2002 by Blackwell Publishing, Ltd. Reprinted by permission. References omitted.

one might find in a typical school for pupils with emotional and behavioural difficulties (EBD). She felt that such pupils might have become 'immune to praise'. Hanko does not give a precise definition or, indeed, terminology of the type of pupil she had in mind. However, her terminology is not that different from that used by the then Department for Education and Employment who designated 'disaffected' pupils as being characterised in terms of their irregular attendance, truancy and difficult-to-manage behaviour.

This paper presents an account of the application of the Assertive Discipline programme in a school for pupils with EBD. It addresses some of the issues raised by Hanko; provides some evidence that praise-based strategies can be effective with all pupils irrespective of their age or state of disaffection; and provides further evidence of the effectiveness of the Assertive Discipline approach.

The Liverpool Study

The study was conducted in one of Liverpool's schools for pupils with emotional and behavioural difficulties. The school seeks to provide for both junior and secondary-aged pupils from around 7 years of age up to 16 years. Two classes cater for junior-age pupils and six for those in the secondary phase. Class sizes are small; the largest class contains 12 pupils and the smallest six. One teacher, together with a Learning Support Assistant (LSA), teaches each class. The school attempts to provide a full and balanced curriculum to its pupils. It uses a variety of approaches to encourage good behaviour including individual counselling, working with the parents and time-out.

The staff at the school asked for training in Assertive Discipline after hearing of its success in one other Liverpool school. The training consisted of three two-hour in-service sessions presented by a trained and accredited Assertive Discipline Leader. The training look place after school over a three-week period.

In order to evaluate the impact of the Assertive Discipline training sessions, trained undergraduate students from Liverpool John Moores University observed a series of lessons. These observations were carried out during the morning teaching sessions. The lessons observed included mathematics, English, religious education, geography, and personal and social education. An initial series of observations was made during the period the teachers were being trained but before they implemented any of the skills or techniques of Assertive Discipline. A second series was made approximately six weeks after the teachers introduced the Assertive Discipline approach in their classes. Each teacher, in each of the eight classes in the school, was observed for 30 minutes. The main purpose of the observations was to gain objective information about the behaviour of the pupils in each class. One method that has been widely used to make objective judgements about classroom behaviour is to record in a systematic way whether pupils are 'on-task' or 'off-task'. Pupils who were judged as being 'on-task' in this study were those who were observed to be doing as the teachers had directed and therefore were deemed to be behaving appropriately. Pupils who were judged to be 'off-task' were those who were not following their teacher's directions and were therefore deemed to be misbehaving. Observers were also briefed to record aspects of the teachers' verbal feedback to pupils.

'On-task'/'off-task' criteria are widely used in educational research to provide a measure of behaviour in the classroom. Merrett and Wheldall devised a system called OPTIC which uses this approach. In this study, observations were made using the Pupil Behaviour Schedule devised by Jolly and McNamara. This schedule was chosen as it allowed the recording of:

- pupil on-task and off-task behaviours;
- the nature of the off-task behaviour;
- the rate of teacher verbal approval and disapproval.

Each pupil was observed in turn every ten seconds and a judgement made as to whether they were on or off task. This was recorded. At the same time a record was made of the teachers' use of verbal feedback to the class.

We were therefore in a position to compare the behaviour of both pupils and teachers before and after the implementation of Assertive Discipline strategies and to use these data as the basis for evaluating the effectiveness of the training.

Results

The results were statistically analysed using a standard 't' test. This test was used to ascertain if the differences between the observations carried out before and after the training were statistically significant or not.

Pupil Behaviour

Pupil behaviour was judged by recording both the on-task behaviour and the number of disruptive incidents in each lesson before and after training. . . .

The difference between, the pupils' level of on-task behaviour before and after training was found to be significant at the $p = 0.01$ level ('t' test: $t = 5.097$, d.f. = 14).

The number of disruptive incidents during the two periods of observation was also recorded. A disruptive incident was classified as a behaviour that stopped other pupils from learning, for example shouting out, disrupting other pupils, arguing or distracting the teacher. . . .

The difference between the two sets of incidents was found to be significant at the $p = 0.02$ level ('t' test: $t = 2.91125$, d.f. = 14).

The differences we found were apparent in all classes. There was no significant difference in the behaviour changes of the youngest classes and those of the older pupils.

Teacher Behaviour

We also monitored changes in teacher behaviour following their training. We are particularly interested in changes in their rate of praise . . . and in the rate of admonishment. . . .

The difference between the praise before and after training was found to be significant at the $p = 0.01$ level ('t' test: $t = 9. 195$ d.f. = 14).

Analysis of these two scores shows them to be significant at the $p = 0.01$ level ('t' test: $t = 10.04$, d.f. = 14).

Conclusions

This was a small-scale study based in a single school. Therefore we wish to be cautious about the over-generalisation of the results. However, this study yielded similar findings to other studies of pupils and teachers in primary schools. When these findings are considered together, a clear outcome begins to emerge. The results of this study, like those in previous work, indicate that training teachers to use Assertive Discipline techniques in their classrooms yielded four positive outcomes.

1. There was an increase in appropriate pupil behaviour. In other words, a higher proportion of children were doing as they had been asked and were actively engaged in the lesson. This improvement was found in all classes, irrespective of the age of the pupils.
2. There was a decrease in disruptive incidents. All classes showed this decrease, which may be related to the fact that more pupils were spending more time on task.
3. There was a dramatic increase in teachers' use of positive feedback. In two cases, this increase was by a factor of eight. Teachers of both younger and older pupils managed to be much more positive than hitherto.
4. All classes showed a reduction in 'telling off' or use of negative state- ments. This applied not only to informal admonishments but also formal recording of consequences within the Assertive Discipline sanctions hierarchy.

It would appear, therefore, that pupils in special school settings do respond to a positive atmosphere in the classroom. This would include a proportion of pupils who may well have had a history of educational failure and who, in the words of Hanko, are so disenchanted with school that they have become immune to praise. Clearly, our results do not support her assertion that, for these pupils, praise-based strategies are ineffective, neither did we find any evidence that this approach was less effective with older pupils.

We suggest that the provision of positive feedback is an essential element in the process of improving both behaviour and learning, irrespective of the age of the pupil. When pupils behave in an appropriate fashion it is important that teachers acknowledge that fact. The key to successful teaching may lie in the way this acknowledgement is delivered. The techniques used for older pupils should differ from those used with younger ones. Canter and Canter suggest that, for older pupils, the use of private rather than public praise is appropriate. The use of individual rewards or certificates may also have limited value with older pupils. Indeed, this point is also made in the study by Lepper, Green and Nisbett. Sutherland also argued that the effect of singling out an individual for an award or special attention might have a two-way detrimental effect. First the receiver of the individual award may cease to work hard when rewards are discontinued; second those who were not rewarded may become disenchanted and switch off. However, these factors do not necessarily apply if:

1. the positive feedback is given privately;

2. the use of positive feedback is widely spread across the whole of the class (in our study this proved to be the case and praise statements were being made at the rate of one every three minutes);
3. rewards are awarded on a group or whole class basis.

We have not suggested that Assertive Discipline has all the answers to all the problems of classroom control or teaching disenchanted 'switched-off' pupils. Canter and Canter say very little about the content of teaching programmes or differentiation, which are both essential if teachers are to encourage very difficult children to become engaged once more in the education process. We do argue that the assertion that praise-based strategies are ineffective with disenchanted and discouraged children is not borne out by our evidence. Our evidence also suggests that when positive feedback to pupils is increased, within the context of a structured approach to classroom discipline as proposed in the Assertive Discipline programme, then the behaviour of the pupils is improved. This improvement was apparent for all pupils in our sample including those described as disenchanted, disaffected and 'switched off'.

POSTSCRIPT

Does the Authoritarianism of Traditional Classroom Management Contribute to Student Disrespect?

Everyone wants it. Parents encourage it among siblings. Teachers describe how it can be expressed between cultures. Students will work for it. Gang members will go to war when it is not shown. Even pop singers like to sing about it. What are we talking about here? R-E-S-P-E-C-T.

Teachers get frustrated when respect is not shown toward them. After all, they are the adults. They do hold advanced degrees. They are supposed to be in charge. When respect is not shown to them, teachers will often "engage" students and "demand' respect. The problem with this approach is that respect is an attribute that is earned and that is given willingly. Respect cannot be coerced out of a student. Probably the poorest management approach that a classroom manager can use is to act like an authoritarian disciplinarian. Authoritarian teachers may not have rules and yet they will readily punish when they see student misbehavior. They respond to student disruptions in a sometimes aggressive, if not hostile, manner. They are intolerant and get frustrated about seemingly trivial matters. They do not seem to care about developing a positive relationship with their students. They discipline students publicly. When students are defiant, they get emotional, if not angry. They compare students. They ask students what they have done wrong. They use labels (like "goof-off") to describe students. They think that students are always misbehaving deliberately. They talk too much when they discipline. They don't consider causes of patterns of escalating misbehavior. They blame the child.

While the above examples represent an extreme perspective, it is true that assertive discipline represents a "traditional form" of classroom management that is more authoritarian than democratic. Assertive disciplinarians believe many classroom teachers labor under some false illusions. These misconceptions include the following:

- All behavior problems can be handled in the classroom without any help from school administration.
- Firm discipline can cause psychological damage to children.
- Discipline problems disappear in the presence of good teaching.
- All misbehavior is caused by deep-seated problems on which teachers can have little direct influence.

In contrast, assertive disciplinarians assert their rights to the following:

- The right to establish classroom rules and procedures so all students can learn
- The right to insist on good behavior from students and to punish misbehavior
- The right to get help from school administrators and parents in managing their children

Assertive discipline has its merits and its demerits. On the one hand, it is simple and easy for the teacher and students to understand. The personal needs of the teacher are met so it satisfies teachers. It requires parent involvement in the behavior-management process, which can motivate change from students and parents alike. On the other hand, traditional discipline approaches such as assertive discipline are destined to instill disrespect from students for multiple reasons:

- Traditional approaches fail to deal with the underlying causes of misbehavior, such as emotional illness, divorce, intolerance, bullying, and social skills deficits, among others.
- Traditional approaches focus on correction over prevention and skills development.
- Traditional approaches fail to promote self-direction and instill dependence.
- Traditional approaches recommend exclusion of misbehaving students.
- Traditional approaches overrely on punishment.
- Constant negative consequences for misbehavior stimulate rebellion and disrespect.

The antidote for a toxic classroom such as the one described is for all behavior managers to consider not only how they are punishing misbehavior but also how they are reinforcing the behavior that is incompatible with classroom disruption. For a more positive classroom atmosphere, most behavior-management texts recommend that the ratio of positive reinforcement to punishment in the classroom should be 4:1. Teachers garner respect by "catching 'em doing something right." They garner more disrespect by spending most of their time in "catching 'em doing something wrong." Traditional classroom management can work, but for respect to flourish, traditional classroom management must be balanced with prevention strategies, positive student-teacher relationship building, and a strong dose of classroom community building and self-discipline.

For well-written articles on the benefits of prevention over punishment to instill a respect in the classroom, the following readings are recommended: K. Tomeczyk, "Prevention, not Punishment," *American School Board Journal* (vol. 187, no. 5, 2000, pp. 60–61) and C. Kamii, "Obedience Is not Enough," *Young Children* (vol. 39, no. 4, 1984, pp. 11–14). For a presentation of the current status of assertive discipline, read L. Canter and M. Canter, *Assertive Discipline: Positive Behavior Management for Today's Classroom* (Canter and Associates, 1992, 2001). For a model of classroom community building as an alternative to traditional classroom management, read A. Kohn, *Beyond Discipline: From Compliance to Community* (Association for Supervision and Curriculum Development, 1995).

ISSUE 7

Is Positive
Reinforcement Overused?

YES: Alfie Kohn, from "Five Reasons to Stop Saying 'Good Job!'"
Young Children (September 2001)

NO: K. Angeleque Akin-Little, Tanya L. Eckert, Benjamin J. Lovett, and Steven G. Little, from "Extrinsic Reinforcement in the Classroom: Bribery or Best Practice," *School Psychology Review* (Summer 2004)

ISSUE SUMMARY

YES: Alfie Kohn, the author of eight books on education and human behavior, believes that positive reinforcement is overused and that, contrary to common belief, may have potentially negative effects on students.

NO: K. Angeleque Akin-Little and Steven G. Little are professors at the University of the Pacific. They debate that the benefits of positive reinforcement far outweigh the detriments to students and offer suggestions for the appropriate use of reinforcement programs in educational settings.

"Good job," "Nice work," "Keep it up," "High five." These are all forms of social reward or praise that many teachers have adopted to show their students that they like the work they are doing. What could be the harm? Who doesn't like to be told that they are doing a good job? Teachers have been admonished to avoid punitive approaches to classroom management. They have been encouraged to find the positive and "catch 'em doing something right."

Alfie Kohn takes the position that while general support and encouragement are necessary student-teacher relationship-building tools, praise for specific student behaviors may have some unintended and insidious side effects. Students desire teacher approval, but teachers may unknowingly take advantage of that need when they exploit that student dependence for classroom control by overusing praise. Furthermore, some students may rely too much on teacher evaluations and become dependent on their teachers. Kohn claims that students need to learn to trust their own judgments so that they can persist with difficult tasks even when the teacher is not there to praise them. When teachers repeatedly praise a child, they may be simultaneously teaching that child that he/she should not trust his/her own feelings. Children must learn to take personal pleasure from a job well done. When teachers overuse praise for every accomplishment a child makes, they may be stealing that child's own joy in learning. In some cases, students who have been praised too much will only engage in a task when they are being constantly rewarded. Some students who become "hooked" on praise will refuse to take risks or try new activities because they fear failure and the loss of all those rewards.

Kohn believes that students need unconditional support and not constant praise. He distinguishes them in that unconditional support is a caring, respectful teacher-student relationship in which students know it is acceptable to think independently, to take chances, to develop values, and that even occasional failure is OK as long as they learn something from it. On the other hand, praise is manipulative and directive and may not instill a sense of self-direction. As alternatives to praise, Kohn suggests that teachers should consider saying nothing, especially when the behavior being reinforced is one which the student regularly displays. The student probably has his or her own good reasons for continuing this behavior and needs no social reward from the teacher. A second approach might be for the teachers just to describe what they saw or to point out the effect that the student's behavior had on someone else. In this way, the teacher is encouraging the child to make his/her own judgments about the act and to self-reinforce. Finally, Kohn thinks teachers should be less directive of students and should ask more questions.

The authors of "Extrinsic Reinforcement in the Classroom: Bribery or Best Practice" are not nearly as worried as Kohn about the presumed detrimental effects of extrinsic reinforcement in the classroom. These authors provide research-based evidence that would refute the personal insights, observations, and claims made by Kohn that intrinsic motivation is of greater value than extrinsic motivation and that social reinforcement by teachers tends to induce extrinsic motivation. As a matter of fact, these authors point to a document published by the National Education Association entitled "How to Kill Creativity" (Tegano, et al., 1991) in which the extreme claim is made that the expectation of reward can actually undermine intrinsic motivation and creativity of student performance. Akin-Little et al. contend that any detrimental effects of extrinsic reinforcement can be avoided by employing best practices in the use of reinforcement procedures in the classroom. They suggest that rewards should not be presented for participation in a task only. Teachers should reward students for task completion or for high-quality work. They also recommend that rewards should not be presented on a single occasion only. Rewards should be used to shape behavior that is either not present in the student's behavioral repertoire or that is present, but at a low level. Furthermore, they propose that once a student has gained a skill, the schedule of reinforcement should be thinned so that the student can find appropriate intrinsic reinforcement in the completion of his or her own schoolwork.

Alfie Kohn

 **YES**

Five Reasons to Stop Saying "Good Job!"

Hang out at a playground, visit a school, or show up at a child's birthday party, and there's one phrase you can count on hearing repeatedly: "Good job!" Even tiny infants are praised for smacking their hands together ("Good clapping!"). Many of us blurt out these judgments of children to the point that it has become almost a verbal tic.

Plenty of books and articles advise us against relying on punishment, from spanking to forcible isolation (time-out). Occasionally someone will even ask us to rethink the practice of bribing children with stickers or food. But it's much harder to find a discouraging word about what is euphemistically called positive reinforcement.

Lest there be any misunderstanding, the point here is not to call into question the importance of supporting and encouraging children, the need to love them and hug them and help them feel good about themselves. Praise, however, is a different story entirely. Here's why.

1. Manipulating Children

Suppose you offer a verbal reward to reinforce the behavior of a child who cleans up her art supplies. Who benefits from this? Is it possible that telling kids they've done a good job may have less to do with their emotional needs than with our convenience?

Rheta DeVries, a professor of education at the University of Northern Iowa, refers to this as "sugar-coated control." Very much like tangible rewards—or, for that matter, punishments—it's a way of doing something *to* children to get them to comply with our wishes. It may be effective at producing this result (at least for a while), but it's very different from working *with* kids—for example, by engaging them in conversation about what makes a classroom function smoothly or how other people are affected by what we have done (or failed to do). The latter approach is not only more respectful but more likely to help kids become thoughtful people.

The reason praise can work in the short run is that young children are hungry for our approval. But we have a responsibility not to exploit that

Copyright 2001 by Alfie Kohn. Reprinted from *Young Children* with the author's permissions. For more information: www.alfiekohn.org. References omitted.

dependence for our own convenience. A "Good job!" to reinforce something that makes our lives a little easier can be an example of taking advantage of children's dependence. Kids may also come to feel manipulated by this, even if they can't quite explain why.

2. Creating Praise Junkies

To be sure, not every use of praise is a calculated tactic to control children's behavior. Sometimes we compliment kids just because we're genuinely pleased by what they've done. Even then, however, it's worth looking more closely. Rather than bolstering children's self-esteem, praise may increase kids' dependence on us. The more we say, "I like the way you . . ." or "Good ___ing," the more kids come to rely on *our* evaluations, *our* decisions about what's good and bad, rather than learning to form their own judgments. It leads them to measure their worth in terms of what will lead *us* to smile and dole out some more approval.

Mary Budd Rowe, a researcher at the University of Florida, discovered that students who were praised lavishly by their teachers were more tentative in their responses, more apt to answer in a questioning tone of voice ("Um, seven?"). They tended to back off from an idea they had proposed as soon as an adult disagreed with them. And they were less likely to persist with difficult tasks or share their ideas with other students.

In short, "Good job!" doesn't reassure children; ultimately, it makes them feel less secure. It may even create a vicious circle such that the more we slather on the praise, the more kids seem to need it, so we praise them some more. Sadly, some of these kids will grow into adults who continue to need someone else to pat them on the head and tell them that what they did was OK. Surely this is not what we want for our daughters and sons.

3. Stealing a Child's Pleasure

Apart from the issue of dependence, a child deserves to take delight in her accomplishments, to feel pride in what she's learned how to do. She also deserves to decide when to feel that way. Every time we say, "Good job!" though, we're telling a child how to feel.

To be sure, there are times when our evaluations are appropriate and our guidance is necessary—especially with toddlers and preschoolers. But a constant stream of value judgments is neither necessary nor useful for children's development. Unfortunately, we may not have realized that "Good job!" is just as much an evaluation as "Bad job!" The most notable feature of a positive judgment isn't that it's positive, but that it's a judgment. And people, including kids, don't like being judged.

I cherish the occasions when my daughter manages to do something for the first time, or does something better than she's ever done it before. But I try to resist the knee-jerk tendency to say, "Good job!" because I don't want to dilute her joy. I want her to share her pleasure with me, not look to me for a verdict. I want her to exclaim, "I did it!" (which she often does) instead of asking me uncertainly, "Was that good?"

4. Losing Interest

"Good painting!" may get children to keep painting for as long as we keep watching and praising. But, warns Lilian Katz, "once attention is withdrawn, many kids won't touch the activity again." Indeed, an impressive body of scientific research has shown that the more we reward people for doing something, the more they tend to lose interest in whatever they had to do to get the reward. Now the point isn't to draw, to read, to think, to create—the point is to get the goody, whether it's an ice cream, a sticker, or a "Good job!"

In a troubling study conducted by Joan Grusec at the University of Toronto, young children who were frequently praised for displays of generosity tended to be slightly *less* generous on an everyday basis than other children were. Every time they had heard "Good sharing!" or "I'm so proud of you for helping," they became a little less interested in sharing or helping. Those actions came to be seen not as something valuable in their own right but as something they had to do to get that reaction again from an adult. Generosity became a means to an end.

Does praise motivate kids? Sure. It motivates kids to get praise. Alas, that's often at the expense of commitment to whatever they were doing that prompted the praise.

5. Reducing Achievement

As if it weren't bad enough that "Good job!" can undermine independence, pleasure, and interest, it can also interfere with how good a job children actually do. Researchers keep finding that kids who are praised for doing well at a creative task tend to stumble at the next task—and they don't do as well as children who weren't praised to begin with.

Why does this happen? Partly because the praise creates pressure to "keep up the good work" that gets in the way of doing so. Partly because their *interest* in what they're doing may have declined. Partly because they become less likely to take risks—a prerequisite for creativity—once they start thinking about how to keep those positive comments coming.

More generally, "Good job!" is a remnant of an approach to psychology that reduces all of human life to behaviors that can be seen and measured. Unfortunately, this ignores the thoughts, feelings, and values that lie behind behaviors. For example, a child may share a snack with a friend as a way of attracting praise or as a way of making sure the other child has enough to eat. Praise for sharing ignores these different motives. Worse, it actually promotes the less desirable motive by making children more likely to fish for praise in the future.

❧◉❧

Once you start to see praise for what it is—and what it does—these constant little evaluative eruptions from adults start to produce the same effect as fingernails being dragged down a blackboard. You begin to root for a child to give his teacher a taste of her own treacle by turning around and saying (in the same saccharine tone of voice), "Good praising!"

Still, it's not an easy habit to break. It can seem strange, at least at first, to stop praising; it can feel as though you're being chilly or withholding something. But that, it soon becomes clear, suggests that *we praise more because we need to say it than because children need to hear it*. Whenever that's true, it's time to rethink what we're doing.

What kids do need is unconditional support—love with no strings attached. That's not just different from praise, it's the *opposite* of praise. "Good job!" is conditional. It means we're offering attention and acknowledgment and approval for jumping through our hoops, for doing things that please us.

This point, you'll notice, is very different from a criticism that some people offer to the effect that we give kids too much approval or give it too easily. They recommend that we become more miserly with our praise and demand that kids "earn" it. But the real problem isn't that children expect to be praised for everything they do these days. It's that *we're* tempted to take shortcuts, to manipulate kids with rewards instead of explaining and helping them to develop needed skills and good values.

So, what's the alternative? That depends on the situation. But whatever we decide to say instead has to be offered in the context of genuine affection and love for who kids are rather than for what they've done. When unconditional support is present, "Good job!" isn't necessary; when it's absent, "Good job!" won't help.

If we're praising positive actions as a way of discouraging misbehavior, this strategy is unlikely to be effective for long. Even when it works, we can't really say the child is now "behaving himself"; it would be more accurate to say the praise is behaving him. The alternative is to work *with* the child, to figure out the reasons he's acting that way. We may have to reconsider our own requests rather than just looking for a way to get kids to obey. (Instead of using "Good job!" to get a four-year-old to sit quietly through a long class meeting, perhaps we should ask whether it's reasonable to expect a child to do so.)

We also need to bring kids in on the process of making decisions. If a child is doing something that disturbs others, then sitting down with her later and asking, "What do you think we can do to solve this problem?" will likely be more effective than bribes or threats. It also helps a child learn how to solve problems and teaches her that her ideas and feelings are important. Of course, this process takes time and talent, care and courage. Tossing off a "Good job!" when the child acts in the way we deem appropriate takes none of those things, which helps to explain why "doing to" strategies are a lot more popular than "working with" strategies.

And what can we say when kids just do something impressive? Consider three possible responses:

- **Say nothing.** Some people insist a helpful act must be reinforced because, secretly or unconsciously, they believe it was a fluke. If children are basically evil, then they have to be given an artificial reason for being nice (namely, to get a verbal reward). But if that cynicism is unfounded—and a lot of research suggests that it is—then praise may not be necessary.

- **Say what you saw.** A simple, evaluation-free statement ("You put your shoes on by yourself" or even just "You did it") tells a child that you noticed. It also lets her take pride in what she did. In other cases, a more elaborate description may make sense. If a child draws a picture, you might provide feedback—not judgment—about what you notice: "This mountain is huge!" "Boy, you sure used a lot of purple today!"

  If a child does something caring or generous, you might gently draw his attention to the effect of his action *on the other person*: "Look at Abigail's face! She seems pretty happy now that you gave her some of your snack." This is completely different from praise, where the emphasis is on how *you* feel about her sharing.

- **Talk less, ask more.** Even better than descriptions are questions. Why tell a child what part of his drawing most impressed *you* when you can ask him what *he* likes best about it? Asking "What was the hardest part to draw?" or "How did you figure out how to make the feet the right size?" is likely to nourish his interest in drawing. Saying "Good job!" as we've seen, may have exactly the opposite effect.

This doesn't mean that all compliments, all thank-you's, all expressions of delight are harmful. We need to consider our *motives* for what we say (a genuine expression of enthusiasm is better than a desire to manipulate the child's future behavior) as well as the actual *effects* of doing so. Are our reactions helping the child to feel a sense of control over her life—or to constantly look to us for approval? Are they helping her to become more excited about what she's doing in its own right—or turning it into something she just wants to get through in order to receive a pat on the head?

It's not a matter of memorizing a new script, but of keeping in mind our long-term goals for our children and watching for the effects of what we say. The bad news is that the use of positive reinforcement really isn't so positive. The good news is that you don't have to evaluate in order to encourage.

NO ↩

K. Angeleque Akin-Little, et al.

Extrinsic Reinforcement in the Classroom: Bribery or Best Practice

Many educational personnel have at least some rudimentary knowledge of the effects of rewards and/or reinforcement on students' behavior in school settings. Observations of classrooms and school settings frequently reveal evidence of some sort of reward system for academic output and/or appropriate behavior. For example, stickers may be given to students for completed assignments or pizza coupons may be given for appropriate classroom behavior. Schools have successfully employed the use of external rewards for decades. The past 40 years have witnessed the success of the use of reinforcement procedures in the classroom.

Along with the research on the effectiveness of external reinforcers in the schools, there has been a rise in concern on the part of some educators and psychologists over the use of reward contingency systems in classrooms across the country. The problem, these researchers assert, is the effect an extrinsic reinforcer may have on a student's intrinsic motivation to perform a reinforced task once the reinforcer for that task is withdrawn. These researchers speculate that if reinforcement strategies are used, an individual's perceptions of competence and self-determination will decrease, thereby decreasing that individual's intrinsic motivation to perform the task. For example, in some teacher guidebooks, teachers are told that the use of extrinsic reinforcement can decrease creativity. Further, many teacher education programs embrace a cognitive theory of education that emphasizes intuition and insight to facilitate learning. In the resulting teaching practices (e.g., discovery learning, constructivism), the teacher does not impart knowledge; rather, the focus is on arranging the environment to help students "discover" knowledge. The accent is on internal, intrinsic machinations with no external reinforcement procedures used. This pedagological instruction may be in direct conflict with research supporting the use of external reinforcers in the classroom and the efficacy of direct instruction. Finally, Kohn goes as far as to state that the use of external rewards, even verbal praise, can be considered bribery to invoke temporary obedience and make children dependent on adult approval. This perspective is prevalent not only in teacher education programs, but in society as a whole. . . .

From *School Psychology Review*, vol. 33, no. 3, Summer 2004, pp. excerpts from 344–52. Copyright © 2004 by National Association of School Psychologists. Reprinted by permission. References omitted.

The present article . . . attempts to review the evidence of the effectiveness of reinforcement programs as currently used in school settings. An attempt is made to define the terms intrinsic and extrinsic motivation. . . . Cognitive investigations that form the basis for criticisms of the use of reward are discussed. . . . Best practice suggestions for both teachers and school psychologists are offered on the use of extrinsic reinforcement in the classroom. . . .

Defining Intrinsic and Extrinsic Motivation

An intrinsically motivated behavior has been defined by Deci as one for which there exists no recognizable reward except the activity itself (e.g., reading). That is, behavior that cannot be attributed to external controls is usually attributed to intrinsic motivation. Consequently, an extrinsically motivated behavior refers to behavior controlled by stimuli external to the task. . . . Subsequent researchers have also attempted to define intrinsically motivated behavior. These definitions have included defining intrinsic motivation as the need for achievement, the need to be effective and competent in dealing with one's environment, the need to conceive of oneself as the locus of causality, or the need to be self-determining and competent.

. . . In general, if the dichotomy between intrinsic and extrinsic motivation is accepted, intrinsic motivation is assumed to be of greater value. This belief is due in large part to the Western conceptualization of the human as autonomous and individualistic. In this view, humans are driven toward self-actualization and any occurrence that impinges on self-determination causes dissonance. Further, the use of extrinsic reinforcement is seen as controlling and/or limiting self-discovery, creativity, and the capacity for humans to reach fulfillment. Interestingly, when this tenet is examined in relationship to the use of punishment, punishment is perceived as less of a threat to autonomy because humans may choose how to behave to avoid punishment.

Cognitive Evaluation Theory

Deci and Ryan's cognitive evaluation theory is based on the assumption that self-determination and competence are innate human needs. Cognitive evaluation theory states that events facilitate or hinder feelings of competence and self-determination depending on their perceived informational, controlling, or amotivational significance. Deci and Ryan divide rewards into two categories: task-contingent rewards that are rewards given for participation in an activity, solving a problem, or completing a task; and quality-dependent rewards that involve the "quality of one's performance relative to some normative information or standard." Task-contingent rewards are hypothesized to detrimentally affect intrinsic motivation by decreasing self-determination (i.e., reward is viewed as a controlling event attempting to determine behavior thereby decreasing self-determination and, consequently, intrinsic motivation). Quality-dependent rewards are also believed to act to decrease intrinsic motivation by reducing one's feelings of self-determination. However, quality-dependent rewards also serve to increase feelings of competence according to Deci and Ryan (i.e., reward is viewed as an informational event indicating skill at a certain task, leading to an increase in feelings of competence, which serves to increase intrinsic motivation). Therefore, it is never clear whether the detrimental effect to self-determination or the incremental effect to competence will be stronger in experiments examining quality-dependent rewards. Thus, for Deci and Ryan, quality-dependent rewards may not decrease intrinsic motivation. The detrimental effect of greatest concern is in circumstances involving task-completion rewards.

Eisenberger and Cameron further divide the task-completion rewards category into the subcategories of performance-independent rewards that individuals receive simply for participation in an activity, and completion-independent rewards given when an individual has finished a task or activity. Cognitive evaluation theory suggests that an individual's intrinsic motivation would be most detrimentally affected upon receipt of tangible, anticipated rewards. Additionally, according to this theory, verbal rewards may be informational, and therefore, increase intrinsic motivation. . . . Events may also be perceived as amotivational indicating an individual's lack of skill, which reduces one's cognitions of competence and, subsequently, intrinsic motivation. . . .

Researchers have suggested that cognitive evaluation theory is not a useful or viable theory and that any decrements in behavior are better explained through learned helplessness or general interest theory. In learned helplessness, the decrement in intrinsic motivation is said to be due to the single reward delivery paradigm utilized by most studies in this area. General interest theory suggests that intrinsic motivation is driven by more than just self-determination and competence needs. Eisenberger et al. propose that rewards must be examined for both content and context of tasks. Rewards that communicate task performance and satisfy needs, wants, and desires can increase intrinsic motivation, whereas rewards that convey a message that the task is extraneous to needs, wants, and desires may decrease intrinsic motivation.

The Overjustification Hypothesis

Another experiment designed and conducted to explore the detrimental effects of reinforcement on intrinsic motivation was the work of Lepper, Greene, and Nisbett. These researchers, using Bem's attributional model, examined individuals currently engaging in a task or activity without the possibility of external rewards. They hypothesized that introduction of extrinsic rewards that can be earned for engaging in that task or activity (i.e., overly sufficient extrinsic pressure) may lead the individual to view his or her actions as extrinsically motivated. Consequently, these individuals may find the activity, in the later absence of these extrinsic rewards, to be of less intrinsic interest.

In this experiment, preschool children were chosen based on their high baseline level of interest in drawing. The participants were divided into three groups: an expected-reward group, an unexpected-reward group, and a no-reward group. Children in the first group were promised and received a good-player award contingent upon their drawing with magic markers. Children in the second group received an award, but were not promised it before hand, and children in the third group did not expect or receive an award.

In subsequent free-play sessions, children from the expected-reward group were observed to spend considerably less time drawing than children from the other two groups. The unexpected-reward and no-reward groups showed slight increases in drawing time. Lepper et al. concluded that their results provided evidence of an undesirable consequence of the use of extrinsic rewards. However, this conclusion does not appear to be supported by the data. If the receipt of the reward were the cause of a decrease in drawing behavior, one would expect both the expected- and unexpected-reward group to exhibit a decrement in drawing behavior. This was not the case.

In an attempt to explain their results, Lepper et al. offered the overjustification hypothesis. According to this hypothesis, if a person is already performing an activity and receiving no extrinsic reward for that performance, introduction of an extrinsic reward will decrease intrinsic interest or motivation. This occurs because the person's performance is now overjustified, resulting in the person's perception that his or her level of intrinsic motivation to perform the activity is less than it was initially. According to this theory, the person subsequently performs the activity less once the reinforcement is removed. . . .

Recent Debate Criticism of Cameron and Pierce

Although this debate originated with Deci's study, it gained impetus in 1994 when Cameron and Pierce conducted a meta-analysis and concluded that reinforcement did not harm an individual's intrinsic motivation. Subsequently, Cameron and Pierce's findings have been criticized as utilizing flawed methodology. Kohn wrote that Cameron and Pierce ignored important findings which suggested that the receipt of tangible rewards is associated with less voluntary time on task as contrasted with the no-reward condition. Kohn further stated that Cameron and Pierce's methodology was flawed because results from studies in which informational praise was delivered (i.e., no detrimental effects on intrinsic motivation expected), with praise delivered that might be construed as manipulative (i.e., detrimental effects on intrinsic motivation expected) were combined to detect an overall effect. Further, Kohn pointed out that, in his view, the more common type of praise in a classroom is the latter, and, therefore, studies that utilized manipulative praise should be examined separately. Kohn continued his criticism against token reinforcement programs by inspecting studies examining the effects of performance-contingent rewards (PCRs). Kohn refuted the idea that the delivery of PCRs can mitigate the detrimental effect on children's intrinsic motivation by stating that in the majority of programs in "real" classrooms, not all children attain the specified criterion level and still obtain rewards. This is in opposition to research studies in which variables are manipulated so that each participant receives a reward. Therefore, Kohn suggested that a very different motivational effect might be expected in an actual classroom. Kohn concluded by expressing his personal belief that adequate justification exists for schools to avoid the use of incentive programs and simply provide children with informational feedback. This informational feedback alone is expected to increase compliant behavior and work output, and maintain initial levels of intrinsic motivation. . . .

In the most recent meta-analysis, Cameron et al. synthesized 145 studies using categorizations similar to those adopted by Deci et al. They found, in general, that rewards do not decrease intrinsic motivation. Although the sample was not homogeneous, an overall effect size was calculated. Cameron stated this overall effect is important because educators and other school personnel often report that all rewards are harmful on motivation. Contrary to Deci et al., Cameron et al. included the categories of high and low initial interest. Notably, they found that rewards can enhance intrinsic motivation, particularly if measured as time on task. This is in accordance with Bandura's finding that most activities have little initial interest for people, but that engagement in the activity may increase interest. This has important implications for schools as many children do not find academic tasks initially appealing. The use of reward then may be used to increase students' time on task and intrinsic motivation for a task. Cameron et al. did not find detrimental effects with the use of verbal praise for either children or college students. Instead, they found significant increases.

In terms of tangible reward, no detrimental effect was found for unexpected rewards or for rewards that were closely tied to specific standards of performance and to success. Detrimental effect was found when rewards were not explicitly connected to the task and signified failure. This last finding is also important to educators who may be attempting to use reinforcement to increase either social or academic behavior. Oftentimes, teachers will set the goals for a student too high. Behavioral principles state that it is important to shape behavior, reinforcing the child's current competencies and giving him or her a chance for success. . . .

Best Practices in the Use of Reinforcement Procedures in the Classroom

In 1991, the National Education Association published a document entitled How to Kill Creativity (Tegano et al.) that stated:

> The expectation of reward can actually undermine intrinsic motivation and creativity of performance . . . A wide variety of rewards have now been tested, and everything from good-player awards to marshmallows produces the expected decrements in intrinsic motivation and creativity of performance. . . . (making) them (students) much less likely to take risks or to approach a task with a playful or experimental attitude. (p. 119)

A review of several educational psychology books reveals a more balanced view of the effects of rewards by including the findings of Cameron and Pierce, along with Deci and Ryan and Lepper et al. This is an encouraging sign because many of the findings in this area support the effectiveness of reinforcement procedures in the classroom and many researchers have criticized the literature on supposed damaging effects.

Additionally, any detrimental effects of the use of extrinsic reinforcement can be easily avoided with the use of these guidelines. Rewards should not be presented for mere participation in a task without regard for completion or quality. Decrements have also been found in the literature when rewards are presented on a single occasion. This is not the most common method utilized in classrooms. In general, reward contingencies used in schools are presented repeatedly with appropriate thinning of schedules utilized when behavior change has occurred. School psychologists are advised to heed this advice when consulting and planning with teachers on the use of reinforcers in the school setting.

Specifically, school psychologists are often asked to aid in increasing the frequency of a number of student behaviors (e.g., math, reading, homework) for which the baseline level of performance is close to zero (i.e., the "unmotivated" child). Maintaining a perspective that these students "should" engage in certain behaviors because of "intrinsic" motivation is unlikely to result in a change in the level of performance. Instead, the efficacious response includes selecting the target behavior(s), determining the current and desired level of functioning, and delivering reinforcers based on a set criterion. This criterion changes as the behavior improves. This entire procedure is based on the principles of shaping through reinforcement of successive approximations of the desired behavior. This practice has been used with both performance and acquisition deficits, with acquisition deficits requiring a slightly different schedule (i.e., continuous) of reinforcer delivery in the initial learning stages. Additionally, to insure that extrinsic rewards have true reinforcing value, the use of a Reinforcer Preference Survey has proven efficacious.

Teachers continually request training in behavior and classroom management techniques such as the procedures discussed above. The irony is that techniques that aid teachers in improving their management skills have existed since Skinner's seminal work on the principles of operant conditioning. Techniques based upon the use of extrinsic reinforcers (i.e., positive reinforcement) work in the classroom. These include verbal praise, token economies, group contingencies, contracts, and others. The question is why teacher education programs are not incorporating these principles into their curriculum. Why is there such resistance to the data? Axelrod suggested that some causes for the lack of both professional and popular acceptability may be that the use of positive reinforcement consumes too much time, attempts to eliminate human choice, and there is little compensation for educational personnel for using these procedures. This is a somewhat discouraging view and one can only hope that future and current teachers, educational personnel, and teacher training faculty make evidencebased decisions when choosing intervention for children and youth.

The polemical papers on both sides of this extrinsic/intrinsic issue, their rebuttals, and the further replies are gradually bearing out a common "bottom line"—the programs that show increased intrinsic motivation are those programs that incorporate the elements of good, comprehensive behavioral intervention: relatively immediate reinforcement, generalization strategies, and individualized intervention. The implication is that any blanket rejection of programmed reinforcement strategies is entirely unwarranted and programmed reinforcement strategies, like any other instructional strategy, should be undertaken in a thoughtful manner after considering the many variables of any classroom situation. . . .

POSTSCRIPT

Is Positive
Reinforcement Overused?

One of the topics most requested for teacher in-service training is classroom management. Akin-Little and her colleagues find this ironic because the techniques to aid teachers in improving their management skills have existed since Skinner's (1953) work on the principles of operant conditioning. They insist that, "Techniques based upon the use of extrinsic reinforcers (i.e., positive reinforcement) work in the classroom." They recommend that teachers should infuse verbal praise, token economies, group contingencies, and contracts, among other behavioral techniques into their classroom-management regimens. In fact, they wonder why more teacher education programs are not incorporating behavioral principles into their teacher education curricula. Among the reasons for resistance to the full implementation of behavioral principles in the classroom is treatment acceptability, as elaborated by Kohn. That is, even though behaviorally based classroom-management principles have the capacity to change student behavior through shaping and successive approximations, some teachers perceive praise to be manipulative and think that it removes human choice. Others feel that positive reinforcement just takes too much time to shape a child into behaving better. The most cynical reason that can be offered for not employing behavioral principles is because there is little reward (i.e., compensation) for education personnel to intersperse these proven principles into their daily instructional curriculum. Akin-Little and colleagues protest that any blanket rejection of social reinforcement by teachers in the classroom is unwarranted as long as teachers take thoughtful steps in applying best practices in the application of behavioral principles. If in fact teachers are implementing social reinforcement programs without expert training, then it may be true that such programs could have unintended outcomes—but that finding would only suggest that teachers need more and better training in the principles that are proven to work, rather than the abandonment of those same principles. Perhaps all teachers should be trained to be able to respond to the challenges sometimes put forth by other teachers, administrators, and parents that, "Positive reinforcement is nothing more than bribery." Their protestations might be as follows:

- While it would be desirable for all children to come to school with internal motivation to learn, some students need external motivation to get started because they don't enjoy the topic, they do not have even the most basic of skills in the area, they have had previous failure experiences in the area, or they do not value education in general.

- Some students such as those with mental, behavioral or physical disabilities may respond best to the immediate motivation provided by concrete reinforcers that are applied immediately after successful performance on a task.
- When students are given reinforcers for "good work," these reinforcers are no more bribes than adults getting paid for their work. In fact, token reinforcers in the classroom have been compared to money since their value is only realized when they are cashed in, just like money earned by adults.
- Finally, bribery is a nefarious act intended to get someone to do something that is immoral that is not in their best interest and that under other circumstances they would not do. In direct contrast, positive reinforcement should not be described as a bribe since it is given only after students have started a classroom activity that is in their best interests and which they most likely would not have undertaken on their own due to lack of internal motivation.

To learn more about Kohn's criticisms of positive reinforcement, read A. Kohn, *Punished by Rewards* (Houghton Mifflin, 1993). For a classic reading on the effects of rewards on student locus of control, read E.L. Deci, "Effects of Externally Mediated Rewards on Intrinsic Motivation," *Journal of Personality and Social Psychology* (vol. 18, 1981, pp. 105–115). For practical ideas on how to move students toward self-discipline, consider reading J.F. Carter, "Self-Management: Education's Ultimate Goal," *Teaching Exceptional Children* (vol. 25, 1993, pp. 28–32).

ISSUE 8

Should Time-Out Be Timed Out?

YES: Christine A. Readdick and Paula L. Chapman, from "Young Children's Perceptions of Time Out," *Journal of Research in Childhood Education* (Fall/Winter 2000)

NO: Robert G. Harrington, from "Time Out: Guidelines for Parents and Teachers," *National Association of School Psychologists* (2004)

ISSUE SUMMARY

YES: Christine A. Readdick and Paula L. Chapman are professors at Florida State University whose child interviews have shown that preschoolers perceive time-out as a punishment, and they are unable to explain why they were placed in time-out, thus reducing its effectiveness.

NO: Robert G. Harrington is a professor in the department of psychology and research in education at the University of Kansas who argues that time-out has been used effectively with preschoolers and elementary students to reduce noncompliance, and he provides guidelines for the effective use of the time-out strategy.

T ime-out is one of the most common classroom management techniques in use today. Time-out is a brief period of usually five minutes or less for which students are asked to leave an otherwise rewarding classroom activity due to their behavior. It provides space and time for the student to calm down, think about what they may have done wrong and to problem solve.

Some critics say time-out increases other maladaptive behaviors commonly associated with punishment such as student withdrawal, student avoidance of the teacher, and passive-aggressiveness. Others believe that students may leave time-out with feelings of anxiety, rejection, and humiliation. Finally, there is another set of critics who contend that since time-out does not specifically teach a replacement behavior to the child, it is a dead end and should be replaced by social skills modeling and instruction.

In order to determine exactly how young children feel about being placed in a time-out area, Readdick and Chapman set out to study 42 young children immediately after they had left time-out. The researchers noted that in their study more children were placed in time-out for noncompliance than for aggression. In other words, these students were disruptive and avoidant in the classroom environment, but they were no threat to others. Results of individual interviews with offending students found that significantly more children than not reported feeling alone, yet safe, in time-out; feeling disliked by their teacher; and feeling ignored by their peers in time-out. Significantly more children reported disliking, as opposed to liking, being in time-out. As many children reported feeling happy in time-out as sad, and the number of students who felt liked by their peers during time-out versus those who felt disliked by their peers was evenly split. While almost two-thirds of the students claimed that they knew exactly why they were placed in time-out, only 50 percent of those children provided reasons for their time-out that corresponded with observations.

Readdick and Chapman conclude that young children perceive time-out as punishment. Furthermore, since many children do not even know why they have been placed in time-out, there is a reduced likelihood that time-out will result in any positive behavior improvement. Most disturbing for these researchers is that teachers were removing students mostly for non-compliance and not for severe aggression.

While Readdick and Chapman admonish teachers about the problematic side effects of time-out and the lack of evidence for social skills improvement, Harrington provides a different perspective regarding the status of time-out. Harrington contends that if teachers follow guidelines for the implementation of time-out, this simple behavioral procedure has the capacity to be a positive source for behavior change. He further contends that there is no necessity for students to feel badly about themselves after leaving time-out. Finally, he believes that time-out can be used not only to diminish inappropriate behaviors but also to teach more appropriate replacement skills. Harrington does concede that time-out is often misunderstood since it is a deceptively simple procedure. Time-out will only work if the activity from which the student is being timed out is undesirable. Time-out may take several attempts to work and may not work on the first trial. It is not uncommon for students to meet time-out with resistance. After all, these students would like to get their way in the classroom.

While Harrington sees time-out as a punishment, he believes that mild punishment used wisely can be a useful management tool. He provides guidelines for the appropriate use of time-out. He recommends teachers not use time-out when there is any doubt about whether a child has the target skill in their repertoire. Teachers should be sensitive to developmental issues and not ask students to perform developmentally inappropriate behaviors, such as asking young children to sit for extended periods of time. He recommends that before being placed in time-out, every student must know the rule that has been broken and know what can be done to improve his or her behavior. Furthermore, he emphasizes that time-out alone will not produce the desired behavior. Teachers must do problem-solving with the offending students, help them to identify ways in which they could be better behaved, and then socially reinforce them for improvement.

YES

**Christine A. Readdick
and Paula L. Chapman**

Young Children's Perceptions
of Time Out

Time out, a brief social isolation and temporary suspension of usual activity, is a discipline technique frequently employed to decrease young children's undesirable behavior in early childhood settings. Originally designed as a technique for the modification of deviant behavior in clinical populations, time out has been embraced by many as a means of quelling an array of undesirable behaviors in noncompliant children, from thumbsucking to crying to hitting others.

While a vast literature details with whom and for what behavior the technique has been successfully or unsuccessfully employed, no one has tapped the perceptions of time out as constructed and held by children themselves. Certainly, young children's understandings of time out and perceptions of self and others vis-a-vis the time out event are interesting and worthy of investigation. More important, however, children's perceptions may provide insights for adults trying to determine the developmental appropriateness of using time out as a guidance technique.

The utility of time out first was demonstrated as a means to reduce tantrums and self-destructive behavior in an autistic child. Each time a deviant behavior occurred, the child was placed alone in a room and allowed to leave only after the tantrum or self-destructive behavior subsided. Applied immediately and consistently, time out has been determined to be most useful in the reduction of aggressive behavior, both verbal and physical.

Proponents of using time out with young children extol its virtues, at least for children 2 or 3 years of age and older. Time out is viewed as an efficient means of providing space and time for the young child to mull over wrongdoings, refresh feelings of guilt, and ponder socially desirable responses in similar circumstances. Consequently, time out appears to remain a popular technique because of the positive reinforcement received by the adult when administering time out to a misbehaving child.

Critics of time out acknowledge that the practice can reduce undesirable behavior; they lament, however, that time out fails to teach desirable behavior. Time out, say these critics, should be reserved for use only when a child is wildly out of control or is a threat to other children. Under these

From *Journal of Research in Childhood Education*, vol. 15, no. 1, 2000, pp. 81–87. Copyright © 2000 by Association for Childhood Education International. Reprinted by permission. References omitted.

extreme circumstances (for example, when the young child is engaged in flagrant hitting or biting), the adult is advised to approach the child physically, get down to the child's level, look him in the eye and tell him calmly what the offense is, and then escort the child to the time out site; the rule of thumb for the length of time out is one minute per year of the child's age. Others recommend selecting a boring location for time out, setting a timer to prevent forgetting the child in time out, announcing time out is over, and seeking the next available opportunity to praise the child for a good behavior.

There is speculation that time out may be hurtful in a number of ways. If the child perceives it as a punishment, time out can have serious side effects that are commonly associated with punishment, including increases of other maladaptive behaviors and withdrawal from or avoidance of the adults administering time out. Furthermore, when escape is impossible, some young children are apt to withdraw and become passive.

Because of the young child's limited knowledge and experience, he or she may ultimately feel anxious, rejected, hurt, and humiliated as a result of time out. Gartrell suggests that, given their social inexperience, young children tend to internalize negative labels, see themselves as they are labeled, and react accordingly. Stone declares time out a dead end for young children at the threshold of social development. Instead, the preschool-age child, who is wrestling with egocentrism and with limited knowledge of social relations, would probably benefit from social skill modeling and instruction.

Because no one has paused to ask children their perceptions of time out and their feelings about being placed in time out, there is no known support, other than suppositional, for these expectations. Therefore, this exploratory study was designed to flesh out young children's views of time out, subsequent to the experience of a time out event in an early childhood education setting.

The following research questions were asked:

1. What feelings about time out do young children express?
2. What perceptions of time out do young children express?
3. What behavioral events are resulting in preschool children being placed in time out by their teachers?
4. What differences in feelings about time out can be identified between children who perceive themselves to be frequently in time out and those who perceive themselves to be infrequently in time out?
5. What is the correspondence of the child's stated reason for being in time out and the observer's view of the reason for the child being in time out?

Method

Participants

Subjects included 42 two-, three-, and four-year-old children. Twenty-three of the children were boys, 19 were girls.

Setting

Observations were conducted in 11 child care centers in a north Florida community that serves primarily working and fee-paying families (60% Caucasian, 35% African American, and 5% other ethnic backgrounds, including Hispanic and Asian American). The centers constituted a convenience sample of sites at which directors reported the use of time out as a disciplinary technique. Observations were performed both in indoor and outdoor classroom environments.

Measure

An interview targeting children's perceptions and feelings about time out was constructed by the first author. The 17-question interview, revised from a 14-item interview employed in a pilot study, was designed to gauge children's views of school, ability to recount the specific event that led to the time out incident, specific feelings about being in time out, and perceptions of time out in general.

Procedure

After receiving parental and teacher permission, observations were conducted at local child care centers by students enrolled in a child study class at a local university. These students had been trained in observation techniques and interviewing skills for a minimum of 30 hours prior to data collection. To minimize bias, the social desirability of time out as a disciplinary technique was not addressed and the exploratory nature of the investigation was emphasized. Each of 40 pairs of observers observed a minimum of 6 hours over a 30-day period and recorded time out events using an anecdotal format.

Each anecdote included a description of the precipitating event (what the child was doing that led to placement in time out), adult direction of the child to time out, location of time out, child behavior in time out, adult release of child from time out, and duration of the time out incident. *Time out* was defined as an occasion in which the child is removed from an activity or group for performing an act deemed unacceptable or undesirable by an adult, and spends time in a designated spot isolated from others at the request of the adult.

Precipitating events expected to lead to time out were aggressive and noncompliant behaviors. *Physical aggression* was defined as the act of striking, slapping, kicking, pushing, biting, or pulling others, or throwing objects at others; *verbal aggression* was described as aiming offensive words at others with the intent to harm another person. *Noncompliance* was designated as refusal to initiate or complete a request made by an adult.

At the conclusion of a time out episode, one researcher would approach the affected child and invite him or her to talk about being in time out. If a child did not wish to participate, that name was deleted and the child was excluded from the study. If the child responded favorably to the invitation to talk about time out, one researcher asked each of the questions, while the other recorded the child's answers. Upon completion of the interview, the child was thanked and encouraged to rejoin the class.

In anticipation of this research project, a pilot study was conducted at a similar child care center. The purpose of the pilot study was to assess the usefulness of an interview measure and develop procedures for training undergraduate students in techniques for accurately recording anecdotal records of noncompliant and aggressive behavior and subsequent time out events, as well as teaching the students interviewing skills. In this pilot study, five students observed and interviewed 15 young children placed in time out. It was determined that the clarity of the operational definition of *time out* assured 100% interobserver agreement. Subsequent modifications to the interview included simplification of wording, omission of two items, and development of five items to better tap into young children's perceptions of time out.

Results

Analyses were made up of cross-tabulations and non-parametric chi-square tests. The results are presented as answers to the following research questions:

Question #1: What feelings about time out do young children express? Children's recountings of their feelings during the incident of time out were measured using seven questions. . . . Significantly more children than not reported feeling all alone, yet safe; disliked by their teacher; and ignored by their peers while in time out. Significantly more children reported disliking, as opposed to liking, being in time out. About as many children declared themselves to be happy in time out as admitted to being sad. Similarly, almost as many children felt liked by their peers during time out as felt disliked.

Question #2: What perceptions about time out do young children express? Children's perceptions of time out were ascertained by six questions. Significantly more children than not were able to describe a precipitating event of some nature, such as "I wasn't playing the right way" or "I was standing on the bookshelves," when asked to tell what had just happened. Significantly more children reported being in time out "a little" than "a lot"; and more declared they would not repeat the behavior that led to the time out incident. Regarding their other perceptions of time out, almost two-thirds of the children reported that an adult told them why they were put in time out. More admitted that they deserved to be in time out than not. Finally, most children expressed some notion about what they needed to do to be released from time out, from "be quiet" to "be good" to "do what I'm told."

Question #3: What behaviors result in preschool children being placed in time out by their preschool teachers? Most children were placed in time out for noncompliance (n = 27). Fewer still were placed in time out for physical aggression (n = 16) or verbal aggression (n = 3) toward others.

Questions #4: What differences in feelings and knowledge about time out can be identified between children who perceive themselves to be frequently or infrequently in time out? Eight children admitted being in time out a lot, while 22 said they were in time out a little. Children who perceived themselves to be frequently in time out differed from their peers who believed themselves to be infrequently in time out on five of seven expressions of feelings. . . . They liked being in time out less, and while in time out, they declared they felt more alone, scared, sad, and disliked by their peers.

Questions #5: What is the correspondence of the child's stated reason for being in time out and the observer's view of the reason for the child being in time out? While almost three quarters of the children acknowledged that they knew why they were put into time out, only a little more than half of those children gave answers that actually corresponded with the observers' anecdotal records.

Discussion

Despite their rosy accounts of liking preschool and having friends at preschool, the young children queried in this study upon release from a time out event expressed largely negative feelings about time out and about themselves in time out. Not only did they not like being in time out, many said they felt sad and scared while in time out. Such negative self-attributions confirm Clewett's (1988) and Gartrell's (1995) expectations regarding the feelings likely to be generated in the very young, socially inexperienced child in time out. The negative impressions of self, vis-a-vis the larger social group expressed here—feeling alone and disliked by one's teachers and disliked and ignored by one's peers—suggest that time out may indeed be perceived as punishment by the very young child, as cautioned by Parke.

The inability of many children to tell why they were in time out or to recall an adult telling them why they were in time out makes it less likely that the specific time out event will be effective in inhibiting future occurrences of the same aggressive or noncompliant behavior. Punishment is more effective when accompanied by a rationale that is understood.

Children in this study were placed in time out for a variety of reasons (e.g., biting, spitting, splashing water out of the sink, not sitting in circle for storytime), yet most were isolated for nonaggressive, noncompliant behavior. Clearly, in these preschool settings, time out is not being reserved consistently for use when a child is wildly out of control or a threat to other children, contrary to the recommendations of Betz. Indeed, many children are receiving time out for trivial reasons that are a far cry from the behavior that the technique was initially meant to address, thus confirming Webber and Scheuermann's observation that time out is a seductively easy reinforcing technique for harried caregivers, who may be eager to get a noncompliant child "out of their hair" for a few moments. . . .

The fact that fewer than half of the young children queried could accurately recall what they had done that resulted in their placement in time out, or refused to recall their misbehavior, despite most declaring that someone had told them why they were in time out, raises doubts that *these* preschoolers, at least, were mulling over their misbehavior, generating feelings of guilt, or pondering alternative desirable responses in similar circumstances, contrary to the expectations of Dobson and Twiford. What is more likely is that these children are withdrawing or acting out in other, even more undesirable, ways. With little direct tuition provided by adults to children regarding the specific misbehavior to correct, it is hard to imagine that the children in this sample, despite their earnest protestations to the contrary, will not misbehave again. . . .

Finally, what is clear is the discomfort of many young children on the heels of being released from a time out. When asked at the end of the interview, "Is there anything else you want to tell me about time out?," one subject offered, "I want to go play," while another implored, "I want to say something good—about my family and toys." . . .

Summary

In this investigation, young children in selected group child care settings were queried individually about their time out experiences and feelings. Despite recommendations that time out be reserved for occasions when the child is wildly out of control or an imminent threat to other children, it appears that time out is being used largely for reasons of noncompliance that give immediate irritation to caregivers. Furthermore, it appears that the consequences of time out, for many young children, may be punitive rather than instructional. . . .

NO

Robert G. Harrington

Time Out: Guidelines for Parents and Teachers

*T*ime out is an often used yet misunderstood behavior management strategy that is available to teachers and parents. Time out refers to *time out from positive reinforcement*. What this means is that a child is placed in an isolated area where he or she is unable to obtain positive reinforcement, such as attention or participation in a desired activity. Time out is based on the principle of punishment, which involves the removal of something pleasant. However, the child can avoid going to time out and missing a desired activity if he or she behaves appropriately now.

Misconceptions Regarding Time Out

There are three major misconceptions associated with time out.

Time out from undesirable activities won't work   Time out will *not* work if the child is missing the skills necessary to perform the desired activity. A child with math anxiety who refuses to complete pages of math worksheets may actually act out to go to time out and avoid math. A child who does not like the food served for supper may actually disrupt suppertime to get out of eating. *Therefore, time out should only be used during activities the child enjoys and can perform.*

Time out may not be immediately effective   The behavior of the child may not change immediately after time out is used. Time out may need to be used over an extended period (1 or 2 weeks) before change is seen. *For the child to learn to eliminate inappropriate behaviors, time out must be used consistently and applied after each misbehavior that has been targeted.*

Implementing time out can be met with resistance   The child may resist initial attempts at using time out. Initially, the child may test the parent by arguing, yelling, swearing, complaining, threatening, intimidating, avoiding, or by asking for leniency ("Just this one time." "Give me one more chance."). Once the child has violated a rule, then time out is applied without discussion.

If the child does not go to time out on the third command, there must be a follow up with *response cost*. At home, the response cost for not going to time out when required might involve missing a favorite TV show that evening or canceling a visit to a friend's house. At school, the response cost might involve loss of free time or reduced recess. *It is necessary to be firm and to have a back-up plan that has been discussed with the child if he or she resists going to time out initially.* At the same time, it is also necessary to teach the child more adaptive behaviors that will help the child obtain the same goal.

Appropriate Uses of Time Out

Time out is used when a child is acting out or is disrupting an activity, such as whining and complaining about a TV show that is being enjoyed by the rest of the family or loudly talking during math instruction. Time out should never be used when there is any doubt about whether the child has the skill being requested. For example, a parent should never place a child in time out for refusing to clean his or her room well unless the parent has told the child what constitutes a clean room, shows the child how to clean the room, and watches while the child demonstrates the ability to clean the room. In addition, time out should not be used for *not* cleaning his or her room because the child is then allowed to escape a task he or she doesn't like to do. In school, time out should not be used as a consequence for not completing work or not attending to instruction. Even an escape for a short period can be reinforcing.

Developmental Issues

Time out is best used with children between the ages of 2 and 12. Children in this age range need the external structure that time out provides. Adolescents require interventions that combine external control and self-management.

Time out may not be effective for all children. For example, some children will act out deliberately to go to time out. This response is more likely to occur if the child does not like the activity that is taking place, such as cleaning his or her room or working on a math problem, if the child is shy and wants to escape the social attention, if the child is the attention seeker and is acting out to get attention from others, or if the child needs help in performing a task such as homework and gets that assistance after going to time out. However, parents and teachers may want to consider the use of time out for children who seek attention. When the time out is implemented properly, it will help to eliminate the reinforcement (the attention) the child obtains for an inappropriate behavior.

Implementing Time Out

Three steps should be followed for time out to be most effective. First, the child should know in advance what the rules are for an activity (bedtime is 9:00 p.m. or staying seated during reading instruction). Second, the child should know that time out will be applied each time with a back-up plan, if necessary, when he or she refuses to comply with the rules. Third, when the child complies with the rules, he or she should be reinforced through social recognition (a smile or a pat on the back), a token (a token that may be redeemed for a tangible reinforcer such as an ice cream at a later time), or preferred activity treatment (if the child behaves appropriately now there will be reinforcement later in the form of a preferred activity, such as having friends visit). Each of these examples shows that it is important to reinforce positive behavior (to catch them being good).

Step 1: State the Rules and Consequences

Make sure you have the child's attention, and establish eye contact at the child's eye level. State a clear, concise, and concrete rule for behavior. In no more than six words, firmly tell the child, "Keep your hands to yourself." Don't say, "Stop hitting." Focus on the behavior that you *want* the child to exhibit and not the behavior you want the child to *stop*.

Direct the child to what you want him or her to do by stating the direction and not by *asking* for compliance. Don't say, "Would you please go to bed now?" Be directive and say, "It's 9:00 p.m. Time for bed." Use visual and physical cues such as a timer to communicate to the child that there are only 5 minutes left before bedtime.

Once you have stated the rule you should turn away from the child to provide the opportunity to comply, and then expect compliance. If the child complies after you give a signal, remember to reinforce for compliance. For example, you might say, "You have cleaned your bedroom just the way we practiced. That shows good listening. Good job." If the child does not comply after you state the positive rule, then begin signaling by counting. "That's 1, that's 2, that's 3." By beginning to count, you are giving the child three chances to comply with the rule. Some children, especially less mature children with Attention Deficit Hyperactivity Disorder (ADHD), a learning disability, or receptive language delays, may need additional time to process the requests.

For children with emotional or learning disabilities you may need to ask them to repeat or rephrase the direction to make sure that they have understood it fully. If the child resists, disengage and do not get into an argument. You should not answer the child's questions about why compliance is necessary now. Lower your voice and become the broken record for compliance by repeating the rule in a firm voice several times.

On those occasions when there are two legitimate options for behavior, you might think about offering the child a choice. For example, if on Thursday evening the child resists going to bed at 9:00 p.m., you can offer the choice, "I will read you a book or you can play your video game for 5 minutes before bedtime, but you must go upstairs to bed when I tell you. What is your choice?" Or, in the classroom, you might offer a child who resists participating in the reading group, "You can stay at your desk and read, or you can read with your group, but you must stay in the classroom and work on reading during our reading period." When a choice is not an option and the rule has been provided without compliance, then time out should be used.

Step 2: Apply the Time Out

When the child has refused to comply, you should first mirror the child's behavior back and direct the child to the time-out area. "You have chosen not to keep your hands to yourself. You have chosen time out." Do not scold the child and do not engage the child in any discussion or argument at this point.

If the child goes to time out, say, "You have made a good choice," and give a reminder, "Think about the rules posted in time out and what you need to do when you come out of time out." If the child goes to time out and is rude and hostile, ignore the rudeness and hostility or say that you will talk about it later. Do not argue with the child because it will usually escalate the inappropriate behavior. When time out is initially introduced children will often be angry and rude because that is how they have learned to get negative attention.

When the time is up for time out always ask the child, "What are you going to do differently now?" If the child is able to state the positive rule such as, "I plan to keep my hands to myself," welcome back the child to the dinner table or classroom and compliment him or her by saying, "You made a good choice, welcome back." If the child is not able to state how he or she will comply, then place the child back in time out for another 5 minutes. After the second time out the child should be asked again, "What do you plan to do differently?" If the child resists, place the child in time out for a third and last time. When the child comes out of time out on the third trial, mirror to the child, "You have chosen not to bahave appropriately. As a consequence your sleep over for this evening (or free time after reading) is canceled." Parents and teachers should be aware that some children may not be uncooperative, but may have difficulty verbalizing what behavior is desired. In these cases, parents or teachers will need to help the child explain what behavior is expected and use their judgment with regard to the appropriate consequence.

How long The time out is for no more than 5 minutes or 1 minute for each year of age below age 5. Never negotiate the length of time out. If the child comes out of time out early, then you can either start the time out over or use response cost as back up. In this case, tell the child, "You have chosen to leave time out early, that will cost you. By your uncooperative behavior you have chosen to not come with us for an ice cream cone this evening (or not have extra computer time this afternoon)."

Time out area Time out should be in an area that is safe, well lit, and well ventilated. A carpeted stairway works well. Avoid placing the child in his or her own bedroom or near a play area with books, toys, and other amusements with which the child can be entertained and not disturbed about being in time out. The child should be monitored and should not be left in a distant area alone. If the child refuses to comply, becomes destructive, or self-injurious, then follow up with *response cost*. The child should be informed in advance that the parent or teacher will take away an activity, treat, or social time in response to the child's non-compliance in time out. In the future the child will see that it is easier to comply upon going to time out rather than lose the special treat, social time, or special activity.

Step 3: Reinforce Good Behavior

It is much more direct and more effective to reinforce good behavior that it is to manage non-compliant and inappropriate behavior. Once a child has begun to comply after time out, it is very important to reinforce the child's new, more frequently appearing appropriate behavior. This should be a very significant focus of a parent's or teacher's behavior management strategy because if appropriate behavior is not adequately reinforced, then the inappropriate behavior may return. Simple strategies to reinforce new, more appropriate behaviors after time out include:

- Cue the child to the new behavior you want demonstrated before having the opportunity to act inappropriately. Verbal reminders and visual cue sheets can be used.
- Use proximity control (close monitoring) to let the child know you are checking to see that there is compliance with rules such as doing homework.
- Shape the new behaviors by reminding the child about which behaviors you like. "I like the way you are waiting until it is your scheduled time to use the Internet."
- Select rewards for good behavior that are reinforcing to the child. Use a reinforcement menu with various rewards listed so that the child selects a reward and does not become satiated to the rewards as is often the case with many children with learning disabilities, ADHD, and Asperger Syndrome.
- At private times ask the child if there are problems with complying with the rules. Help the child to problem solve and compromise if appropriate.
- Be prepared to make an instructional or physical adaptation to the environment if the child has a legitimate reason for not being able to comply. For example, children with ADHD may not be able to sit for more than 5 minutes even though the homework or seatwork assignment is 30 minutes long. In this case, the assignment should be split into 5-minute segments using a timer. The child will need clear directions, both verbal and written, about what needs to be done. At the end of 5 minutes the child should be provided positive redirection and told to take a short 1-minute break to stand, stretch, get a drink of water. After the break the child should be redirected to the next 5-minute chunk of the task. Over time, the child is directed to work in his or her seat for longer times with proximity control, positive redirection, and breaks until the goal is reached.

Summary

Time out is a behavior management strategy that focuses on eliminating inappropriate behaviors and, at the same time, teaching and reinforcing the positive behaviors that are desired. Time out, when used properly, can be a very effective behavioral intervention for improving children's behavior.

POSTSCRIPT

Should Time-Out Be Timed Out?

At the crux of the debate about whether time-out should be "timed out" is the assumption that all good behavior management will work only if the behavior manager knows exactly several key points about the strategy: what it is, who should receive it, when to apply it, how it should be implemented, where it should be done, and why it works. There is much misunderstanding about the proper application of time-out and that may be leading to at least some of its misuse and negative effects.

When time-out is implemented effectively, it can potentially have four beneficial effects. Time-out eliminates opportunities for reinforcement; time-out itself is punishment since the child is placed in a small space without much other stimulation to calm down and think about what he or she needs to do; time-out is extinction since the child can receive no attention from the teacher or the rest of the class for whining, complaining, and acting out; and time-out is positive reinforcement since the student can gain prosocial attention when the child decides to follow the classroom rules.

What can be done to increase the probability that these effects will take place? First, classroom managers must understand that time-out is based upon a simple principle. When behavior managers understand the principle, they will find that time-out can reduce problem behavior as well as increase self-control; if the principle is not followed, time-out will not work. The time-out principle is that when a classroom manager removes a student from the opportunity to earn or receive new reinforcers, then disruptive behavior will decline over time. What is important is that the classroom environment must be rich in reinforcers; if it is not, then the time-out principle has been violated and time-out will not work. Furthermore, if the student does not perceive the rewards as reinforcing and refuses to work for them, then once again the time-out principle has been violated and time-out will not be effective in reducing disruptive behavior.

There are some simple reasons why time-out can fail. Teachers may send students to time-out to punish them for misdeeds; to permit the student to calm down, reflect, and make a better plan; or to get rid of the child for the time being. Only the first two reasons will result in a reduction in misbehavior. All classroom managers should evaluate very closely why they are sending a student to time-out. According to Readdick and his colleagues, children perceive time-out as punishment—which it is. When Readdick laments that as many children feel happy in time-out as those who feel sad, we shouldn't be surprised because time-out is meant to be mildly aversive. After all, if it were an enjoyable environment, students would want to go there. An even split was found in the number of students in time-out who felt liked by their peers compared to those who felt disliked. Once again, this finding should not be surprising

136

since time-out may eliminate some acting-out behavior. After all, the student in time-out isn't enjoying the laughs and giggles from the student audience anymore now that he or she is in time-out. Finally, Readdick is concerned that teachers use time-out for noncompliance and don't reserve it for more severe cases of disruption. This criticism is a bit confounding since most experts recommend its use for mild disruptions such as noncompliance. For severe disruptions that erupt into shouting matches or fights, in-school suspension is recommended whereby the student is taken out of the classroom to calm down and problem-solve about what he or she needs to do to go back to the classroom and join the others. A disconcerting result from Readdick and colleagues' research is that two-thirds of children claimed that they knew why they were placed in time-out, and only 50 percent of those reasons were correct. All children should know exactly why they are being placed in time-out. If they don't know, then there isn't much hope that they will know how to make their behavior more acceptable.

The lesson to be learned in this controversy is that no classroom-management procedure, however simple, can be effective if it is not properly applied. When behavior-management regimens do not work, teachers and consultants should ask themselves two important questions: Was the classroom environment reinforcing to the child? Was the time-out procedure applied according to recommended quidelines? It may be entirely possible to turn a failed strategy into a successful one.

Some useful resources for learning creative ways to implement behavioral procedures including time-out into a classroom setting are P.A. Alberto and A.C. Troutman, *Applied Behavior Analysis for Teachers*, 6th ed. (Merrill Prentice-Hall, 2003); M.M. Kerr and C.M. Nelson, *Strategies for Addressing Behavior Problems in the Classroom*, 4th ed. (Merrill Prentice-Hall, 2002); and R.C. Martella, J.R. Nelson, and N.E. Marchand-Martella, *Managing Disruptive Behaviors in the Schools* (Allyn and Bacon, 2003). For information on specific applications of time-out with students with emotional disturbance, you are directed to D.B. Center and S. McKitrick, "Disciplinary Removal of Special Education Students," *Focus on Exceptional Children* (vol. 20, no. 2, 1987, pp. 1–10), V. Costenbader and M. Reading-Brown, "Isolation Timeout Used with Students with Emotional Disturbance," *Exceptional Children* (vol. 61, no. 4, 1995, pp. 353–363), and L.H. Cuenin and K.R. Harris, "Planning, Implementing and Evaluating Time Out Interventions with Exceptional Students," *Teaching Exceptional Children* (vol. 18, 1986, pp. 272–276). For a fascinating treatise on the legal aspects of timeout, read M.L. Yell, "Timeout and Students with Behavior Disorders: A Legal Analysis," *Education and Treatment of Children* (vol. 17, no. 3, 1994, pp. 293–301).

ISSUE 9

Is Punishment an Effective Technique to Control Behavior?

YES: Shannon R. Brinker, Sara E. Goldstein, and Marie S. Tisak, from "Children's Judgements about Common Classroom Punishments," *Educational Research* (Summer 2003)

NO: John W. Maag, from "Rewarded by Punishment: Reflections on the Disuse of Positive Reinforcement in Schools," *Exceptional Children* (Winter 2001)

ISSUE SUMMARY

YES: Shannon R. Brinker, Sara E. Goldstein, and Marie S. Tisak are professors in the department of psychology at Bowling Green State University. They contend that children think that conventional punishment works best for conventional classroom transgressions, but removal punishment (e.g., grounding) works best for moral violations. In either case, children believe that punishment works.

NO: John W. Maag is a professor in the department of special education and communication disorders at the University of Nebraska–Lincoln. He contests that while conventional punishments may make a classroom safer for the moment, they fail to teach socially appropriate behaviors.

There is much controversy about whether any form of punishment should ever be used in the classrooms. Some say that the unintended side effects of punishments far outweigh the potential benefits. Another major complaint is that punishment is not effective. One way to test the effectiveness of punishment is to ask the children receiving the treatment.

In one study conducted by Brinker and colleagues, third- and fifth-grade students were asked about their perceptions of presentation punishment (e.g., sending the child to the principal's office) and removal punishment (e.g., taking away a reward) with respect to their use in cases of moral infractions against other students or conventional transgressions such as chewing gum in class. These researchers were interested not only in the frequency of these types of punishment but also their perceived effectiveness in reducing these two forms of student misbehavior. Overall, these authors found that children perceived presentation punishments as occurring most often in the classroom and as possibly more effective than removal punishment. Higher frequency of presentation punishment may be associated with higher satisfaction since children prefer consistency. Interestingly, children believed that removal punishments were more effective for moral violations against other children and less effective in cases of noncompliance and other conventional classroom transgressions. Perhaps students believe that removal punishment is more deserved after a moral infraction than it is after a conventional violation.

Treatment acceptability is important if teachers are to avoid resistance from their students. Brinker found students think mild punishment is fair and reasonable. That is a useful finding that supports punishment as an effective technique to correct misbehavior.

There is another point of view however that posits that punishment is not only ineffective but that it is harmful and can actually increase disruptive behavior. John Maag bemoans the fact that most teacher discipline for student disruptions involves various forms of punishment such as removal from the classroom, fines, restitutional payback, and in-school and out-of-school suspensions and expulsions. Maag concedes that punishments such as in-school and out-of-school suspensions for violent students may make the school safer, but then he quickly adds that punishment does little to teach students new socially appropriate behaviors. He feels that some classroom managers punish reflexively but overlook the long-term benefits of positive reinforcement. Finally, Maag believes that the side effects of routine punishment far outweigh the benefits and that positive reinforcement should replace punishment as a first-line strategy in classroom management.

**Shannon R. Brinker, Sara
E. Goldstein, and Maria S. Tisak**

➡ **YES**

Children's Judgements about Common Classroom Punishments

In every classroom, teachers must make decisions concerning punishments on a daily basis. Because the purpose of punishment is to keep a behaviour from recurring, it is critical that punishments are effective and appropriate, particularly from the perspective of the recipient. Students' perceptions can serve as valuable tools for deciding on classroom management techniques. Moreover, it has been argued that considering the perspective of the student is particularly important given current trends to attend to students' rights with respect to education.

Surprisingly, only a few studies have specifically focused on students' perspectives of classroom discipline. However, the existing studies on this topics highlight its importance. For example, Tulley and Chiu investigated student preferences for three types of discipline styles: (1) rules/reward punishment, in which a teacher has control over the choice of punishment; (2) relationship/listening, in which the teacher listens to the child and then decides the punishment; and (3) confronting/contracting, in which the teacher and child choose the punishment together. Findings indicated that children greatly preferred the confronting/contracting approach to the other two styles. The authors interpret this finding as demonstrating that children do have an interest in determining the types of interventions used in their classrooms (*ibid.*).

In another study, Elliott examined students' perceptions of two different types of punishments: presentation punishments, which involved presenting the child with an aversive stimulus (e.g. sending a child to the principal's office) and removal punishments, which concerned removing a positive stimulus (e.g. taking away free-time from the child). Students rated presentation punishment as more effective and acceptable than removal punishment. This finding was supported by Tulley and Chiu, who used anecdotal descriptions provided by sixth-graders. The students were asked to describe a recent instance in which they had broken a rule, to explain how the teacher disciplined them, and if that punishment was effective. Presentation punishment was rated as effective, whereas removal punishment was generally rated as ineffective.

A related but separate issue with regard to the type of punishment is children's perceptions of who the punishment affects. Research has found that children consider whether or not their peers are affected when making judgements about a punishment. Elliot *et al.* reported that children generally prefer interventions that have negative consequences for the individual, as compared to the whole class. Likewise, students would rather have misbehaviours addressed privately, as opposed to a more public reprimand. Illustrative of this point is that students report that home punishments are more desirable than are school-based punishments.

Furthermore, students prefer explanations for why particular behaviours are unacceptable, and tend to prefer explanations that do not include teachers' perceptions of personal annoyance or of personal difficulty in teaching. Instead, students prefer explanations that incorporate clear statements of rules and explanations that clarify why rules help maximize the classroom learning environment.

An additional factor that children consider when evaluating a punishment is the type of behaviour that resulted in punishment. Research demonstrates that children differentiate between moral infractions (concerns of justice, fairness, rights, and welfare—e.g. hitting) and conventional infractions (pertaining to arbitrary rules of conduct intended to aid in the coordination of social interactions—e.g. where students sit in a classroom). Children believe that behaviours such as hitting and stealing (i.e. moral transgressions) are more wrong than conventional violations. Additionally, when asked what other children do that would be considered wrong, young children cite moral transgressions (i.e. hitting, stealing), in contrast to other types of infractions. Likewise, children believe that rules that correspond to moral behaviours are more important than rules pertaining to conventions. Children also believe that violation of a moral rule should result in greater punishment than violation of a conventional rule.

Children's conceptions of appropriate punishment also vary depending on the type of infraction that has occurred. Children perceive that it is appropriate for a teacher to respond to a moral violation by referring to the unfair or hurtful nature of the act or by asking the offender to consider how it makes the other child feel. In contrast, with regard to a conventional transgression, children believe that teachers ought to remind the transgressor of the rule of express concern over the disruption that the act caused. Additionally, Nucci found that students make judgements about whether a teacher is an effective socialization agent based on perceptions of whether the teacher appropriately punishes violations that occur within their classrooms.

With the exception of Nucci, research addressing students' perceptions of classroom punishments typically has asked students about punishments in general, rather than in response to specific types of rule violations. Thus, more research is needed to ascertain whether the type of transgression influences students' judgements about the reprimand. For instance, it may be that students perceive particular punishments to be fairly effective in response to a moral violation (i.e. a serious infraction that has consequences for others), but not in response to a conventional transgression (i.e. a less serious misbehaviour that breaks an arbitrary rule of social conduct).

The purpose of the present study was to extend previous research by investigating children's thinking about two types of common punishments used by teachers in a classroom setting: removal punishment (the removal of a pleasant stimulus, such as taking away a reward) and presentation punishment (the presentation of an unpleasant stimulus, such as sending the child to the principal's office). Of interest was children's perceptions of the frequency of particular punishments in response to specific infractions, as well as how effective children perceived particular punishments to be with regard to the same misbehaviours. The punishments were evaluated for two different types of rule violations: stealing from another child (a moral infraction) and chewing gum in class (a conventional transgression).

Third- and fifth-grade students were chosen as participants based on past results demonstrating that children in this age range are sensitive to the type of infraction when judging teacher punishment strategies. Children in both age groups were expected to evaluate the punishments differently for the moral and conventional infractions. It was also predicted that fifth-graders, due to their advanced developmental level, would consider removal punishment to be more effective than would third-graders.

Participants

Participants were 45 students from the third and fifth grades attending school in a rural area of the Midwestern United States. There were 26 third-graders (M = 8.5 years; 12 females and 14 males) and 19 fifth-graders (M = 10.53 years; 12 females and 7 males). The children were white and from middle-class, two-parent families.

Measures and Procedures

The participants were administered a questionnaire containing two short vignettes depicting hypothetical misbehaviour in the classroom. One vignette was about a child who chews gum in the class, when chewing gum is against the rules (a conventional transgression), and the other vignette depicted a child who steals another classmate's markers (a moral infraction). Vignettes were adapted from past research investigating children's conceptions of similar types of infractions. Vignettes were presented in random order and the gender of the vignette characters were matched to that of the participants (i.e. male participants were given stories about male children, and female participants were given stories about female children).

Each vignette was followed by a series of questions pertaining to six different punishments (two questions per punishment, for a total of 12 questions after each vignette). Six questions pertained to perceptions of punishment frequency (i.e. how often participants think that the punishment is used by teachers), and six involved judgements about punishment effectiveness (i.e. how effective students think that the punishment is when it is used by teachers). For each vignette, the order in which the frequency/effectiveness questions were asked was randomized. Approximately half of the participants received questions about punishment frequency first, and the remaining students were presented with questions about effectiveness first. Questions are described in greater detail below.

As noted above, participants were asked questions about six different punishments. Three of these items were punishments that involve the removal of a pleasant stimulus (i.e. removal punishments) and the remaining three items involved the presentation of an unpleasant stimulus (i.e. presentation punishments). When participants were evaluating the frequency of punishment, the scale ranged from 1 (never) to 4 (very often). With respect to the effectiveness of punishment, the scale ranged from 1 (not good at all) to 4 (very good). Based on their content, the following three punishments were determined a priori to be removal punishments:

1. time-out at/by the teacher's desk
2. losing recess
3. losing points towards a reward.

The following three punishments were considered to be presentation punishments:

1. sent to the principal's office
2. warning of future punishment
3. made to apologize and to promise not to repeat the behaviour.

Questionnaires were administered in a mid-sized group format by the first author. The researcher read the instructions aloud and then asked the children to continue reading and filling out the questionnaire on their own. . . .

Results and Discussion

Students in the present study perceived that their teachers utilized presentation punishments (i.e. punishments involving presenting a student with an aversive stimuli, such as making a student apologize) more often than removal punishments (i.e. the removal of a privilege or pleasant stimulus, such as giving a student time-out). Students reported that this was the case for a moral infraction (i.e. stealing) and for a conventional transgression (i.e. chewing gum in class). Students also perceived presentation punishments as more effective than removal punishments in response to both types of infractions. Thus, children appear to believe that teachers are using punishments that are relatively effective. That is, the punishments that students reported to be executed most often are also the punishments that students believed to be most useful.

These results are consistent with the findings of past research, demonstrating that students find presentation punishments more acceptable and effective than removal punishments. Given research demonstrating that students prefer teachers to be consistent in this punishment behaviour, this perception of greater effectiveness in conjuncture with greater perceived frequency may reflect a general preference for consistent types of punishment. Alternatively, students may simply find it more aversive to be presented with something positive than have something taken away, thus making them believe that presentation punishments are more effective.

Another major finding pertained to the way that children viewed removal punishments in response to the two different type of infractions. Children reported that teachers used these types of punishments more often in response to the moral infraction, as compared to the conventional infraction. Likewise, participants also believed that removal punishments would be more effective after the moral violation than the same type of punishment would be after the conventional violation. There are several interpretations for this finding. One, perhaps students were considering frequencies of punishments when considering how effective the punishments would be, in that they anticipated that the particular punishment would consistently follow a moral infraction, but not a conventional infraction. Thus, if they could 'count on' something positive being taken away after a related violation, they perceived this type of punishment to be relatively effective in such situations. Additionally, this finding may reflect thinking consistent with prior findings demonstrating that children believe that rules prohibiting moral infractions are more legitimate and important, and that punishment is more deserved after a moral infraction than it is after a conventional violation. Therefore, if children believe that punishment is comparatively legitimate, important and deserved in light of moral infractions, they may also believe that those who get punished may be relatively more impacted by the reprimand, and thus will be less likely to repeat the offensive behaviour.

Interestingly, no age or gender differences emerged in the way that children were thinking about the punishments. . . .

[There was a] lack of age differences in the present study. . . .

Although children's perceptions are not an objective measure of whether or not the punishment effectively reduces the occurrence of the unwanted behaviour in the future, children's perceptions can certainly serve as one index of a punishment's utility. Involving children in their own behaviour modification plans has been found useful in the context of therapy and is arguably a desirable approach for teachers to consider. For example, given that children in the present study found removal punishments to be relatively ineffective in light of conventional violations, teachers may wish to respond to conventional infractions with a presentation punishment. . . .

NO ↩

John W. Maag

Rewarded by Punishment: Reflections on the Disuse of Positive Reinforcement in Schools

. . . Probably more than any other recent publication, Kohn's book, *Punished by Rewards* (1993), crystallized the rejection of techniques based on positive reinforcement, and struck a chord that continues to resonate throughout education and society. Although Kohn's arguments have been well received by much of the educational profession, his conclusions ignored significant bodies of literature that provided more support for behavioral procedures than he acknowledged. Nevertheless, ideas such as Kohn's have found an apparently wide and receptive audience. Axelrod believed that techniques based on positive reinforcement lack popular and professional acceptability because they are time-intensive, offer little compensation for educators, contradict popular views of developmental psychology, threaten special interest groups, are socially unacceptable, and demean humans. Ironically, punishment—also a behavioral technique—is widely accepted because it agrees with popular notions about school discipline. . . .

Embrace punishment because it is easy to administer, works for many students without challenging behaviors, and has been part of the Judeo-Christian history that dominates much of our society. Therefore, the purpose of this article is to consider why educators find punishment to be a more acceptable approach for managing students' behaviors than positive reinforcement and to argue that the latter is much more effective than the former.

Three propositions are put forth to support these assumptions. First, positive reinforcement is ignored and misunderstood because of a strong cultural ethos that encourages punishment. Second, the punishment paradigm that permeates education distorts teachers' knowledge of several important terms associated with managing students' behaviors. Third, although contrary to the beliefs of many educators and Kohn, positive reinforcement is a universal principle that occurs naturally in every classroom. Therefore, educators should plan its occurrence to increase appropriate behaviors rather than running the risk of it haphazardly promoting inappropriate behaviors. . . .

Why Positive Reinforcement Is Ignored and Misunderstood

Freedom versus Coercion

Techniques based on positive reinforcement are often perceived to threaten individuals' freedom as autonomous human beings. Ironically, punishment, which is the opposite of positive reinforcement, appears much more acceptable because of the perception that it does not threaten individuals' autonomy—people believe they are free to choose to behave in responsible ways to avoid punishment. . . .

As well as being perceived as less coercive than positive reinforcement, punishment is also viewed as a highly effective way for society to control its members. . . .

This well-ingrained historical and cultural ethos has resulted in a kind of *paradigm paralysis*—"a condition of terminal certainty"—that prevents people from understanding techniques based on positive reinforcement and acknowledging their effectiveness. The paralysis has completely fortified the punishment mentality that permeates education and much of society.

The Punishment Paradigm

A punishment paradigm has evolved, and been advocated for, since biblical times and is reflected in the proverb "spare the rod and spoil the child." Besides having history on its side, a punishment mentality has been perpetuated for the simple reason that punishing students has traditionally been highly reinforcing to teachers.

Punishment often can produce a rapid—although often temporary—suppression in most students' inappropriate behaviors. Furthermore, because punishment techniques may be quickly and easily administered, teachers have found them quite desirable to suppress a variety of classroom disruptions. For example, a teacher may find a student's "obnoxious" behaviors to be aversive. Being sent out of the classroom to sit in the hall or principal's office may be punishing if the student finds exclusion from others aversive. Consequently, the teacher has been reinforced for sending the student out of the room because that act terminated the unpleasantness of the student's behavior. . . .

The property of punishment that teachers find reinforcing (e.g., sending a student out of the room) leads to a related, and undesirable, phenomenon called the "negative reinforcement trap." Patterson coined this term to explain coercive relationships that sometime evolve between parents and children, although its emergence can also be observed between teachers and students. In the previous example, a student was removed from the classroom for engaging in behaviors the teacher found obnoxious. If the student lacked the necessary skills for performing the stipulated assignment or found it boring, then being removed from the classroom negatively reinforced the student's performance of obnoxious behaviors because these behaviors terminated the perceived unpleasantness of the assignment. Consequently, teachers and students have often been caught in a trap in which both individuals were negatively reinforced for engaging in counterproductive behaviors.

There is another very powerful reason why punishment continues to be used—it works for about 95% of students attending public schools. Despite the fact that students' behaviors have recently become increasingly violent and challenging for teachers to manage, most students attending public schools nevertheless behave fairly well. Consequently, mild forms of punishments, such as the use of verbal reprimands, fines, or occasional removals from the classroom, typically control most students' behaviors. However, these types of consequences are ineffective for about 5% of students who display the most challenging behaviors (i.e., those that do not respond to traditional forms of punishment).

The paradigm paralysis mentality proceeds in the following manner: Because mild forms of punishment work for most students, then the solution for teachers with the 5% of students with the most challenging behaviors is to simply punish them severely and more often. This reaction, although easily foreseen, results in the application of *linear interventions*. For example, if a student stays after school for misbehaving, the problem is presumed to have been addressed by the consequence. But what if the student misbehaves again? The linear solution would be to keep the student after school for 2 days, then 3, and so forth. This type of solution is simply "more of the same" and seldom works. In fact, if punishment were effective, it would be used less rather than more frequently, a point that is elucidated upon shortly.

Ignoring Data

Researchers have typically relied on empirical data to convince people of the effectiveness of a particular technique, model, or approach. If this tactic worked, applications of positive reinforcement would have already enjoyed much more widespread acceptance and implementation because the successful clinical, educational, and real-life applications are truly remarkable. The effectiveness of this body of research has been well documented in various journals and books over the past 20 years. Unfortuantely, empirical data has little effect because people often only see that for which they are looking. . . .

The solution to this problem may not be to keep trying to inculcate teachers with data supporting the effectiveness of positive reinforcement. . . . Instead, the solution is to describe positive reinforcement in a way that is congruent with teachers' existing notions about behavior management and present techniques as easy to apply. Specific recommendations for doing so are described in the last section of this article.

Punishment Paradigm: Distorting Reality to Perpetuate Misunderstanding

. . . The paradigm of punishment tends to distort reality and perpetuates misunderstanding of four common and important terms associated with students' behavior: discipline, punishment, reinforcement, and rewards.

Positive Reinforcement and Discipline

Positive reinforcement is often misunderstood because it is rarely associated with discipline. Instead, many teachers and parents wrongly assume the terms "discipline" and "punishment" are synonymous. For example, a quick glance at the disciplinary practices appearing in the policies and procedures handbook of any public school in this country would reveal an exclusive focus on punishment: in-school and out-of-school suspension, expulsion, fines, detention, restitution, and even corporal punishment in some states. Yet according to the *American Heritage Dictionary*, discipline refers to "training that is expected to produce a specific character or pattern of behavior, especially training that produces moral or mental improvement." A key word in this definition is *improvement* that means "to increase, develop, or enhance." Conversely, punishment, by definition, does one thing—decreases behavior. Simply because a student's inappropriate behavior may be suppressed with punishment does not guarantee that the student knows what appropriate behavior should be performed in its place. Rutherford and Neel stated that in many cases, the use of punishment leaves the development of desirable behaviors to chance. . . .

Positive Reinforcement and Punishment: Function over Form

In order to understand discipline better, it is helpful to examine the concepts of positive reinforcement and punishment more thoroughly. . . . The key consideration in the definitions is that positive reinforcement and punishment are not *things* but rather *effects*. The effects are to either increase or decrease a behavior. Therefore, the statement made by some teachers, "I've tried positive reinforcement, and it doesn't work," is oxymoronic because, by definition, if a consequence did not function to increase behavior then it was not a reinforcer. Nevertheless, many teachers continue to believe that positive reinforcement and punishment are things that are either received or removed. . . .

Students who repeatedly receive verbal reprimands, are sent out of the classroom, or receive suspensions are not being punished: They are instead being positively reinforced. The adage "negative attention is better than no attention" certainly applies here. Teachers expect students to behave well, and consequently ignore them when they do so, but usually give them negative attention when they behave poorly. Adult attention, even if it is negative, is a powerful reinforcer—especially for students with the most challenging behaviors who typically receive very little positive attention. . . .

The distinction between form and function is similarly not well understood when applied to the use of punishment. Here is a telling example encountered by the author. A teacher was disturbed that a student frequently did not bring his reading book to class. As a result, the student was required to write 100 times, "I will remember my book." Most teachers would probably view this consequence as a kind of punishment. Yet what behavior is the teacher trying to decrease—remembering the book? This unfortunate case illustrates how punishment is often misunderstood and can be misapplied with counterproductive results. Not coincidentally, the student in this example was embarrassed about his learning disability in reading. Therefore, "forgetting" to bring the book to class served the function for him to avoid what he considered to be more aversive—being embarrassed in front of his peers when asked to read—than having to repeatedly write sentences.

The Contradiction of Reinforcement and Rewards

The functional definition of positive reinforcement frequently does not help some teachers get past the stereotypical notion that it is a manipulative tool created to coerce students into behaving appropriately. Consequently, reinforcement continues to be viewed by some educators as tantamount to bribery, undermines students' abilities to become self-directed, and quells internal motivation. The problem with this assertion is that many teachers incorrectly equate the terms reward and reinforcement. Unlike reinforcement, a reward is, in fact, a *thing* given to acknowledge an accomplishment. Other words for reward are "merit" or "prize." A reward may or may not function as a reinforcer. . . .

Many teachers are puzzled as to how talking nicely to a student, for example, could be punishment because punishment certainly must be something unpleasant. However, once teachers understand that reinforcement and punishment are effects rather than things, their ability to managing students' challenging behaviors will increase dramatically. But first, it is important to address the issue of external reinforcement stifling motivation.

There is an irony in the belief that Kohn and many teachers hold that providing external reinforcement will stifle children's internal motivation: These individuals often have few qualms that administering external punishment will cause the same problem. In other words, why would externally applying reinforcement but not punishment stifle internal motivation? The answer has nothing to do with motivation, but rather that misapplications and misunderstandings are perpetuated by a cultural ethos condoning punishment and eschewing reinforcement.

The Naturally Occurring Phenomena of Positive Reinforcement and Punishment

Some teachers have said, "I don't believe in using reinforcement." This statement is as logically absurd as saying, "I don't believe in gravity." Just because someone may not like something does not consequently abolish its existence. Reinforcement and punishment are naturally occurring phenomena— all behaviors are followed by certain consequences. If a behavior increased, then the consequence functioned as a reinforcer; if a behavior decreased, then the consequence functioned as a punisher. . . . If a person asks someone a question and that person responds positively, then question asking has been reinforced and the interaction will continue. On the other hand, if a person asks someone a question and that person either walks away or responds negatively, then question asking has been punished and the interaction will terminate.

The Propriety of Reinforcement

With great effort, opponents of reinforcement can sometimes be convinced that it is a naturally occurring phenomenon; nevertheless, they continue to argue with its propriety. Their specific objection is usually to its planned use to elicit certain behaviors in others. This position on reinforcement is as ridiculous as arguing whether gravity is good or bad—both are naturally occurring phenomena. Furthermore, this position takes teachers' foci away from the meaningful task of analyzing interaction patterns and reinforcement contingencies that exist in classrooms in order to restructure them to increase desirable student behaviors. To ignore this ecologically important aspect of behavior management is to allow reinforcement to occur randomly and run the risk of it increasing students' inappropriate behaviors. Nevertheless, many teachers continue to believe that techniques based on positive reinforcement have been tried and have failed. This belief is not only a self-contradiction but also fallacious. Techniques based on positive reinforcement have rarely represented a dominant approach to managing students' behavior.

Perhaps part of the problem educators have in understanding and correctly using techniques based on positive reinforcement is the perception that they either require too much effort or do not work well enough. This perception makes it easy for people to fall into dichotomous thinking—techniques based on positive reinforcement either work perfectly or they do not work at all. . . .

Good Is Not Good Enough

. . . In spite of their empirical support, techniques based on positive reinforcement are seldom used correctly. Part of the problem may be that when techniques based on positive reinforcement are used, they are often implemented haphazardly and inappropriately. Many teachers still believe that techniques based on positive reinforcement consist of nothing more than providing students with M&M candies or stickers when they are "being good." Behavior management is much more—analyzing behavior, deciding what to change, collecting information on the behaviors of concern, using schedules of reinforcement, and monitoring progress—not to mention the plethora of techniques based on positive reinforcement that run the gamut from those that are teacher-directed to those that are student-directed.

Managing students' challenging behaviors effectively is a "good news-bad news" story. The good news is that the technology has long existed to develop, implement, and monitor effective behavioral interventions for managing students' challenging behaviors. The bad news is that this process takes considerable time and effort. One of the major impediments in having educators put forth the effort to develop and implement techniques based on positive reinforcement is that many do not believe it is their job to manage students' behavior.

The Way Things Are and Could Be

There is a prevailing view that teachers' primary responsibility is to teach students academic behaviors and to control (i.e., bring into alignment) their socially inappropriate behaviors. Some teachers, and even entire schools, have developed elaborate management plans to control students' challenging behaviors. This "control mentality" is pervasive throughout education and places teachers in a reactive, instead of proactive, position when managing students' challenging behaviors. Managing students' challenging behaviors effectively will continue to be a frustrating endeavor until teachers view misbehavior as an opportunity for increasing positive social interaction rather than being something to be punished. For example, most teachers would readily agree that when students make mistakes in division, the goal is not to "punish" or decrease division behavior. Rather, procedures are implemented to provide students with the correct strategy and practice to increase their competence in division. The same logic should apply to students' challenging behaviors. . . .

The literature is replete with studies documenting very low, and in many instances nonexistent, rates of positive teacher statements directed to students when they perform desirable behavior. Even more disturbing, teachers typically give students attention only when they perform inappropriate behaviors. Ironically, teacher praise has been supported as among one of the most empirically sound teacher competencies. The irony is that because teacher attention is so effective, it nevertheless is being used primarily when students misbehave.

It is equally disappointing that teachers fail to see the powerfully reinforcing value in such natural human behaviors as eye contact, smiles, kind words, physical proximity, and social interaction. All too often teachers justify not using positive reinforcement by stating that they "expect" students to behave well. Ironically, they have no difficulty "reacting" to students when they behave poorly. Furthermore, simply having the expectation that students "should" behave well, especially those with the most challenging behaviors, is a prescription for failure and frustration. The use of the word "should" is a classic example of teachers engaging in a common type of irrational belief: demandingness. Demandingness is a magical and ineffective attempt to change events to a more desirable outcome without engaging in any behavior other than saying either the word "expect" or "should."

Implications for Practice

Effectively changing students' behaviors requires teachers to also change their behaviors, which, in turn, requires that they understand how positive reinforcement is congruent with their values and that the techniques are easy to apply. . . . There are a variety of easy-to-implement recommendations for using positive reinforcement. Several of them are presented here.

1. *Catch Students Being Good.* Catching students being good is one of the easiest and most effective ways for dealing with students with challenging behaviors. . . . As a general rule, the second time a teacher gives a student a verbal warning should be a cue for that teacher to catch the student being good. Ironically, and unlike punishment, teachers only have to catch students being good occasionally. Intermittent reinforcement can maintain high rates of students' appropriate behaviors. On the other hand, punishment is most effective when it is delivered continuously. Therefore, what takes less time and effort:

observing a student occasionally to positively reinforce him or observing the student continuously to punish him?

2. *Think Small.* There is an interesting reaction some teachers have to students with challenging behaviors: They expect students with challenging behaviors to behave better than students without behavioral challenges. For example, some teachers expect students with attention-deficit hyperactivity disorder (ADHD) to sit quietly and pay attention longer than students without this disorder. . . . The solution is for teachers to set small goals for students and then reinforce successive approximations of behaviors toward that goal. For example, if a student is chronically late to class by 10 min or more he should be reinforced when he makes it through the door in 5 min. Once he begins to make improvements in the desired direction, future behavior changes become much easier.

3. *Have a Group Management Plan.* There are two reasons why it is easier to manage specific students with challenging behaviors when the entire class is well behaved. First, group management plans make use of intermittent reinforcement that maintains high levels of appropriate behavior. Second, it is easier to implement a more intensive individual positive reinforcement intervention once a classwide management plan is in place. . . . [One] approach is the Good Behavior Game. Three appropriate behaviors are listed on the chalkboard. Prerecorded random tones are played on a tape recorder during a lesson. When a tone sounds, the teacher places three marbles in a jar if everyone in class is engaging in one of the three appropriate behaviors. The class earns a reinforcer (e.g., movie or popcorn on Friday) if the jar is filled with marbles by the end of the week.

4. *Prevent Behavior Problems.* Punishment is less likely to be used when teachers anticipate and prevent behavior problems from occurring. It is easier to prevent behavior problems than to try to reestablish control. The following strategies work to enhance a positive classroom climate for both students with and without challenging behaviors. First, teachers should establish classroom rules that specify appropriate behaviors and the positive reinforcement students earn for performing them. Second, teachers should strive to have 70% of their day devoted to students being academically engaged. Third, teachers should not let students with challenging behaviors sit next to each other. Fourth, teachers should spend as much time as possible walking around the classroom to monitor students' behaviors and subtly reinforce them.

5. *Use Peer Influence Favorably.* Peer influence exists in every classroom. Students with challenging behaviors have learned that the easiest way to get peer attention, either positive or negative, is to misbehave. Therefore, teachers should use peer influence in a socially constructive manner. A common mistake some teachers make is to override the influence of peers with punishment. For example, a teacher may punish a student for making animal noises in class. However, the student may be receiving reinforcement from peers in the form of smiles, comments, snickers, or subtle gestures. The punishment must be severe to override the reinforcing value of peer attention. The most effective way to use peer influence positively is to implement a group management technique such as one described previously.

The most effective behavior managers are teachers who acknowledge that reinforcement and punishment occur naturally and, consequently, analyze and modify environmental, curricular, and instructional variables to promote appropriate behavior. These teachers work hard to positively reinforce appropriate student behavior and ignore misbehavior when it does not interfere with other students' learning, classroom routines, or is otherwise reinforcing. They also sparingly use reprimands and only in an even-handed, matter-of-fact tone. Students view these teachers as people whose attention is valued, whom they want to be around, whom they enjoy interacting with, rather than as a watchdog to be feared because of the punishment they may dole out. . . .

POSTSCRIPT

Is Punishment an Effective Technique to Control Behavior?

Previous researchers have found the involvement of students in the development and implementation of their own classroom interventions for misbehaviors to be a desirable goal. Brinker agrees with this perspective. Given the broad use of punishment, it is an interesting question to ask whether students think that punishment works. Brinker's findings suggest that both males and females in the third and fifth grades think that presentation punishment (e.g., time-out) is an effective means for reducing minor classroom misbehaviors but that removal punishment (e.g., denial of a participation in a preferred activity, such as a party) is relatively ineffective with conventional classroom rules violations. Removal punishment should be reserved for moral infractions between two students, specifically when one student does something wrong toward another. Research like this that can result in deeper insights into how students perceive punishment can make a useful management technique work even better.

What Maag finds most perplexing is that while teachers are so convinced about the benefits of punishment, these same teachers still regularly report that they would like more in-service training about "what works" in classroom management. Doesn't punishment work? Maag contends that positive reinforcement works, but teachers resist it; punishment does not work as well, but teachers embrace it. If these apparent logical inconsistencies are true, then presumably teachers either are not receiving the classroom management training they need, or the training has not enlightened them sufficiently about the punishment paradigm discussed above. That may be precisely why punishment is so attractive to teachers but so ineffective in the long run.

What is most interesting about these two articles is that perception can effect the choice of classroom management procedure. It is important to consider what teachers and students think about forms of classroom management and how acceptable they may be to each of them. Unfortunately, some teachers may choose a classroom management strategy based upon what they believe and not upon what works. This stance would appear to be logically unjustifiable. Both positive reinforcement and punishment will occur naturally in any classroom environment whether teachers deliberately manipulate the contingencies or not. Maag makes the case that it is better to be deliberate about classroom management than to leave it to the randomness of environmental control of behavior. Thus, he recommends planning for proactive behavior management by employing mostly positive reinforcement over punishment. Brinker recommends that punishment is what students expect for their infractions and that is what they should get.

How should this punishment-praise conundrum be resolved? Perhaps the best resolution is to understand the limitations of each approach. Mild punishment is best used to suppress student misbehavior at the moment, but it cannot be expected to produce new replacement skills in students. In other words, when preventive techniques have failed, mild punishment may be used as a last resort, but good behavior management requires that punishment should always be paired with reinforcement to improve good student behavior.

Recommended readings on the controversies surrounding punishment as a classroom management strategy are R.E. Buchart, *Classroom Discipline in American Schools: Problems and Possibilities for Democratic Education* (State University of New York Press, 1998, pp. 19–49) and H.J. Freiberg, ed., *Beyond Behaviorism: Changing the Classroom Management Paradigm* (Allyn and Bacon, 1999, pp. 3–20). For commentary on alternatives to punishment, these readings are recommended: I.A. Hyman and P.A. Snook, *Dangerous Schools.* (Jossey-Bass, 1999) and A. Kohn, *Beyond Discipline: From Compliance to Community* (Association for Supervision and Curriculum Development, 1996).

ISSUE 10

Should Character Count?

YES: Maurice J. Elias, Margaret C. Wang, Roger P. Weissberg, Joseph E. Zins, and Herbert J. Walberg, from "The Other Side of the Report Card," *American School Board Journal* (November 2002)

NO: David Elkind, from "Character Education: An Ineffective Luxury?" *Child Care Information Exchange* (November 1998)

ISSUE SUMMARY

YES: Maurice J. Elias is a professor at Rutgers University and vice-chair of the leadership team of the Collaborative for Academic, Social, and Emotional Learning (CASEL). Elias and his colleagues believe student success depends on more than just test scores and that teachers should pay as much attention to student behavior and character as they do to student grades.

NO: David Elkind, professor emeritus at Tufts University and a prolific writer, researcher, and lecturer, believes that character education is a luxury that public schools cannot afford. He contends that there is no research to support the practice and that it detracts from valuable teaching time.

Character development has become a hot-button issue for several reasons. First, teachers are pressured to use their days mostly in direct academic instruction. Character education is often seen as an "add-on," a goal that may be a good idea but not central to the mission of education. Secondly, character education is based in the investigation of virtues, values, and morals. In character education, students are taught criteria for making choices in their lives, to attend to the effects of their personal choices on themselves and others, and to be critical thinkers about what they are learning in class and implications for their own value systems. What can be frightening to educators and empowering to learners is that with character education, students are being taught to live according to the courage of their convictions, to make choices and live by them. These choices can even get down to a very personal level. For example, students may make a decision to befriend an "outsider," someone who is not in their clique of friends, even though they risk ostracism from the group themselves.

The question arises whether students should be taught how to make personal life decisions employing the traits of good character. Could it be possible that character development is an essential part of good classroom management? Could it be that teachers inadvertently teach character development whether they deliberately choose to or not because everyday they teach students about their own value systems by how they act, what they like, what they choose to teach, how they respond to various topics, and what topics get them excited? With this perspective in mind, some important questions arise: Should character be fostered deliberately? Should it be taught? Should it be encouraged? In other words, should character count?

In a compelling article, Maurice Elias and colleagues contend that student success depends on more than simply test scores and achievement. They believe the "other side of the report card" where schools traditionally evaluate student behavior and attributes of character development are just as important. Many of the student attitudes and attributes that they hold dear are ones that other authors, such as Daniel Goleman, have referred to as emotional intelligence. They insist that it is just as important for students to be educated emotionally as it is to stimulate their intellects because without emotional intelligence, students may never realize their full potential. They believe that teaching positive attitudes toward cooperation, compromise, goal persistence, personal responsibility, personal initiative, and leadership development are essential to education. Furthermore, these authors have found that when teachers instruct students in social-emotional competencies and ethical decision making, the classroom climate becomes more supportive, academic performance improves, and individual behavior is less egocentric and more respectful of others in the classroom.

Elias and colleagues recommend that schools seeking to encourage character development should identify character virtues that they would like to develop in their students, teach students about these virtues and actively practice and reinforce these virtues, employ character education to prevent behavior problems, develop student coping skills that are compatible with good character such as problem-solving conflict resolution, and provide opportunities and recognize student participation in service learning in the broader community in which the school resides.

In sharp contrast, David Elkind is much more critical of character education and frames it as an "ineffective luxury" that schools cannot afford. He contests assertions that character education has demonstrated benefits and maintains that precious instructional time should be put to much better use on instructional activities. He asserts that pressure to implement character education curricula is driven by traditionalists who believe that their values should be the ones taught and that without guidance, student behaviors will spiral out of control.

Elkind provides several reasons why he believes that character education curricula are ineffectual. He believes that there is no agreement about what character virtues should be taught. Furthermore, he believes that schools should not be used as a platform for social reform. Parents are the best teachers of morality and virtue, and students are not likely to take ethical stances that their parents do not hold. Teachers need to teach character by modeling character, making moral decisions that they share with their students, and acting on those decisions as they would hope their students would be able to act someday.

Maurice J. Elias, et al.

 **YES**

The Other Side of the Report Card

Student success depends a great deal on what we call "the other side of the report card." Students who are actively engaged in class and come prepared, who cooperate with their peers, who resolve conflicts peacefully, who complete their work, who attend school often and on time, and who demonstrate initiative and leadership are more likely to succeed in school and, ultimately, in life.

If these characteristics are so important, why don't newspapers rank schools in terms of the social and emotional aspects of education as well as test scores? In life, doesn't it matter who shows up, who works well with others, who can solve problems, who is prepared for what must be done, who can function as part of a team, and who is an ethical person? Are these attributes any less important than algebra, geometry, chemistry, and spelling?

With the recent focus on the academic side of the report card, we risk losing sight of the other side—the side that reflects how we live with one another, whether we are inclined toward peace or war, and whether we have the skills we need to avoid violence and alcohol and drug abuse. The interpersonal life of schools rests on the character of the people involved and the skills they need to carry out their tasks effectively. The skills of sound character and citizenship have recently been termed emotional intelligence or social and emotion learning. However, their importance was recognized from the earliest days of public education in the writings and advocacy of Horace Mann.

Skills for Academic and Life Success

Research conducted by the Collaborative for Academic, Social, and Emotional Learning and the Mid-Atlantic Regional Educational Laboratory for Student Success (a U.S. Department of Education regional laboratory) is yielding a clearer picture of the skills and competencies students need for academic and life success. Our research confirms that social and emotional factors affect academic grades and school performance. Furthermore, we have found that enhancing social-emotional competencies, in combination with a positive, supportive classroom and school climate, can improve academic performance.

A number of teachable skills underlie positive child development and academic performance. These skills include knowing and managing emotions, recognizing strengths and areas of need, showing ethical and social responsibility,

From *American School Board Journal*, November 2002, pp. 28–30. Copyright © 2002 by National School Boards Association. Reprinted by permission.

taking others' perspectives and sensing their emotions, respecting others and self, appreciating diversity, setting adaptive goals, solving problems, listening and communicating clearly, building relationships, cooperating, negotiating, and managing conflict nonviolently, and seeking and giving help.

Teachers who review this list tell us it captures the skills they know students need to put their knowledge to productive use and to live as responsible citizens in our increasingly complex society. Indeed, think about any of the character traits we want students to have, such as respect or honesty. What are the skills necessary to act respectfully and honestly and to conduct your life with these traits as guiding principles? Almost any answer would include skills from the above list.

Teachers and teacher educators alike should be aware of research and field-tested methods for building these skills in students. (See the box on page 30 for more information.) And the same skills can help parents be more supportive of the work of educators.

School Conditions for Success

What kinds of schools create the conditions under which students' cognitive, affective, and interpersonal growth flourishes? Our field studies at CASEL and research by the Character Education Partnership support the view that systematic attention to the other side of the report card enhances and promotes academic learning. Such attention—or the lack thereof—influences how children conduct themselves in the classroom; how they respond to lectures, cooperative learning groups, tests, projects, and all the personal and interpersonal tasks in school through which learning takes place; and the direction of their ethical and moral compass.

The research also strongly suggests that schools must organize themselves effectively if students are to develop sound character and see themselves and their learning as positive resources for their families, schools, workplaces, and communities. Skills and knowledge must be imparted in a way that reinforces and exemplifies these behaviors if students are to learn to participate actively in the institutions that allow for a free and democratic society.

Schools of social, emotional, character, and academic excellence generally share five main characteristics:

1. A school climate that articulates specific themes, character elements, or values, such as respect, responsibility, fairness, and honesty;
2. Explicit instruction and practice in social-emotional learning skills.
3. Developmentally appropriate instruction in ways to promote health and prevent problems.
4. Services and systems that enhance students' coping skills and provide social support for handling transitions, crises, and conflicts.
5. Widespread, systematic opportunities for positive, contributory service.

These schools send messages about character, about how students should conduct themselves as learners, about the respectful ways staff members should conduct themselves as educators, and about how staff and parents should conduct themselves as supporters of learning.

Many such schools have incorporated social-emotional learning or character education into their overall mission statements or school board policies. They have ongoing, coordinated, research-based programs to teach skills for social and emotional learning and to infuse character into various aspects of the school routine and environment. These schools also devote time to preventing problems such as bullying and other forms of violence; alcohol, tobacco, and other drug use; and pregnancy.

The most forward-looking of these schools organize student support and guidance services that anticipate situations rather than merely react to them. They provide assistance for children as they and their families face life crises and challenges, rather than wait until academic or behavioral problems are obvious. These schools also teach all students conflict-resolution skills, since all of them will experience many interpersonal conflicts in school and the community. Finally, these schools put a strong emphasis on high-quality service-learning experiences, certainly at the high school level, but also, in many cases, in earlier grades.

Implications for School Boards

These research findings have clear implications for those concerned with educational policy and school governance. For those who believe, as we do, that excellence in education can and must include both sides of the report card, here is what research shows we must ask of our schools—and the implications of those findings:

- *Sound classroom structure and function are based on a foundation of caring relationships.* Schools must be organized to provide each student with a caring connection, ideally to another adult but at the very least to a peer mentor. Students must feel welcome in their schools and know that their presence matters to educators at least as much as to peers. This is why bullying and peer harassment are so insidious. They raise questions in children's minds about how much adults care about their safety. Those who are not victims may breathe a sigh of relief, but they don't feel entirely safe—their turn could be next.
- *Students function better and learn more effectively when they are encouraged to have clear, positive goals and values, to manage their emotions and make responsible decisions, and to set goals for their own learning while pursuing the academic goals that must be reached to function well in our society.* Education must be explicitly goal oriented. Students need to know why they are in school and what they are working to accomplish. They need to define goals for learning so they will internalize what they learn and not simply forget it. (Such goals are especially important in the areas of health, character education, and the prevention of violence, pregnancy, and drug abuse.)
- *Students behave more responsibly and respectfully when given opportunities for moral action and community service.* From the earliest grades, students must have ways to contribute to their classrooms, schools, communities, municipalities, and the larger world. This starts with putting away the toys in kindergarten as a service to classmates and extends to such efforts as interning with legislators, working with model United Nations programs, and working on behalf of the poor and homeless.

- *A challenging academic curriculum that respects all learners motivates and helps them succeed.* Educators must aim as high as possible for each student and convey their belief in that student's potential. The goals of education must be to inspire students and extend their boundaries, rather than discourage them through negative evaluation. A realistic culture of "you can" and "let's find ways to achieve success" must predominate over a culture of "you can't."
- *The school staff must be a caring, moral community of learners and must model as well as teach caring and moral behavior.* Educators cannot expect more from children and teens than they do from themselves. Administrators are responsible for seeing that this is the case and cannot relegate it to secondary status when faced with competing demands.
- *The opportunities for a child to achieve moral probity and to reach social, emotional, and academic goals are enhanced when the school, parents, and community collaborate.* Schools must make ongoing efforts to reach parents, especially those who are hardest to reach. Many immigrant parents, single parents, and parents who have limited academic skills are unwilling, unable, or just plain afraid to interact with the school. The most effective schools have reached these parents through, for example, meetings in churches and other faith-based facilities, multilingual cable television programs and parenting materials, and meetings that include family dinner and child care. The message to parents is that perhaps the most important things they can do are to read to their children, become involved in their learning, provide guidance and supervision, and create a climate in which kids come to school everyday emotionally, physically, and nutritionally ready to learn.
- *The concerns of students with special needs must be fully integrated into the mainstream functioning of the school as much as possible.* School and special services administrators must work cooperatively to ensure that character education, health, and drug- and violence-prevention programs are delivered to special education students as well as to their peers. Those who need the messages most must get the messages most clearly and frequently.

A New Standard

Students' success in school and their preparation for active engagement in a complex, participatory democracy depend greatly on the other side of the report card. We must organize our schools so that they promote both academic and social-emotional excellence. Indeed, the important message of recent research is that enhancing children's social, emotional, ethical, and academic development is one inseparable goal, rather than a set of competing priorities. This goal defines the educational standards for the 21st century.

This perspective poses challenges for those who are responsible for school policy and governance. The following steps can help a school district "go public" with this set of concerns:

- Introduce evidence-based instructional programs that promote students' social and emotional development.
- Communicate the importance of this instruction to students and parents.

- Outline clearly what social and emotional skills and positive character attributes are priorities, and assess progress being made in those areas.
- Modify items on the other side of the report card to carefully reflect these areas and ensure that they are rated seriously and carefully by teachers and combined with other indicators as deemed necessary.
- Summarize these data to look systematically at how well students, and schools overall, are doing in these areas, and share the results with parents and the community.

If educational leaders and policy makers provide students with school experiences that integrate academic, social, and emotional learning, character education, and education for service and citizenship, we will have the best chance in recent memory to truly leave no children behind.

NO ⬅

David Elkind

Character Education:
An Ineffective Luxury?

Character education is a luxury that we cannot afford. It has absolutely no demonstrated benefits and consumes precious instructional time that could be put to much better use. Today's teachers are already overwhelmed with demands to get students to meet state mandated academic standards as well as to teach drug, multicultural, and antibias curricula. In this pressured climate, character education is a needless additional burden. The truth is that he effort to put character education into our schools is driven by moral, rather than academic, concerns. These curricula are advocated because the larger society feels that its traditional values are threatened and that delinquent behavior appears to be spiraling out of control.

Before I make my case that character education is a time-consuming frill, however, a bit of history is necessary to demonstrate its societal, rather than its pedagogical, origins.

Character Education Since the Beginning off the Century

Character education was initially introduced as a curriculum into our schools around the turn of the century and was retained for a few decades thereafter. The waves of immigration of that time worried many established Americans who feared the immorality and lawlessness of the incoming hordes. Moral education in the schools was one way to help prevent thievery and vandalism by inculcating moral values while the children were still young. Such education was also seen as a defense against the increasing secularization of American society as a consequence of its growing industrialization and urbanization.

After World War I, the demands for character education subsided. For one thing, immigration was greatly curtailed so the worries on that score lessened. In addition the newly emerging social sciences tried to distance themselves from religion, regarded as unscientific. For example, Gordon Allport at Harvard argued that personality (a system of measurable traits) rather than character (a system of unmeasurable values) was the proper subject for psychological

Child Care Information Exchange, November 1998, pp. 6, 8–9. Copyright 1998 by Exchange Press Inc. (WA). Reproduced with permission of Exchange Press Inc. (WA) as conveyed via Copyright Clearance Center. References omitted.

investigation and, by extension, for educational consideration. The post World War I rejection of moral education was aided and abetted by the research of Hartshorne and May in the late 1920s who demonstrated that moral education was unrelated to children's moral behavior. Finally, the growing evidence of the virulent racism and anti-semitism in Nazi Germany, and its strong support in this country (e.g., Henry Ford and Father Cauglin), made concern with morality a highly sensitive topic.

For all these reasons and probably more, moral education was all but defunct in our schools until the 1960s. The events of the 1960s—the Vietnam War, the Civil Rights Movement, the Women's Movement, and Watergate—all served o once again raise our moral temperature.

More heat was generated by social science with the research of psychologist Lawrence Kohlberg who elaborated and extended Piaget's studies of moral development to include the advanced morality of adulthood. The timing was fortuitous because of the heightened awareness of the social, educational, and economic inequalities in our society. Kohlberg's work was widely disseminated and became required reading in our psychological and educational psychology textbooks and the basis for much new research on moral development, as well as new programs of moral education and "values clarification" in our classrooms.

Although the new moral education initiatives were largely instigated by the moral and value conflicts of the '60s, they were aided and abetted by other societal changes. With the movement of women into the workforce, the increased rate of divorce, and a growing number of single mothers and fathers, parents had less time to engage in moral and values training at home Character education programs, introduced to counter the social inequities brought so violently to the surface in the 1960s, have now been appropriated to fill the void left by the growing decline of moral training in the home. What began as a reaction to a societal crises was continued as a remedy for changes in the family. Schools are now expected to compensate for the diminished role of parents as purveyors of mural values and virtues.

Why Character Education Curricula Are Ineffectual

In preparation for writing this article, I did a web search and found hundreds of character education sites. These sites included: a variety of character education partnerships; character education curriculum projects; character education resources; character education fur children of the world; and a character education home page. Clearly, character instruction is now a major enterprise for many educators all over this country and around the world. To reiterate the theme with which I began, the preoccupation with moral education is both ineffectual and needlessly time consuming.

Character education is ineffectual because it attempts to use our schools to solve social problems that originate elsewhere. Using the schools in this way has not worked in the past and is not likely to succeed now. School busing, for example, did not solve the segregation and racism problems in our society, and one might make the case that they may have made them worse.

Busing didn't work because the adults in children's lives did not integrate. Parent of white children did not entertain African-American parents in their homes nor vice versa. At home, children could such get virulent racist messages that might undo any positive experiences they had at school. Children learn racism, much as they learn tolerance, from parents and other significant adults, not from one another. Peers can reinforce these attitudes but not create them.

I believe a similar argument can be made for the uselessness of character education. First of all, it is not even clear what we mean by such education. My thesaurus, for example, has 53 entries for "character." The most common definition, the one employed in educational circles is that of the "good person" who exemplifies such virtues as honesty, truthfulness, fairness, generosity, locality, and fidelity. Many character education programs focus upon honesty and fairness, which are values that are basic to the society of schools. Yet even if we concentrate upon these values, two major problems remain. One of these is developmental, the other is situational.

With regard to the development of honesty and fairness, we need to first recall that children's understanding of these values changes with age. School-age children, for example, make up hypotheses (sometimes called lies) to explain certain events such as their having lifted something from a store. Once their hypotheses are formed, children really believe in them and often bend the facts to fit them. What is a lie from an adult standpoint is really not a lie from the perspective of children's construction of reality. This does not mean we condone either taking things (dishonesty) or lying (untruthful-ness) but only that we take account of developmental considerations.

When, for example, children confront us with a hypothesis as to how something came into their possession, the best approach is to leave the question open and to check out the hypothesis with the child—not to assume dishonesty and untruthfulness.

This example illustrates a couple of points about effective character education. First, to be effective, such education must take place in the context of a lived experience. Secondly, the most powerful lesson is the teacher's modeling of fairness and lack of prejudgment. The child's hypothesis about how he or she obtained something may in the end be true. By not rushing to prejudgment, and by giving the child the opportunity to elaborate and to test out his or her hypothesis, the teacher provides a model of objectivity and fairness that the child can internalize and use as a guide in future, similar situations. Moral values are best taught by example in meaningful, everyday situations.

The second issue in moral education is that moral behavior itself is very situational. In my college classes I often present my students with two different moral dilemmas. One of these places them in a phone booth where they discover that, thanks to a fault in the connection, they can call anywhere in the world without putting money in the coin slot.

The other situation puts them in the college bookstore at the checkout counter where a friend is at the register. While engaged in conversation, the friend inadvertently gives the student the wrong change, $10 too much.

Most students say they would take advantage of the phone company's largesse but not of their friend's mistake. They explain that the phone company overcharges them anyway and that they are entitled to the free calls. On the other hand, because they believe the friend will have to make up for the register shortfall out of his or her pocket, they would return the extra money.

There is thus a clear difference between moral knowledge and judgment and moral behavior. To the extent that character education is intended to instill moral knowledge and judgment, it will have little or no impact upon children's choices in problematic situations. There is simply no close connection between *knowing* what is right and what is wrong and *doing* what is right and what is wrong, Sometimes this comes about because of value clashes. For example, our desire to tell the truth may conflict with our loyalty to a friend when the truth might get him or her into trouble. Moral dilemmas of this sort are the rule, not the exception.

Conclusion

The current time and effort spent in character education is largely wasted and uses up precious time that could be much better spent in other instructional activities. The hope that character education curricula in our schools will help reduce the immoral behavior of youth flies in the face of what we know about the chasm between moral knowledge and moral behavior.

This is not to say, however, that effective moral education does not take place in our schools. It does. As I suggested above, character is best taught not by a curriculum but rather by example. Teachers—who are competent, caring, and sensitive to children's needs—are the best purveyors of moral values. In the end, taking some of the pressures off teachers, and supporting and encouraging them in their efforts, will do more for character education than any curriculum ever could, or ever will.

POSTSCRIPT

Should Character Count?

In recent years, there has been a renaissance in interest in teaching self-discipline as a means of motivating students to be better behaved. This may be due in part to the decline in the role of organized religion serving as a paragon of morality and as a repository for moral teaching. This institutional change has left a void. Some would say that character education has developed to fill that moral chasm by identifying character traits that define the moral American citizen and that could guide the self-discipline of the next generation of students. Some critics of character education would characterize the major goal of character education programs as indoctrination. Proponents argue that the role of schools in character education is to instruct students in the democratic beliefs and virtues that have made America great. The goal of character is to prepare students to be good citizens both in and out of the classroom, both as students and as adults.

What is obvious about the character education debate is that there are no simple answers. There never are when it comes to issues of ethics and morality. One fundamental issue that would appear to be central to this controversy over whether character education should be taught is whose virtues or values should be taught? Should the values and virtues be chosen by the school, the teachers, the students, or the parents? Or should a combined decision-making process be attempted? Can character education be sensitive to the cultural differences in our schools, or is character nothing more than a rigid set of postulates that must be followed despite the cultural, religious, racial, or ethnic context? If character development is a matter of exposure to values and the ethical decision-making process, how should schools respond if students do not arrive at the ethical decisions that schools would like? For example, what happens if students arrive at the ethical conclusion that all forms of diversity should be tolerated on the school campus? What happens if this tolerance flies in the face of current state statutes and school mission statements? Should schools reteach character development until the students "get it right," or should students be allowed to hold their own beliefs about ethical situations as long as they are based upon their own value systems? Some would invoke claims of "secular humanism" if this situation were allowed to persist. Some would say that students should adopt the values of their parents and are not capable of arriving at their own values-based decisions.

Another problem that character educators encounter is whether moral behavior is situational or whether it is a character trait. If moral behavior is a character trait, then one must question the extent to which this trait is open to modification. In addition, it is not clear how character changes depending upon the cognitive developmental capacity of the students being instructed.

For example, surely preschoolers do not have the same moral capacity as abstract-thinking later adolescents. On the other hand, if moral behavior is situational, then perhaps students could learn the principles of character education but be unable to apply them in specific situations or come to the "wrong" decision given the personal dynamics of a specific ethical dilemma.

A third obstacle to character education arises when one considers how character education should be taught. Should students be instructed in the elements of good character as in learning a code of good conduct that the school proffers? If that were the case, then the role of the teacher would be to teach and for the students to learn and practice the code of conduct. Teachers would reinforce students for demonstrating those designated virtues. On the other hand, if character education is a process whereby students learn a decision-making model for moral behavior, then schools must be willing to accept the fact that students have some role in self-determination and self-discipline. In this framework, students would be encouraged to "question authority," as the car bumper stickers herald. This approach calls for a measure of individual freedom and student freedom of dissent from popular views. With the indirect approach, students would be given the reasoning, problem solving, and principles of ethics that could inform their own ethical conclusions. Schools give up control under these conditions.

Despite the challenges to character education, the notion that students live in a classroom community where they participate in a social contract with other students, and where they have rights and responsibilities is appealing. Character education is also appealing as a preventive strategy for classroom-management problems. In addition, an important part of indirect methods of character education is problem solving, which has been proven to be a valuable tool in many forms of classroom management. Perhaps the most compelling feature is that the decision to teach character education takes a lot of character on the part of schools too. Character education says that there are virtues that we as a school hold dear and that we want to encourage these virtues among our students. Taking a stand in public education by committing to character education can be a risky business precisely because it is difficult to please all of the public all of the time. Perhaps, that is why character education has primarily been the domain of private, religiously based schools.

For excellent reading on the history and foundations of character education, the following text is recommended: B.E. McClellan, *Moral Education in America: Schools and the Shaping of Character from Colonial Times to the Present* (Teachers College Press, 1999). An excellent source of information on a program to develop character among students is T. Lickona, *Character Matters: How to Help Our Children Develop Good Judgment, Integrity, and Other Essential Virtues* (Touchstone, 2004).

Office of Safe and Drug-Free Schools

The Office of Safe and Drug-Free Schools is an organization of the federal government that provides financial assistance for programs related to drug and violence prevention, develops policies, and assists with creating a national research agenda on preventing drug use and school violence.

```
http://www.ed.gov/about/offices/
        list/osdfs/index.html
```

American Association of School Administrators

The American Association of School Administrators (AASA) is a professional organization developed for national and international educational leaders. The mission of this organization is to support and develop effective school system leaders who are dedicated to the highest quality public education for all children. This site provides a collection of crisis management and response plans from various states as well as articles that are specifically related to safe schools.

```
http:www.aasa.org/issues_and_insights/safety/
```

National Education Association

The National Education Association addresses the importance of parental involvement with education. There is a strong correlation between parental involvement and a student's academic and behavioral success within the school setting. This site provides parents with a better understanding of testing, specific subject areas, and how to become more involved with their children's school.

```
http://www.nea.org/parents/
```

The ERIC Clearinghouse

The ERIC Clearinghouse is an organization sponsored by the Council for Exceptional Children in order to disseminate research-based information. This online document takes a comprehensive view of school-wide behavior management in terms of recent research. Effective behavior supports, unified discipline, and placement options are discussed.

```
http://ericec.org/digests/e563.html
```

American Civil Liberties Union

The American Civil Liberties Union Web site provides information related to the constitutional rights of students and discusses these rights in terms of recent court cases.

```
http://www.aclu.org/StudentsRights/
        StudentsRightsMain.cfm
```

PART 3

School-Wide Management Strategies

*B*ehavior management is not only important in the classroom, it is important at the school and district levels as well. School-wide and district-wide behavior-management programs provide needed support to the strategies that teachers apply in their own classrooms. Without a broad school-wide plan for increasing positive student behaviors (such as social skills) and for decreasing inappropriate behaviors (such as bullying), more severe student misbehaviors are likely to manifest and maintain themselves within a school setting. Research-based behavior-management systems are also imperative because they provide for ongoing education and for a back-up management plan outside of the classroom for more serious student behaviors, such as aggression. These school-wide management interventions have included bully-proofing education, cultural sensitivity training, parent education, and profiling potentially violent students. Not all of these systemic interventions for misbehaving students have been met with universal acceptance, however. Many strategies and policies are implemented within school buildings and across districts that appear to be appropriate responses to issues of school safety or behavior management. However, in many cases, we find negative aspects of policies and practices that are potentially harmful to some students. Some have claimed that certain school-wide interventions restrict student rights. The issues discussed in this section address the major areas of school-wide behavior-management interventions and their ramifications for students. The following issues are thought-provoking in terms of school-wide management strategies.

- Can Bully-Proofing Change School Climate?

- Are Culturally Sensitive Practices Attainable?

- Are Parent Education Programs Effective?

- Can Profiling Help Identify Potentially Violent Students?

- Are Schools Violating Student Rights?

ISSUE 11

Can Bully-Proofing Change School Climate?

YES: Christopher H. Skinner, Christine E. Neddenriep, Sheri L. Robinson, Ruth Ervin, and Kevin Jones, from "Altering Educational Environments Through Positive Peer Reporting: Prevention and Remediation of Social Problems Associated with Behavior Disorders," *Psychology in the Schools* (vol. 39, no. 2, 2002)

NO: Charles Go and Shelley Murdock, from "To Bully-Proof or Not to Bully-Proof: That Is the Question," *Journal of Extension* (April 2003)

ISSUE SUMMARY

YES: Christopher H. Skinner and Christine E. Neddenriep are professors at the University of Tennessee. They suggest that perhaps a more effective strategy to change school climate and social relationships through bully-proofing is to teach peers to report the incidental positive behaviors of bullies rather than tattle on their misbehaviors.

NO: Charles Go is a youth development advisor in Alameda, California, and Shelley Murdock is a community and youth development advisor in Pleasant Hill, California. They contend that students can be both bullies and victims as part of a continual cycle and that bully-proofing programs that label youths as either victims or bullies will not "fix" the bullies.

Bullying is reported each day in America's public schools. Bullying can take on many forms, including verbal bullying or teasing, physical bullying or fighting, shunning or deliberately excluding individuals from a group, and sexual bullying.

One strategy that has been offered to reduce the incidence of bullying behavior is bully-proofing, whereby classes or the entire school are taught how to avoid bullying, deescalate bullying when it does occur, respond to bullies on the spot, and report incidents. Many programs have been developed to prevent and intervene in cases of bullying, and many schools have zero tolerance policies. Their response to bullying typically is to punish the offender. Of course, schools cannot punish a bully if they do not first receive a report of bullying. Consequently, it is not unusual for victims of bullies to be taught assertiveness and how not be victimized. They have a right to be treated with respect, not to be teased, not to be pushed and shoved, not to be deliberately shunned, and not to be sexually harassed. When these behaviors occur, they have the right to ask the bully to stop. If the bullying does not stop, then they have the right to leave the situation and report the incident to an adult in the school such as a teacher, counselor, or principal. Some students perceive the act of reporting the bully as "tattling," which is a social taboo many students cannot overcome. The problem with the typical "report and punish" approach to bully-proofing is that punishment fails to teach more socially appropriate replacement behaviors to the bully, such as friendship-making skills, problem-solving conflict resolution, and anger control. Furthermore, so-called bullies who express antisocial behaviors often do not feel accepted and supported by the school. As a result, they become socially isolated and have little opportunity to practice the very social skills in which they are deficient.

As a slight modification and alternative to the status quo of bully-proofing, Skinner and cowriters recommend that bullies be reinforced for prosocial behaviors through two procedures called positive peer reporting and "tootling." With positive peer reporting, students are taught to recognize and report prosocial behaviors of a target child, which are then reinforced individually with tangible rewards by the teacher. An extension of positive peer reporting is tootling. With tootling, classmates work toward a group contingency once a group goal has been met for frequency of helping behaviors. The philosophy is that if victims can tattle or report on the inappropriate behavior of a classmate, then perhaps they can be taught to recognize and tootle or report the prosocial behaviors as well. Could it be that positive reporting of prosocial behavior is a beneficial enhancement and addition to the traditional "report and punish" bully-proofing that is epitomized in tattling? Skinner and his colleagues seem to think so, and given the inexpensiveness of this procedure, this strategy could be applied not just to individual classrooms but to the entire school.

A competing perspective is expressed in the research and commentary provided by Go and Murdock. They contend a major assumption of all bully-proofing programs is that it is relatively easy to identify the bully and victim even when the teacher was not present during the bullying event. It is further assumed that if bullies are punished or taught new replacement skills the bully will cease and desist and become a better classroom citizen. Go and Murdock suggest that two alternative possibilities must be taken into consideration. First, it may not be so easy to distinguish the bully from the victim because a student can alternate between being a bully and then a victim. Second, it may be possible that bullies are bullying others because they have been bullied. When bullies are victimized, they may be reacting to their sense that they are not safe and do not know what to do to make themselves safe. Could such a finding mean that attempts to bully-proof schools are in vain? Is it fair to label a student a bully when in fact he or she may be retaliating from being bullied yesterday? Perhaps bully-proofing programs need to be rethought with this information in mind.

Christopher H. Skinner, et al. **YES**

Altering Educational Environments through Positive Peer Reporting: Prevention and Remediation of Social Problems Associated with Behavior Disorders

Within educational environments, punitive systems have been designed to prevent students from engaging in incidental antisocial behaviors. These systems often take the form of rules that identify unacceptable behaviors and specify consequences and processes for delivering those consequences contingent upon those behaviors. Typically, these systems are independent group contingencies. The group aspect of the contingency indicates that each individual receives the same consequence (i.e., punishment) contingent upon the same antisocial behavior. The independent aspect signifies that students are punished for their own behavior, rather than their peers' behavior. These characteristics of rules address concerns about fairness and equal protection, and make students responsible for their own behavior.

In many instances, these punitive systems may be effective in preventing students from engaging in incidental inappropriate behaviors. However, as with any contingency, these independent group punishment procedures are not equally effective across all children. When specific children persist in engaging in incidental antisocial behaviors, despite these punitive systems, they may be referred for psycho-educational assessment and diagnosed as having behavior or social-emotional disorders. Thus, in some cases, children with behavior or social-emotional disorders are children who engage in high rates of incidental antisocial behavior under environmental conditions designed to punish those behaviors.

In this article, punitive systems designed to prevent antisocial behavior are described and analyzed. After discussing possible negative side effects associated with using peers to monitor and report incidental antisocial behavior of their classmates with behavior disorders, the focus shifts to procedures designed to encourage incidental prosocial behavior. Methods, theory, and research related to two procedures that encourage peers to monitor and report classmates'

From *Psychology in the Schools*, vol. 39(2), 2002, pp. 191–202. Copyright © 2002 by John Wiley & Sons. Reprinted by permission. References omitted.

appropriate prosocial behaviors are reviewed and analyzed. Finally, directions for future applied and theoretical research are provided.

Peer Participation with Independent Group Punishment: Tattling

One problem associated with punishing antisocial behavior is that educators often have difficulty monitoring antisocial behavior. Because incidental antisocial behaviors are often punished, one way to avoid punishment is to avoid detection. Hence, students may still engage in these antisocial behaviors, but learn to avoid being caught. In this manner, merely punishing antisocial behaviors can teach children to avoid detection and be sneaky, rather than to behave prosocially.

Because it is not possible for teachers to monitor each student's behavior, students help with this task by observing and monitoring their peers' behavior and reporting inappropriate behaviors to authority figures, (i.e., tattling). This entire system, based on peer monitoring and reporting of classmates' incidental inappropriate behaviors (i.e., tattling), seems to have evolved in a similar manner in diverse education environments.

Social Side Effects of Punishment and Tattling on Students with Behavior Disorders

Research suggests that teachers spend more time focused on and responding to inappropriate as opposed to appropriate behaviors. By encouraging students to monitor and report peers' incidental antisocial behavior, tattling and punishment procedures may have a similar effect on students. This may cause social problems for students with behavior or social-emotional disorders who may engage in higher rates of these incidental antisocial behaviors than their peers. Specifically, encouraging peers to monitor and report *only* incidental antisocial behaviors may inadvertently cause classmates to ignore prosocial behaviors of students with behavior or emotional disorders. Consequently, peers' perceptions of classmates with social-emotional or behavior disorders may be inaccurate, unbalanced, and harsh because they are based primarily on inappropriate behaviors. In this manner, tattling and punishment systems may encourage students to socially reject or neglect peers with behavior disorders.

Research examining peer rejection has typically utilized classroom sociometric measures, asking children to nominate peers whom they like the most and peers whom they like the least. Children receiving a high number of liked-least nominations and a low number of liked-most nominations are considered rejected. Students who receive few nominations (either liked-least or liked-most) are considered neglected. Those students who demonstrate aggressive, withdrawn, or inattentive-hyperactive behaviors are more likely to be rejected. Also, those students who are socially rejected and/or neglected by peers are more likely to experience other school-related problems, engage in delinquent behavior, and experience mental health problems. Furthermore, the additive effect of both aggression and peer rejection in boys has been shown to produce the poorest outcome in adolescence.

Many students who are rejected or neglected by peers may repeatedly experience their peers' rejection over time, despite changes in peer groups. Coie and Dodge found that almost half the children rejected in fifth grade continued to be rejected over a 5-year period. Thus, peer rejection may be persistent and children may continue to reject some children despite changes in the student's behavior over time. In addition, the emotional impact of peer rejection detrimentally increases as the peers' rejection is persistently experienced over time.

Social Skills Mastery

School psychologists, educators, teachers, and counselors have tried different strategies and procedures to enhance the social interactions of students with behavior disorders. Perhaps the most common procedure is to teach students appropriate prosocial behaviors. Researchers have developed social skills curricula that are designed to teach appropriate social behaviors. Additionally, some teachers develop and plan their own lessons designed to teach prosocial behaviors such as sharing, waiting their turn, and asking for and/or giving help.

Researchers who reviewed studies on social skills training have found that such procedures are effective for teaching students appropriate social behaviors; however, few have shown that such procedures alter students' incidental social behaviors within their natural environment. There are several reasons why social skills training programs may not result in improved social behavior within natural environments. One limitation of most social skills training programs is that they focus primarily on skill acquisition. In many cases, children with behavior disorders may have already acquired social skills. Thus programs that are designed to teach skills may be addressing the wrong problem. Acquisition is merely the first stage of skill learning. If skills are to be functional, students must maintain those skills, become fluent with those skills, be able to generalize those skills to appropriate natural environments, and adapt those skills as environmental contingencies change.

Opportunities to practice acquired skills have been shown to be effective and may be necessary to enhance skill fluency and maintenance. When these opportunities to practice acquired skills occur in natural environments, then generalization and adaptation may be enhanced. This is particularly important with respect to social skills mastery. Because social environments are fluid and cues are subtle it is difficult to identify behaviors that will consistently be reinforced, punished, or ignored across social settings and over time. For example, interrupting a speaker with a funny remark may yield social reinforcement (e.g., laughter) in some situations, while in other subtly different situations such behavior may be socially punished. Thus, successful use of social skills requires students to constantly alter their behavior based on subtle and perhaps difficult to discriminate differences across social situations. . . .

Unfortunately, research suggests that students who are rejected or neglected (e.g., students who are aggressive, withdrawn, or hyperactive) may receive fewer opportunities to develop their social skills within natural incidental social situations. For example Ladd, Price, and Hart showed that negative peer nominations at the beginning of the school year predicted less peer contacts at midyear. Similarly, negative nominations at midyear predicted fewer peer contacts at the year's end. Thus, these students who need more exposure to natural social learning situations in order to develop and master social skills may actually receive fewer opportunities to have their social skills shaped through incidental learning. This lack of social interaction can adversely impact on the development and mastery of social skills, thereby hindering the students' ability to establish subsequent social relationships. . . .

Encouraging Incidental Prosocial Behaviors

While preventing and decreasing inappropriate behaviors is an important goal in any school system, schools are not meeting their educational goals if inappropriate behaviors are not replaced with appropriate behaviors. Merely helping students acquire appropriate social behaviors is unlikely to be sufficient to prevent or alleviate social problems, unless those behaviors are supported in their natural environments.

Incidental Learning: Taking Advantage of the Situation

Incidental opportunities for teaching and shaping appropriate prosocial behaviors often occur in educational environments. For example, a student may notice that a peer's pen has run out of ink. Without prompting, the student quietly offers the classmate one of her/his extra pens. An unplanned, incidental prosocial behavior has just occurred. Although the teacher could have used this incidental event as a learning experience for the students involved and their peers, there are several reasons why this opportunity to praise, reinforce, encourage, and/or teach these appropriate prosocial behaviors is often lost.

The most basic reason why the previously mentioned prosocial behavior (i.e., offer a peer a pen) could not be used as an incidental learning experience is because the teacher did not directly observe the prosocial behavior. In many instances, teachers may not directly observe prosocial student-helping-student behaviors. Even when teachers directly observe prosocial behaviors, they may not be aware or cognizant of these behaviors. Teachers often spend so much time and cognitive energy monitoring students' inappropriate behaviors that they may not be aware of all the incidental prosocial behaviors that occur during daily classroom activities. . . .

A final problem with the previously described scenario is that, even if the teacher did observe the appropriate behavior and reinforce the student for helping her/his classmate, other students may not learn from this event. Punishing students who misbehave may suppress misbehavior rates in other students. In a similar vein, reinforcing students for behaving prosocially may increase prosocial behaviors in other students. However, this learning is unlikely to occur if other students are not informed of, or do not directly observe, their peers' appropriate behaviors and the related reinforcing event.

Positive Peer Reporting and Tootling

Beginning in their early school years, without formal instruction, students learn to monitor and report incidental instances of peers' inappropriate behaviors (i.e., tattle). If students can learn at an early age to monitor and report peers' inappropriate behaviors, then they could learn to monitor and report appropriate prosocial behaviors.

Grieger, Kaufman, and Grieger published the first study in a line of research documenting the benefits of having peers report prosocial behaviors of other peers. In this first study, kindergarten teachers told their students (90 participants) that they would be given an opportunity to name one student who had done something nice for them during play period. Students who were named were then allowed to select a happy face. Providing opportunities for peers to report prosocial behaviors resulted in increased cooperative play and decreased aggression.

Next, two promising peer-reporting procedures will be described that may encourage students to focus on and report their peers incidental prosocial behaviors. The first procedure, positive peer reporting (PPR), has been shown to be effective in altering the social status of students with behavior disorders and enhancing the quality and quantity of social interactions in these students.

The second procedure, tootling, is designed for classwide implementation. The tootling and PPR programs described are based on similar assumptions. PPR is based on the assumption that some students with social interaction problems may have acquired appropriate social skills (e.g., they engage in appropriate social behaviors), but may be ostracized by their peers because they engage in these behaviors less frequently than their peers. Thus, the goal of the program was to enhance reinforcement for prosocial behaviors by having peers publicly acknowledge those appropriate behaviors that were already occurring in the students' natural environments. Furthermore, it was hoped that public acknowledgement would alter peers' perceptions of targeted students.

The tootling program is based on the assumption that peers spend so much time monitoring classmates' socially inappropriate behavior that they may not be aware of, respond to (e.g., socially reinforce), or value incidental prosocial behavior. Thus, this program is designed to enhance classroom environments by increasing the probability that peers will engage in incidental student-helping-student behaviors and also increase their awareness of and appreciation for these behaviors.

Positive peer reporting (PPR).   PPR is a relatively simple procedure that has been used in residential and educational settings to enhance peer interactions and peers' perceptions of students who are socially rejected or neglected. . . . Instead of reporting inappropriate instances of behavior, children are told they will have the opportunity to earn reinforcement (e.g., tokens) for noticing and reporting a peer's positive behavior. The procedures are then explained to the students. First, a target student is randomly selected as the "Star of the Week." During a specified time of day (e.g., last 10 minutes of homeroom), a group session is held where peers are given the opportunity to report aloud any positive behaviors they observed from this student that day. Students typically require training with practice and feedback in order to learn to identify examples of positive behaviors (e.g., Billy shared his soccer ball at recess). The behaviors reported must be deemed by the teacher as specific and genuine in order for the child reporting the behavior to receive reinforcement.

Ervin et al. used PPR to improve the social interactions and acceptance of a 13-year-old socially rejected girl in a residential treatment setting. The procedure consisted of classmates reporting positive behaviors of the target child to the teacher (but with the target child present) during the last 5 minutes of math class. Peers' positive comments were awarded points that could be exchanged later for tangible or activity reinforcement. . . . Results showed that PPR decreased negative and increased positive social interactions with peers. Additionally, peers rated this student more favorably following the intervention.

Subsequent studies conducted at Boys Town investigated the effects of similar interventions. Across these three investigations, there were nine target students. Data suggest that the PPR procedure or a modified version of this procedure increased the percentage of positive interactions with peers for all nine target students and enhanced peers' perceptions of target students for eight of the nine target students. Additionally, Bowers et al. found that a modified PPR procedure decreased negative peer interaction rates.

Researchers also investigated the effects of PPR on social initiation and cooperative statements. Robinson found that PPR increased target students' rates of initiating social interactions with peers. However, the peers who provided the positive reports did not increase their social initiations with target students. Jones et al. evaluated the effects of PPR on students' cooperative statements. Target students were three children from the middle school who were identified by their mathematics teacher as rejected. Three times per week, cooperative learning groups of three were formed to complete math assignments. Following cooperative learning activities, 5-minute sessions were held where peers provided the target child with positive comments about behaviors and the target child was encouraged to provide three reciprocal comments to peers. During cooperative mathematics activities, all three participants' mean percentage of cooperative statements increased during intervention phases, with median peer acceptance ratings also increasing from preintervention to postintervention. . . .

Classwide positive peer reporting: Tootling.   During the PPR procedure, students are encouraged to focus their attention on a specific student's prosocial behavior. Another program developed by Skinner, Cashwell, and Skinner employs interdependent group contingencies to reinforce the entire class for reporting incidental prosocial behaviors of any classmate. . . . The tootling and PPR programs share some common procedures. With both procedures, brief group instruction is used to train students to report positive behaviors and reinforcement procedures are used to encourage students to report peers' incidental positive behavior.

There are several procedural differences between PPR and tootling. PPR targets specific children, often children who have been socially rejected. During tootling, all children are encouraged to monitor and report prosocial behaviors of *all classmates*. The behaviors targeted are also somewhat different. PPR targets general positive behavior while during tootling only reports of classmates actively helping peers are reinforced. During PPR, students publicly report target student positive behaviors. However, during tootling, students write reports of students helping students on index cards throughout the school day and turn them into the teacher at the end of the school day. Thus, reports of peers' positive behaviors are not made public. Finally, the tootling procedure employs an interdependent group contingency and feedback system similar to Ervin et al., where all tootles or reports of peers helping peers bring the class closer to earning a group reward. Despite several procedural and conceptual differences, both procedures are designed to structure the environment that enhances peer relationships.

Research on the tootling program has just begun. Two studies have been published where tootling procedures were implemented in general education second-grade and fourth-grade classrooms. These studies have shown that students can quickly learn to provide these written reports and the interdependent group contingency increases rates of tootling, while students report many incidental instances of prosocial behavior (e.g., a second-grade class provided 72 reports one day). Researchers continue to investigate the impact of tootling on students' social behaviors and perceptions of peers.

Summary and Future Research

Students with behavior disorders may be more likely to be rejected by peers and receive fewer opportunities to interact with peers in unstructured social situations. Thus, these students may receive fewer opportunities to develop and master their social skills. PPR has been shown to increase both positive peer interaction rates and target students' initiation of social interactions, while decreasing negative peer interaction rates of socially rejected children. Longitudinal research is needed to determine if these enhanced social interactions occasioned by PPR procedures provide neglected or rejected students with more opportunities to develop social skills within natural environments and whether these additional interactions can improve their social skills and their social status.

Although research on PPR and tootling is promising, there are several important limitations that should be addressed by future researchers. To date, PPR and tootling studies have shown that peer relations or peer reporting rates return to baseline levels when intervention is withdrawn. . . . One potential reason that behaviors might return to baseline levels is the failure to address stimuli (both antecedent discriminative stimuli and reinforcing stimuli) for behaviors that compete with socially desirable behaviors. Thus, future researchers should determine if reducing reinforcement for socially inappropriate behavior in natural environments may enhance the impact of these programs. Also, researchers should determine if gradually fading PPR procedures enhances maintenance.

Research designed to describe and specify the causal mechanism responsible for positive outcomes should allow research to enhance these outcomes. It seems unlikely that a few praise statements each day could have much impact on social interactions if taunting, tattling, and intimidation continue at other times and in other settings. However, empirical data from the studies reviewed and anecdotal information from teachers suggests that praise and tootling transfer to more natural contexts and reduce inappropriate peer inter- actions outside of the structured praise sessions. In order to more fully account for the behavioral processes responsible for improved peer relations, future researchers should determine what other specific social behaviors are occa- sioned in target students and peers by PPR by collecting data on social interac- tions during class, at breaks, or at recess.

Understanding the causal mechanism(s) responsible for positive out- comes has applied implications. During the PPR program, peers provide *public* verbal praise to students with behavior disorders for their incidental prosocial behaviors. This public praise may cause students with behavior disorders to ini- tiate more social interaction with children. Additionally, students who provided the verbal praise may be less likely to neglect or avoid the students who they praised. If outcomes are dependent upon the public praise statements, then one way to enhance these procedures may be to increase rates of public praise. Fur- thermore, if public praise is the causal mechanism, then children whose behav- ior is sensitive to peer attention may respond more favorably to positive peer reports. However, for other students (e.g., high-school students) public praise may be aversive stimuli (e.g., embarrassing stimuli). Therefore, public PPR may not be effective with these students.

It is possible that these PPR procedures are effective primarily because they increase peers' awareness of a rejected student's prosocial behavior. If this is the case, then outcomes may be enhanced through procedures designed to maxi- mize students' awareness of all prosocial behaviors (e.g., tootling). Regardless, identifying the causal mechanism(s) responsible for the effectiveness of PPR procedures should enhance practitioners' ability to predict conditions (e.g., stu- dents, context, social environments) where PPR procedures are likely to be effec- tive and strengthen these procedures in order to maximize their effectiveness.

Proactive punishment systems may be needed to prevent incidental anti- social behavior. The attention and energy placed into developing and imple- menting these systems may teach children that inappropriate behaviors are unacceptable, but do little to suggest that society values incidental nondramatic prosocial behaviors. Thus, future researchers should determine if implementing programs designed to encourage prosocial behaviors may help shape adults who value and respect incidental prosocial behaviors.

Few simple yet effective strategies for promoting positive peer relations have been developed. The current article describes research and theory that sug- gests that encouraging peers to monitor and report their classmates' incidental prosocial behaviors can enhance social relationships. The procedures described require little time as children quickly learn the steps in monitoring and report- ing a peer's appropriate behavior. Furthermore, implementing these procedures within educational settings requires few additional resources. Thus, the strate- gies described in this article might also prove to be efficient and effective school- based prevention procedures. Given the heightened sensitivity in our culture to problems that may stem from peer isolation and rejection (e.g., school vio- lence), future research should investigate whether schoolwide implementation of these or similar procedures may prove to be effective proactive strategies for promoting adaptive skills and enhancing peer relationships among all children.

**Charles Go and
Shelley Murdock**

To Bully-Proof or Not to Bully-Proof: That Is the Question

Introduction

Since the tragic Columbine school shootings, many programs have been created to prevent such incidents from recurring. The most popular response is the institution of "bully-proofing" programs in schools. Programs are based on the assumption that in school, youth are either bullies or victims. It is further assumed that if we identify all the bullies and provide intervention services, we will prevent a repeat of the Columbine school shooting.

Using a psycho-social theory of development, where the focus of adolescence is identity formation, we hypothesize that it is possible for youth to be both a bully and victim as part of their developmental process. Second, a youth could have been bullied, and, in response, he/she would bully others. Both could have implications in the way we intervene and design our youth violence prevention programs. In the study discussed here, we examined the relationship between a youth's sense of safety and bullying and victimizing behaviors.

Methods

Participants

We surveyed youth in three middle schools in a diverse urban city in California.

- Questionnaires were administered to 3542 students; 1137 (45%) were completed and returned.
- The majority of the youth were ages 14 (29%), 13 (31%), 12 (28%), and 11 (12%).
- Fifty-seven percent were females; 43% were males.
- Ethnically, 35% identified as African-American, 36% as Hispanic/Latino, 13% as Asian, 12% Mixed/Other, 2% American Indian, 1% Pacific Islander, and 1% White non-Hispanic.
- School grade level showed that 36% were in eighth grade, 29% in seventh grade, and 35% in sixth grade.
- Youth self-reported most frequently received letter grades were A's (22%), B's (39%), C's (32%), D's (5%), and F's (2%).

From *Journal of Extension*, vol. 41, no. 2, April 2003. Copyright © 2003 by Extension Journal. Reprinted by permission. References omitted.

Measurements

The questionnaire was anonymous and confidential. It was translated into Spanish and Vietnamese. Teachers administered the questionnaire during a class period at the respective middle schools. To allow for national and state comparisons, we used highly reliable and valid questionnaire items from the National Youth Risk and Behavior Survey and the California Healthy Kids survey. For the purposes of this article, we focus on whether the middle school youth engaged in the following behaviors within the past 12 months:

- School perpetrator/bully behaviors (been in a physical fight, used a weapon to threaten or bully someone, sold drugs to someone, been arrested by the police or sheriff)
- School victimization (been offered, sold or given illegal drugs, been teased or "picked on" because of your race, gender, disability, been threatened or injured with a weapon, had things stolen or deliberately damaged)
- Safety issues (how safe do you feel in school, how safe do you feel in your neighborhood).

Results

Frequencies

In response to the perpetrator or bullying questions, 36% of the youth reported having been in a physical fight; 9% used a weapon to threaten someone; 6% sold drugs; and 11% had been arrested in school at least once during the past year. In answer to the victimization questions, about 20% of the youth reported they were offered, sold, or given drugs at least once in school during the past year. Also within the past year and occurring at least once, 24% had been teased because of their race; 10% had been threatened with a weapon; and 29% had property stolen.

When asked about sense of safety, approximately 84% of the middle school youth reported feeling very safe or safe in their neighborhoods, while approximately 16% felt unsafe or very unsafe. Further, about 70% reported feeling very safe or safe while at school, while 30% reported feeling unsafe or very unsafe. This suggests that youth felt safer in their neighborhoods than in their schools.

Bivariate

Using t-tests, we found significant gender differences in the perpetrator behaviors. On average, boys were more likely to be involved in perpetrator behaviors (fighting, using a weapon, selling drugs, being arrested) than girls . . . were. But note that we also found no significant gender differences in victimization and safety issues. Despite their perpetrator behaviors, the boys were just as likely to be victimized as girls and were no more likely to feel safe than girls were.

Further, the perpetrator/bully variables were significantly correlated. Youth who had been in a physical fight were more likely to use a weapon, . . . sell drugs . . . , and have been arrested . . . than those who had not been in a fight.

Of note is that youth who had been arrested were more likely to have used a weapon . . . and sold drugs . . . than those not arrested.

The victimization variables were also significantly correlated. Youth who were offered or sold drugs were more likely to have been teased . . . , threatened with a weapon . . . , or had property stolen . . . from them.

Interestingly, there were also significant relationships between the perpetrator/bully variables and victimization variables. For example, youth who had been arrested were more likely to have been offered or sold drugs . . . , teased . . . , threatened . . . , and had property stolen. . . . On the other hand, youth threatened with a weapon were more likely to have been in a physical fight . . . , used a weapon . . . , sold drugs . . . , and been arrested. . . .

School safety was significantly correlated with neighborhood safety. . . . Also note that both school safety and neighborhood safety were negatively correlated with all the youth perpetrator and victimization variables.

Conclusion

We hypothesized that a youth could be a bully and a victim as part of the developmental process. The correlation analyses indicate that there is indeed a significant relationship suggesting that a youth can be a bully and a victim in a continual cycle. This finding lends support to the notion that adolescent youth, in the process of the struggle between social/cultural issues and the individual, may exhibit both bully and victim behaviors.

In addition, the data suggests that adolescent bully and victim behaviors may be coping responses to the youth's lack of a sense of safety. It is interesting to note that school and neighborhood safety were negatively correlated with all the youth perpetrator and victim behaviors. Perpetrators do not feel any safer than their victims do. It is most likely because they know their victims may retaliate.

Implications for Programs

Both findings have distinct programmatic implications. The first finding implies that programs that simply label youth as victims or bullies and then seek to "fix" the bullies will not work. Depending on the situation, both behaviors may be exhibited by the same youth. A more effective approach may be to monitor the youth's development (e.g., process of youth identity formation) over time and across incidents. The focus should be supporting and providing youth with positive youth development activities that allow them to try out a variety of roles and challenge norms without the use of bullying behaviors.

The second finding indicates that programs that focus on youth bully and youth victimization may not be effective. Instead, we suggest that programs should focus on increasing all youth's sense of safety because sense of safety decreased both youth perpetrator/bully behaviors and victimization behaviors.

POSTSCRIPT

Can Bully-Proofing Change School Climate?

An age-old lament has been applied to bullying: "Boys will be boys." Some teachers and parents parrot this axiomatic statement as if bullying is an inevitable state of affairs, as if bullying is a rite of passage, as if bullying could actually toughen the spirit of the victims. Sadly, such tacit acceptance of this long-time problem behavior provides no relief for the victims and no behavioral improvement for the bully.

Levels of violent student-student behavior have increased in recent years. An estimated 160,000 U.S. students miss school each day due to bullying (Lee, 1993). The fallout from bullying can be generational since youths who bully others are more likely to have children who are bullies (School Safety News Service, 2001). An estimated 6 percent of all students are bullied and also bully others (Department of Education, 1998). Bullying among school children is quite common. Nearly one in four students in grades four to six will be bullied, and nearly 80 percent of middle and high school students report being bullied. Students who are friendless are more likely to bully others than children with a strong support group and those who participate in extracurricular activities.

Bullying has made it to the front pages of our newspapers and our TV screens due in part to the infamous school shootings at Columbine. These perpetrators were at once both bullies and victims. They sought revenge against other students who had ridiculed them. There is yet another reason why bullying has become front-page news: According to a 1999 case heard by the U.S. Supreme Court, school districts may be held liable if they do not keep all students emotionally and physically safe while they are attending school.

Correlates of bullying behavior are all negative outcomes, as might be expected. Male bullies have positive attitudes toward using more violence. Females may coach their friends to ostracize an individual whom they have bullied to add insult to injury. Long-term bullies have a 60 percent chance of a criminal conviction by age 24. Victims of bullying are truant from school, express negative attitudes toward school, and have a higher frequency of mental health problems (Epstein, Plog, and Porter, 2002).

Many approaches to reduce the incidence of bullying on school campuses have been offered. One of the most well-known researchers on the topic of bullying (Olweus, 1991, 1993, 1996) has suggested that all good bully interventions should be schoolwide and all such programs should have three components: developing awareness; involving teachers, parents, and students in finding solutions; and creating a caring school climate through promotion of a "caring majority." Olweus has developed an approach called "bully-proofing" where schools teach students about the various forms of bullying, they teach students to report bullying, and the schools provide the appropriate punishment.

The question of whether bully-proofing can change school climate does not have a straightforward answer—it's complex and less than perfectly clear. On the one hand, Skinner proposes that "tootling" or reporting of helping behaviors of bullies may be an efficient modification and enhancement to the "report and punish" regimen of bully-proofing since the reporting now focuses on the improvement of the prosocial behavior of bullies. On the other hand, positive peer reporting may create the caring majority that Olweus deems so important to any viable bully-prevention program. The problem arises as to who will develop and carry out these bully-prevention programs. Could tootling be effective at the high school level? Would victims of bullying actually be willing to find "good" in their perpetrators and report it? Wouldn't victims of bullying want to avoid the bully and perhaps reap their own form of retribution? While tootling is an interesting concept, one has to wonder about the viability of its implementation in schools. Would teachers be willing to provide a group contingency for positive improvement of group social skills? How could teachers be motivated to see the deescalation of bullying, both in and outside their classrooms as part of their personal and professional responsibility? What role could a building plan play in the development of a schoolwide plan to manage bullying?

Go and Murdock's data suggest that programs such as "bully-proofing" may not be reliable because it can be impossible to identify who is the bully and who is the victim unless a teacher was present at the time. Bullies are sneaky and will often bully in the shadows or will extort their victims not to tell. Victims may exact revenge against their bully and become bullies themselves. It is not uncommon for both parties to point their fingers at each other when asked the inevitable question, "Who started it?" Perhaps, a more equitable approach might be to problem-solve and develop a solution-based contract with agreed-upon actions and contingencies for performance between the two parties that would reduce the probability of future bullying. Perhaps students prone to involvement in bullying relationships should be encouraged to learn new social skills and develop a more positive support group by being involved in extracurricular activities either in or outside of school. Perhaps instead of focusing on individual student safety, schools should focus on all students' sense of safety—when students feel generally safe at school, bullying and victimization tend to decrease.

For an excellent treatise on bullying and a bully-proofing program to prevent it, check out D. Olweus, *Bullying at School: What We Know and What We Can Do* (Blackwell, 1993) and D. Olweus, *Bullying Prevention Program* (Center for the Study and Prevention of Violence, 2000). Two other valuable intervention packages for management of bullying include: U.S. Department of Education, *Preventing Bullying: A Manual for Schools and Communities* (U.S. Department of Education, 1998) and H. Hops Walker and C. Greenwood, *Recess: A Program for Reducing Negative-Aggressive Behavior* (Educational Achievement Systems, 1993).

ISSUE 12

Are Culturally Sensitive Practices Attainable?

YES: Laurel M. Garrick Duhaney, from "Culturally Sensitive Strategies for Violence Prevention," *Multicultural Education* (Summer 2002)

NO: Judy Groulx and Cornell Thomas, from "Discomfort Zones: Learning about Teaching with Care and Discipline in Urban Schools," *International Journal of Educational Reform* (January 2000)

ISSUE SUMMARY

YES: Laurel M. Garrick Duhaney is an assistant professor in the department of educational studies at the State University of New York at New Paltz. Garrick Duhaney suggests that when culturally sensitive behavior-management strategies are employed, school violence can be reduced.

NO: Judy Groulx and Cornell Thomas are associate professors in the department of educational foundations and administration in the School of Education at Texas Christian University. They contend that teachers working in urban schools enter the field of teaching with misconceptions about students of color and consequently feel uncomfortable in their behavior management because their university coursework did not adequately prepare them.

There is a large disparity between the cultural backgrounds of many teachers and their students. Groulx and Thomas report that approximately 90 percent of our teachers today are Caucasian and from a middle-class background. This is in sharp contrast to the rising percentage of minority students in America's schools. Projections estimate that Caucasian students will soon become the overall minority when compared to non-Caucasian students (representing just under 50 percent of the total school population). Therefore, cultural understanding and sensitivity must be an important factor in classroom management.

Variations in cultural backgrounds often include subtle and sometimes not so subtle differences in attitudes, beliefs, and values. When considering classroom and behavior management, cultural differences can include variations in expectations regarding adult/child interactions, communication, discipline procedures, and expectations with regard to fairness and respect. All of these areas are represented within behavior-management strategies both at the classroom and school building level. If educators are not aware of these differences or do not respect and respond to these differences, additional difficulties with student behavior can be created.

A strong component of behavior and classroom management within schools is to assist with violence prevention. When considering decreasing and hopefully eliminating violent behaviors, educators must consider the behavior-management strategies that are being utilized. Inappropriate or ineffective responses to behavior can quickly increase the incidence and severity of unwanted behaviors from students. Various research articles have commented on the inequitable number of punitive management strategies (i.e., suspensions) dispensed to minority students. The question about what causes the unequal distribution of punishment has been debated. Can it be that minority students display behaviors that are less acceptable than non-minority students? Or, is it that there may be some stark differences in values and attitudes? The latter seems to be a likely explanation. Cultural differences are a factor. Educators and students do not see eye-to-eye on every issue. For example, if students perceive their teacher as being disrespectful to them, they may respond in an equally disrespectful manner, thus increasing the likelihood that the teacher will respond punitively.

The rising contrast in cultural backgrounds between educators and students begs the question as to whether educators are implementing behavior-management methodologies that complement the diversity of their students. Based upon their research, Groulx and Thomas report some stark differences between new teachers and their students in urban areas. They describe many young teachers as entering the classroom with a "well-intentioned colorblindness" and view issues such as the curriculum and behavior management with ideals of equity and democracy. In other words, they see the world as fair and set the values of the classroom around their values. In contrast, many of their students do not see the world as impartial and do not have values that directly correlate with many educators.

On the other hand, Duhaney's article takes a much different approach. She brings to light various differences between minority students and their needs as well as addressing appropriate methods toward making classrooms and schools culturally sensitive. The focus in this article is proactive. She discusses creating an environment that fosters comfort, safety, and respect. She also discusses intergroup harmony and group-oriented behavior-management programs.

There are various questions surrounding this issue. For example, to what degree is culturally sensitive behavior management present within our schools today? Do cultural differences play a major role in some of the behavior-management difficulties that educators and students experience? Is it imperative that teachers spend more time during their education learning about these differences and how to respond? If so, who is responsible for this education?

YES 🡐

Laurel M. Garrick Duhaney

Culturally Sensitive Strategies for Violence Prevention

Violence is initiated by those who oppress, who exploit, who fail to recognize others as persons—not by those who are oppressed, exploited, and unrecognized.

—Paulo Freire, "Pedagogy of the Oppressed"

The problem of violence in schools, which is part of the general problem of violence in society, has not only become a nationwide dilemma, but is viewed as a critical cultural and educational issue facing schools today. Schools seem preoccupied with the stereotypic negative images of Black adolescent violence which depict these students as lawless, morally depraved, and outside the social order. Moreover, concerns for violence have become, for some school administrators, the highest priority for reform and intervention. For example, in the 1993–1994 school year, the Association of California School Administrators made efforts to reduce violence in schools their top priority.

Although violence in schools is portrayed by some (e.g., the electronic and print media) as having increased significantly in the last few years, reports from the field remain mixed. A survey of ten innercity public high schools in California, Louisiana, New Jersey, and Illinois found one out of every five students (and one out of every three males) reported being shot at, stabbed, or otherwise injured with a weapon at school or on their way to or from school. Furthermore, a 1994 survey by the National School Boards Association of 700 suburban, urban, and rural school districts revealed that 75 percent of the administrators believe violence in the schools is worse now than it was five years ago.

However, youth crime and violence have been declining for several years. Based on gross numbers and percentages of all crimes, youth crimes peaked in the mid-1970s. Since then, the number of youth arrests has dropped significantly. By 1990, the youth arrest rate had fallen to 15 percent of all arrests, down from a high of 26 percent in 1975. Therefore, "the perception that this generation of young people is more violent than ever in terms of raw numbers is suspect, if not simply false."

Likewise, the stigmatizing portrayal of poor children of color, especially African-American males, as being the chief perpetrators of violence in schools

From *Multicultural Education*, no. 4, Summer 2000, pp. 10–17. Copyright © 2000 by Caddo Gap Press. Reprinted by permission. References omitted.

rather than the main "victims" of punishment in school is troubling. Evidence of a disproportionate number of African-American students—students classified as educationally or trainable mentally retarded, or as students with behavioral or emotional disorders—and in some cases, Latino students, who are subjected to various forms of school discipline, can be found in many school districts nationwide.

National and local studies report that culturally and linguistically diverse students are more likely than White students to receive corporal punishment, are up to three times more likely to be suspended, and are three to eight times as likely to be expelled. Based on these disturbing statistics, it appears that under the facade of ridding the public school of violence, children of color are too often being barred from school and unfairly treated.

Unquestionably, schools should be made safe, even if the analysis of crime statistics suggests an overstatement of the problem of school violence. Notwithstanding the crime statistics, several schools have implemented violence prevention programs in an effort to maintain safe schools. But although social science researchers highlight the significance of cultural factors that can either strengthen or weaken the likelihood of a violent response to problem-solving, in the main, violence prevention programs have the tendency to either overlook, over-simplify, or underrate the potency of cultural factors.

Violence prevention programs should address specific cultural concerns, including cultural values and norms, and should be preventative and remedial rather than overly punitive. Furthermore, such programs should seek to build strong interpersonal and caring relationships between teachers and students.

Given schools' abstraction with Black adolescent violence and their need for greater recognition of the importance of cultural factors as a key to the success of their violence prevention programs, this article will discuss cultural influences on behavior, theoretical assumptions about culturally diverse students, and culturally sensitive behavior management strategies that educators might consider in their efforts to curtail school violence. These strategies are intended to be culture-specific and culture-fair, to humanize school environments, and to encourage a sense of community and collective responsibility. An underlying premise of these suggestions is that by changing their own thinking and ways of behavior, teachers may have the greatest impact on their students' violent behaviors.

Cultural Influences on Behavior

Schools are locations where we find polyethnic classrooms. As a result, one way of trying to understand cultural influences on behavior has been to focus on the diversity of ethnic groups that exist in the classroom. An examination of ethnic influences on behavior finds substantial differences in behavioral ratings from different social classes, with children of lower-class backgrounds receiving higher problem scores and lower social competence scores than those from higher-class backgrounds. It, therefore, appears that the insinuation that African-American and Hispanic adolescents display more violent behaviors than White adolescents is a false impression, since class seems to influence behavior more than ethnicity.

A second way of attempting to ascertain cultural influences on behavior is for schools to be cognizant of, and attentive to, cultural orientations and nuances. Culture is, in part, an aggregation of beliefs, habits, values, and practices that form a view of reality. Culture serves as a filter through which students view and respond to the behavioral demands of the classroom environment. Cultural diversity is important, but particularly so, when students from African-American, Hispanic, Native-American, and Asian groups are members of the classroom community. The reality is that the cultural orientation most prevalent within students of color differs significantly from that of the White middle-class classroom community. While African-American students' fate is controlled, in large measure, by invisible standards based on skin color, the White classroom community perceives that society reinforces and acknowledges their existence. When these two orientations meet in the classroom, the incongruent behaviors that emerge can lead to violent confrontations.

A third way of probing cultural influences on behavior is to examine the deculturalization of the culturally and linguistically different child. Broadly conceived, deculturalization is a process by which individuals are deprived of their culture and then conditioned to other cultural values. Deculturalization does not mean a loss of a group's culture, but rather failure to acknowledge the existence of their culture and the role it plays in their behavior.

As a result, there is a need for an approach that addresses the issue of deculturalization. Such an approach requires, at a minimum, that teachers restructure the curriculum to reflect cultural diversity. It is, however, important to note that inclusion of different cultural experiences in the curriculum may not be embraced by some teachers and students. To circumvent such a problem teachers should recognize subtle and unintentional biases in their own behavior, and begin instruction with an emphasis on self-awareness of each student's own culture.

Schools' deculturalization or assimilation policies can result in classroom misbehavior and opposition to teachers. Teachers who engage in deculturalization practices can drive students from the safety of their ethnic groups. At the same time, many of these teachers fail to draw minority students into a sense of belonging in the wider society. Similarly, some teachers who engage in deculturalization practices have the tendency to ignore minority culture and replace it with the macroculture or larger American culture.

Theoretical Assumptions about African-American Students

Given the differences in cultural orientations of students of color and the White, largely middle-class classroom community, educators should focus more attention on cultural dimensions of behavior when they plan disciplinary measures to curb students' violent behaviors. The following theoretical assumptions about cultural groups underscore recommendations for culturally sensitive behavior management strategies that are presented later in this article. While many of the theories may apply to other cultural groups, the theoretical assumptions delineated here primarily focus on African-American students as a way to focus the discussion.

Heritage of Caring

African-American students have a heritage of caring. Studies of African philosophy chronicle an emphasis on interdependence and cooperation among tribal and community members. Yet, African-American students' heritage of caring, connectedness, altruism, and selflessness are threatened by racial and economic oppression, by a history of vilification, exclusion, and unequal educational opportunities which has resulted in a growing cynicism among African-American children and youth at the incongruities of the social justice system.

These circumstances, along with "elements of self-denigration, the fraying of social bonds, the loss of a shared sense of community" and the "nihilistic threat of meaninglessness, hopelessness, and helplessness," feed destructive behavior, crime, and violence. Given this depiction, schools might focus their violence prevention programs on at least one psychosocial task of adolescence, moral development. In so doing, violence prevention programs would address African-American students' hunger for self-value, meaning, and identity and would serve to "cultivate systems of culturally based values that guide just and caring social behavior."

Behavioral Style

Schools have meticulously designed behavioral norms that require conformity, submissiveness, quietness, teacher-focused activities, and individualized, competitive noninteractive participation of students. However, many African-American students are non-compliant to these expectations and may prefer activity (referred to by Boykin as behavioral verve), speak out of turn, and be teacher/adult-directed. This conduct is often viewed as disruptive behavior within the school culture.

As a result, teachers and African-American students have divergent views about appropriate classroom behavior. This divergence results in some teachers being overcritical of African-American students' behavior, and African-American students receiving more negative behavioral feedback than their White counterparts. This differential treatment has evoked expressions of astonishment, bewilderment, and anger over the negativism evident in teachers' judgments of African-American students. Moreover, in an attempt to elicit the behavioral responses they value, some teachers focus on control and classroom management issues, which contributes to African-American students being disproportionately represented in the suspension, expulsion, and discipline statistics of schools.

Research has demonstrated that African-American students' walk affects educational decisions and placement. Neal and Bridgest investigated the effects of African-American adolescent males' movement styles on teachers' expectations and reactions. One hundred thirty-six predominantly female, Euro-American teachers were shown a videotape of non-standard walk (characterized by a tilted head, swaggered bent posture, one foot dragging, an exaggerated knee bend) and standard walk (characterized by a straight head, erect posture, coordinated leg and arm swing, a steady brisk pace).

The teachers were given a Likert-type scale and asked to rate their reactions and expectations to the students' walk. Results of the study showed that teachers perceived students with nonstandard movement styles as: (a) lower in achievement than students with standard movement styles; (b) higher in aggression than students with standard movement styles; and (c) more likely to need special education services than students with standard movement styles.

Communication Style

Cultural variations in communication also impact behavioral norms and expectations in the classroom. Researchers have noted that African-American students often discover that their communication styles differ from those promoted by the school. African-American speakers are perceived to be more animated, more persuasive, more active in the communication process, and thus more confrontational because of this style. Some teachers have observed that African American students, when asked questions, appear to be caustic or sarcastic in their responses.

On the other hand, many teachers who are predominantly White, tend to be oriented toward a passive style, which gives the impression that they are detached and literal in the use of the language. For example, researchers report that teachers who are White give more verbal and nonverbal criticism and display more negative nonverbal behavior when interacting with African-American students than with other students. These stylistic variations may invoke feelings of anger, aggression, and violence in African American students.

Culturally Sensitive Behavior Management Strategies

The search for solutions to the problem of violence in schools has resulted in myriad strategies that range from more intrusive measures such as the installation of metal detectors in schools to other less punitive approaches such as conflict resolution and mentoring programs. Though some of the less intrusive strategies for reducing violence in schools have proven successful, the overall momentum appears to be biased in favor of more intrusive approaches that disproportionately impact students of color.

Although numerous strategies have been designed for students who display violent and aggressive behavior in schools, several of these approaches do not appear to be specifically designed for students from culturally diverse backgrounds. The strategies presented here are intended to be culture specific, non-punitive, and non-intrusive. These culturally sensitive behavior management strategies advocate that teachers create humane environments for learning; know their students; empower students from culturally diverse backgrounds to develop a positive self and racial identity; build intergroup/intragroup harmony; support students in their moral development; abandon punitive and psychological practices that contribute to violence; and promote opportunities for involvement of culturally and linguistically diverse families.

Create Humane Environments for Learning

There is evidence of destructive interpersonal dynamics between some teachers and the students with whom they work. Many student-teacher relationships are characterized by apprehension, distrust, and disrespect rather than compassion, regard, and sensitivity. Schools need to create more humane learning environments, not only to counter escalating violence, but to transform social relationships in school, so that culturally diverse students feel more connected, esteemed, and empowered. Schools should foster a strong sense of collective responsibility and should enable students to become self-actualized. To become self-actualized, individuals need to be accepted and to develop self-esteem.

The classroom should be perceived by students as a community—a place where students feel cared about and where they are encouraged to care about each other. The students should sense that they are valued and that they matter to each other and to the teacher. Teachers who employ strategies that facilitate a classroom community should:

a. emphasize care and trust above restrictions and threats;
b. ensure that unity and pride (of accomplishment and in purpose) replace winning and losing;
c. ask, help, and inspire each student to live up to such ideals and values as kindness, fairness, and responsibility;
d. provide each student multiple opportunities to think about, discuss, and act on their values, while gaining experiences that promote empathy and understanding of others; and
e. meet each student's need to feel competent, connected to others, and autonomous.

Know Your Students

Teachers can successfully build a humane learning environment by getting to know the students with whom they work. There often are great gaps between how students and teachers perceive each other and how students perceive themselves.

A clarity of perception may be obscured by the fact that many teachers, especially those who work in urban school districts, do not reside in the communities in which they work and therefore know very little about their students or the community in which their students live. Furthermore, many of the students who live in and attend schools in urban communities differ in race, and have vastly different experiences than the majority of their teachers who are White, female, and from middle-class backgrounds.

Yet several schools operate on the premise that teachers should view all students the same, although there are numerous studies on teacher expectations that have demonstrated that race, class, and gender have considerable influence over the assumptions that teachers hold toward students. Moreover, an unpleasant result of the lack of knowledge that teachers have about their students is the reality that some teachers fill the knowledge void with stereotypes based upon what they have read, heard, or seen in the media—which is often negative (e.g., African-American students are violent and come from dysfunctional homes). This negative stereotype often leads to a breakdown in communication and deterioration in the relationship between teachers and their students.

There are several strategies that teachers can use to enhance their knowledge of students from culturally diverse backgrounds. Banks provides the following examples of books that teachers can read: Balm in Gilead: Journal of a Healer, Sara Lawrence Lightfoot's biography of her mother, one of the United States' first African American psychiatrists; and Bank's Teaching Strategies for Ethnic Studies, historical overviews of various U.S. ethnic groups. Banks also recommends Peters' Eye of the Beholder, a videotape that uses simulations to show the cogent effects of discrimination on adults. The videotape features Jane Elliott, who attained fame for her well-known experiment in which she discriminated against children on the basis of eye color to teach them about discrimination. Eyes on the Prize II, the award winning history of the Civil Rights Movement, is a film that contains historical and sociological information about the experiences of different ethnic and racial groups that teachers can view.

Teachers can analyze and clarify their values regarding the readings, video, and film by asking several questions such as: How did the book, film, or video make you feel? Explain how the book, film, or video give you a better understanding of students from diverse backgrounds?

Empower Culturally Diverse Students to Develop a Positive Self and Racial Identity

A stable concept of self, both as an individual and as a member of a racial minority group, is essential to the healthy growth and development of one's self. Development of a positive cultural identity involves synthesis of external experiences within the context of cultural, school, and societal influences. Therefore, programs that seek to curtail students' violent behaviors should also help them to feel good about themselves and their race, and equip them with the skills to repudiate racism and unacceptable negative stereotypes.

People of color—African Americans, Hispanics, and Native Americans—are distinctly subordinate economically and their children are particularly hard-hit by poverty. For example, in 1988 the percentage of African-American children living below the poverty line was three times that of White children. Many of these children not only live in poverty, but they attend schools that are in need of human and material resources. Poverty and certain theoretical orientations (e.g., deficiency orentation) can eclipse these students' sense of personal and racial pride, and may cause them to physically harm those who thwart their sense of dignity and racial pride.

Furthermore, some students from culturally and linguistically diverse backgrounds have to deal with the opinion that as members of poor families, they are genetically flawed and that their failures in school reflect that flawed inheritance. They (especially African-American students) also face those who attribute their failures in school to factors ranging from the use of Black English to a lack of moral integrity and stability. Using the cultural deprivation model to explain the lower achievement of students from culturally different backgrounds has led educators to disproportionately label a substantial number of African-American students as mentally retarded and assign them to special education classes. Furthermore, teachers who subscribe to the cultural deficiency model often give up on African-American students and have low expectations for them.

The deficiency model prevents many teachers from critically examining their beliefs and attitudes, and to reflect upon how these might contribute to violent and non-productive behaviors among culturally and linguistically diverse students. Culturally and linguistically diverse students who live in impoverished conditions, who attend poor schools, who must face negative views about their race and of themselves, and who daily confront racism, could benefit from teachers who hold positive views of them and of their race. They could benefit from teachers who get to know more about their backgrounds and their strengths, and from teachers who use this knowledge as a bridge to the dominant culture.

Without the help of supportive teachers, many students from culturally and linguistically diverse backgrounds will feel stripped of their dignity and sense of self, and will feel powerless to act in non-violent ways towards individuals and conditions that cheat them of their values.

Strategies that teachers can employ to foster students' self and racial identity include the use of multiethnic content that incorporates positive and realistic images of racial and ethnic groups in teaching materials in a consistent, natural, and integrated fashion. However, teachers need a sound knowledge of the history and culture of ethnic groups in order to successfully integrate multiethnic content into the school curriculum. Teachers can involve students in vicarious experiences with students from various racial and ethnic groups.

For example, teachers can utilize films, videos, children's books, recordings, and photographs to expose students to members of different racial, ethnic, and linguistic groups. Vicarious experiences are especially important for students in predominantly White, Latino, or African-American schools or communities who do not have much direct contact with members of other racial, ethnic, and social-class groups. Teachers also can provide positive verbal and nonverbal reinforcement for the color brown.

Moreover, students can be empowered to develop positive self and racial identities by teachers who not only promote positive expectations for students' achievement, but who use cooperative learning in their classes. Cooperative learning situations can help to reduce prejudice which negatively impacts the self and racial identities of a significant number of students from culturally and linguistically diverse backgrounds. Allport, in his contact learning theory, noted that prejudice can be reduced if interracial contact situations or cooperative learning situations encompass these characteristics

a. students experience equal status;
b. encounters are cooperative rather than competitive;
c. students have shared goals; and
d. contacts are sanctioned by authorities such as teachers, parents, and principals.

Banks notes that research on cooperative learning activities indicate that Mexican-American, African-American, and White students develop more positive racial attitudes and choose more friends from outside racial groups when they participate in group activities that have the conditions identified by Allport.

Build Intergroup/Intragroup Harmony

As racial and sex-based crimes continue to increase in our society, it becomes increasingly important for teachers to promote intergroup and intragroup harmony in their classrooms. Teachers need to provide the knowledge and skill training to empower not only their culturally diverse students, but all students, to work and socialize with members of their own cultural groups as well as students of different cultural and social groups.

Curricular activities designed to promote intergroup and intragroup harmony will help students to resist crime and violence, not only in their schools, but in their communities. Classroom teachers should try to develop in their students respect, appreciation, and tolerance for individuals and groups that are different from themselves. When teachers develop in their students positive attitudes toward tolerance and acceptance of diversity, there will usually be more intergroup and intragroup harmony in their classrooms.

To facilitate intergroup and intragroup accord in the classroom, teachers need to establish a supportive, warm classroom environment that will enable all students to feel comfortable, to let down their defenses, to communicate honestly, and to discuss their differences. Equally important, teachers also need to help students to understand the causes of intergroup and intragroup conflicts and to determine what they can do to eliminate them.

Creative drama can be used for students to experience potential sources of conflict, and to accomplish intergroup and intragroup harmony. Creative drama provides students the opportunity to think about and identify with the point of view of another person. Teachers can ask students to generate a list of topics or situations that may cause intergroup and intragroup conflicts. Some topics that might stimulate class discussion and students' involvement include the following:

- If a student called a member of a different racial or linguistic background names, would you join in? What would you do if you were the victim of the name calling?
- A student has accused you of "acting black" or of "acting white," what will you say or do?
- It has been rumored that a classmate is of a different sexual orientation. A group of students has planned to attack him or her after school. What will you do?
- Your parents only allow you to befriend members within your own racial and ethnic group but you want to socialize with members of other groups. How could you persuade your parents to change their minds?

Guidelines should be established for setting up successful creative dramatic situations for reducing intergroup and intragroup conflicts. Pamela Tiedt and Iris Tiedt provide the following guidelines for setting up a successful role-play situation, and these approaches can also be applied in establishing creative dramatic situations.

- Use props such as hats or masks to help students assume their roles.
- Set a time limit.
- Give [students] an explicit, detailed situation or explanation to get started. Or have them draw the plot elements (who? what? where?) out of a box.
- Start with focused sessions before more complex situations.

Support Students in Their Moral Development

As recipients of injustice and a lack of care from the general society, students of color stand to benefit from an emphasis on moral development. Educators should examine how cultural norms affect the differential experiences, values, and construction of caring.

While some researchers suggest that adolescents are deeply concerned with moral values and principles, others intimate that adolescents, in organizing their moral thinking and feelings, have highlighted issues of unfairness in their accounts of real-life moral conflict and choice. In light of the importance of moral development, violence prevention programs should:

a. encourage students of color to develop their sense of justice and help them to act in accord with their values;
b. guide students of color toward moral solutions that acknowledge their own and others' rights and relational experiences; and
c. empower students of color to assume leadership opportunities afforded by participation in school government and extracurricular activities, particularly those that emphasize social commitment, political advocacy, and democratic change.

A significant number of traditional American schools relegate moral development to the aspects of the hidden curriculum rather than to the overt curriculum. However, moral development should be taught explicitly. One way that this can be accomplished is to help students to resolve moral dilemmas by allowing them to think through conflicting and realistic moral issues. These moral dilemmas and issues can be presented to students through the use of carefully designed case studies.

Abandon Punitive and Psychological Practices That Contribute to Violence

A sometimes overlooked practice that may contribute to violence is victimization of students by teachers, administrators, and other school staff. A legally and socially sanctioned disciplinary practice such as corporal punishment, which is most often used with students of color and students from low socioeconomic backgrounds, may increase students' ire, hostility, and aggression against peers, school staff, and school property.

Moreover, these practices may cause profound, and sometimes long-lasting, emotional harm. While there are mediating factors (e.g., respect for the person administering the punishment, parent support) that prevent some students who receive corporal punishment from becoming aggressive, almost all violent delinquents have a history of receiving corporal punishment.

Psychological maltreatment, which may consist of various verbal assaults such as systematic bias, prejudice, emotional neglect, derogatory statements, sarcasm, ridicule, and name calling, is another practice that may contribute to violence in schools. Data reveal that many students are recipients of, and witnesses to, verbal maltreatment which may result in feelings of frustration, anger, and thoughts of revenge against perpetrators of verbal abuse.

As with corporal punishment, the frequency of psychological maltreatment in schools is often a function of the socioeconomic status of the school population. Research suggests that culturally diverse students from low-income families are at greater risk than are other students of being psychologically abused.

A few studies suggest that there may be a correlation between verbally abusive educator behavior and increases in student misbehavior. Many educators, psychologists, and students are aware of incidents where teachers and administrators' verbal assaults triggered violence in already aggressive students. Three retrospective studies suggest that more than one-half (50 to 60 percent) of students experienced at least one occurrence of maltreatment by an educator which lead to some stress symptom, including aggression. A series of studies which used the My Worst School Experience Scale identified 105 specific psychological reactions to both physical and psychological maltreatment.

Group-oriented behavior management strategies (e.g., group free-token responsecost system, token economy systems) can serve as positive alternatives to punishment and corporal punishment. Salend identified several advantages of group-oriented systems, such as the promotion of group cohesiveness and cooperation among class members, support of the class in solving classroom problems, adaptability to a variety of behaviors and classrooms, and presentation of a positive, practical, and acceptable method of dealing effectively with peer related problems.

Teachers should be prepared to deal with several potential problems when using group-oriented strategies. For instance, sometimes one student will prevent the class from receiving reinforcement by repeatedly engaging in violent and disruptive behavior. If this should occur, the offender should be removed from the group system and dealt with individually.

Moreover, since group-oriented management systems can result in scapegoating and negative peer pressure, teachers should carefully observe the impact of the group systems on students and implement strategies (e.g., select target behaviors that are of benefit to every student in the group, using heterogeneous grouping) to minimize these negative effects.

Affective education strategies (e.g., humor, values clarification, life space interviewing, class meetings, peer mediation) can be used in place of punitive and psychological practices that contribute to violence. These strategies can assist students in clarifying their values and feelings, and can provide students insights into their attitudes.

Affective education strategies seek to promote students' behavioral, emotional, and social development, and help students to resolve conflicts by enhancing their self-concept. Another benefit of affective education strategies is that they empower students to feel good about themselves. Moreover, "students who feel good about themselves and know how to express their feelings tend not to engage in problem behaviors."

Promote Opportunities for Involvement of Culturally and Linguistically Diverse Families

Culturally and linguistically diverse families play an important role in supporting their children and youth who exhibit problems of aggression and violence. Parent and family support networks are often the bridge to long-term solutions to problems of aggression and violence. Culturally and linguistically diverse parents and families should have direct involvement in developing and implementing intervention programs. Their participation in schools' disciplinary programs is crucial, especially when one considers the increasingly diverse school population and the relatively limited cultural and linguistic diversity among teachers.

Culturally and linguistically diverse families possess a wealth of knowledge that can enhance educators' understanding of children's behavior. Families also have preferences for disciplinary strategies that school personnel might well consider in their efforts to discipline children. Research has shown that in Asian cultures, where it is important not to embarrass the family, children may be disciplined by the use of ostracism, limited verbal feedback, and shame.

African-American families, families from the Caribbean, and other cultural groups may employ disciplinary measures such as the "evil eye," verbal humiliation, and denial of privileges. Some Native-American families believe that the behavior of each member reflects on the community and a child's misbehavior may result in the child apologizing to group members, being excluded, or temporarily being the target of verbal disapproval.

Schools should empower culturally and linguistically diverse parents and families to participate in overall efforts to curb violence in schools. This is especially essential when one reviews research on parental involvement that too often shows a pattern of apathy rather than active involvement among minority families, especially African-American families.

Minority families' passivity might be attributable to feelings of intimidation from schools, resulting in their reluctance to participate in schools' violence prevention programs. Strategies for involving families from culturally diverse backgrounds in violence prevention programs include the following. First, parents and families should be included as policymakers through schoolbased parent advisory committees. Second, parents and families can be encouraged to provide support to other families with students who are exhibiting violent and aggressive behaviors. Third, for parents and families who are intimidated by schools, interactive formats consisting of one teacher and one parent or small groups may facilitate the sharing of information. Fourth, teachers can seek the input of parents and families, who for various reasons cannot come to school, in writing or they can solicit parental input over the telephone.

Conclusion

Violence of any proportion is harmful, and violence in schools is especially so. It is, therefore, important that schools try to solve the problem of school violence, not only because it results in physical and emotional scars, but because it impacts students' abilities to learn and succeed in school.

Furthermore, it is difficult for teachers to teach and for students to learn in the absence of certain standards of behavior, mutual respect, and a system of values that helps students to develop self-control and self-direction. Teachers have the power to help students of color deal with situations that can potentially cause them to act violently. As teachers plan their violence prevention programs, they should consider the inclusion of culturally sensitive behavior management strategies such as the ones delineated in this article.

Judy Groulx and
Cornell Thomas

 **NO**

Discomfort Zones: Learning About Teaching with Care and Discipline in Urban Schools

Our education students are a classic reflection of the demographic mismatch between public school teachers and their students. Approximately 90 percent of teachers are White and middle-class, while their learners consist of steadily increasing numbers of non-white, as well as ESL or bilingual children and youth, from low-socioeconomic families and neighborhoods. Like their counterparts in the research literature, our students typically begin their teacher preparation sequence of courses holding cherished images of their future careers in middle-class or affluent, mostly-White schools just like the ones where they grew up. As recently as the beginning of this decade, we used to arrange field experiences and student teaching placements for them that allowed them to stay mostly in their comfort zones. Not anymore.

Changes began with our venture into a professional development school (PDS) partnership with three elementary schools reflecting the demographics of our city: one was in a Hispanic neighborhood, one in an African-American neighborhood, and the third enrolled an even mix of Hispanic, Black, and White children. Many of the relationships we formed with teachers and administrators at our partner schools have continued, and matured, while others were ended more or less amicably as the formal grant period for the PDS project came to a close. Neither our School of Education nor our PDSs engaged in dramatic reforms or restructuring as we had initially envisioned. Yet, we were never the same. Once we had moved out of our comfort zone, we continued to seek and develop urban school collaborations and experiences for ourselves and our students. We recognized as never before that problems in urban schools are made especially complex because of the ways that schools reproduce and magnify all the shortcomings of our society. Now, we are more aware of the implications of our students' initial expectations, and as our awareness grows, so does our dissatisfaction. We continue searching for ways to guide our students' expectations in directions that will encourage them to teach in urban schools and help them learn how to do so successfully.

This study is an exploration of some disturbing findings that arose from surveys gathered during our first semester (1992) in the PDS project and up to the present, that continued to unnerve us throughout that project and that reverberate well into our current efforts to encourage our students to teach out of their comfort zones. The findings had to do with the cross-currents between learning about management and discipline, and learning about multicultural teaching. A comment made by an education student who had been placed at a PDS site for her 12-week student teaching assignment exemplifies these findings. It illustrates her personal discomfort as well as many wider and deeper concerns we face in urban teaching. In response to a survey question asking "How successfully did you learn to manage your class?" she wrote, *"Trial and error; no one guided me—I felt alone—both my teachers were black and experienced; they just told me to be mean, but they didn't say how."*

As they confront their first experience, solo and responsible for a classroom full of children, the primary concerns of many of our student teachers have to do with management and discipline, which is typical of almost all new teachers and student teachers. Discipline is hard enough with one's own children; witness the consistent popularity of books on parenting, the repeated outcries in the media about the increasing failure of parents to raise responsible, law-abiding citizens. But teachers must discipline "other people's children," a matter of enormous complexity and ambiguity as discipline concerns intersect with multicultural principles.

To openly share deep values and beliefs about one's own and others' cultures and backgrounds is excruciatingly difficult. Issues of racism, prejudice, and discrimination lurk at the edges of conversations, and frequently people do not know how to talk directly about such issues for fear of giving offense. Discussion participants may retreat into abstractions by making politically correct and socially acceptable affirmations, or they may end up on the spot, forced into a position of defending or explaining their feelings or having to act as a spokesperson for their group whether or not they believe themselves as representative of anyone but themselves. Yet, in trying to help new teachers and inexperienced administrators think through how they are going to discipline urban schoolchildren from diverse backgrounds, we must not only foster discussion, but also help shape future decisions and actions they will take, because these decisions can make all the difference in the world to the children in their care.

This study is framed around the following questions: 1.) How does the research literature on multicultural education inform teacher educators as we try to scaffold preservice teachers' and administrator candidates' experiences in learning about discipline with urban schoolchildren? 2.) What kinds of approaches can we take toward discipline and multicultural issues in our university-based teacher and administrator preparation courses? 3.) What kinds of connections can we foster in the field where we work with children, teachers and administrators in multicultural urban settings? Interspersed with these questions are data gathered from our preservice students and student teachers that lend immediacy to our analysis and validity to our questions, if not our evolving answers. Names of the actual schools referenced in student comments have been replaced with aliases.

Findings from Past Research

A rich body of research literature on multicultural education provides us with an impressive analysis of urban teaching problems. While discipline issues provided an entry point, we quickly found that there are inextricable links among many related issues. Problem areas center around preservice teachers' entering beliefs and misconceptions, the failure to interconnect multiculturalism and discipline issues with considerations of curriculum and instruction, and underdeveloped understandings of multiculturalism.

The Beliefs and Misconceptions of Entering Preservice Teachers

In urban schools, issues of discipline can quickly become tangled with issues of racism. As mentioned earlier, teachers are likely to be White and middle-class, while students in urban schools are likely to be poor and non-White. While minority children's parents prepare them to confront discrimination and prejudice as a fact of life, Whites have been brought up to believe that democratic values play out fairly in society. Those who have power are least aware of its existence. Paradoxically, they are taught to espouse equality and equity, but their idealistic beliefs can lead to dysconscious racism, a denial of White privilege along with an intention to disregard color in an attempt to be impartial. Wrote one of our students, *"I didn't really teach to individuals. I taught as if they were all equal until otherwise necessary to change thoughts about them."* This well-intentioned colorblindness may be based on a desire to act fairly with all children, but it can be as harmful as active prejudice, because it can make a person of color feel invisible. It refuses to recognize and deal with the valid experiences that nonwhites know to be true and real every day.

When our students encountered urban schoolchildren and met up with that reality, we saw two main reaction patterns. One was shock. *"It was new to work with students who couldn't afford shoes, clothes, etc. I never realized how much some parents don't support kids. Some issues I ran into were unbelievable." "Most didn't sleep enough at night." "Their social backgrounds were very far from my experience." "We need a course in counseling!" "Very different! It was a shock to see how some of those kids lived. Children were dealing with problems I never even knew about at that age!"*

A concurrent reaction was to construct a deficit model as a way to deal with the shock. Having participated in monocultural environments all their lives, many Whites of European background lack a cultural identity except to see themselves as "normal." Out of this logic develops the idea that kids or situations not within their realm of previous experience are therefore *not* normal; for example, note one student's pride in commenting that *"I learned to treat them as human beings, as normal children."* This logic further assumes that living outside the assumed "norm" causes deficiencies in school performance and automatically puts children at-risk for failure. By logical extension the child's parents and home lives are labeled deficient, as well. *"I could definitely tell which were the kids who had absolutely nothing." "The at-risk kids at Morrow Elementary come from horrible home lives. The kids that were in my room did not have normal two-parent homes. Many of their parents were in jail and had siblings who were drop-outs. The School of Ed. could not have prepared me."*

Once these two patterns of reactions develop, out of shock and a deficiency perspective, a potentially vicious cycle winds into place. Teachers are in denial that schools might be reflecting the dominance of powerful White, middle-class values and privileges. They see the effects of poverty but without acknowledging the social realities that perpetuate that poverty, they are prevented from understanding why some urban minority students decide to battle the system. Many students will do so in nonconstructive ways, by being aggressive, refusing to work, being late, or simply tuning out. In some cases, to do well in school seems to them a betrayal of their own identities. Teachers rapidly fall into a pattern of blaming children's home lives as the main detriments to learning, which makes them insensitive to ways that their own behavior as teachers, and the policies of the school might also be major factors in children's failure. "By making believe that failure is something that kids do, as different from how it is something that is done to them, and then by explaining their failure in terms of other things they do, we likely contribute to the maintenance of school failure." These insensitivities make the urban school a place where street-survival values begin to win out, where students believe it's the teachers' job to "make them learn" and teachers react by threatening suspension, or where teachers and students make a tacit agreement to trade off student compliance for academic credit, just for showing up. Demoralized teachers will then continue to see only sullen, apathetic or ill-prepared, "deficient" students, and the self-fulfilling prophecy perpetuates.

Other misperceptions develop out of the unfortunate correlation between social class differences and parental attitudes and experiences regarding school. Middle-class parents are more likely to have had some degree of success in school themselves. They know how to speak the same language as the teacher. They often know how to negotiate on their child's behalf when there are academic or disciplinary problems. They know how to read and work with their children at home. They know how to make other educational resources available to their children—the library, the museum, scouting, lessons in art or dancing or judo—and they have the means to access them. All these parental skills and privileges save their children from having to act out in school and enable them to cope and even succeed with the standard curriculum. To a teacher it may thus look like the "normal" middle-class kids not only achieve more, but are better behaved, while the others, the lower-class and often non-white kids, are "deficient," lacking not only in academic skills *but also in values.*

Broken Links

Another important factor in this cycle of discomfort and negative perceptions is a failure to see linkages between disciplinary matters and matters of instruction or curriculum. As novices, new teachers have incomplete and fragmented schemas about teaching. Their concerns are often compartmentalized: children's behavior is seen separately from their academic regimen. Even veteran teachers fail to realize that student apathy and anger might be reactions to insensitive and oppressive curricular and instructional decisions. Administrators and staff specialists also routinely locate learning and behavior problems in the children rather than in the curriculum or the school environment. Instruction, motivation, and management are a seamless whole, but many teachers don't see that. What they do see are children who are restless at best and hostile at worst. The children become the focal point of pathological inquiry; teachers see them as the problem rather than considering the wider teaching-learning process as an important source of their troubling behavior.

A test-driven curriculum exacerbates the problem. Teachers today are increasingly vulnerable to accountability pressures, which become part of a routine mentality. Test performance priorities surround them at school and may force blind conformity to a competency-driven curriculum that can quickly become boring, irrelevant, and alienating when children's individual strengths and needs are ignored. Management problems increase markedly when instruction does not allow choices for appropriate, engaging learning activities. Yet, in the "pedagogy of poverty," traditional teaching models prevail: establish learning objectives based on task analyses, give information, ask questions, give directions, make assignments, monitor seatwork, give tests, settle disputes, punish noncompliance, mark papers, give grades. Teachers relentlessly proceed in lock-step through standardized texts, scripted lessons and meaningless worksheets, while they struggle to motivate and control the children. . . .

Undeveloped Understandings of Multiculturalism

All of the above problems are compounded when the standard curriculum consists of "White studies" which continue to benefit the dominant members of our society and ignore the needs of the rest. Furthermore, the very definitions and central models that schools use for teaching, learning, and performance are geared toward the middle-class, White learner. A growing body of research suggests a wide variety of ways that instruction can be made culturally congruent so that teachers can relate more successfully with minority children's interests and ways of thinking and behaving. If taken with an essential caution against overgeneralizing, studies of different ethnic group characteristics provide many insights on the unique perspectives that can be so different and crucially important when interpreting children's behavior. . . .

Some writers have argued that multicultural teaching stops short unless the teacher also learns how to enable children from all backgrounds to critically analyze the social ramifications of their different group memberships, at school and in their future lives. Too often, multiculturalism is perceived as a strategy, a way to react *to* diversity, a means for individualizing instruction to meet only certain students' needs. Ultimately, multiculturalism has to become a pervasive mindset that aims to empower all children to understand themselves, one another, and the imperfect system in which different cultures now exist. Others argue that it is patently ridiculous to expect 22-year-old females to act as central change agents in the lives of children facing poverty, racism, and all the challenges of an unjust world. These arguments point out to us that teacher education programs need to deliberately locate themselves relative to reform and at least help their fledgling teachers gain an initial awareness of all that multiculturalism might imply.

University Coursework

Classes for students preparing to become teachers and administrators represent our first, best opportunity to promote thoughtfulness, based on awareness. While education students are away from the immediate demands of children and the incessant pressures within school contexts, we can make it our goal that they discover as much as possible about themselves, about diversity, about the nature of children and learning, and the ways of schooling.

Awareness of Beliefs

As teacher educators, we need to avoid working from deficit orientations about our own education students. We may anticipate the likelihood that they may resist or deny ideas about racism and how schools help perpetuate social injustice, but we must build on the strengths that they bring into teacher preparation, just as we hope to teach them to build on their children's strengths. With few exceptions, education students passionately declare that a primary motivation for entering the teaching profession is a sense of caring for children, but it is a naive sense of caring that is easily challenged by children and youth who don't exhibit or seem to share much joy in learning. To build positively on their initial notions of caring, we have to help educators attend carefully to their beliefs about what children bring from home to school.

Teachers who ignore, dismiss or devalue what their children bring from home are showing them a lack of respect, trust, and caring. Children should not have to earn their teachers' respect in order to access teachers' full attention, expertise, and commitment. Rather, teachers should begin with automatic, full respect and afford all children with their very best efforts. All children enter school with plentiful sets of knowledge, but that knowledge too often goes unrecognized. It may not be in English, or it may be incompatible with current school ideology. Children may be dirty when they come to school, may lack the social graces we prefer, and may possess a weak vocabulary and poor academic skills. Their curiosities are deemed unacceptable, and their stores of information on standard academic topics are seen as hopelessly inadequate. Tracked into the "low" group, they get instruction that is watered down and lessons that rarely move beyond basic, low-level skills. As their strengths are discounted and their opportunities for success diminish, children's disillusionment and anger grow, and they withdraw or become proficient at disrupting the teaching and learning process. Thus they behave in ways unconducive to what their teachers perceive to be "normal," right, and good. Neither the child nor the educator may understand this behavior until we see it as an outcry for help. . . .

When teachers automatically give respect to children, they maintain high expectations for all of them. They may modify instructional methods, but in ways that enhance opportunities for making connections, helping students bridge gaps between what they already know and what they are to learn. Trust grows from the assurance that the teacher will work from the children's library of information, not finding fault in students' abilities but instead discovering past experiences, strengths and previously learned knowledge to build on. This is fundamental to the way we all learn. Connective activities bring relevance and personal meaning to new information. Therefore our own foundations courses for teachers must manifest the same trust and respect for their potential abilities through connecting their sense of caring to active, engaging pedagogy.

Multicultural Awareness

Many writers agree that multiculturalism should be infused throughout teacher preparation, not added-on as though it were a marginal concern to be dealt with in a separate class or as an extra chapter in a book. Our student teachers told us we needed *"More classes on cultural difference. Practical classes, not BS what a book says. Speakers. Real life would be good!"* They said they felt as though they had experienced a broken-record, academic repetition of multicultural principles. *"I was bombarded with multiculturalism—we did this in every class and it was always the same information."* I suspect that this impression may have arisen from "teaching in a vacuum" on the part of education faculty. As professors we must move out of our disciplinary comfort zones where theories from psychology and sociology, reading or math or science instruction, special education or child development or administration lie isolated in their separate domains. Students too easily reject textbook information that they see as disconnected and not relevant to actual teaching, as evidenced by such comments as, *"All of the theory is great to know, but with cultural differences sometimes not practical."* . . .

Awareness of Linkages

We argue that not only multicultural principles, but also discipline and curriculum theories should also be integrated and revisited across the education program. We can help teacher educators avoid the tangled knot of denial, harmful generalizations and misunderstandings by proactively, carefully weaving together the important strands of thinking about teaching and administration across the whole context of university-based education courses. While we may not be able to directly affect or control the cultural forces that have potential to damage children and overwhelm our teachers, we can focus on the decisions that educators do have power to make. Teachers and administrators need to see that curricular choices, instructional strategies, and the discipline system in any school can all work in synchrony, recognizing and valuing children's differences while also modeling and sustaining a belief in the dignity of all humans.

One way to link together all these issues is through analyzing case studies, which can not only connect different theories, but can also act as bridges to and from field experiences. We can create highly relevant cases out of our own students' and cooperating teachers' experiences and stories. The raw material is plentiful and immediately accessible; evidence comes again from our surveys:

"When I had a situation with a student who thought I had a vendetta against him, my teacher gave me practical things I could say individually to the boy." "Only after some incidents arose and my cooperating teacher gave me some suggestions did I improve." "I sat down with my cooperating teacher after school and would talk about situations, concerns, and would take notes on suggestions on how to handle or manage future situations." Filled out with details, these episodes could provide bases for potentially rich analyses.

Another vehicle for fostering linkages across different content areas is the use of portfolio assessment. The portfolio is made to order for fostering reflection, whereby the developing teacher looks critically inward at her own practice and outward at institutional practices that influence the behavior of her children as well as her own decisions and actions. Where semesters and separate course assessments create artificial boundaries, portfolios help to foreground student development as a whole process. . . .

In the Field

If the university classroom is the arena for increasing awareness of self, students, and linkages among concepts and theories, then the school is where awareness can be—and often is—submerged under the press of immediate decisions and actions. Frequently we saw the vicious cycle of lack of awareness, negative perceptions and low expectations come to life as our students moved out of their comfort zones into field experiences in urban schools.

Negative assumptions about urban teaching begin even before experiences bear them out, and when teachers expect urban children to be undisciplined and unmotivated, their perceptions will reinforce their beliefs. They characterize their children's disruptiveness and disrespect as permanent traits. Even on occasions when children are well-behaved, teachers attribute it to some sort of exception, a "good day." A teacher can fall victim to this way of thinking even after preparation in a program that expressly supports social reconstructivist philosophy, as exemplified by the anguished report of a recent graduate:

> I have felt very alone and hopeless . . . most days I end the school day very disappointed, exhausted, and emotionally broken. . . . I spent all of my energy and emotions on classroom management and trying to understand what it is that drives these students to be so disrespectful and cruel . . . I was a complete outsider to my students' real lives . . . I know their likes, dislikes, hobbies, and attitudes, but I still feel as though I cannot understand them as people. I cannot understand their motives to act so mean and violently to each other . . . I am not a part of their African-American or community culture.

Cantor points out that this student's story shows that she lost sight of the societal forces affecting her students' lives and instead began to judge students' families and their values as deficient.

We saw similar reactions taking shape in our own students. During a seminar for graduate students seeking teacher certification, one intern shared a classic case of culture shock as she began her first week with African-American students in a high-school business class. Their academic skills were weak and their motivation was low. She poured out her worries, about how difficult she found it to motivate and gain rapport with the students. She was afraid she would be unable to gain their respect. She expressed amazement at how boisterous and outspoken they were, and at one point she exclaimed, "They just have no values!" This prompted an intense reaction among the group. "Oh, yes they do so have values! They have strong values—loyalty, resourcefulness, courage—they may not express those values in a way that you can see them right now!" This little story has a happy ending: the intern found immediate, relevant ways to transform her textbook concepts into applications that drew her students in, and she invited business people from their community to speak with the students and lend credibility to what she wanted them to learn. She began to win the students' respect, but perhaps more importantly, she also saw their strengths and gained respect for their viewpoints. She and her fellow interns rediscovered what we had tried to talk about in classes, but now it was real. "For genuinely effective urban teachers, discipline and control are primarily a consequence of their teaching and not a prerequisite condition of learning. Control is completely interrelated with the learning activity at hand. . . ."

Not all stories have happy endings, however. Many comments from our student teachers gave evidence that harmful generalizations had begun to form, beliefs that we had failed to prevent or counteract. *The kids these days are exposed to so much at a young age. They are getting into trouble and have attitudes that show they don't care what you do to punish them. They are apathetic and we need help in dealing with this!!" "They want/need discipline. They like routine. Some are only used to harsh discipline (yelling, banging books) which is hard for me to do, but they respond to it."*

These reactions alarmed us. How naive we were to think that simply removing students from their comfort zones would lead them to independently develop culturally responsive pedagogy or to construct appropriate or healthy coping methods for disciplining children from different and diverse backgrounds. Field work in a diverse setting cannot be assumed to be positive if students are unprepared and still fearful of children and parents who are so different from themselves. Raw experiences by themselves can backfire and lead to stereotyping and oversimplification unless there is sustained reflection about alternative ways to consider discomforting issues. In some cases, sensitive supervisors or thoughtful cooperating teachers skillfully provided safe arenas in which students could talk about their feelings, compare their perceptions to other possible viewpoints, and test out different strategies with their children. . . .

We have since developed a variety of early field experiences and practice that allow our students to encounter diversity beginning with their first education classes and every semester thereafter. For example, students in a literacy curriculum course work to assist immigrant families in their first encounters with all the different contexts that require them to speak English. In another course, students confront historical, philosophical and sociological issues of schooling by attending class at an urban elementary school not far from campus. Rather than losing an opportunity to share their many spontaneous questions and reactions, members of the class write to a web-based discussion board before their next class session. This format allows the professor to monitor and join in as students express their shock, denial, or indignation, and to intervene to guide their ongoing inquiry toward seeking to understand rather than offering judgment. . . .

Despite our growing engagement in urban teaching, some of our findings suggest that even after their culminating field experience, many students wanted to hold onto a premise that teaching, and discipline as well, should consist of procedures to follow, step by proper step. They wanted prescriptions. *"I wish I had known more about discipline for the children from this socioeconomic background." "It would be helpful to have suggestions for actual behaviors or verbal things I could say to students in situations." "It would be beneficial to talk about different kinds of misbehavior—the outwardly defiant types, passive defiance, non-defiant but hyperactive, and the other types (i.e. not having materials, being tardy) that are more inconveniences than real troublemakers. Knowing how to recognize and handle these different types would be very helpful." "If we are to work successfully with diverse students, we need to know what specific behaviors demonstrate successful work and what behaviors to avoid."*

These comments indicate that our students still sought methods and techniques, which we should not deny. Yet, there is more to it. When they focus on the need to teach the curriculum, and on the need to use whatever behavioral techniques are handy for making the process "work," they ignore the art and the heart of teaching. We want them to move beyond their idealistic and simplistic notions of teaching, because discouragement and burnout set in quickly unless they anchor their work in the value of the young people they will teach, regardless of how shocking and different their backgrounds may be. While we help answer their questions about what steps to follow, we must also insist they keep their focus on the fundamental step, on how they start building connections by first valuing who each child is and what each one knows. We all internalize meaning better when new knowledge is discovered out of our own experiences, and we all work harder to understand when we see how something connects with our own reality. We all know what the "aha" moment feels like; it is a revelation, a joy, and the teacher's ultimate vicarious reinforcer.

In between the joyful moments, when we send our students out into the field, we need to help them build expectations that they will be learning from both good and bad examples. In some schools, discipline practices will be inconsistent. Teachers may deliberately ignore the misbehavior of some children because they fear that the youngsters will challenge their authority and charge racism. They are reluctant to confront misbehaving students for fear of their own safety, or threats from parents or older siblings. Neither teachers nor principals will try to communicate with some parents because they have reason to believe the parent will severely punish the child later on. Unfortunately these avoidance tactics are based on fear rather than care, and they will only perpetuate the problems. Nevertheless, our student teachers may have to grapple with similar problems and they will have colleagues who will make avoidance decisions based on this form of learned helplessness. But it will do no good to blame or condemn any of the involved parties. *"Student teachers should be taught that there are no perfect students, perfect schools, perfect communities or perfect teachers."*

It is not to the student teachers' benefit to see only models of excellence. If we expose students to only the best, exemplary situations, we make the mistake of catering to their need for teaching to appear neat and simple: one student wrote, *"I wanted a school where I could truly test my skills so far without distractions that come with lower socioeconomic backgrounds."* She saw pluralism as an obstacle to her development when it should have been an asset. She saw children's backgrounds as distractions, instead of crucial resources for understanding and meeting their needs and also for enriching everyone else in the class. . . .

We must all learn to grow through all experiences, especially from those that are less than ideal. If we try to guarantee success only through working with philosophically compatible partners, how will students react when their beliefs are inevitably challenged later on? *"I felt a lot of pressure from other teachers who did not believe in what we were taught."* Some cooperating teachers seemed to want to sabotage students' ideals, as illustrated by comments from one student who had two different six-week student teaching placements back-to-back: *"After completing my second experience, with a wonderful teacher, I felt like I could do anything. If I had gone into my first assignment with this level of confidence, I know that I would have done more for the kids. I would have stuck by what I believed in."* This was not the only student who reported feeling that her beliefs were attacked and undermined during student teaching. Like their counterparts in other studies of student teachers, many seemed to be vulnerable, for example: *"One of the teachers did not hold the same beliefs that I did. This made me doubt my beliefs as a teacher. I felt that what I had believed for four years was wrong. The teacher tried to convince me that what I had learned did not work in the classroom. My other student teaching experience was wonderful because the teacher shared the same beliefs that I did." "Everyone is entitled to their own opinions, but, for a student teacher, this is hard. They need to be with someone who shares the same teaching philosophy. I started to doubt what I had learned at TCU. I thought that it just didn't work."* Neither we nor our students should expect all teachers and administrators to share congruent viewpoints and priorities. However, we must prepare our students to survive this dissonance, even to benefit from it. We must also help them to view their own understandings in a state of continual evolution and renewal. . . .

Conclusions

To turn toward a brighter side of our findings, we heard from many students who experienced rewarding and positive instances of competence and caring at our partner schools. *"The atmosphere in the school was critical because the other teachers were so supportive of me and willing to back me whenever I had done the right thing." "Being at Jose Martinez Elementary was extremely beneficial because I had never been exposed to children of other backgrounds. I learned so much. I grew up in an all-white community and it was so helpful to be in a school different from my own." "I attempted to learn more about the culture that I was involved with. I made sure that the parents, as well as the children, knew that I was there because I cared about them."* Thus we knew that for many students we succeeded in counteracting the shock, the constructing of deficit models and harmful stereotypes, and the undermining of core beliefs and values as our students acclimated themselves to their urban school settings. . . .

One key element in these successes was sustained conversation that allowed for safe, nonjudgmental validation of feelings, and offered multiple opportunities for sharing and exploring alternative perspectives. Again and again we heard about how university supervisors, cooperating teachers, and fellow students provided invaluable support and *"made all the difference in the world to the experience and how much is learned." "The meetings I had with my advisor and other student teachers seemed to help ease the burden. We found a way to turn frustration into something positive."* Such conversation may appropriately include critical evaluation of some situations and disagreement with decisions a teacher or administrator may take. However, we must strike a thoughtful balance; we must articulate what we strongly believe to be right, but we want not to sit in self-righteous judgment of others. We should prefer to take a "collaborative resonance" approach that shares and owns problems together with teachers and administrators, rather than critically pointing them out in their settings.

A second key element is to keep up a steady search for urban schools where we can build alliances with effective principals and their best teachers. Just as we encourage education students to look always for children's strengths and to build upon what children bring to their learning, so we should look for the special strengths within each urban school faculty, staff, and community. We will find teachers who have positive expectations, who allow choices within a secure structure, who ask for children's responsibility rather than their obedience, and who act as "warm defenders" of their children.

When we do find our allies, teacher educators need to advocate for them and find resources to engage in collaborative professional development *with* them. School change takes place in different layers, beginning with personal transformations and moving toward collective transformations, which ultimately affect institutional reform. Our work can progress at the personal and collective levels, at least. Culturally responsive teachers need content materials and knowledge about instructional practices that will enable them to reach their children, communicate successfully with parents, and shape their classrooms into learning communities. These are resources that schools of education can help provide. Just as children can be taught strategies for self-control, cooperation, defending against bullies, or appropriate ways to express frustration, so adults can learn how to detect nonverbal signals of trouble before it takes place, to help angry children save face, or to invite children and parents to voice complaints and help set policies together with teachers and administrators. Because our collaboratives must include the children's parents, it means that we teacher educators also must push ourselves to venture beyond our comfort zones to learn more about school communities where we send our students. All of us can create opportunities to develop these skills together. . . .

One final element is to trust the power of children. They so readily demonstrate their curiosity and affection and resilience when we enable them! We must nurture one another's moral commitments and our affective lives in teaching as well as our cognitive engagement in educational problem-solving.

Trusting in student capital and their remarkable learning capacities can diminish barriers along both their and our own pathways to success, because in a community of learners, we all help sustain each other. *"The kids need us."* *"I found so much satisfaction working with these children."* *"I love the children at Morrow—they are what kept me going and made my job worthwhile."* For all of our coursework and field experiences, discussions and analyses to make ultimate sense, we must begin and end with the fundamental importance of developing and cultivating respectful, trusting, and caring relationships with students. If teachers begin by internally caring for the well being of students, then their goals will focus on student self-empowerment and authentic learning rather than compliance and test performance. We must take time in teachers' preparation to help them broaden their understandings of caring and discipline, and learn how these can play out even in zones of discomfort.

POSTSCRIPT

Are Culturally Sensitive Practices Attainable?

Most educators would agree that classrooms and schools should be culturally sensitive to their students. The challenge comes in making it happen, especially when many educators believe that it is already happening. Should districts and state departments take a more in-depth view of specific cultural issues within the curriculum and behavior-management plans? Would outside evaluators be more objective in determining if there is a strong match between culturally sensitive practices and the student population? Further evaluation of culturally sensitive practices as well as continued training of future and current educators are factors to seriously consider.

Secondly, both articles differ in their response to creating a more culturally sensitive environment. Duhaney discussed various strategies for the school and staff to incorporate, while Groulx and Thomas proposed that much of the onus falls on university training programs. Many universities are requiring courses in multicultural education. However, is this sufficient to truly train educators to implement a culturally diverse behavior-management program? Is it the responsibility of universities to make sure that new teachers are fully aware of the various nuances in cultural differences and how to employ appropriate behavioral management strategies and curricular strategies? Can this be accomplished in a semester course? Should universities make more room in an already tight university training program?

The demographics of our school population have changed and will continue to change. The shift is toward a much more culturally diverse population while there is still a less diverse teaching population. The alignment of student needs and the skills of educators certainly plays a role in the educational success of all individuals as well as decreasing the behavioral-management issues that are present in our schools today.

Suggested readings include J.A. Banks, *An Introduction to Multicultural Education,* 2nd ed. (Allyn and Bacon, 1990), H.R. Milner, "Reflection, Racial Competence, and Critical Pedagogy: How Do We Prepare Preservice Teachers to Pose Tough Questions?" *Race Ethnicity and Education* (vol. 6, no. 2, 2003, pp. 193–208), A.H. Miranda, "Best Practices in Increasing Cross-Cultural Competence," in A. Thomas and J. Grimes (eds.), *Best Practices in School Psychology,* 4th ed. (The National Association of School Psychologists, 2002), and L.T. Zionts, P. Zionts, S. Harrison, and O. Bellinger, "Urban African American Families' Perceptions of Cultural Sensitivity within the Special Education System," *Focus on Autism and Other Developmental Disabilities* (vol. 18, no. 1, 2003, pp. 41–50).

ISSUE 13

Are Parent Education Programs Effective?

YES: Kathleen Vail, from "Teaching the Parents," *American School Board Journal* (September 2001)

NO: Amy E. Assemany and David E. McIntosh, from "Negative Treatment Outcomes of Behavioral Parent Training Problems," *Psychology in the Schools* (vol. 39, no. 2, 2002)

ISSUE SUMMARY

YES: Kathleen Vail is an associate editor of *American School Board Journal*. Vail believes that perhaps the best way to help students with their classroom misbehaviors is to first help their parents learn better ways to raise their children at home.

NO: Amy E. Assemany is a professor at the State University of New York at Albany, and David E. McIntosh is a professor at Ball State University. They argue that parent education programs are likely to fail, citing premature parental dropouts, parental failure to engage and participate, and failure to maintain gains when parent educators do not consider the contextual factors of socioeconomic disadvantage of the family, family dysfunction, and severity of the child's externalizing behaviors.

Parental involvement is an important component in the degree of a student's success, increasing the odds that a child will find more value and success within the classroom. Parents and educators have been working together for many years in an effort to improve education for children. It is a natural partnership. In addition, educators are knowledgeable and experienced regarding issues of child development and managing behavior. Teachers who are in tune with their students can often offer support to parents regarding difficulties they may be having with their children. Because there is a natural relationship and educators are chiefly concerned about the well-being and education of children, schools and school districts have engaged in offering parenting education courses in order to share knowledge about child development, education, and basic parenting skills.

There have been many articles and research studies that promote the positive aspects of parenting courses offered through schools. Vail discusses the challenges that parents face trying to meet the various demands that are placed on them, such as enough time. Although there are issues about how parents are approached, Vail believes that it can be done successfully. Providing an open, respectful, and responsive program will go far in guaranteeing parental involvement and participation. Surely, this will lead to greater ties between home and school and greater student success.

Conversely, Assemany and McIntosh bring to light the fact that the majority of studies and reported results from parent education programs have not included the negative outcomes, such as those parents and families who drop out of programs prematurely, those who do not fully engage in the treatment aspect of programs, and the outcomes of those students whose families did not benefit from a parenting education program. These authors provide evidence that parenting education programs are often not effective for a percentage of the population. Specific variables and characteristics are discussed that increase the chances of lowered success. However, it is clear that parenting education is often not effective.

Therefore, should schools and educators engage in teaching parents? Is this an endeavor that is worthwhile? On one hand, it appears to be a positive venture, but can it also have negative consequences or be only minimally helpful?

Kathleen Vail  **YES**

Teaching the Parents

These days, everyone seems to have an opinion on how parents should be raising their children. Parenting manuals multiply on the bookstore and library shelves, talk shows feature parenting experts, specialized magazines target the parents of kids of different ages. Despite this jumble of information, schools report that more and more children arrive in their classrooms defiant, aggressive, disruptive, or depressed. It's probably not surprising, then, that educators and school leaders increasingly see the need to dispense parenting advice of their own.

Blame it on the societal problem of your choice: the breakdown of the nuclear family, the rise of postmodernism, the weakening of community ties, the prevalence of poverty, mobility, or divorce. But whatever the reason, many families are struggling with a lack of support, knowledge, and time. Most large urban or suburban school districts (and quite a few smaller ones) attempt to fill that void with various kinds of education for parents. Programs range from occasional classes and workshops to semester-long sessions and support groups, as well as visits into the home and even maternity wards. The programs vary, but the notion behind parent education is the same: The best and perhaps only way to help students is to first help their parents.

"So many problems are spilling into schools," says Linda Johnston, executive director of Practical Parent Education, a parent education program run by the Plano (Texas) Independent School District. "We must nurture the parents to help the child, to hold their hands and fill their needs."

Not everyone, however, is enthusiastic about school-sponsored parenting classes. Anne Henderson, parent involvement researcher and coauthor of *A New Generation of Evidence: The Family Is Critical to Student Achievement*, cautions that schools could appear patronizing when they offer to teach parents how to raise their children. In some communities where the families are mostly African-American or Latino and the school employees are mostly white, parent education might result in a culture clash between middle-class professionals in the school building and working-class parents.

"Parents I've spoken with in the past 25 years are ambivalent about parenting classes," says Henderson. "There is an element of condescension. Parents pick up on that."

Parent educators say these concerns can be addressed, and parents can be drawn in without making them feel they are being chastised. The key, they say,

Reprinted with permission from *American School Board Journal*, September 2001, pp. 23–25.

is to make sure parents are comfortable, respected, and welcome and that they have opportunities to build relationships with school staff members and other parents. As Jeana Preston, head of the parent involvement program for San Diego City Schools, puts it, "The focus is not on 'fixing' parents."

Although parent education programs look and feel different from district to district, the people who run them agree on a few essential points: First, if parents don't feel welcome, they won't come. Second, the classes must be an opportunity for parents to meet school staff members and each other and discuss their problems and issues. When parents form what researchers call "social capital," both schools and families benefit.

Drawing Parents In

Educators and parents alike have long recognized the importance of parent involvement in schools, but attention has grown over the past decade. Some federal programs, including Title I, require schools that receive federal money to develop a parent involvement component. Parent education is one way that schools try to draw parents in, and Title I money is often used to pay for parent classes.

Research shows that parent involvement is important in schools, Preston says, but some kinds of involvement are better than others. "The type of parent involvement that benefits the child most academically is how parents support children at home," she says. At first, her plans for a parent education program in the San Diego schools were met with skepticism. People said parents would never, after a day's work, board buses with their children and attend parenting classes. But Preston, who has headed the district's parent involvement program for 10 years, was convinced parents would do all this and more to help their children succeed in school.

Many schools use the name Parent University to cover an array of parenting classes. It could be a casual one-time seminar or a weekend workshop. Or it could be San Diego's Parent University, which runs 40 classes per school year quarter (like a university schedule) while providing child care and transportation.

Preston came up with the idea after reading an article by James Traub in the *New York Times Magazine* (Jan. 16, 2000). Traub's article said, among other things, that schools could do a great deal to help children from poor families, but they could not influence what goes on in a child's life outside school. Preston disagreed. She believed schools could—and should—offer to help parents support their children academically, have high expectations for them, and help them learn effective ways to discipline and communicate. She set up a program that was longer and more rigorous than many said was practical, but Preston believes the difficulty makes the parents value the experience more.

Classes run for nine weeks in the evening at a San Diego high school and are taught in English and Spanish by district teachers who receive a stipend. Topics include working with teachers to reduce homework hassles; improving your child's reading; increasing study skills; ideas to help your child do better in school; effective discipline; understanding your child's behavior; and helping your child make good decisions.

"We would like all parents to know at what level their child is performing and how to help [the child] at home," says Preston. "It's almost criminal if you don't give parents support."

Last year, 530 parents from 10 targeted low-income schools attended at least one class at Parent University. Every parent who completes a class receives a certificate—and some parents frame their certificate and hang it up at home. Preston hopes the program will grow with the help of private and business donations, and she'd like to start daytime classes and add sessions for parents of infants and toddlers, as well as school-age children.

The First Teachers

Attempts to reach parents before their children come to school are already showing up in some school readiness programs. Parents as Teachers, for example, is a national program that stresses parents are their children's first and most important teacher. The program, which started in Missouri and is run through and supported by school districts, has four parts: home visits, parent group meetings, screening for health or developmental problems, and linking parents to community resources. The program is in 2,600 schools nationwide—including all schools in Missouri, where it's required by state law.

"Most districts are delighted" with Parents as Teachers, says Barb Sander, the head of parent educator training for Missouri. "Children are coming to school ready to learn. Schools spend less money on special education and remediation. Parents get involved with the schools."

New parents in participating school districts receive pamphlets at the hospital about Parents as Teachers. Families, who can stay in the program until their child is 5, are assigned a trained educator who visits with the parents monthly. Parents also can attend regular classes to learn about developmental issues, and how to handle problems with eating, sleeping, toilet training, and language development. These services are available until the child is ready for kindergarten.

Sander says the program is based on the premise that many parents—middle-class parents included—don't receive a lot of training about child-rearing or parenting. "We strengthen their confidence in parenting," says Sander. "Some young families are at a loss."

Practical Parent Education—which started in Plano and is spreading to schools around the country—picks up where Parents as Teachers leaves off, at kindergarten. In Plano, the program runs from 12 to 20 classes, often going into churches, community centers, and businesses to reach busy parents. Small support groups for parents also meet regularly. Curriculum for the classes, which has been developed by Practical Parent Education staff, includes such topics as understanding your role as a parent; developing trust within the family; understanding parenting and power; and accepting and growing through transitions.

"We really believe there are different levels of parent involvement," says Johnston, the program's executive director. "If we stay at the surface, we won't get results. We must go deeper."

Another program that is growing nationally is FAST (Families and Schools Together), which was created by social worker Marilyn McDonald, a professor at the University of Wisconsin. McDonald's program takes a different approach. Parents come with their families to eight weekly sessions. With the help and support of a team of school staff and community members, the families do group activities and have a chance to meet other families with children of the same age.

"There are no lectures and no handouts," says McDonald, who worried that people wouldn't come if they felt they were on the receiving end of a lecture. "Parents are afraid they won't be respected for their own knowledge and experience."

If You Hold One, They Might Come

Parenting is a personal subject, and as Anne Henderson points out, attempts to teach it smack of condescension if they're not handled with sensitivity. Experienced parent educators know they have to present their classes in a positive manner or no one will attend. Here's their advice:

- **Be persistent.** Overcoming wariness of the program—and of school in general—is the first order of business. "At first, parents were suspicious," says McDonald. "We had to develop recruiting strategies." One of those strategies is persistence, and recruiters make repeated visits to homes to tell families about the program. They ask parents to come to one class, rather than committing right away to the whole block of sessions. McDonald found that 80 percent of the parents who attended the first class returned and ended up completing the program. "Once you find there's no hidden agenda, you'll come back," she says.
- **Don't single parents out.** Another strategy is to open programs to all parents in the school system, rather than targeting a specific group of parents. That way, participants don't think they're being singled out because they've done something wrong.
- **Hold classes where the parents are.** "Getting parents there is a challenge," says Johnston. "Some parents aren't comfortable in school." Those who didn't have positive experiences at school themselves aren't especially eager to go back, she says. The Practical Parent Education program combats that resistance by going outside schools to where parents are: churches, community centers, and even businesses.
- **Have a diverse staff.** Having teachers of the same ethnic or cultural background as the parents lends credibility to the program, says Johnston, whose program serves a predominantly Latino population.
- **Offer child care.** Another way to entice parents is to have an attractive and well-developed child care program. San Diego's Preston says children like the child care program so much that they're just as eager to attend as their parents. Both Parent University and FAST use this time to help children develop academically, mentally, and emotionally.
- **Build relationships.** An important component of parent education is the opportunity for parents to form relationships with other parents, as well as with teachers and other school staff members. FAST, for example, gives parents an opportunity to meet other families with children.

When the sessions are over, parents are encouraged to attend monthly meetings with other parents to continue to strengthen their relationships. "High stress and social isolation can collapse even the strongest family," says McDonald. "Schools are suffering from this. Parents will abuse and neglect their children if they're isolated and stressed."

Results, Tangible and Intangible

Working with the Wisconsin Center for Education Research, McDonald developed a research instrument to determine whether children in FAST benefited academically from being involved in the program. The results, she's happy to say, look good. Two groups of children—a rural American Indian population and students from inner-city Milwaukee—were compared to control groups. Two years out of the program, the FAST students showed less anxiety and aggression, longer attention spans, and improved academic performance. FAST is now in more than 600 schools in 38 states and five countries.

Aside from McDonald's work, though, there's scant research on whether parent education boosts academic achievement or improves student behavior or even helps parents become more involved in schools. Its effectiveness aside, some observers worry that parent education doesn't reach the parents who need help and support the most. But parent educators are convinced the programs help parents in sometimes intangible ways. Not only do parents learn to support their children in school, but, in turn, they feel supported by a larger community, which includes the school system. And when parents feel supported, that translates into health and stability for children.

Says Preston, "The whole community does better when children do better in school."

NO ↵

Amy E. Assemany and
David E. McIntosh

Negative Treatment Outcomes of Behavioral Parent Training Programs

The positive outcomes of behavioral parent training (BPT) programs have been well documented and provide justification for these treatments to be considered "best practice" or "empirically supported" for most populations. Yet, valuable information can be gained about the effectiveness of behavioral parent training programs by examining the circumstances and mechanisms involved in negative treatment outcomes or the "treatment failures." Unfortunately, these negative outcomes have not received as much attention in the literature as the positive treatment outcomes of behavioral parent training programs. The present review has three purposes: (a) to define and outline the literature on negative treatment outcomes of behavioral parent training programs, (b) to examine the literature on variables predictive of negative treatment outcomes, and (c) to suggest future directions of study in the hope of improving treatments to the sizeable minority of families who experience negative treatment outcomes.

Behavioral Parent Training Programs

Behavioral parent training (BPT) programs are often recommended for preschool children exhibiting a clinical level of disruptive behaviors and their parents. The disruptive behaviors targeted by the treatment often include temper tantrums, noncompliance, aggression, defiance, stealing, and destruction of property. If untreated, the conduct problems exhibited by children often become increasingly debilitating over time. Children who do not receive or respond favorably to treatment are at risk of developing a wide range of problems later in life, such as interpersonal problems, juvenile delinquency, poor school performance, school dropout, substance abuse, adult crime, and antisocial personality disorder. A number of BPT programs have been supported steadily by efficacy studies describing the outcomes for families that complete the treatment. Examples of such BPT programs are the Living with Children Program, a group discussion/videotape modeling program, Parent-Child Interaction Therapy, the Helping the

From *Psychology in the Schools*, vol. 39(2), 2002, pp. 209–215, 217–219. Copyright © 2002 by John Wiley & Sons. Reprinted by permission. References omitted.

Noncompliant Child program, and the Delinquency Prevention program. These programs share similar treatment goals, procedures, underlying assumptions, and outcomes. Each of these programs have been identified by the Task Force on Effective Psychosocial Interventions initiated by Division 12 of the American Psychological Association as either "empirically supported" or "probably efficacious."

In general, empirically supported BPT programs have demonstrated short-term and long-term efficacy for the majority of families who completed the training. The short-term effects include improvement in the target child's behaviors, such as increased compliance to parent's directives, and decreased oppositional and aggressive behaviors; along with enhanced parenting skills in the form of parents spending more time attending to and rewarding their child's positive behaviors, and giving better, more appropriate commands, warnings, and discipline. When short-term effects have occurred as a result of BPT, they often have generalized to settings other than an outpatient clinic, the typical location of service delivery. For example, for many families decreased disruptive behaviors have been documented in the home, school, and community settings.

Support of the long-term effects of BPT for some families who complete the treatment has been documented in the literature. Due to the difficulties inherent in longitudinal research, limited data exist to support the long-term effects of BPT. Nevertheless, the existing studies suggest reductions in clinically significant disruptive behaviors for many children assessed 1 to 2 years after completing PCIT, and sustained improvements in parenting skills for many parents who successfully completed treatment.

Negative Treatment Outcomes of Behavioral Parent Training

Despite the scores of outcome studies demonstrating the numerous benefits of BPT programs for the treatment of young children with conduct problems and their parents, a consistent mention of negative outcomes of BPT programs also exists in the literature for a sizeable minority of families. Three types of negative treatment outcomes occur in BPT programs and have been examined to date. They are: (1) high rates of premature family dropout, (2) failure of parents to engage and truly participate in treatment throughout the process, and (3) failure of the parents and child to maintain positive changes made in treatment at follow-up. The high rate of sporadic participation, premature dropout, and behavioral outcomes remaining in the clinical range for a considerable number of families present a major obstacle to successful BPT, limiting the effectiveness of these "empirically supported" treatments with particular families.

The study of negative treatment outcomes has received less attention in the literature than the documentation of positive outcomes. This relative oversight of the topic of negative treatment outcomes resulted primarily from two factors: excitement about the promise of BPT programs after many positive effects were observed for families who engaged fully in the treatment, and lack of publication of studies not demonstrating positive results or statistically significant effects. Behavioral parent training programs offered psychologists working with families of children with conduct problems one of the first effective treatments available for this population. As a result, it is not surprising that the vast amount of scholarly writing in this area focused strictly on the benefits and promise of the treatment, and not on the negative treatment outcomes occurring for a sizable minority of families who participated. Coupled with the reporting of exciting, positive findings, the tradition of journals to publish only studies with statistically significant effects leads to an underrepresentation of literature about the negative outcomes of treatment. Stoiber and Kratochwill argue that negative results of empirically supported interventions offer valuable information to the field in that a pattern of negative results is likely indicative of particular conditions under which a treatment is not effective. Without the reporting and examination of information about families who are not satisfied or helped by BPT programs, the effectiveness of this treatment for this population may not improve.

Premature Termination

The first negative treatment outcome, high rates of premature family dropout, appears to be the most studied out of the three types of negative outcomes discussed in the BPT literature. A literature review conducted by Forehand et al. discovered that out of 45 parent training studies published in eight popular journals between 1972 and 1982, only 22 (49%) studies contained dropout data. This data indicated that the reported dropout rate in parent training in those years was 28%. Consistent with the 49% rate of reporting dropout data in parent training outcome studies, published reports of the five BPT programs with the most empirical support have not always included the number of families who prematurely dropped out of training. These efficacy studies frequently report the positive outcomes of the treatment, yet do not specify that these outcomes only occurred for families who completed treatment. No information is available about those families not completing treatment, other than the fact that they received no treatment at the time of the study.

When treatment dropout rates have been documented in reports of BPT programs, the data have varied. Reported dropout rates range from 8–48%. Notably, reports of treatment dropout rates have been the lowest when Webster-Stratton's BPT program has been used. The high rate of premature termination has a number of ramifications, including the fact that families who drop out are less likely to improve compared to families who complete treatment, families with significant impairment remain untreated, and costs for the provision of clinical services for all families frequently increase. Overall, data on BPT treatment dropout rates suggest that a sizable number of families qualified to receive BPT do not complete the treatment, and therefore do not benefit from the therapeutic gains observed in most families who complete these "empirically supported" treatments.

Poor Treatment Engagement

The second negative treatment outcome discussed in the literature, failure of the parents to engage and truly participate in treatment throughout the process, has not received much mention in the literature on BPT programs. Specific parental behaviors that have been defined as insufficient treatment engagement include inadequate treatment session participation (e.g., refusing to participate in role plays or discussions), dissatisfaction with the treatment regimen (e.g., hostile interactions when the therapist makes suggestions), sporadic attendance, and noncompliance (e.g., not completing homework assignments); these behaviors have been also referred to as resistance in the literature. Although insufficient data exists about treatment outcomes specific to parents who resist BPT or do not fully participate in treatment, it is likely that resistive parental behaviors compromise the potential positive effects of full participation in BPT programs.

Lack of Maintained Progress

The third negative treatment outcome, failure of the parents and child to maintain positive changes made in treatment at follow-up, refers to both the lack of maintenance of skills at posttreatment assessment, and the assessment of the child's behavior to have returned to a clinical level of impairment at posttreatment. Despite favorable results upon completion of a BPT program, researchers have begun to acknowledge the limited benefit of those treatment gains if the child's overall adjustment at the follow-up assessment was not maintained in the normal or nonclinical range of functioning. Serketich and Dumas commented after conducting a meta-analysis that only a small percentage of available BPT outcome studies were methodologically rigorous enough to allow for an analysis of the clinical utility of BPT at follow-up. In other words, very few studies examined whether the impact of treatment continued to make a difference in everyday functioning over time by conducting a follow-up comparison of experimental and control groups with clinically sensitive measures. When clinical significance has been examined, long-term follow-up studies suggest that 30–40% of parents who participate in treatment rate their child's behavior in the clinical range at the time of follow-up assessment. This finding indicates that after the completion of treatment, the functioning of many of the children treated continued to measure in the clinical range.

Summary

Behavioral parent training programs have a relatively long history of success in the treatment of most young children with conduct problems and their families. Successful completion of BPT programs has led to numerous short-term and long-term positive outcomes. Although less studied, a sizeable minority of families do not benefit from BPT programs and instead experience negative treatment outcomes. Included under the umbrella of negative treatment outcomes is a family who prematurely drops out of treatment, does not engage in the process of treatment, or does not demonstrate positive gains following BPT. Historically, families who have not completed the prescribed treatment have not been described in published outcome studies, nor has research finding negative treatment results been published by major journals. However, the relatively small number of studies focused on this population provides valuable information about characteristics that appear shared among families at-risk for experiencing negative treatment outcomes. This literature suggests that despite being "empirically supported" for most participants, not all families in need of BPT are benefiting at this time from such treatment.

Contextual Variables Predictive of Negative Treatment Outcomes

As a result of studies describing the negative outcomes of BPT, researchers began to document child, parent, and family characteristics associated with negative treatment outcomes. In the literature, these characteristics are also commonly referred to as contextual variables impacting treatment outcome. . . .

The BPT literature on contextual variables associated with negative treatment outcomes indicates three consistently mentioned characteristics predictive of poor outcomes: socioeconomic disadvantage, family dysfunction, and severity of the child's externalizing behaviors. The first two of these characteristics include in each category a number of related variables that appear associated with each other, yet fall under the broad category of either socioeconomic disadvantage or family dysfunction. The following review of the literature on contextual variables will detail the three characteristics suggested by research to be predictive of poor outcomes.

Socioeconomic Disadvantage

The powerful association between socioeconomic disadvantage and negative treatment outcomes has been demonstrated repeatedly in the literature. Since the early 1980s, BPT researchers have associated poor treatment outcomes or premature treatment termination with families of low socioeconomic status. Dumas and Wahler, publishing in the early 1980s, defined socioeconomic disadvantage as the presence of at least four out of six risk variables. The risk variables comprising their Socioeconomic Disadvantage Index were family income (below $13,000), maternal education (no college education), family composition (one-parent household), family size (three or more children), source of referral (social agency referral), and area of residence (high crime neighborhood). These six risk variables defined the variable socioeconomic disadvantage in the early 1980s.

From the mid-1980s to the mid-1990s, criteria used to define socioeconomic disadvantage in the literature began to expand. A few additional risk variables were added to the definition of socioeconomic disadvantage, namely, ethnicity (minority status), type of insurance (Medicaid), inadequate housing, and unemployment. Moreover, during this time, researchers began to suggest specific variables underlying the influence of the broad characteristic of socioeconomic disadvantage. For example, ordinary daily inconveniences experienced by those who are socioeconomically disadvantaged, such as inflexible and demanding work schedules, a lack of child care coverage, and unreliable transportation, were suggested as variables subsumed under the broad category of socioeconomic disadvantage that may be adversely impacting treatment participation. Thus, with time, scholars have acknowledged the complexity of the variable socioeconomic disadvantage and broadened the variables included in the definition of the term.

The more recent BPT outcome studies, conducted in the latter half of the 1990s, continued to expand the definition of socioeconomic disadvantage. Some studies during this time hinted at the interconnectedness of contextual variables by making reference to "socioeconomic disadvantage and related family conditions" and the "adverse effect of poverty and its accompanying stressors." Included in the definition of socioeconomic disadvantage were variables such as the educational and occupational attainment of the family, family income, receipt of public assistance, mother's age, family structure, minority group membership, and type of insurance.

Evident from the review of outcome studies reporting the association between socioeconomic disadvantage and negative BPT treatment outcomes, the criteria used to define the variable has changed over time. As more research is conducted in this area, the trend appears to be the inclusion of more variables under the broad category of socioeconomic disadvantage. At different times in the BPT literature, all of the following variables have been included in various definitions of socioeconomic disadvantage: family income, maternal education, family composition, family size, source of referral, and area of residence, ethnicity, type of insurance, occupational attainment of the parent(s), mother's age, inflexible and demanding work schedules, a lack of child care coverage, and unreliable transportation. The number of variables used to define this family characteristic in and of itself indicates the broadness of the category of one's socioeconomic situation; subsumed under this category are many variables, some directly a result of poverty and others considered associated stressors.

Family Dysfunction

The second category of family characteristics predictive of negative treatment outcomes is family dysfunction. This variable has also been identified since at least the early 1980s as predictive of poor BPT outcomes or premature termination from BPT. Earlier research identified variables such as mother insularity, maternal depression, the presence of the father, marital violence, and maternal psychopathology to be driving the association between family dysfunction and negative treatment outcomes. The term, "mother insularity," first described by Wahler, Leske, and Rogers refers to mothers who have few and/or aversive day-to-day social contacts. Moreover, the limited social contacts are not with friends, but most often with family or social service agents, and are usually not initiated by the mothers. These parental-interactional variables were considered the influences accounting for the association between family dysfunction and negative BPT outcomes. Maternal psychopathology typically was defined as the mother's reported history of psychological/psychiatric symptoms or disorder for which she had sought professional help at least once since the child's birth.

Behavioral parent training outcome studies conducted between the mid-1980s and mid-1990s continued to include variables such as parental psychopathology, especially maternal depression, father's presence, insularity, and marital violence under the umbrella category of family dysfunction. However, similar to the definition of socioeconomic disadvantage, additional variables were added to the definition of family dysfunction and were linked to the variance in negative treatment outcome explained by family dysfunction. Variables that were added to the definition included negative life stress or high family stress, cognitive factors of the parents, such as their perceptions of their children's behavior, marital discord, parental substance abuse, and parental criminal record. Negative life stress refers to life events such as relocation of a family, a family death, and unemployment that increase the general stress level of the family. To measure the mother's perception of her child's problematic behavior, standardized behavior rating scales were completed by the mother upon intake. Externalizing behavior ratings in the clinical range indicated the mother to perceive her child to have a high level of behavioral distress.

As with the variable, socioeconomic disadvantage, researchers have expanded the definition of the broad-based category of family dysfunction over time. More specific variables have been found that better explain the variance of the association between family dysfunction and negative treatment outcomes during the last 20 years of BPT research. Since the mid 1990s, BPT outcome studies have continued to expand the list of variables subsumed under the category of family dysfunction. New variables listed in the literature as increasing the level of family dysfunction that is adversely related to positive treatment outcomes are poor parental interpersonal relations, poor parental health, and adverse and harsh child-rearing practices. These variables together with those previously mentioned from earlier years of research form a list of the specific variables predictive of negative treatment outcomes generally referred to as family dysfunction.

Severity of the Child's Conduct Problems

The third characteristic, severity of the child's externalizing behavior, is different from the first two in that it is similarly defined across studies, and is not an umbrella term for a number of smaller variables closely associated. In general, this variable is defined as the intensity and frequency of the child's conduct problems and antisocial behaviors present at the time of treatment. Some minor variation has occurred in the definition of this variable across studies, resulting often from the measures used to define the problem behaviors. However, for the majority of studies, the meaning has referred to the severity of dysfunction of the referred child.

In a study conducted by Kazdin, a number of measures of child dysfunction were assessed and entered into a discriminant function analysis to determine which, if any, aspects of child dysfunction were predictive of negative treatment outcomes. An interview was used to assess the total number of conduct disorder symptoms and antisocial behaviors exhibited by the child, using the Diagnostic and Statistical Manual of Mental Disorders. Also included as measures of child dysfunction were the total number of delinquency behaviors based on a self-report measure, and the behavior problem score on the Child Behavior Checklist. Kazdin found that out of the four measures of child dysfunction utilized, only two, the total number of conduct disorder symptoms and the self-reported delinquency, were predictive of negative treatment outcomes in BPT programs. The results of this study indicated that one of the ways families who experience negative treatment outcomes differ from those who do not was the severity of the dysfunction of the referred child, specifically in the number of Conduct Disorder symptoms and delinquent behaviors reported at the beginning of treatment.

Summary

The BPT literature on contextual variables associated with negative treatment outcomes indicates three consistently mentioned characteristics predictive of poor outcomes: socioeconomic disadvantage, family dysfunction, and severity of the child's externalizing behaviors. The third characteristic, severity of the child's externalizing behavior, is defined as the intensity and frequency of the child's conduct problems and delinquent behaviors presented at the time of treatment. This literature affirms the importance of these contextual variables in the treatment of this population, and suggests that these variables may strongly influence the overall effectiveness of BPT for families presenting to treatment with contextual stressors. . . .

POSTSCRIPT

Are Parent Education Programs Effective?

Is it the responsibility of schools and educators to provide additional instruction on parenting? Schools are a likely entity to engage families in regard to their children, but is it overstepping a boundary that should be established? Educators have a large role in education, and adding the role of teaching parents can seem like another responsibility and role that may not be appropriate.

Educators trying to provide parenting education may find themselves in situations where they can become intimately involved with various family issues. In many cases, they may not have the skills to deal with a variety of the complex problems that families are facing. For example, families with mental illnesses, substance abuse issues, significant health issues, or environmental stressors such as parental unemployment may be beyond the scope of what can be addressed in a parenting course offered by educators. Second, families may feel that educators may not understand their family dynamics, background, or issues. This can lead to disengagement and possibly resentment on the part of families.

Conversely, because schools are a public entity and are probably the closest institution and organization to most families and their children, it stands to reason that schools can offer assistance to parents. In many instances, families are not receiving any support or further education from any other entity. Caring educators with a working knowledge of child needs and principles of behavior management can provide some support to parents even if they are not able to reach all parents.

It does stand to reason that effectiveness studies and program evaluations of parenting education courses should be evaluated and well understood by those who engage in these types of programs. Understanding this information will allow educators to make the most informed decision about parenting education.

Suggested readings include L.K. Elksnin and N. Elksnin, "Teaching Parents to Teach Their Children to Be Prosocial," *Intervention in School and Clinic* (vol. 36, no. 1, 2000, pp. 27–35), A.L. Jacobson and J. Engelbrecht, "Parenting Education Needs and Preferences of Parents of Young Children," *Early Childhood Education Journal* (vol. 28, no. 2, 2000, pp. 139–147), T.J. Lewis and C. Daniels, "Rethinking School Discipline Through Effective Behavioral Support," *Reaching Today's Youth: The Community Circle of Caring Journal* (vol. 4, no. 2, 2000, pp. 43–47), and W.D. Wood, III, and J.A. Baker, "Preferences for Parent Education Programs among Low Socioeconomic Status, Culturally Diverse Parents," *Psychology in the Schools* (vol. 6, no. 3, 1999, pp. 239–247).

ISSUE 14

Can Profiling Help Identify Potentially Violent Students?

YES: Gale M. Morrison and Russell Skiba, from "Predicting Violence from School Misbehavior: Promises and Perils," *Psychology in the Schools* (March 2001)

NO: Kirk A. Bailey, from "Legal Implications of Profiling Students for Violence," *Psychology in the Schools* (March 2001)

ISSUE SUMMARY

YES: Gale M. Morrison is a professor at the University of California at Santa Barbara, and Russell Skiba is a professor at Indiana University. They share the perspective that students who are involved in various types of school-based offenses and subsequent disciplinary actions are at increased risk for later violence and other unsafe behaviors that threaten the overall safety of school campuses. They argue that the propensity for violence may be mitigated depending upon the response of individual school disciplinarians.

NO: Kirk A. Bailey, who is a professor at the Hamilton Fish Institute on School and Community Violence at George Washington University, raises suspicions about how profiling for violence might violate the constitutional rights of students, including protections against discrimination, unlawful search and seizure, and privacy.

One option for preventing school violence is identifying and targeting those students who are likely to commit violent or aggressive acts and then intervening. Because violence in schools is so devastating to the students, staff, and community, wouldn't it be ideal to prevent violent acts before they happen? Just imagine if school staff would have read the warning signs emitted by the two individuals responsible for the Columbine school shootings. If educators are more astute at reading early warning signs, intervention steps can be put into place that may decrease—and ideally eliminate—the likelihood of a student committing a violent act.

Identifying individuals who are at high risk for unwanted behavior has been studied scientifically, and methods for identifying these individuals have been developed. If this is applied to students, educators may be more likely to identify and implement specific interventions that will target the characteristics of concern and decrease the incidence of violence in schools.

A publication developed by the U.S. Department of Education entitled "Early Warning, Timely Response: A Guide to Safe Schools" was created following a directive President Clinton commissioned to the Department of Education and the Department of Justice. These two entities in conjunction with various other national educational and mental health organizations developed this guide. The purpose is to assist educators and families in identifying children with behaviors of concern and subsequently put these children in contact with professionals to begin appropriate intervention. One of the key purposes of understanding early-warning signs is for adults to intervene with children in a timely and effective manner.

In light of this, Morrison and Skiba clarify the issues related to early-warning signs and identification of potentially violent students. The authors outline the best understood characteristics of students who are most likely to engage in violence. They also discuss the variations in discipline procedures and philosophies by school personnel. They advocate for early intervention and for utilizing the most reliable methods of identification for future violent behaviors. Early identification includes taking into consideration the variables that impact the action of students such as the environmental context.

Bailey takes a much more skeptical approach to early identification of potentially violent students. He discusses the practice of profiling and identification in terms of the social science methodology and argues against its direct application in school environments. He states that educators who are the most likely to evaluate the behavior of students are not always objective parties because of their relationships with students. Bailey also discusses the various constitutional violations and possible legal implications with the practice of early identification.

233

**Gale M. Morrison and
Russell Skiba**

 **YES**

Predicting Violence from School Misbehavior: Promises and Perils

The outbreak of high visibility violence in schools in the past few years has led to an intensive search for behavioral and emotional precursors that could provide a prediction of which students might be at-risk for committing such acts. Nationally, a number of resources have become available that attempt to provide some guidance to school staff, parents, and students.

A logical place to look for students who would be likely to commit acts of school violence is on the rolls of school discipline cases. In fact, a history of discipline problems has been listed as a warning sign in the U.S. Department of Education document "EarlyWarning, Timely Response: A Guide to Safe Schools." A common assertion is that the best prediction of future behavior is past behavior; therefore, those students who have exhibited previous antisocial behavior at school would be expected to be those most likely to exhibit this behavior in the future. Indeed, students who exhibit chronic patterns of school discipline involvement are highly likely to experience future school adjustment problems. Walker and Sprague found that the number of discipline contacts during the school year for an individual child was one of three salient predictors of arrest status in the 5th and then again in the 10th grades. In addition to the perspective of individuals' contribution to school violence, there is concern about the systemic contribution of high levels of overall disciplinary disruptions in a school to acts of more serious violence.

The question addressed in this article is whether or not a focus on school discipline records and patterns of disciplined behavior can improve risk predictions and inform the prevention or reduction of antisocial behavior in schools. We examine school discipline systems and the students that are most likely to be involved in them. Given this information, we then discuss the validity of predictions of subsequent violence or disruption and possible sources of error in these predictions.

School Discipline Processes and Targets

When defining the nature and scope of school discipline, it is important to recognize that school-wide discipline includes multiple settings (e.g., classroom, playground, halls, cafeteria) and can be implemented at a group or an individual

From *Psychology in the Schools*, vol. 38(2), March 2001, pp. 173–184. Copyright © 2001 by John Wiley & Sons. Reprinted by permission. References omitted.

level. This article focuses on the discipline methods at the school-wide level; that is, office referrals, suspension, and expulsion. Surprisingly, there have been a limited number of studies of school discipline procedures and outcomes. Yet, there has been some consistency in these research findings on the major reasons for office referrals, suspensions, and expulsions.

While focus on school discipline is most often directed to serious issues of drugs, gangs, and weapons in our schools, the data have consistently shown that these are not the most frequent problems with which school administrators wrestle. A national survey conducted by the National Center on Educational Statistics asked school principals to list what they considered moderate or serious problems in their schools and found that the problems principals deal with most frequently at both the elementary and secondary level are non-violent or less violent behaviors such as tardiness (40%), absenteeism (25%), and physical conflicts between students (21%). The critical incidents that are the typical focus of school safety debates are seen relatively infrequently: drug use (9%), gangs (5%), possession of weapons (2%), physical abuse of teachers (2%). These national findings are consistent with research on disciplinary incidents at the school level. Similarly, in studies at the district or school level, the behaviors that most frequently result in office referral appear to be disobedience and general disruption, defiance, and physical contact/fighting.

Out-of-school suspension is among the most common consequences for disciplinary infractions. . . . Suspension appears to be used with greater frequency in urban areas than in suburban or rural areas. As might be expected with such high rates of usage, school suspension is not always reserved for the most serious or dangerous behaviors. Fights or physical aggression among students are consistently found to be among the most common reasons for suspension. Yet, school suspension is commonly used, as well, for a number of relatively minor offenses, such as disobedience and disrespect, problems of attendance, and general classroom disruption. In fact, students are suspended for more serious offenses (e.g., drugs, weapons, vandalism, assaults on teachers) relatively infrequently.

Suspension and expulsion procedures exclude students from the school setting for specific amounts of time. In the case of expulsions, this exclusion may be permanent. Each of these disciplinary actions has a set of due process guidelines that are outlined by state and local educational agencies. Most states provide guidelines for the behaviors that cause a student to be subject to suspension or expulsion, most recently as a result of zero-tolerance philosophies and federal legislation. According to a study by The Civil Rights Project of Harvard University, 41 states have laws establishing grounds for suspension and 49 have these guidelines for expulsion. All of these states require a recommendation for expulsion for possession of firearms, weapons, or other deadly weapons. Eighteen states specify that possession, use, or distribution of drugs on school campuses serves as grounds for expulsion. Other expellable offenses include willful or continued defiance of authority or disruptive behavior and habitual profanity. Some form of zero tolerance policy appears to have become the norm for the most serious infractions. Defining zero tolerance as mandating predetermined consequences or punishments for specified offenses, the National Center on Educational Statistics reported that more than 90% of all schools report having zero tolerance policies for weapons or firearms, almost 90% for alcohol or drugs, and 79% for violence or tobacco.

In contrast to suspension, school expulsion appears to be used relatively infrequently as compared to other disciplinary options. Morrison, D'Incau, Couto, and Loose reported that expulsion appears to be reserved for incidents of moderate to high severity, although there is some doubt as to whether students who are expelled are always those who are the most troublesome or dangerous. Zero tolerance policies, mandating expulsion for certain types of events, have apparently led to the expulsion of many children and youths who would be considered "good students."

The Challenge of Prediction: Multiple Sources of Variance

In using disciplinary data for early identification, one is seeking to use the discipline event to predict which students are likely to be at-risk for violence or disruption in the future. Although the stability over time of school misbehavior offers some promise for prediction, it is critical to note that predicting from school discipline is not a *univariate* but a *multivariate* process of prediction. That is, the process of school discipline is highly complex, involving student behavior, teacher reactions, administrative disposition, and even local, state, and national politics. Thus, a model of prediction from school disciplinary incidents must be similarly complex, accounting for all of these levels.

Office discipline referrals represent an initial level of discipline designed to manage disruptive behavior at school. Sugai, Sprague, Horner, & Walker defined office discipline referral as "an event in which (a) a student engaged in a behavior that violated a rule or social norm in the school, (b) the problem behavior was observed or identified by a member of the school staff, and (c) the event resulted in a consequence deliver by administrative staff who produced a permanent (written) product defining the whole event." Even within this apparently simple event, however, there are numerous sources of variance. For example, the nature of office referrals differs between schools depending on the unique rules and ways of referring, implementing the consequence, and formalizing (recording/reporting) the event. There will also be considerable within-school variation, depending on the tolerance level different teachers have for similar behaviors, and their skill at handling the behavior at the classroom level.

Once the office referral is made, there will be additional variation at the level of administrative disposition. The use of suspension and expulsions involves a good degree of latitude (within state-mandated limits) on the part of the school administrators and school board, and will thus result in considerable variance in the use and severity of these consequences at the school and district level. Finally, variations in school discipline philosophy can influence the use of these processes within these limits.

In the sections that follow, we attempt to outline some additional sources of variance in school discipline contributed by individual differences, as well as variation contributed by implementation of the process of school discipline.

Student Behavioral Characteristics, Discipline, and the Prediction of Violence

Individual differences that predict violence.   Risk models for the prediction of juvenile delinquency often focus on the individual characteristics of the child. Some of the individual characteristics identified in this research include: (a) problem behavior evident beginning at ages 4 and 5, (b) engagement in a variety of problem behaviors (overt and covert), (c) problem behavior exhibited in a variety of settings (home, community, school), and (d) display of extreme aggression. Difficult temperament in early childhood has been identified as an individual characteristic that may interact with a problematic, ineffectual parenting style. Patterson's work has emphasized the role of coercive child-rearing techniques in the development of antisocial behavior in children. Gresham, Lane, & Lambros suggested that attention be given to subtypes in the prediction of youth violence. They focus on the description of the "fledgling psychopath" or children who exhibit comorbidity of hyperactivity-impulsivity-inattention and conduct problems. These children are at markedly greater risk for later psychopathology and/or chronic offending.

Walker and Sprague identify five risk factors associated with delinquency and youth violence: "(a) the mother and/or the father has been arrested, (b) the child has been a client of child protection, (c) one or more family transition has occurred (death, divorce, trauma, family upheaval), (d) the youth has received special education services, and/or (e) the youth has a history of early and/or severe antisocial behavior." With the exception of the last factor, these factors are all system-involvement factors, indicating factors in the child's environment or evidence that maladjustment of some kind has come to the attention of authorities. Additional factors mentioned by the American Psychological Association (APA) in 1993 include factors associated with problem behavior, including early involvement with alcohol and other drugs, pervasive exposure to media violence, association with deviant peer groups, and easy access to weapons.

Many of the individual and family characteristics described above are likely correlates with involvement in school discipline processes. Eckenrode, Laird, and Doris reported that students with substantiated reports of abuse or neglect were significantly more likely to be referred for school discipline and somewhat more likely to be suspended, especially at the middle and high school level. Morgan-D'Atrio et al. reported that, of students who were suspended, 43% at the high school level and 38% at the middle school level had clinically elevated scores on one or more student *and* teacher subscales of the Child Behavior Checklist. It is important to note, however, that there was wide variability in the characteristics listed for individual students, ranging from aggression to thought problems, to delinquent behavior to somatic complaints. Thus, while individual and family characteristics in general may predict who will be referred or suspended, the specific relationship between those characteristics and school discipline can be expected to be highly variable among disciplined students.

The problem of predicting future behavior.   Thus, although it is possible to identify the types of *problems* that predict future violence or disruption, the problem of predicting which *students* will commit acts of violence is a thorny one. First, the possibility of this prediction assumes that there is causal homogeneity, that some subset of variables measured for all participants will account for a significant proportion of variance in a multivariate statistical model. This assumption is repeatedly challenged by research literature that suggests that there are multiple subtypes and a variety of developmental trajectories that describe this population. Most research has focused on markers or correlates, not on the developmental or causal processes through which antisocial behavior develops across time.

Another limitation of the multivariate prediction model is that these predictions are limited in the extent to which they approximate a full accounting of the variance in the equation. While a certain subset of variables have been shown to be "best predictors" of youth aggression (see characteristics identified above), there is still considerable variance for which the equation does not account; thus, the likelihood of many false positives and false negatives is high. Indeed, it has been noted that less than 50% of children with extreme antisocial behavior become antisocial adults or continue to exhibit antisocial behavior in their later childhood or teen years. Gresham notes that the difficulty evident in these predictions is partially due to the relatively high "base rates" of behavior problems in young children. Many children do not continue with patterns of antisocial behavior as they continue through their school years or into adulthood. Predicting future behavior from childhood patterns is extremely difficult. In parallel, predicting extreme acts of violence from patterns of rule breaking at school is difficult as well. Realistically, involvement in school discipline processes is just one of a cluster of student characteristics that may play a part in a developmental process that leads to violence on school campuses.

In short, not all students who have risk factors associated with antisocial behavior or delinquency involve themselves in rule-breaking behavior. Risk and resilience theory suggests that students who do not end up with negative outcomes, despite the existing risks, have some individual resiliency or protective factors within the environment that allow for more positive trajectories. The net effect of the presence of such protective and resilience mechanisms is that the prediction model, if accounting for only individual risk factors, becomes less accurate.

An additional challenge to accurate prediction is that research that identifies and studies markers does a poor job of documenting the contribution of environmental influences to antisocial behavior. This omission is particularly problematic in the discussion of school discipline markers. While student behavior is a salient contributor to disciplinary referral, so are teacher tolerance and classroom management skill, administrative decision-making, and even local and national politics. As we discuss later in this article, these variations in school environment create a variety of situational contexts that muddy the prediction for individual behavior. School contexts do have a powerful influence on violence when it is seen as SCHOOL violence as opposed the YOUTH violence. . . .

Environmental Contributions to School Discipline

In a multivariate model, the best predictions come from accounting for as much variance in the equation as possible. Most research to date has focused on the individual characteristics that may lead a student to break rules, sometimes in a violent fashion. It is more difficult to document and account for the effects of risk and protection within the environment, yet it is apparent that classroom and school characteristics contribute a significant source of variance to school disciplinary events and outcomes.

Classroom and school predictors of school discipline.   Classroom and school characteristics are a significant source of variance in predicting school disciplinary actions. At a molar level, schools have been implicated in the contribution to antisocial behavior through practices such as punitive disciplinary practices, lack of clarity about rules, expectations and consequences, failure to consider individual differences and overall high rates of academic failure. Hinshaw notes that academic failure in the early school years contributes to frustration, peer rejection, and concomitant aggressive behavior.

At a molecular level, classroom and school variation appears to make a substantial contribution to who is referred or suspended. In one investigation at the middle school level, two thirds of all disciplinary referrals came from 25% of the school's teachers. Rates of suspension are also influenced by a variety of school factors. Schools with higher rates of suspension have been reported to have higher student-teacher ratios and a lower level of academic quality, spend more time on discipline-related matters, and pay significantly less attention to issues of school climate. Indeed, Wu et al. reported that school and district characteristics, such as teacher attitudes, administrative centralization, quality of school governance, and teacher perception of student achievement, explained a greater proportion of the variance in school suspension than student attitudes and behavior.

Differing discipline philosophies/implementation.   Administrative philosophies and variations in interpretation and implementation of rules and policies are a major source of variation for discipline referral, suspension, or expulsion rates at the school level. Bowditch reported that repeated school violations constituted the most frequent reason for suspension in the innercity school she studied, and found that the disciplinarians in troubled urban schools often view their role in large measure as dealing with persistent "troublemakers" who challenge the institution's authority.

In contrast to the view of school discipline measures as a discipline "event" and a way to control student behavior, there is increasing recognition that students who break the school rules are in need of some additional form of academic, social, or personal assistance. The provision of this assistance, as part of the punishment, could potentially enhance the protective factors in the child's environment or enhance their personal resilience. For example, in one study school administrators interviewed about the topic of school discipline revealed that they used the office referral or suspension event as an opportunity to contact the parent and bring them into the circle of concern about the student's behavior. Some would also use these events as an opportunity to pull in support from community agencies, depending on the needs of the student. These system-level actions have a potential to interrupt the negative trajectory of student misbehavior.

Morrison et al. noted that school principals' beliefs about children who misbehave and about the nature and cause of their misbehavior were important determinants of whether they approached discipline from a punitive or learning perspective. Two overall approaches were distinguished. The first approach was an emphasis on the rule-breaking behavior and the desire to deliver consequences. The overall driving theme for these principals was the need to control the students' behavior and a perspective about the behavior that was "black-and-white" (i.e., a rule was broken, the student *must* suffer the consequence). These principals did not necessarily see the need to involve the parent or bring in external resources to provide for support and possible remediation. The second approach was characterized by a focus on potential contributing influences for the rule-breaking behavior. These principals explored the issues with the parents and sought out resources to assist the child and their family with ongoing problems. Their emphasis was on assisting the child to improve their behavior and overall school functioning. In general, schools who had principals that endorsed the first, "get tough" approach had more suspensions than those who endorsed the second "student support" approach. Principals in the second group were more likely to explore and pursue non-punitive consequences for the behavior in question. Related to the question of prediction, the principals who adopted a supportive, non-punitive approach would be contributing inadvertently to error in the prediction of violent behavior; they would be instrumental in bringing protective factors and resilience into the lives of these students, helping them to decrease their use of aggression or rule-breaking behavior.

Suspension/Expulsion As an Intervention

The Latin root of the word discipline is "to learn." Thus, given a literal interpretation, all forms of school discipline such as office referrals, suspension, and expulsion should be designed for student learning. However, given the influence of zero-tolerance policies and mentalities, the main "learning" message is that the student's behavior is not acceptable and will not be tolerated. These discipline events typically are designed as just that . . . an event. The purpose of the event is to send a message to the student and to others, that a line has been crossed and the punishment is exclusion from the setting. This view of discipline begs the questions (a) Is the event as a punishment effective? and (b) In the case of students with disabilities, have important educational rights have been denied?

Part of the prediction question related to suspension and expulsion is the impact of those disciplinary measures on the student and on their future behavior. Very little research has documented the effects of these disciplinary actions as measures of change. Although they are designed as punishment (i.e., setting events designed to decrease the target behavior), it is unclear whether or not student behavior changes in a positive fashion as a result. In fact, some experts argue that school disciplinary consequences may accelerate the course of delinquency by reducing supervision and increasing the opportunity to associate with deviant peers and putting the student at odds with potential source of adult support at the school. However, some students who are disciplined, such as the "first-timers" described by Morrison and D'Incau, do respond with an awareness of avoiding trouble in the future and with the benefit of heightened vigilance by family and school personnel through supervision and support. Thus, given the unknown contribution of disciplinary processes to future student behavior, predicting from records of discipline events is of questionable utility.

There is very limited professional or research literature about "best practices" for suspension and expulsion. Over the past 20 years, a handful of articles have appeared that address the use of "in-school" suspension as an alternative to avoid total school exclusion; however, data-based evaluations of these strategies are limited and do not begin to answer the plethora of questions that need to be addressed. These questions include (a) Are student outcomes improved as a result of the intervention? (b) Are subsequent discipline referrals reduced? and (c) Are school-wide rates of discipline reduced?

Sugai et al. present a multilevel system of school-wide discipline strategies, noting that students who exhibit different types and different levels of severity of antisocial behavior will need different types and intensities of intervention to arrest and prevent future behavior. The relevance of this model for the prediction of violent behavior at school is that the prediction of violent behavior may be different at each of these levels. A number of other researchers have proposed preventive models that focus on school-wide reform and a comprehensive combination of program components with documented effectiveness such as skill training (conflict resolution/social skills), parent involvement, classroom and school-wide behavior management, functional assessment and individual behavior plans, school safety planning, and school and district data management systems.

Although these authors advocate for proactive, preventive school-wide discipline plans, at the point where a student is being excluded from school for disciplinary purposes, there is little to guide school personnel in how to make such actions part of a learning, improvement process. In recognition of the potential problem with denying education to a student, some states do mandate an alternative form of education for excluded children, as does the IDEA legislation for students with disabilities. As alternative programs continue to expand in response to increased disciplinary vigilance of the past few years, best practices for alternative programming will need further examination and explication.

Goodness-of-Fit Between Individuals and Systems

In the previous paragraphs, we outlined discipline practices that potentially have an impact on student outcomes. The variations in these practices will contribute to either positive or negative student trajectories. It is important to recognize that these trajectories develop over time. It is likely that the influence of a discipline "event" will be affected by the numerous environmental and individual circumstances that accompany the event. In this sense, the student's behavior and the system's reaction to that behavior are in constant interaction. The ultimate outcome for the student will be influence by the extent to which there is "goodness-of-fit" between the child's characteristics and the school's approach to discipline. Students with a high number of risk factors for delinquency may fit better in a school where the principal or school leader in charge of discipline takes a broad view of the student's behavior and garners support to keep that student in school and behaving in productive ways.

Conclusions

Any effective early warning system must meet two important criteria. First, as an early identification and screening system, it must yield reliable and consistent predictions. Thus, early warning signs must be capable of being reliably measured, so that there is a high level of certainty that the behaviors and students identified are those that most need assistance. Second, a primary requirement, perhaps the most important requirement, for early identification is that it enables effective intervention or treatment. The U. S. Department of Education guide *Early Warning, Timely Response* counsels that the primary use of any early warning system is not to target troublemakers, but to provide help for at-risk students identified through such a system. Unfortunately, accurate prediction may be a double-edged sword: a high level of accurate prediction of future disorder from present behavior may simply mean that our treatments have not been particularly effective in influencing the trajectory of disordered behavior.

In school discipline, as in much of education and psychology, the ability to predict disorder seems to far outrun the ability to positively influence the course of disorder. Studies of school suspension have found that up to 40% of school suspensions are due to repeat offenders, suggesting that this segment of the school population is decidedly not "getting the message." Tobin, Sugai, and Colvin reported that, contrary to their original hypothesis, students suspended in the 6th grade were more likely to be referred or suspended in middle school, prompting the authors to conclude that for some students "suspension functions as a reinforcer . . . rather than as a punisher." In the long term, school suspension appears to be moderately correlated with school dropout. From a standpoint of prediction, these data suggest that school suspension may be a useful predictor of future disorder. From a standpoint of treatment, however, these data provide a rather distressing insight into the failure of current disciplinary approaches to positively affect long-term outcomes.

In this article, we developed the case that students who are involved in the types of offenses that are disciplined by school systems are at-risk for a variety of negative outcomes, some of which may be violent and unsafe behaviors that threaten the overall safety of school campuses. However, the extent to which we can make accurate predictions from past discipline histories to future violent incidents is compromised by the variations in discipline practices among school campuses and limitations in capturing other environmental sources of risk and protection. Because the science of prediction has yet to capture these sources of error, we propose an alternate goal for educators. While we recognize the importance of protecting school campuses from the dangers of violent behavior, educators should attempt to undermine the science of violence prediction by making process of predicting future behavior from past behavior more error-prone; that is, they should institute effective school-wide prevention programs that address antisocial behavior early. Educators can thereby "bust" the predictions by making them meaningless and irrelevant in students' lives. Effective educational, behavioral, and mental health interventions may serve to interrupt the negative trajectories of students who would be expected, from past behavior, to commit the violent offenses of the future. Early warning systems, then, to be effective would need to factor in the presence (or lack of) effective early interventions, the nature of school administrator discipline philosophy, and the availability (or lack of) of secondary and tertiary intervention possibilities in order to provide "accurate" warning signs.

Kirk A. Bailey

NO

Legal Implications of Profiling Students for Violence

In April 2000, the Secretary of the Department of Education, Richard W. Riley, announced his opposition to the use of behavioral profiling systems to identify potentially violent students in schools, in a speech to school counselors in Chicago. Secretary Riley went on to state "[w]e simply cannot put student behaviors into a formula to come up with an appropriate response." The Secretary's comments are some of the latest in a longstanding debate over the use of violence-prediction tools to identify potentially violent students before they unleash their carnage on an unsuspecting school or community.

On the other side of the issue, parent groups, students, and law enforcement who see the daily press reports of school violence, teen shootings, and similar tragedies throughout America are calling for effective ways to prevent school violence. . . . In light of the level of violence affecting America's youth, it only seems natural that as each new school shooting grips the public's attention, parents, teachers, school officials, and policy-makers would demand a profile of school shooters to identify the source of potential violence before it erupts. Typically, a profile identifies a person likely to commit an act (usually criminal) of a certain type. These types of profiles are developed from extensive research and analysis of the crimes and behaviors of actual perpetrators: terrorists, drug couriers, and assassins, for example. The assembled information is compiled to identify the key characteristics of each type of crime and the corresponding characteristics of the type of person most likely to commit that type of crime. Accordingly, they are used to assess all persons in a given location or under a particular set of circumstances to determine if they match the profile and represent a potential threat to the safety of others.

A youth violence profile would most closely resemble the dangerous passenger profile used by the Federal Aviation Administration to identify possible drug couriers and terrorists in the airport setting. First, both are based on the methodology just described. Second, both are utilized in specific, highly insular environments—namely, an airport or a school. Third, they identify potentially violent individuals from a large population of highly similar individuals most of whom are engaged in innocent behavior. Finally, the assessment based on the profile is done under significant time constraints; time is of the essence in deciding on a profile match before a person boards a plane, or enters a school.

From *Psychology in the Schools*, vol. 38(2), March 2001, pp. 141–153. Copyright © 2001 by John Wiley & Sons. Reprinted by permission. References omitted.

Predicting violent activity in the school context raises a host of legal and ethical concerns. These concerns center on the validity (meaning the profile's ability to measure what it purports to measure and conformance to accepted scientific standards), and use of profiles as social science evidence, the impact of potential discrimination, search and seizure; and implications for privacy and the use of student records. The use of profiles as social science evidence will be addressed in the initial section of this article regarding "General Validity," while the search-and-seizure aspects of profile usage are addressed under the second section, "Profiles as Grounds for Search and Seizure." The third section, "Constitutional Issues: Access to Education Services Based on Profiles," addresses constitutional issues involving referral of students to alternative education based on profile matches. The implications for student privacy are discussed in the fourth section on "Privacy and Educational Records." This article attempts to outline the breadth of these issues without suggesting concrete answers. . . .

General Validity: Objectivity, Over-Inclusiveness, Evidentiary Issues

The general validity of a profile depends on the circumstances of its use. There is no governing legal rule or case involving a youth violence profile or the use of a profile in a school setting. As discussed in the Introduction, however, profiles have been used in a number of other settings and their validity assessed by the Supreme Court and a number of lower federal courts. The courts have avoided ruling on broad cases involving profiling, instead focusing on the specific facts of individual cases. Based on this body of law, it may be said that where a profile is used as an investigation tool to assist the determination of the need to stop and search a suspect, it is generally regarded as a valid practice (*U.S. v. Lopez*, 1971). . . .

Profile Objectivity

Typically, the Supreme Court requires that an "[e]ffective profile is one that may be 'objectively employed by the ticket seller [teacher] without requiring any subjective interpolation'" (*U.S. v. Bell*, 1972). In U.S. v. Lopez, despite upholding the general use of a profile in an airport-search context, a lower federal court suppressed the use of the profile because its objectivity and neutrality had been compromised. The court was concerned with the elimination of fundamental terrorist characteristics established by research, the addition of "an ethnic element for which there [was] no experimental basis" and the requirement of "an act of individual judgment on the part of airline employees" (*U.S. v. Lopez*, 1971). The court went on to state "[t]he approved system survives constitutional scrutiny only by its careful adherence to absolute objectivity and neutrality. When elements of discretion and prejudice are interjected it becomes constitutionally impermissible" (*U.S. v. Lopez*, 1971). The court suggested that the appropriate remedy for this oversight lies in the continuous supervision and control of personnel who have the power and authority to use the profile (*U.S. v. Lopez*, 1971).

Clearly, the court is concerned that profiles be free from issues of race and prejudice and supported by a thorough analysis of the factors involved in the profile. The concept of neutrality implies that the implementation of a profile will be free of any bias based on impermissible factors, such as race, religion, gender, or a host of other classifications, which our society deems an inappropriate base for judging individuals. Presumably, this also includes the absence of bias based on prior association of the parties involved, meaning that there should be no significant or compelling personal history between teachers and students that suggests unfairness, animosity, rancor or the like. Moreover, it seems reasonable to suggest that the limits of this neutrality stretch to prohibit even the appearance of bias in the implementation of a profile. Even the suggestion of unfairness or inappropriate application of a profile threatens to undermine its validity and acceptance by the general public and the affected population namely, youth, teachers, school officials, and parents.

Issues of individual discretion are somewhat cloudier, however. The law is concerned primarily with an individual employee's discretion regarding the factors included in the profile in the first instance rather than the exercise of judgment in applying those factors. This concern is particularly compelling in the case of a youth violence profile where numerous and differing risk factor lists exist that might be used as profiles. Our brief foray into this area revealed different formulations compiled by the Centers for Disease Control, the American Psychological Association, the U.S. Department of Justice, and the U.S. Department of Education. With so many, the risk of individual decisions at the classroom or school levels seems greatly heightened.

Yet, it may be impossible to ensure that the required objectivity and neutrality is present because, simply and fundamentally, schools and airports are too different. In an airport, strangers come together for a brief time for a utilitarian purpose (travel), while schools, in contrast, are places where people form long-term, intimate, personal relationships focusing on social and cooperative goals. It may well be that in the context of an airport or other public place that a profile will be implemented in a fashion that allows for its objective use. Usually in such a highly public setting, the passengers, travel agents, airline personnel, security officers, and others are largely unknown to each other. This anonymity promotes a greater level of tolerance for the unavoidable diversity one is likely to encounter during travel. In this scenario, security officials are more likely to utilize a profile in an objective manner—all they have to go on is the factors listed in their profile, and they are actively seeking those individuals who meet several of the criteria and disregarding at a moment's reflection those who do not. Under such circumstances, the security officers do not have time or inclination to consider subjective factors such as concerns about past actions of individuals, beliefs about political or social issues, personal habits or hobbies, or relationships with other members of the traveling community.

The situation is exactly the opposite in the school setting. In most cases, the students, teachers and administrators in any given school will be relatively well known to each other, at least in their immediate group of association. Teachers will be reasonably familiar with the lives, interests, problems, hopes, dreams, and fears of many of their students. In fact, as a society we hope that teachers will concern themselves with such matters. Consequently, teachers will be aware of those students who excel or are "problem" students. Under such circumstances, the probability that a profile might be applied subjectively and selectively increases dramatically. An integral part of the growth and learning process involves exploration of the bounds of social acceptance through a process of rebellion and antipathy to authority. While some of this behavior may rise to the level of violence or criminality, much of it remains relatively harmless and free of violence. Students exhibiting such behavior tend to generate more attention, however, and will certainly be well known to their teachers and the school administration. Moreover, these same students are likely to score high on the factors associated with any profile, if for no other reason than they are more highly visible among the student population, or consume the greater part of a teacher's time. For these reasons, it is not altogether clear that a profiling tool could be described accurately as "objective."

In any case, what is clear is that the use of a profile requires an objective and neutral application of the its elements and that employees should not be allowed the freedom to include or omit factors based on their subjective perspectives.

Profiles as Evidence: Over-Inclusiveness

In contrast to the investigation context, profile evidence is not admissible, generally, in a court proceeding to establish guilt, on the rationale that profile evidence represents a type of character evidence, which is disfavored by American courts, except in limited circumstances not applicable here. The view is that such evidence would be "too sweeping and over inclusive, and hence potentially misleading to juries and unfairly prejudicial to defendants."

Typically, a profile includes a number of factors that taken individually would result in the selection of almost any individual in a given circumstance or locale as a potential match to the profile, and most of these individuals will be innocent of any wrongdoing whatsoever. This is especially true in the case of a youth violence profile in light of the relative infancy of the predictive tools and the imprecision of existing measures.

The social science research in this area concerns itself with several factors including the level of positive prediction (accuracy), the sensitivity of the profile, and interrelationship of these two factors. The odd dynamic is that as the level of accuracy increases, the level of sensitivity decreases, and vice versa. In other words, as prediction (accuracy) improves, the effort becomes less precise in solving the problem of violence because a significant number of violent youth will not be identified by the profile. On the other hand, as sensitivity is improved, the effect is to identify more persons who do not belong in the prediction. . . .

In any case, the sensitivity dynamic is the over-inclusiveness problem commonly associated with profiles. These profiles are based on samples of compiled data regarding the known characteristics of known shooters. As such, they focus on the characteristics of a known population, heighten the impact of those characteristics on selection and improve the level of sensitivity. In doing so, however, they cast their net too wide and include youth who will not exhibit violence but who may possess one or more of the identified risk factors.

This over-inclusiveness problem severely diminishes the general validity of a profile and presents serious constitutional issues discussed in a separate section below.

The dynamic between profile accuracy and sensitivity does suggest some policy implications worth a moment's reflection, however. If sensitivity is society's concern, namely to account for all the violent youth, then the intervention program used in response should be positive, educational, and nurturing rather than punishing and retributive. This is so because we are likely to identify youth who may be at-risk but will never commit a crime or exhibit any violent tendencies. Inflicting a penal-type solution on these youth would exacerbate their problems, while a strong educational and social skills approach promises great returns in terms of their employment prospects, social development, contribution to society, and savings to the criminal justice system. However, if programs and interventions aimed at the potential outcome, youth violence, are harsh, punitive, and penal in nature, then greater predictive strength (accuracy) will be needed and should be desired. This argues for placing as much emphasis on accuracy as possible because society will want to guarantee that those who are subjected to limitations on their educational opportunity and civil rights are a true threat.

Clearly, however, this latter approach is fraught with difficulty, so much so that it proves unworkable. The greatest legal objection is that it somehow implies that youth may be deprived of certain rights or opportunities based on their *potential* for violent or criminal acts, rather than the act or wrongdoing itself. Our legal tradition abhors this approach. The U.S. v. Lopez court remarked disapprovingly on this very subject in stating:

> Undoubtedly there are persons with objectively observable characteristics who provide a higher statistical probability of danger than the population as a whole. But our criminal law is based on the theory that we do not condemn people because they are potentially dangerous. We only prosecute illegal acts. Putting a group of potential violators in custody on the ground that this group contained all or nearly all of the people who would commit crimes in the future would raise the most serious constitutional issues. (U.S. v. Lopez, citing Williams, Bonkalo, Woods)

For these reasons, profile evidence is generally avoided as a basis for the potential deprivation of liberty or rights, especially as evidence to be used in a formal trial or hearing. As a matter of policy however, it is worthwhile to consider how such evidence would be treated if the general prohibition did not exist. . . .

Youth violence profiles ultimately will be constructed according to standard methods of scientific inquiry such as surveys of school shooters and the compilation of statistics and risk factors for youth to identify trends. Yet, it is not clear that these profiles have been assembled to date according to standard and accepted lines of scientific inquiry, which is not to suggest that the social science identifying particular risk factors for violence among youth is invalid, but only that it cannot fairly be said to have been developed with the purpose of serving as a law enforcement tool in mind. At a more fundamental level, the social science methods that assemble these risk factor analyses often represent aggregated information regarding the risk that a given population will be involved in a specific behavior. This aggregation provides useful information about the group at risk for violence but may not have significant predictive ability when focused on individuals. In this light, a profile might be useful in identifying a "hot spot," a community, neighborhood, or school, more at-risk than others that needs additional prevention and intervention efforts.

In addition, few could argue that social scientists, educators, or policy-makers have had sufficient time to evaluate the effectiveness of these profiles as predictive tools. To bolster this argument, there clearly has not been sufficient time to subject these profiles to independent testing and verification or for them to gain general acceptance in the scientific community. Moreover, to improve the predictive strength of these profile models as applied in individual cases, a more complete understanding of the correlation between a profile and the outcome it addresses is needed. Therefore, more empirical data are necessary. A significant problem, however, is that referencing back from school shootings to assemble a profile is probably mathematically flawed in that it over-samples those individuals who are clearly positive for the violence outcome (Derzon & Wilson, 2000). This over-sample contributes to the over-inclusiveness of profiles when they are applied to a general population, as previously discussed.

In sum, these considerations indicate that a legitimate profile will be one based on objective and neutral factors, established by comprehensive research and replication, and accepted generally by the scientific community. Lacking these assurances, schools, education leaders, and the general public would be justified in treating profiles with significant skepticism. The presence of these conditions, however, will improve the use of profiles by practitioners and enhance their treatment in areas of the law considered in the remainder of this article. We now turn to those additional issues.

Profiles as Grounds for Search or Seizure

In some circumstances, a list of risk factors for youth violence or a profile of a potentially dangerous student may be used as grounds to stop a student for questioning or to search his or her possessions or person. There is no Supreme Court case addressing the use of risk factor lists or profiles in the school setting. Consequently, we must turn to the Court's leading decisions on search and seizure in the school setting in combination with its jurisprudence on the use of passenger profiles used in airports for guidance regarding the issues implicated by the use of a profile in a school.

Generally, school officials may search a student "if a search is justified at its inception and is conducted in a manner reasonably related in scope to the circumstances" (*New Jersey v. T.L.O.*, 1985). The reasonableness standard is intended "to ensure student's rights [will] be invaded no more than necessary to maintain order in schools, not to authorize all searches conceivable to school officials" (*New Jersey v. T.L.O.*, 1985).

A search will be justified where there are reasonable grounds for suspecting a search will reveal contraband or evidence that a student is violating school rules. The scope of the search is permissible when the measures used are reasonably related to the objective of the search and not excessively intrusive given the age and sex of the student and nature of the infraction. Accordingly, school officials may inspect a student's bag (purse, backpack, duffel) and clothing for hidden weapons, cigarettes, and drugs when they have reason to do so: e.g., a tip, observation of materials associated with drug use, bulges characteristic of weapons, the student lacks the proper school pass and acts excited or aggressive when confronted by school officials. Security officers may stop and frisk a student and proceed on reasonable suspicion resulting from the stop.

In addition, the court has expressly approved the use of "probabilistic" profiles in the airport setting to identify potential drug couriers or terrorists (*U.S. v. Sokolow,* 1989). The basis for this conclusion rests on the notion that while "[a]ny one of [the] factors is not by itself proof of any illegal conduct and is quite consistent with innocent [activity] . . . taken together they amount to reasonable suspicion" (*U.S. v. Sokolow,* 1989). In these circumstances, the fact that a list of factors giving rise to reasonable suspicion are also part of a profile "does not somehow detract from their evidentiary significance . . ." (*U.S. v. Sokolow,* 1989). Numerous other cases have allowed the search of individuals, particularly in the airport setting, based on their identifications through the use of a profile and noted that under the circumstances the officers possessed reasonable suspicion to stop a suspect (*U.S. v. Riggs,* 1972).

In short, profiles contribute to the formation of reasonable suspicion authorizing school officials to stop and search students for suspected wrongdoing. So long as they are used in an investigatory manner, consistent with the requirement for reasonable suspicion to stop an individual, they are probably a valid tool. Caution must be exercised however, to ensure that the scope of the search does not exceed the original justification for the search, namely that the search is consistent with the profile factors. However, the appropriateness of profile use in the school setting may be questioned at a fundamental level.

Critical Zones

The difference between the use of a profile in an airport setting and a school setting involves a fundamental question about the similarity of the settings in the first instance: Are they really the same or are there significant differences between them that impact whether it is reasonable to use a profile?

Airports are recognized as a "critical zone," where more intensive and intrusive searches are reasonable in light of the extreme risk to life and property represented by weapons in a plane. The notion that airports are a critical zone rests on the extreme vulnerability of the individuals utilizing the air-travel system. As stated by the Fifth Circuit Court of Appeals, the need for heightened security in airports as an "exceptional and exigent situation" is based on a variety of factors:

> At the core of this problem is the hijacker himself. In some cases, he is a deeply disturbed and highly unpredictable individual—a paranoid, suicidal schizophrenic with extreme tendencies towards violence. Although the crime of air piracy exceeds all others in terms of the potential for great and immediate harm to others, its undesirable consequences are not limited to

that fact. Among other things, it has been used as an avenue of escape for criminals, a means of extorting huge sums of money and as a device for carrying out numerous acts of political violence and terrorism. Perhaps most disturbing of all is the fact that aerial hijacking appears to be escalating in frequency (*U.S. v. Moreno*, 1973).

For these reasons, it is reasonable to implement the most effective and comprehensive prophylactic measures possible to ensure the safety of an airport, airplanes, and the traveling public. Consequently, few question the need for metal detectors, multiple checkpoints, video surveillance, or the use of profiles to identify potential terrorists in the airport setting.

In contrast, it is not altogether clear that a school is a "critical zone," as it is understood in the airport setting. Strong arguments exist on both sides. First, individuals at a school (students, teachers, administrators, staff) may readily escape a situation rapidly escalating towards violence. They can leave a room, jump out a window, or desert the campus location altogether if they feel their safety is threatened. Their choice to do so does not necessarily present them with the threat of imminent death represented by escaping an airplane flying at 30,000 feet.

In addition, the potential for harm is somewhat lesser in a school setting. A terrorist can destroy an entire plane with a bomb or well-placed gunshot, killing hundreds of people with a single, brief act. However, the school shootings that have occurred to date, while horrible, have not claimed hundreds of lives, and the average incident of violence involves person-on-person violence harming single individuals or small groups. It is harder in the school or community setting for a perpetrator to harm a great number of individuals than it is in an airport setting. No judgment of the relative importance of airport or school violence in human, emotional, or personal terms is intended by these comments, only recognition of the difference in scale involved in each circumstance.

Finally, and perhaps foremost, the perpetrator in a school setting, whether a highly motivated gang member, homicidal teen or garden-variety bully, is generally not the crazed fanatic associated with acts of international terrorism. It seems unfair, and at least an overstatement, to describe these youth as "paranoid, suicidal schizophrenics with extreme tendencies to violence," the concern so eloquently stated by the Fifth Circuit (Moreno). . . .

On the other hand, strong arguments support viewing schools as "critical zones." Perhaps the most persuasive argument rests on the American belief in the fundamental value of children and our concern for preserving the safety and innocence of young people. As a society we place a high premium on protecting our children, often couched in terms of fulfilling the promise of our most precious resource and preserving a legacy to our future.

In addition, schools are a critical zone in light of their salience as a target for domestic terrorism in its many possible forms. Clearly, the use of a school as an intended target would afford significant leverage in forcing compliance by political leaders, school districts, or wealthy parents with any number of demands. Whether a lone disaffected teen or a highly organized gang, a school would present a unique opportunity to extort money, compel political action, or bargain for release of fellow gang members.

Consequently, the use of profiles to identify potentially violent individuals is probably justified as an investigation technique to the extent schools are viewed as "critical zones" deserving heightened levels of security. Significant legal hurdles remain, however, before a profiling tool may be used for other purposes in the school environment.

Constitutional Issues: Access to Education Services Based on Profiles

Beyond the investigation context, the use of a profile in the school setting may implicate constitutional protections in a variety of ways. Primarily, we must be concerned with the due process and equal-protection concerns of using the profile to assign the student to specific services or educational environments. This section seeks to explore the scope of the former issue. Before proceeding, however, please note that the focus of this issue is to define the minimum level of services that must be afforded all students equally. . . .

Generally, constitutional law requires that all individuals be afforded equal enjoyment of fundamental rights (*Neil Broadly et al. v. Meriden Board of Education et al., 1992*, citing *Campbell v. Board of Education*, 1984). The protection of equal enjoyment grows out of equal protection law, which requires that individuals affected by a governmental action or statute be treated uniformly; in other words, that the rights, privileges, or responsibilities imposed on an identified segment of the population apply equally to all members of that group (*Franklin v. Berger*, 1989, citing *Reynolds v. Sims*, 1964, and *Cleburne v. Cleburne Living Center*, 1985). This does not mean pure or absolute equality, rather it requires that government classifications stand on reasonable grounds (*Franklin v. Berger*, 1989).

What constitutes reasonable grounds will depend on whether the classification or government action affects a fundamental right or an "inherently suspect" group. Where state action infringes on a fundamental right or impacts an "inherently suspect group, strict scrutiny will apply, requiring that the state action be narrowly tailored to achieve a compelling state interest" (*Reynolds v. Sims*, 1964, and *Cleburne v. Cleburne Living Center*, 1985).

Accordingly, when a youth violence profile is utilized as a matter of school policy to identify and refer students to an alternative education program, to the extent the profile selects students based on race, ethnic background, or gender, it will clearly have constitutional problems. An "inherently suspect" group has traditionally been defined as a "discrete and insular minority" subject to "invidious discrimination" and is commonly understood to include racial minorities and ethnic groups (*Cleburne v. Cleburne Living Center*, 1985). There are almost no circumstances under which such a classification can be argued to be a narrowly tailored attempt at achieving a compelling government interest. Of course, the presence of such factors in a profile is unlikely for exactly this reason, and notably the factors identified in most risk factor lists that could be utilized as profiles do not include any of the prohibited factors.

The fact of selection according to a profile probably does not create a "discrete and insular" group deserving of protection under constitutional standards. Several courts have ruled that special education students or exceptional students are not considered a "discrete and insular minority" deserving heightened judicial protection (*Neil Broadly et al. v. Meriden Board of Education et al.*, 1992). Accordingly, a class of violators of school rules, or potential violators of school rules does not seem discrete and insular or deserving of exceptional judicial protection. . . .

It has been longstanding belief that the government has a compelling interest in ensuring a strong system of education, necessarily implying it is free of violence. In *Brown v. Board of Education* (1954), the Supreme Court observed:

> Education is perhaps the most important function of state and local governments. . . . It is a principal instrument in awakening the child to cultural values, in preparing him for later professional training, and in helping him to adjust normally to his environment. . . . It is doubtful that any child may reasonably be expected to succeed in life if he is denied the opportunity of an education (*Brown v. Board of Education*, 1954).

For this reason, school officials have a strong obligation, both moral and legal, to take action in dealing with undisciplined youths, who may potentially threaten the welfare and safety of the other children in attendance. School safety is probably not a compelling enough interest to select youth for attention by prevention or intervention programs based on race, however. Race-based classifications are upheld only in situations designed to remediate past discrimination, such as in college admissions (and even this purpose is under serious question). Maintaining school security is critically important to the well-being of young people, but probably not so important as to justify race-based classifications to maintain order. In fact, such methods in schools would run counter to decades of judicial interpretations and development of social norms explicitly aimed at removing race-based classifications from all manner of education practice. To insert such considerations back into the educational environment would play to the worst instincts and base assumptions about violence in America.

Even if the state has a sufficient interest in using a profile under some circumstances, it may find difficulty in arguing that the profile is reasonable, much less "narrowly tailored," in achieving its goal due to concerns about objectivity and over-inclusiveness discussed earlier. The issue of objectivity questions whether a youth violence profile can be described as such when the basic elements of the profile may not yet be established with any general scientific agreement and when the application of a profile in the school setting may be tainted by subjective concerns, teacher-student relationships, and other appearances of bias. Requiring that a profile be objective does not require that it be the best possible method of achieving the government's interest. It simply means that it must bear indications of validity, fairness, and reliability that society as a whole would be prepared to recognize as proper. The absence of agreed-upon profile factors makes it difficult to describe a profile as a reasonable, for if it were so, general agreement would seem a relatively easy matter. More important, a reasonable approach by the government surely would not allow for the potential of bias and tainted application by those charged with implementing the profile. A reasonable method would encourage fairness and protect both teacher and student alike from the possibility or temptation of misuse, prejudice, or animosity. A reasonable formulation of a youth violence profile would make allowances for the close and familiar circumstances of a school setting to ensure it accurately identified those most at risk.

A more compelling concern regarding the reasonableness of profiles stems from the tendency of such tools to be over-inclusive in their scope. As previously discussed, these profiles, which are keyed to be highly sensitive to select all youth who may be violent, tend to identify individuals engaged in perfectly innocent and normal activity. Reducing this likelihood entails improving the accuracy of the profile, but the corresponding effect is to reduce the sensitivity of the tool, meaning that fewer potentially violent youth are identified. So, if the very construction of the profile oscillates between better accuracy and better sensitivity, can the profiling tool be accurately described as reasonable? We miss more potentially violent youth than we actually identify and include too many innocent youth with these methods, making the existing technology in this field too speculative to be reasonable in the eyes of the constitutional law.

For these reasons, it seems unwarranted to consider profiling a reasonable attempt at achieving the government's interest in preserving safe schools and a strong educational system. Logic dictates that to the extent that a profile is not reasonable in achieving the government's stated objectives, it cannot be narrowly tailored to achieving those ends. Consequently, serious doubt exists regarding the constitutionality of profiles as a selection mechanism for many school programs aimed at at-risk youth.

Privacy and Educational Records

The development of passenger profiles enjoyed extensive cooperative efforts between a variety of law enforcement agencies including the Federal Bureau of Investigations (FBI), Department of Justice, Customs Service, Secret Service (Department of Treasury), Federal Aviation Administration, and the Central Intelligence Agency. The frightening prospect of the intersection of profiling and database interconnectivity was anticipated by the Lopez court when it observed "employing a combination of psychological, sociological, and physical sciences to screen, inspect, and categorize unsuspecting citizens raises visions of abuse in our increasingly technological society" (*U.S. v. Lopez*, 1971). Other commentators have pointed out that marketing and insurance companies have collected personal information on databases, while the government has gathered information as well for Social Security purposes, public school operations, commercial regulation, and national defense. In particular, they have observed that "[a]irport security officials have longed for the day when they would have access to these databases for the purpose of singling out potential terrorists."

So, the natural question concerns the next step in the development of youth violence profiles: Will school safety efforts involve data sharing across education, health and human service, and juvenile justice resources to personalize profiles? If so, what information will be included and who will have access to it? The leading federal statute on the use of school-based information regarding students, the Family Educational and Privacy Rights Act (FERPA), ensures that students and their parents will have access to students' records, be able to correct erroneous facts, and be notified when that information is shared with other schools, organizations, or entities. This parental access and control of student records extends to profile-match information.

Family Educational and Privacy Rights Act (FERPA)

The important student records issue rests on the classification of a profile, or more specifically, the profile match regarding a particular student, as an educational (medical) record or a disciplinary record. Generally, FERPA requires that schools obtain prior written permission from a patent before releasing the educational records of a student to an individual, agency, or organization. Federal funding may be denied if a school maintains a policy or practice that does not require this prior parental permission. Educational records are defined in the statute as "those records, files, documents, and other materials which (a) contain information directly related to a student; and (b) are maintained by an educational agency or institution or by a person acting for such agency or institution."

Accordingly, educational records may include attendance records, academic information, general administrative records, and records of extracurricular activity to name only a few examples. In addition, educational records may include a variety of medical records such as psychological evaluations and the results of Rorschach tests used for diagnostic purposes. Based on this definition, it seems clear that information relating to a student's match with a profile would be considered an educational record under FERPA. . . .

On the other hand, the statute exempts certain information from the definition of educational records, only one of which is important for our discussion; namely, "records maintained by a law enforcement unit of the educational agency or institution that were created by that law enforcement unit for the purpose of law enforcement" are not considered education records. Despite this exemption, schools may include information concerning disciplinary action taken against a student for conduct that "poses a significant risk to the safety or well-being of that student, other students or other members of the school community" in the educational records of a student (FERPA). Thus, to the extent a profile is utilized by school security to promote law-enforcement purposes, profile-match information may be a disciplinary record, exempt from consideration and treatment as an educational record.

Consequently, when the profile match is viewed as a medical or psychological record, it qualifies as an educational record. In contrast, if it is a security or law-enforcement record it will be a disciplinary record and may be treated as exempt from a student's educational records *or* may be included in educational record. In the latter situation, notice to the student's parents and permission prior to release is not required. Consequently, parents may not necessarily be informed of the existence of such information on their child or be afforded an opportunity to review and correct the information if necessary.

Sharing Educational Records

The confidentiality of juvenile records (educational and medical) has long been regarded as a compelling state interest, requiring trial courts, state agencies, and school districts to take reasonable steps to ensure that privacy is maintained. So, for example, juvenile educational and medical records may be sealed in court proceedings despite a presumption that such proceedings are open to the public and media (*State ex rel Garden State Newspapers v. Hoke*, 1999).

Reporting information collected by a school to an outside agency or another school is a delicate matter, but one squarely addressed by FERPA provisions. Generally, a school that discloses an educational record must take three steps:

1. Make a reasonable attempt to notify the parent (or student of age of majority).
2. Provide a copy of the record that was released.
3. Provide a hearing if requested (34 Code of Federal Regulations 99.34).

A school may disclose information to another school or institution that the student is attending if the student is enrolled or receives services from the other institution and the preceding conditions are met. In addition, student disciplinary records may be shared between schools attended by the student in question, provided that the teachers or school officials have a "legitimate educational interest in the behavior of the student." Consequently, sharing a profile match on a student with another school will probably be permissible regardless of the classification of the information as a disciplinary record or an educational record. Schools generating such information will simply need to ensure that the recipient school has a legitimate educational interest in the child, a relatively easy obstacle to overcome. . . .

Sharing student records with law-enforcement personnel is also specifically provided for in FERPA, which allows disclosure of even personally identifiable information from educational records without the consent of student or parents to state or local juvenile justice officials or in health and safety emergencies. Exceptions of this type are sufficiently broad to even allow possession of a criminal defendant's school records by a prosecutor when the records had no apparent relation to the case being prosecuted. . . .

The area of difficulty rests in the release of educational records to non-law-enforcement or school agencies such as the media, social service agencies, or private companies. At least one court has held that newspapers may be entitled to receive and publish criminal investigation and incident reports compiled by school security, where such reports do not contain information required for enrollment or attendance, or academic data, because these reports are not exempt from disclosure under state public records law nor protected as "educational records" under FERPA (*Bauer v. Kincaid*, 1991). So, we return full circle to the record-classification issue. If profile-match information is regarded as a disciplinary record its release to media organizations may be permissible. Moreover, the release of that information may or may not require notice to the parents. In contrast, if it is considered an educational record, the possibility that the information may be withheld from the media is greater and the protections afforded parents and student through notification and a hearing must be maintained.

Conclusion

Clearly then, the use of profiling techniques present truly formidable concerns when focused on youth violence issues and used in an educational setting. The rush to stop the violence in our schools is understandable in light of the school shootings in the last three years and the chronic levels of violence among youth. The expansion in, and arguably effective, use of profiling in other areas such as law enforcement, drug interdiction, and terrorism prevention, promotes the notion that such techniques will bring the same results for schools.

Schools are different places, however, with different rules, norms, and customs than airports or other places where profiles are commonly used. In a school, how a problem is addressed is often more important than the purported message of any given lesson. Consequently, administrators, teachers, and school safety officers walk a very delicate balance between ensuring a safe environment through the use of all the methods potentially available to them, and creating a sense of fear, paranoia, infringement of personal rights, and violation of constitutional guarantees through the use of those same methods. As we have seen, in the investigation context, profiles are generally useful tools so long as they lead to proper assessment of reasonable suspicion to stop an individual. Profiles present more problematic constitutional issues where they are used as tools for referring a student to alternative education or counseling services. Even if it doesn't implicate these issues, it may be an invalid tool because it may not be a reasonable method of achieving the government's interest in safe schools. In addition, profiles present significant school record-keeping and right to privacy problems depending on whether they are educational records or disciplinary records. All of these issues rest on fundamental concerns about the general validity of profiles as scientific tools: their objectivity, accuracy, sensitivity, tendency to be over-inclusive, and general acceptance in the scientific community. For these reasons, the use of profiles involving youth in a school setting is highly problematic and controversial.

POSTSCRIPT

Can Profiling Help Identify Potentially Violent Students?

How far should schools go in terms of school safety and intervention with those individuals who may be the most likely to commit violence? Is it a responsible and valid endeavor for administrators and school personnel to identify specific individuals? Conversely, aren't school personnel responsible for keeping all students safe? What if a student displayed various warning signs, no intervention attempts were implemented, and a there was a violent outcome? Wouldn't most think that educators should have attempted to intervene?

Schools are often in a gray zone when it comes to maintaining a safe learning environment. The debate is how far educators should go in maintaining a safe environment while treating all individuals with equity and respecting individual rights. As Bailey pointed out, identification methods applied in other settings, such as airports, may not be appropriate to apply to school settings for obvious differences between the two environments.

A final caveat for consideration is that if early warning signs are to be noticed and appropriate interventions put in place, are educators the ones who should be identifying these students? It is possible that individuals who have developed relationships and opinions about students may not be the most objective parties in terms of identification? The methodology in selection and reading signs may lose its authenticity if someone has preconceived notions and opinions. On the other hand, educators may be some of the closest individuals to students and may recognize signs that other adults would not. What is the solution?

Suggested readings include E.P. Mulvey and E. Cauffman, "The Inherent Limits of Predicting School Violence," *American Psychologist* (vol. 56, no. 10, 2001, pp. 797–802), K. Dwyer, D. Osher, and C. Warger, *Early Warning, Timely Response: A Guide to Safe Schools* (U.S. Department of Education, 1998), S. LaFee, "Profiling Bad Apples," *School Administrator* (vol. 57, no. 2, 2000, pp. 6–11), and M.K. Burns, V.J. Dean, and S. Jacob-Timm, "Assessment of Violence Potential Among School Children: Beyond Profiling," *Psychology in the Schools* (vol. 38, no. 3, 2001, pp. 239–247).

ISSUE 15

Are Schools Violating Student Rights?

YES: Sam Chaltain, from "Is Freedom Safe?" *Teaching Tolerance* (Spring 2002)

NO: Benjamin Dowling-Sendor, from "Seeing Red Over Speech," *American School Board Journal* (March 2003)

ISSUE SUMMARY

YES: Sam Chaltain is the coordinator of the Freedom Forum's First Amendment Schools Project in Arlington, Virginia. Chaltain offers data that suggest that many teachers do not know the five freedoms protected under the First Amendment to the Constitution, and if they do not know the freedoms, they cannot be expected to protect student rights. Chaltain believes that in fostering student rights and related responsibilities, schools foster safer schools.

NO: Benjamin Dowling-Sendor is an authority on school law and is an assistant appellate defender of North Carolina in Durham. Dowling-Sendor contests that schools are being placed in the middle between defending the rights of students who want an education and those who would disrupt the school climate. Through case law, Dowling-Sendor demonstrates the levels of incivility that have crept into our schools and how schools must walk a tightrope to show that whatever student misbehaviors are encountered, schools may restrict student speech only if they have a well-founded fear of classroom disruption.

"Congress shall make no law respecting an establishment of religion, or prohibiting the free exercise thereof; or abridging the freedom of speech, or of the press; or the right of the people peaceably to assemble, and to petition the Government for a redress of grievances.

— The First Amendment to the U.S. Constitution

The five freedoms guaranteed to all citizens of the United States under the First Amendment to the Constitution, which was passed in 1791, include the freedoms of speech, religion, press, assembly, and petition. These basic freedoms allow all citizens to express themselves in various venues and styles, both in speech and in general expression. It also allows for practicing a religion of choice, assembling in groups, and petitioning the government to right a wrong through litigation or by other action.

The first amendment applies to all levels of government, which includes public schools. In 1943, the Supreme Court upheld the First Amendment rights of students who refused to salute the flag for religious reasons in the case of *West Virginia v. Barnette.* This landmark case solidified the protection of students in public schools under their First Amendment rights.

First Amendment rights protect individuals to the point that their actions do not infringe on the freedoms of others or that one's expression does not cause significant harm to another. What is viewed as one person's freedom of expression can become controversial if another is extremely offended or harmed. This issue can be particularly complicated for school administrators who are trying to enforce a safe and free environment for all students while still upholding the constitutional rights of all.

Dowling-Sendor discusses a court case in which students were suspended because of potentially offensive t-shirts they wore to school. The school district's argument is that they were within their rights to suspend the students due to the impending harmful outcomes of wearing clothing that may offend and incite members of another group of students. This, in turn, could lead to additional tensions and problems between student groups within the school. The court did not completely agree with the school district in this particular case and outlined specific reasons why.

Chaltain discusses the likelihood that teachers and administrators are often violating the First Amendment rights of students in the public school setting. He discusses the need for schools to be democratic in nature in order to teach students to become an active part of our democratic society. In addition, Chaltain makes an argument that schools that are the most democratic and tolerant produce safer environments for learning.

Are schools allowing freedom of expression, or are student's rights squelched in the name of order and submission? Do freedoms guaranteed to individuals by the First Amendment allow for all opinions to be heard no matter how offensive? Should schools have a slightly different stance on First Amendment rights when trying to maintain a civilized and comfortable learning environment?

YES

Sam Chaltain

Is Freedom Safe?

Stephanie Cuadrado has had enough. "I don't even see why you teach us this stuff, Mister," she barks. "All this doesn't mean a thing to me, because nobody respects what we have to say in this school anyway."

My U.S. History & Government class is talking about the First Amendment and the rights of students. Stephanie's initial burst of anger sets the tone for the rest of the class, who redirect our subject and launch into a series of disturbing stories of humiliation and powerlessness at school. Stephanie goes on to relate a particularly unnerving experience.

"This hall monitor stopped me last week," she begins, her facial muscles constricting at the memory. "I told him I was on my way to class and I couldn't afford to be any later because there was a test, but he just laughed and said, 'You shouldn't even bother. You're never going to graduate anyway.'"

The day that event occurred, I was teaching at a large public school in New York City, where I was still new enough to question the accuracy of my students' stories. As the semester progressed, however, I witnessed firsthand the charged atmosphere between adults and students at school. Simply put, the administration felt the only way to treat students like Stephanie, who could be gruff and confrontational, was by authoritarian rule. It was easier, in the interest of discipline and "safety," to remove their voices from the school's inner workings.

This rigidity may have produced a desirable code of silence and order during fire drills, but it also prevented the students from developing a set of ethical standards they could use to make informed, responsible decisions. As a result, I watched students get pushed and prodded until they became what was expected of them: troublesome kids with too much attitude and a penchant for making the wrong decisions.

Although many schools in America do create a positive sense of community and provide their students with the necessary intellectual and moral "equipment" for living, too many do not. For students like Stephanie, it is clearly not enough to isolate American civics to the classroom. How can we also find ways to model and apply the democratic principles we are charged with teaching, and help ensure that *all* members of the school community have a voice in the decisions that shape the learning process and their lives?

From *Teaching Tolerance*, no. 21, Spring 2002, pp. 30, 32–35. Copyright © 2002 by Southern Poverty Law Center. Reprinted by permission.

Fear of Freedom

As a starting point for answering this question, the First Amendment Center and the Association for Supervision and Curriculum Development (ASCD) conducted a national survey to discover what public school teachers and administrators think about the role of the First Amendment in schools. The study was commissioned to coincide with the launch of *First Amendment Schools: Educating for Freedom and Responsibility,* a multi-year partnership between ASCD and the Center that is designed to transform how schools model and teach the civic framework of the First Amendment.

Here are some of the key findings from the study:

- Although educators demonstrate greater knowledge of First Amendment freedoms than the general public, roughly one in five cannot recall any of the five freedoms.*
- While a majority of educators (63%) rate American schools "excellent" or "good" regarding First Amendment education, just 28% of the public give the same rating.
- By more than a two-to-one margin, educators disagree that "students at public high schools should be allowed to report on controversial issues in their student newspapers without approval of school authorities."
- Despite recent national guidelines on religious expression that were distributed by the Department of Education in 2000, an alarming 69% of teachers and 39% of administrators were "not at all" familiar with them.

Given this widespread lack of understanding, the current willingness to restrict student rights is not surprising. What results, however, is a belief that students should learn *about* democracy but not necessarily be allowed to *practice* democracy—at least not in the school setting.

Because of this "fear of freedom," educators and students are increasingly finding themselves on opposite sides of an ideological divide, with both sides battling to decide whose version of the First Amendment will win out. The most recent examples suggest just how much is at stake:

- A 16-year-old boy was suspended for lampooning his band teacher on a private Web site. The boy sued, claiming his First Amendment rights had been violated. Eventually, school officials were forced to settle with the student by writing him a letter of apology and paying him $30,000.
- Just weeks after the school shootings in Santee, Calif., a New Jersey school adopted a zero tolerance policy to increase school safety. Despite their good intentions, the policy resulted in nearly 50 suspensions in the first six weeks, most of which were meted out to children between 5 and 9 years old. Police files were opened on all those suspended, including the kindergartners.

---

*In case you've forgotten, the five freedoms are those of religion, press, speech, assembly and petition.

- The Louisiana Civil Liberties Union filed suit on behalf of an 11-year-old Muslim student who refused to accept a Bible from her principal. She had already been forced to participate in a classroom quiz about Jesus. Commenting on the lawsuit, the student's mother said, "The issue here is not whether one religion or faith is better than another, but about forcing one's faith on another person with no respect for that other person's right to practice their own beliefs." In September 2001, a federal court ruled that the distribution of Bibles by the school violated the Constitution.

This confusion about First Amendment principles presents two key challenges to schools and communities: First, how do we reform education about the First Amendment for school officials as well as for students? Second, how can we help educators and communities develop school cultures that encourage intellectual openness, protect dissent and cultivate civility and respect so that *how* we debate becomes as important as *what* we debate?

Ask Charles Haynes, the First Amendment Center's Senior Scholar, and he'll tell you that's where the First Amendment Schools Project comes in. According to Haynes, the project is "built on the conviction that the five freedoms protected by the First Amendment are a cornerstone of American democracy and essential for citizenship in a diverse society.

"What our nation's schools need to understand," says Haynes, "is that the First Amendment isn't part of the reason for unsafe schools; it's the solution that helps to create safer schools."

Any school interested in applying First Amendment principles will carry out that mission in varying ways, since the program doesn't establish a series of mandates. Instead, according to Haynes, "what unites First Amendment Schools is not one view of democratic education or the First Amendment, but rather an abiding commitment to teach and model the rights and responsibilities that undergird the First Amendment."

Echoing Haynes' sentiments, Dr. Gene Carter, executive director at ASCD, believes the project's goals became even more vital after the terrorist attacks of Sept. 11, 2001.

"At ASCD," says Carter, "we believe that schools have an obligation to provide students with the guidance they need as they wrestle with these new complex and emotionally laden issues. We believe that in a democracy, it is essential that schools provide students with access to reliable information and a variety of perspectives so that they can develop their capacities to make educated, rational and compassionate judgments. Schools need to help students carefully weigh questions about the meaning of justice, the balance between our civil liberties and public safety, and our responsibilities to one another as citizens and human beings."

First Amendment Schools

Although one of the goals of the First Amendment Schools Project is to develop an initial group of ten project schools, the main objective is to provide valuable resources to *all* schools. "And it may surprise you," says Haynes, "but there are a number of schools out there that are already applying First Amendment principles and achieving success."

One such place is McLean High School, located in the suburbs of Virginia. According to Becky Sipos, a member of McLean's English department and the faculty advisor to the school's award-winning newspaper, *The Highlander*, "the school has a strong commitment for students to learn civic virtue and moral character." One way the school accomplishes this, says Sipos, is by actively applying First Amendment principles in the school's culture. *The Highlander* is the centerpiece of that commitment. "We really emphasize the importance of a free press," says Sipos. "We stress the ethical responsibilities of reporters to be accurate, balanced and fair, and we analyze our coverage periodically to make sure that we are covering the entire school, not just popular groups and activities."

Sipos notes that the emphasis on rights and responsibilities is not limited to the school paper. "The values of McLean—respect, responsibility and integrity—and our honor code are taught to freshmen the first week of school as part of our Freshman Ethics Seminar." In addition, she says, "the administrators are very supportive of First Amendment principles. The principal comes to the newspaper classroom for regular press conferences and gives the students easy access to ask him difficult questions. And the administrators send memos reminding teachers of religious holidays so that teachers will take care in respecting the religious practices that are not well known."

Similarly, Park Day, an independent school in Oakland, Calif., approaches education from the belief that each child is unique and that children should be encouraged to learn, to think, to pursue their own curiosity, and to develop a strong sense of values. Unlike McLean, however, Park Day is granting these freedoms to elementary-age children.

Mona Hallaby, a teacher at Park Day and the author of the recent book *Belonging: Creating Community in the Classroom*, believes that the first way to achieve this sense of community in young children is by holding weekly class meetings. At the meetings, teachers help students "see the cause and effects of their actions, name their conflicts, and feel the public repercussions for their actions." As the year progresses, said Hallaby, "all the members of the classroom begin to feel safe, because they are seen and recognized as members of a classroom community."

Hallaby believes there are two central principles to which all educators should adhere: "One, positive change cannot occur in isolation. In order for children to feel supported, the whole class, not just their teacher, must be cheering for them, and believing that transformations can occur. And two, classroom power has to be shared among its members. Children are more likely to learn if they're included in the process of running the classroom and making decisions."

Martha Ball, a lifelong educator from Salt Lake City, Utah, couldn't agree more. "I use First Amendment principles as my classroom management tool," she said, "and it always surprises me to see how many of my students have never been asked directly by a teacher to participate in determining the shared values of their class."

Several years ago, Ball witnessed her students at Butler Middle School struggle with the growing pains of increasing diversity in their community. Under Ball's leadership, however, Butler "has [since] created a mini-experiment in liberty, about how we can learn to live with our deepest differences, and create an atmosphere of respect for the rights of others." By Ball's own admission, "it's taken time, but if the adults believe in the principles, and work to model them fully and honestly, then the result will be students who are more sensitive to the rights of others, and who have a greater awareness of what it means to live and work for the common good."

Ball and the other teachers at Butler begin this "mini-experiment" the second day of class each year, by developing and voting on a class code of conduct. "What they discover," observes Ball, "is that everyone is interested in one central principle: respect. Once that is established, I show them that our list of rules means nothing, nor does our commitment to respect, unless we understand the *responsibility* we each have to guard those rights for one another.

"What we teach our students all day," Ball says, "is about how societies are formed and what people have historically held to be most important. But our students need to understand what it means to *live* in a democracy, and what our ideals look like and feel like when they are applied throughout a community. If our children aren't taught in schools how to exercise these rights with responsibility, then who will teach them, and where will they learn this valuable lesson?"

But can we do all of this in our schools?

We must. In fact, our need to do so is even more urgent than before. As President Bush said soon after the Sept. 11 attacks, "freedom and fear are at war, [and] the advance of human freedom, the great achievement of our time and the great hope of every time, now depends on us." He may be right. But that means educators have a unique responsibility. As Martha Ball made clear, it is unrealistic to ask students to defend First Amendment principles if we don't help them learn about what it is they're defending.

The Hon. Learned Hand—one of the country's greatest judges and certainly the judge with the greatest name—warned us against becoming too complacent in our appreciation of these freedoms. As he said, "I often wonder whether we do not rest our hopes too much upon constitutions, upon laws, and upon courts. These are false hopes. Liberty lies in the hearts of men and women; when it dies there, no constitution, no law, no court can save it."

Or, in the words of another great legal mind, Justice William Brennan, "the framers knew that liberty is a fragile thing, and so should we."

Seeing Red Over Speech

Is the word "redneck" racially divisive? Does wearing a shirt with that word on it create ill will or hatred? Should such clothing be banned in school?

According to a New Jersey circuit court case, the answers to these questions depend on the unique history of a school district. They show that drafting and enforcing a policy on student expression is not for the faint of heart and that even in an era when courts are sympathetic to school officials trying to create a sound educational climate, regulating the expressive content of students' clothing can be fraught with uncertainty.

The facts in *Sypniewski v. Warren Hills Regional Board of Education,* as summarized by the 3rd U.S. Circuit Court of Appeals, point to a district determined to eliminate and reduce ongoing racial tension. They also illustrate how difficult it is for school boards to write and enforce policies that properly regulate student speech.

Tension Leads to Policy

The Warren Hills School District was hit by a number of racially charged incidents during the 1999–2000 and 2000–01 school years. They included a student wearing a Halloween costume of overalls, straw hat, and black face with a noose tied around the neck; students wearing shirts bearing the Confederate flag; the formation by some white students of a racist, "gang-like" group called "The Hicks"; the observance by some white students of "White Power Wednesdays"; a student waving a large Confederate flag down a hallway; and distribution of racist material from the Internet.

The tension sometimes erupted into conflict. A white student who had African-American friends was harassed at home by a large group of white teenagers who physically threatened him and called him a "nigger lover." In another incident, a fight broke out between a white student and a black student.

The continuing racial hostility led Superintendent Peter Merluzzi and the school board to take action. The board studied racial harassment policies adopted by other districts around the nation. On March 6, 2001, the board adopted a policy from a Kansas school district that had been upheld the previous year by the 10th U.S. Circuit Court of Appeals in *West v. Derby Unified School District.*

The relevant portion of the Derby Unified policy provides that "District employees and student(s) shall not racially harass or intimidate other student(s) or employee(s) by name calling, using racial or derogatory slurs, wearing or possession of items depicting or implying racial hatred or prejudice. District employees and students shall not at school, on school property, or at school activities wear or have in their possession any written material, either printed or in their own handwriting, that is racially divisive or creates ill will or hatred."

Examples cited in the policy included clothing, articles, material, publications, or any item that denotes Ku Klux Klan, Aryan Nation, white supremacy, Black Power, Confederate flags or articles, Neo-Nazis, or any other "hate" group. This list was not intended to be all-inclusive.

The incident that triggered the Warren Hills case occurred just two weeks after the board adopted the policy. On March 22, 2001, Thomas Sypniewski, a Warren Hills Regional High School senior, wore a T-shirt containing "country humor" by comedian Jeff Foxworthy. The shirt listed "Top 10 Reasons You Might Be a Redneck Sports Fan," none of which were racist.

Thomas and his brothers wore Foxworthy shirts to school several times before the board adopted the racial harassment policy. On those occasions, the T-shirts did not cause any disruption, and no students or school employees objected to the shirts.

On March 22, 2001, Thomas wore his Foxworthy shirt to school again. The shirt did not cause any problems until the last period, when security guard Neil Corley sent Thomas to Vice Principal Ronald Griffith's office. Although the shirt contained prohibited sexual innuendo and mentioned alcohol, Griffith was worried that the word "redneck" would be "offensive and harassing to our minority population" and might even lead to violence, given the history of racial problems at the school.

When Thomas rejected Griffith's option of wearing the shirt inside out, Griffith suspended him for three days. The next day, Thomas' brother Brian wore his Foxworthy shirt to the middle school. Robert Griffin, the middle school's vice principal, told Brian that he and Superintendent Merluzzi had decided that the shirt was not offensive and that it did not violate school rules. The school board, however, upheld Thomas' suspension and said administrators should have taken disciplinary action when Brian wore his short to school.

Thomas and his brothers sued the school board and school administrators in federal district court. Their main claim was that the racial harassment policy and Thomas' suspension violated the First Amendment's Free Speech Clause. By the time the case arrived in the 3rd Circuit on appeal, the questions facing the court were whether the ban of the Foxworthy shirt and the racial harassment policy were constitutional.

Linking Words to Beliefs

In a 2-1 decision, the 3rd Circuit generally upheld the racial harassment policy, but it struck down a small portion of the policy and ruled that the school board's prohibition against the Foxworthy shirt violated the Free Speech Clause.

Writing for the majority, Judge Anthony Joseph Scirica based his analysis on the Supreme Court's landmark 1969 decision about student expression, *Tinker v. Des Moines Independent Community School District.* In *Tinker,* the Supreme Court ruled that school officials could regulate student expression—including expressive clothing—if such expression "materially disrupts classwork or involves substantial disorder or invasion of the rights of others . . ." The court stressed in *Tinker* that school officials could not regulate student expression unless they have specific and well-founded reasons for expecting disruption. "Undifferentiated fear or apprehension of disturbance is not enough to overcome the right to freedom of expression," the court stated.

Note that since the shirt was not lewd and Thomas did not wear the shirt at a school-sponsored activity, two subsequent decisions that give school officials greater power to regulate lewd or school-sponsored student expression did not apply—*Bethel School District No. 403 v. Fraser* (1986) and *Hazelwood School District v. Kuhlmeier* (1988).

Judge Scirica noted that courts have upheld bans against the display of Confederate flags, but only when a school or school district has had a history of racial problems that establishes a well-founded fear of disruption.

But, of course, the issue here was not a shirt displaying the Confederate flag—just a shirt with Jeff Foxworthy jokes. Scirica noted that no disruptions had occurred when Thomas or his brothers had worn the shirts, including on the day of Thomas' suspension. The question, Scirica wrote, is whether the incidents of disruption due to racial hostility in the Warren Hills schools "involved sufficiently 'similar'—or otherwise related—speech to permit an inference of substantial disruption from the T-shirt."

School officials contended that, in the context of the racial tension in the Warren Hills schools, the word "redneck" had come to refer to racism and to words and symbols associated with racism. In short, they argued, clothing with the word "redneck"—like clothing with the word "hick" or with the Confederate flag—had become symbols of "The Hicks" gang. They also argued that it was reasonable for school administrators to expect that a shirt with the word "redneck" would cause disruption and contended that they should be able to ban such a shirt to control gang activity.

Judge Scirica rejected the school officials' argument. Although the words "redneck" and "hick" certainly are similar in meaning, Scirica explained that "[t]he offensiveness of 'hick' in the present context derives not from its meaning, but from its relationship to the gang-like group, The Hicks. Other words do not necessarily become offensive by being synonymous with such symbols . . ."

"Ultimately," Scirica wrote," 'redneck' and 'hick' must be similar not definitionally, but with respect to their associations with a disruptive group and its disruptive behavior. . . . Otherwise, we would be required to conclude that the school could also ban 'hillbilly,' 'peasant,' and the like."

Scirica wrote that schools that seek "to suppress a term merely related to an expression that has proven to be disruptive . . . must do more than simply point to a general association. It must point to a particular and concrete basis for concluding that the association is strong enough to give rise to well-founded fear of genuine disruption."

In other words, school officials had to show that the Warren Hills district and the words "redneck" and "Hicks" are so closely linked that students would naturally regard "redneck" as an obvious symbol or code for "The Hicks" racist beliefs and activities. Scirica concluded that the evidence in this case did not show such a tight link.

Questions About the Policy

Judge Scirica then considered whether the racial harassment policy itself, apart from its potential application to Foxworthy shirts, complied with the First Amendment. Scirica broke this issue down into three questions: Is the policy overly broad? Is it too vague? Does it amount to improper discrimination based on the content of expression?

As Scirica explained, a regulation of speech is overbroad if it prohibits expression that the Constitution protects as well as expression that the Constitution does not protect. The judge observed that the school board properly adopted the policy to contend with a particular problem—racially hostile expression—that had caused genuine disruption and could lead to more. However, disagreeing with the 10th Circuit decision in *West,* Scirica found that one facet of the policy—the prohibition against clothing or material that creates "ill will"—was overly broad.

Scirica emphasized that protection of unpopular expression that causes discomfort or hurt feelings "is at the core of the First Amendment." In contrast, the judge concluded that the policy's prohibition against clothing or material that is "racially divisive" or creates "hatred" satisfies the First Amendment because those terms connote conflict and strong feelings that could lead to serious disruption.

Without the term "ill will," Scirica concluded, the policy "is constitutionally permissible in the context of the Warren Hills School District and its recent unpleasant history. This reliance on the background of turmoil at a particular place and a particular time means that the policy would likely be unconstitutional in another school district, or even in Warren Hills at a different time."

Judge Scirica readily answered the other two questions about the policy. It is not too vague, he wrote, because the policy it is easy to understand and obey even though it is imprecise. Also, although the Free Speech Clause normally prohibits government regulation of speech based on its content, the law carves out an exception for regulation of student expression in elementary and secondary schools to prevent disruption and to maintain an environment suitable for education.

Judge Max Rosenn agreed with most of Scirica's majority opinion about the policy, but he dissented from the conclusion that the term "ill will" was overly broad. In Rosenn's view, the history of racial conflict in the Warren Hills school district indicated that "ill will" could lead to disruption. Rosenn also contended that the ban of the Foxworthy T-shirt satisfied the Free Speech Clause.

No Clear Formula

This case—and the conflicting opinions among the courts—illustrates the daunting complexity of Free Speech Clause analysis and the resulting difficulty in drafting and enforcing policies that regulate student speech. As Judge Scirica pointed out, the school board "made a good faith effort to respond to a serious disciplinary problem without unduly restricting students' expression."

Indeed, the 3rd Circuit largely upheld the racial harassment policy. But the importance of freedom of expression in our nation's law and values led the court to scrutinize the policy carefully and to reject the "ill will" language and the application of the policy to the Foxworthy shirts.

In the final analysis, the most important lesson to learn from this case is that—in light of the strength of our free speech tradition—school officials may regulate student speech (apart from school-sponsored speech or lewd speech) only if they have a well-founded fear of disruption. Unfortunately, the law does not give school officials a clear formula to guide them in making such a decision.

As Judge Scirica explained, that decision depends entirely on the unique conditions of a particular school district at a particular time.

POSTSCRIPT

Are Schools Violating Student Rights?

There are so many issues surrounding the First Amendment that are being continually debated in the current climate such as the right to burn our flag, tobacco advertising, speech that includes hate toward others, pornography, and even the content of some rap songs. There is a continual question in the minds of many about the extent of freedom of expression, and courts are continually asked to rule on these questions.

When considering public schools, educators have to be aware of these issues and how they should respond to issues of freedom while trying to provide an open educational environment for all students. In the case presented in the Dowling-Sendor article, the students were suspended over the possibility of potential disruption to the school environment based upon past incidents. Did the school go too far in its response? The court majority opinion said yes, but a dissenting court opinion said no. This opinion was given by one judge who stated that the "ill will" expressed by the t-shirt could lead to disruption within the educational environment and thought the ban of the t-shirt was appropriate.

Even while courts hand down rulings regarding the First Amendment rights and how they are protected, there are disagreements even among judges. The difficult question for educators is how do schools provide for the constitutional rights of individual students while still maintaining a safe environment that protects the rights of all?

Suggested readings include R.P. Grandmont, "Judicious Discipline: A Constitutional Approach for Public High Schools," *American Secondary Education* (vol. 31, no. 3, 2003, pp. 97–117), B. Dowling-Sendor, "Stop the Presses?" *American School Board Journal* (vol. 190, no. 10, 2003, pp. 44–46), M.M. McCarthey and L.D. Webb, "Balancing Duties and Rights," *Principal Leadership* (vol. 1, no. 1, 2000, pp. 16–21), J.A. Stefkovich and M.S. Torres, Jr., "The Demographics of Justice: Student Searches, Student Rights, and Administrator Practices," *Educational Administration Quarterly* (vol. 39, no. 2, 2003, pp. 259–282), and P.T.K. Daniel, "Violence and the Public Schools: Student Rights Have Been Weighed in the Balance and Found Wanting," *Journal of Law and Education* (vol. 27, no. 4, 1998, pp. 573–614).

Gun Free Schools Act of 1994

This site provides guidance to states and local entities regarding the Gun-Free Schools Act of 1994, which is part of the Improving America s Schools Act (reauthorization of the Elementary and Secondary Education Act of 1965 (ESEA), Public Law 103-382).

```
http://www.ed.gov/legislation/ESEA/
           sec14601.html
```

National Mental Health Association

This fact sheet, provided by the National Mental Health Association, presents information on the symptoms, diagnosis, recent research, and treatment of conduct disorder.

```
http://www.nmha.org/infoctr/factsheets/74.cfm
```

National Association of School Psychologists (NASP)

Mental health needs and their subsequent care within the schools is addressed, including a position statement by NASP. Specific information for educators on the mental health needs of children is provided, along with federal education policies that support expanding mental health services within schools.

```
www.nasponline.org/advocacy/healthcare.html
```

National Institute of Mental Health

This site provides detailed information that describes mental disorders and how medications are used for children.

```
http://www.nimh.nih.gov/publicat/medicate.cfm
```

American School Board Journal

This site provides an article from the *American School Board Journal* that focuses on the causes of aggression in children as well as appropriate steps for intervention within the school and classroom setting. Information is provided from various professionals and experts in the field of children and behavior.

```
http://www.asbj.com/2003/06/0603research.html
```

PART 4

Severe Behavior Challenges

*S*chool districts and their public constituencies occasionally face-off when it comes to managing students with extreme behaviors and significant behavioral difficulties. Public expectations for school safety and federal mandates for school achievement require school districts and school administrators to abide by various standards, expectations, and legal statutes. In response, schools have developed codes of conduct and zero-tolerance policies. On the other hand, blanket policies are often ineffective in all situations. The challenge for schools is to meet the needs of all students—as varied as they are—in a manner that provides an appropriate education for all in attendance. The range of student needs requires that management strategies are sensitive and specialized.

The challenges to the management of more severe student misbehavior are varied. How should zero tolerance be applied? Can all students be instructed within public education regardless of the severity of behavior problems? Who is responsible for the primary treatment of mental health problems—the school or parents? Can medications be helpful when more traditional classroom-management techniques have not been successful? Can explosive behaviors be dealt with effectively through suspensions and expulsions? Is there ever a circumstance when student restraint is justifiable? Important questions are raised regarding these policies and practices related to managing more severe behavioral problems. In Part 4, we address the pros and cons of these practices.

- Does Zero Tolerance Work?

- Can Schools Provide Effective Intervention for Adolescents with Conduct Disorders?

- Should Schools Treat the Mental Health Needs of Students?

- Are Antidepressant Medications an Appropriate Treatment for Students?

- Are Suspensions and Expulsions Viable Responses to Violent Behaviors?

- Is Student Restraint Ever Justifiable?

ISSUE 16

Does Zero Tolerance Work?

YES: W. Michael Martin, from "Does Zero Mean Zero?" *American School Board Journal* (March 2000)

NO: Jeanette Willert and Richard Willert, from "An Ignored Antidote to School Violence: Classrooms that Reinforce Positive Social Habits," *American Secondary Education* (Fall 2000)

ISSUE SUMMARY

YES: W. Michael Martin, supervisor of the office of elementary education for the Loudon County (VA) public schools, suggests that zero-tolerance policies are necessary to keep public schools safe for all children but claims that zero tolerance does not necessarily mean that an offending student must be suspended or expelled. He offers alternative remedies.

NO: Jeanette Willert, an assistant professor and coordinator of secondary education at Canisius College in Buffalo, New York, and Richard Willert, a child and family therapist at Condrell Counseling Center in Orchard Park, New York, counter that zero tolerance does not work since it blames the child as being traumatized and incapable of reform. These authors believe that schools should begin to teach students tolerance for others, coping skills, cooperative learning strategies, and pro-social communication skills as ways for violent students to manage their own anger.

Asignificant law related to zero-tolerance policies is the Gun Free Schools Act of 1994, which Congress enacted in order to provide for safer school environments. The law states that a mandatory expulsion should go into effect for any student bringing a weapon to school grounds. Some school districts have also extended zero-tolerance policies to include other infractions such as drugs, alcohol, and fighting. The controversies over zero-tolerance policies are easily produced. The fact that there are so many variations among incidents begs the question as to whether an automatic expulsion is fair to students in particular situations. Second, the effectiveness of expulsions as a result of a zero-tolerance policy is also consistently questioned. The ultimate goal of zero-tolerance policies is to create safer schools, but do they?

Martin argues that school administrators are put in controversial situations when enforcing zero-tolerance policies, specifically the Gun Free Schools Act. He evokes the phrase "damned if you do and damned if you don't" in reference to enforcing a strict policy that almost always upsets parents, the community, and students alike. He sympathizes with school administrators who are in a tough position because they have to take a stance on an issue that is controversial. Ultimately, Martin provides clear and practical suggestions for managing the enforcement of a zero-tolerance policy. Can school administrators afford to take chances when it comes to the safety of students, especially given the tragic violent incidents that have taken place in schools across the country and made national headlines in the not-so-distant past? Martin concludes that the safety of children is the goal, and it is worth the struggle of enforcing a policy that is put into place to protect students from an otherwise potentially horrendous outcome.

Arguing another position, Willert and Willert believe that an alternative plan should be put into place to keep schools safe from violence. These authors discuss that significant violent incidents are typically a result of individuals practicing aggressive and violent responses over time because these are the only skills in their repertoire. They suggest that one of the most effective ways to treat violent behavior is to address it on a daily basis within the classroom through educational methodologies that teach new skills and strategies to deal with anger. How can zero-tolerance policies work when they do not teach individuals new skills? Expulsions, as a result of zero-tolerance policies, just become a method of handling a behavior that has little to no educational value. It often also produces no significant and long-lasting behavior change. If this is the case, are we ultimately reducing violence in our schools by implementing zero-tolerance policies?

W. Michael Martin  **YES**

Does Zero Mean Zero?

Walking home from school, a 9-year-old boy removes an object that looks like a gun from his book bag and shows it to his friends. Someone notifies the principal, who is later told by the child's mother that the object is indeed a gun—albeit a BB gun that doesn't work anymore.

How would you respond to this incident?

Some context might help. In 1994—long before Jonesboro, Paducah, and Littleton—Congress passed a law called the Gun-Free Schools Act, which required states to approve zero-tolerance laws on weapons or risk losing federal funds. In response to a state law, the district in which this incident occurred adopted a policy requiring that students be expelled for possessing "Category A" weapons, such as guns and knives, and outlined a range of disciplinary consequences—from expulsion, to suspension, to counseling—for possession of "Category B" weapons, with specific attention given to "toy" or "look-alike weapons."

Given such clear-cut categories, it might seem unlikely that any conflict would arise over this issue. We in education know better.

The principal suspended the boy for 10 days and recommended expulsion. However, the boy's father contended that the boy and his mother had incorrectly used the term BB gun to refer to a "Nerf-style" toy that shoots soft foam projectiles.

The superintendent then reduced the suspension to two days, based on the father's statement, and decided not to forward the case to the school board for an expulsion hearing.

A reasonable compromise? Many in the media didn't think so. "Killing Common Sense With a Toy Gun," read the headline in a *Washington Post* column. It was a typical reaction.

A Balancing Act

I'm familiar with the 9-year-old's case because it happened in my district—the Loudoun County Public Schools in Northern Virginia. As an administrator, I'm also familiar with the frustration voiced by colleagues who never anticipated working in an atmosphere of constant conflict that causes them to question

From *American School Board Journal*, vol. 187(3), March 2000, pp. 39–41. Copyright © 2000 by Dr. W. Michael Martin. Reprinted by permission.

even the simplest of decisions. "You're damned if you do and damned if you don't" is a phrase used all too frequently by school administrators: damned if you zealously enforce zero tolerance (a policy mandated by the state and Congress), and damned if you're seen as too lax or too tolerant of weapons violations at your school.

The Loudoun case might not be the best from which to draw conclusions about the impact of zero-tolerance policies. However, it demonstrates the difficult trail yet to be forged by principals in such an environment—an environment that requires an administrator to possess an increasingly sophisticated understanding of the law and the common sense to apply the law on a situational basis.

School administrators must constantly weigh the rights of the individual student (and his or her parents) against the rights of the entire student body (and their parents). To that end, some school boards and superintendents are beginning to look for a middle ground between "automatic" expulsions for weapons violations and "laissez-faire" messages resulting in inconsistent enforcement.

Some school districts have adopted the position that the authority to expel rests solely with the school board and that principals should simply forward serious weapons violations to the board, along with their findings and possible extenuating circumstances. This approach closely resembles the procedure followed in the past, when principals were given broader discretion in determining what constitutes a serious weapons violation. The trouble is, even when special circumstances exist and the disciplinary action is significantly less than the maximum allowed, parents of the disciplined student—and, sometimes, other interested parties—might question the judgment used by school administrators and disagree with their decisions.

By now, most of the country probably knows the case of six high school students who were expelled after a brawl at a football game in Decatur, Ill. The school board initially expelled the students for two years but reduced the punishment to one year after Illinois Gov. George Ryan and the Rev. Jesse Jackson intervened. Jackson argued that the one-year expulsions were still too severe and organized several demonstrations to call attention to the disproportionate number of black students expelled in many urban districts. In early January, a federal judge upheld the expulsions, saying people should be able to attend a football game "without a violent confrontation erupting in the stands."

A Knife and a Threat

Another case that attracted national publicity last year involved a 13-year-old boy who was disciplined after taking a kitchen knife away from a female friend who reportedly had been contemplating suicide. This case also occurred in the Loudoun County schools.

The boy put the knife (which the girl had concealed in a notebook binder) in his school locker. The girl, meanwhile, told some other students, who informed school authorities. School personnel found the knife in the locker and immediately suspended the boy for 10 days, pending action by the district superintendent.

The details of the girl's subsequent discipline, if any, were not disclosed to protect her confidentiality. However, the boy requested to have his disciplinary hearing open to the public and the news media. And once again, Loudoun was criticized by members of the media who said the district was being too unyielding with its zero-tolerance policy.

A closer look shows that the policy was administered more flexibly than many in the news media contended. True "zero tolerance" would have resulted in permanent expulsion, since the student admitted that he had violated the district's weapons policy. In this case, the student was suspended for the remainder of the semester (about four months) because, according to school officials, he should have immediately handed the weapon to a teacher or administrator for safekeeping.

The student and his parents, represented by a lawyer from the Charlottesville, Va.-based Rutherford Institute, appealed the superintendent's decision on the grounds that the zero-tolerance policy was harsh and the punishment too severe. A disciplinary panel made up of three school board members unanimously upheld the recommendation for long-term suspension.

Stephen H. Aden, chief counsel for the Rutherford Institute, claimed that the school system denied the student due process by disregarding the "motive and intent" of the student. But while a four-month suspension is by no means a minor consequence, the boy's "motive and intent" seem to have weighed heavily in the school system's decision not to expel him.

Perception and Reality

The recent escalation of zero-tolerance weapons policies was predicated on the perceived increase in school-related shootings, but it's important to note that the actual statistics showed a 30 percent decrease in such incidents during the 1997–98 school year. This misconception thrived due to a tremendous growth in the reporting of school-related shootings—especially those high-profile cases where multiple deaths occurred in traditionally tranquil settings.

Knowing that children are safer at school than practically anywhere else, school boards and superintendents should try to alleviate the public's apprehension and reduce criticism. First, they should publicize their weapons policy, highlighting the consequences for noncompliance and defining the weapons that are considered deadly and dangerous, for which possession would result in a mandatory expulsion. The district also should acknowledge that only certain special circumstances may be taken into account when determining the appropriate consequence.

These circumstances might include:

- Age of the offender
- Ability of the offender to comprehend the requirements of the policy
- Intent of the offender
- Effect of the presence of the weapon (Was another party threatened or frightened?)
- Past disciplinary record of the offender.

It's important to acknowledge the public's concerns—and then address them through a sound violence-prevention plan. It's also important to publicize some of the safeguards in the plan without compromising the plan's integrity.

Finally, the district should discourage building-level administrators from rushing to judgment in determining whether or not possession of a particular weapon falls under a mandatory expulsion requirement.

Handling a Violation

The news media can play a valuable role by disseminating information on board policies to the community at large. Unfortunately, however, news coverage thrives on conflict, whether that conflict is an international crisis or a controversial decision at a high school. And while parents and students may talk freely to reporters, school administrators—bound by confidentiality requirements—are often portrayed negatively in news coverage of a school conflict. In addition, advocacy groups, such as the Rutherford Institute, often provide legal representation to families who find themselves in conflict with a school board or its policies. This combination of events results in a one-sided media flourish in which the school system and its administrators become silent victims while attempting to protect the rights of the student.

The following suggestions might help the principals in your district avert communication pitfalls in administering zero-tolerance weapons policies:

> **Don't dilute the policy message.** School districts must not soften their stance on weapons violations by appearing to back off from their resolve to keep schools weapon-free. The majority of parents are looking for reassurances that their children are protected by the policies and practices guiding the administration of the schools.
>
> **Be clear about consequences.** Publicize the kinds of situations in which a weapons violation will result in a mandatory expulsion. This information could be presented in conjunction with the "special circumstances" listed earlier.
>
> **Be careful with evidence.** When a weapon is confiscated, maintain a clear "chain of possession" to avoid the possible argument that the evidence presented is tainted or fraudulent.
>
> **Take time to do things right.** Principals who have dealt with weapons violations advise their colleagues to clear their calendars for at least five days if such a violation occurs. It will take a substantial amount of time to meet with the offender, victim, witnesses, and their parents—not to mention the time spent in discussions with central office administrators and, possibly, the board's attorney.
>
> **Prepare a communication plan for school employees and the public.** Taking every precaution to protect student confidentiality, the principal should inform faculty and staff that a weapons violation has occurred. Describe what actions were taken to ensure a safe environment and how this will be communicated to students and parents (announcement, assembly, newsletter, and so on). Staff members should be reminded not to discuss the incident and to

direct inquiries to either the principal or the district public information officer.

Coordinate responses to the media. When contacted by members of the media, all representatives of the school district should provide similar responses. This practice requires a minimal amount of coordination and time but will reap tremendous public relations benefits if the system is viewed as honest, unified, and professional in its handling of the incident.

Don't say, "No comment." If confidentiality requirements prevent open disclosure of details, explain to reporters that information will be made available only after the rights of the child involved have been fully protected.

Most school leaders will never have to deal with the aftermath of a weapons violation that results in serious injury or death. An increasing number, however, will have to deal with the enforcement of "one-size-fits-all" policies aimed at curtailing the number of weapons entering the schools. If we prepare our administrators, our staffs, and our communities for stricter policies but show a lack of resolve in their enforcement, then we lose credibility with all of our constituencies. If, on the other hand, we do intend to "draw a line in the sand," then we must be ready to deal with parents and their advocates who continually try to redraw the line for their children.

Trying to balance strict policy enforcement with practical procedural implementation is the greatest public relations challenge facing today's school administrators. But remember: Any school would rather gain a reputation for zealously enforcing a strict weapons policy than receive notoriety for a shooting incident. And communities will support their schools' efforts to increase safety and decrease violence—as long as schools don't lose sight of common sense.

NO ↵

Jeanette Willert
and Richard Willert

An Ignored Antidote to School Violence: Classrooms That Reinforce Positive Social Habits

Violence That Becomes Habit

In truth, school violence can be better understood when viewed as the extreme expression of bad habits—as the expression of routines of aggressive behavior that have been learned and practiced over time. When children lack a repertoire of successful, peaceful ways to express anger and resolve conflict, they sometimes learn an aggressive, violent way of responding which becomes habitual and ever more extreme. The most extreme act—killing—reflects this gradual development of aggressive habits combined with a tunnel vision focused on slights and rejections. The accumulation of these experiences eventually prompts an extreme response.

When a child feels rejected and powerless in life, then television, movies, music, and video games can serve as models for an alternative world where the powerless feel strong, where they can react decisively in dealing with opposition. Although an aggressive act can result from having seen or experienced trauma, aggressive acts are far more often the result of the repeated practicing of aggression, simulated or real, combined with the receiving of gratification from that practice. Over time, aggressive response becomes a habit, its gratification—for instance, a feeling of mastery converts the young person from a learner to an actor. Harris and Klebold, in their absorption in violent, virtual-reality video games, illustrate this process. In all likelihood, a finding will eventually emerge that every adolescent gunman had both repeated exposure to, as well as, repeated practice in expressing violent aggression. (And the confusing part is that aggressive sports like football may contribute less to this development than the "fantasy" aggression of the video game and arcade.)

High schools and middle schools have always had groups—jocks, fraternities, cheerleaders, sororities, nerds, brains, losers, earth-dogs, Goths, rockers, gangs. Within the school these groups fall into a kind of hierarchy—some are widely admired by fellow students, teachers, parents, and administrators and some are labeled as offenders with varying degrees of estrangement from the mainstream. James Harris, prosecuting attorney in the Paducah, Kentucky killings of

From *American Secondary Education*, no. 1, Fall 2000, pp. 27–33. Copyright © 2000 by Ashland University Weltmer Center. Reprinted by permission. References omitted.

members of a prayer group, believes that school cliques had a strong influence on Michael Carneal, who killed three of his middle school classmates. Michael was a member of the "Zoo Crew," a self-named group of kids who were labeled by others as nerds and misfits.

In the spate of school shootings that have occurred in the last two years, the shooters have spoken about their resentment toward being teased, bullied, and belittled by some of their classmates, particularly by popular cliques such as "the jocks." Eric Harris and Derek Klebold had been active in athletics before high school; however, by the time they took up arms against their school and classmates, they viewed athletes as their enemies.

In case after case, evidence mounts that kids who commit violent crimes in schools have given clear signals about their anger and resentment. What can be done to counteract the toxic buildup of hatred and alienation in some young people?

In dealing with violence, schools need to be more vigilant in looking for signs of aggressive behavior in students. Aggressive students need to be offered a variety of counseling options to reveal and address their frustrations. Certainly, schools need to supervise their halls, grounds, and classrooms more closely. The signs of an adolescent gunman's asocial behavior have frequently been reported only after the fact. Beforehand, no one seemed to really be taking the signs seriously, partly because it is difficult to discern the difference of idle threats or "blowing off steam" from threats with serious intent.

Halls and classrooms are full of angry threats and name calling. The "signs" of violence are overlooked in schools because there are so many "signs" of violence in the ordinary behavior of American children. Separating serious intent from "blowing off steam" becomes impossible. Even professional counselors have difficulty making these discriminations; their tactic in the wake of Columbine and other school shootings is to take all threats seriously. Amid all this concern, it is easy to forget that statistically schools remain the safest place for children to be.

Counseling and Its Limitations

More important, in the long run, than even the identification and treatment of potentially violent and estranged young people is the need for preventing the development of aggressive habits by teaching appropriate responses to frustrations and anger. Just what are these appropriate, alternative responses to aggression? It is a telling and disturbing possibility that many Americans would not find this an easy question to answer. A paucity of well-established alternatives appears to be a fact in our culture. Americans of all ages lack a repertoire of ways to express anger and resolve conflict.

Yet, most Americans could come up with some form of "You need to talk about it." And some of the solutions to school violence have been rooted in this idea. Counseling, peer mediation and peer tutoring have all been promoted as solutions for reducing the likelihood of violence in schools and they do provide an alternative to uncontrolled threats and aggression in the halls; yet each fails to incorporate day-to-day activities of the classroom. Only peer tutoring puts a non-alienated student in regular contact with an alienated student, the apparent goal being that the alienated student will be "helped" academically and become more socially integrated as well.

However, peer tutoring has several hazards. First, it puts two people into close contact—one who has been rejected by the group to which the other belongs. The overt goal of remediation is being delivered by a member of the rejecting group. Second, it presumes that alienated students are academically deficient, when in reality they may simply be refusing to participate. In actuality, some of those who have been responsible for school violence have done reasonably well academically. Third, tutors are given very little in the way of tools for dealing with a peer who may be alienated and angry. For all these reasons, it is unlikely that peer tutoring, will effectively reach those whose habits and choices are leading them to become more violent.

Habits are hard to break, especially when they have been practiced for a very long time and when practiced provide quick and much-needed relief from frustration. Those who struggle with their reliance on drugs, alcohol, tobacco and even food provide powerful support for this contention. For schools to cope with violence, they must teach children pro social ways for responding to each other and to frustration: violence needs to be conceptualized as a habit which needs to be prevented.

Effecting Change

Any solutions to changing students' behaviors and habits which ignore the central activities in schooling—teaching and learning—will probably fail. Effecting change in large systems is challenging. To alter some of the ways young people perceive and treat each other in school settings, however, requires a significant change. For teens to get beyond the labeling of cliques and to see their classmates as full human beings, significant change must occur in students' interactions in school.

Change involves three elements—knowledge, skills, and motivation (the hardest piece). How can these elements be related to school violence? First, knowing someone and understanding how that person can feel in given circumstances humanizes interactions and diminishes the power of the simple label of nerd, Goth, jock, etc. Second, building social skills of listening, sharing, joint problem solving, and group collaborating in small groups within the classroom is a powerful method for weaving a strong social fabric. And third, the hard part, motivation. Is it possible that more humanizing of relationships among classmates and more willingness to listen and accept different behaviors could have altered the angry, desperate thinking of Kip Kinkel, Luke Woodham, Michael Carneal, Derek Klebold, Eric Harris and other teen-aged killers?

If their complaints of being teased, bullied and belittled arc to be believed and if their bankrupt skills for coping with frustration and alienation are truly considered, how can we not clearly see the need for developing sensitivity and coping skills within our classrooms on a daily basis? Only through a consistent instilling of habits of listening, valuing, and sharing can we start redefining the ways kids perceive and treat each other.

Advantages of Collaborative Learning and Social Skills Training

Training teachers to use collaborative learning and to integrate social skills training in their classrooms is an effective step in promoting social and character goals. The key to their success is that they offer systematic and developmental approaches for reinforcing good habits on a day-to-day basis. Rooted in the theories of John Dewey, Jean Piaget and Lev Vygotsky, collaborative learning, and its attendant component of teaching social roles and interaction, promotes the view that learning is spurred by students being actively engaged with both the subject and their fellow learners.

In an article that appeared in The Education Digest, Friedland wrote that a shared trait of the recent school shootings is that the perpetrators felt rejected or ridiculed by their peers. He believes a warmer and more supportive school environment could identify such outcasts and work to defuse their hostility and alienation before they are driven to commit violent acts. He criticized the tendency of American classrooms to instill competitive and self-centered messages: "Do your own work." "Do not help others." "Be responsible only for yourself." Such messages condition young people to be isolated and detached. Frequently, their attitude is "What's in it for me?" He reports that in periodic surveys, students in both middle and high school view their classrooms to be competitive and unfriendly.

Friedland suggests that cooperative learning actively promotes and develops teamwork, pro-social skills, and a strong sense of belonging and unity. The attitude shifts from "What's in it for me?" to "What's in it for us?" That is a significant shift.

Dr. Spencer Kagan, researcher and author, believes that our society has lost the ability to cooperate and that the social structures that once upheld cooperation no longer prevail. He asserts that the schools have to assume this responsibility by teaching core values such as honesty, caring, responsibility, accepting others, empathy, tolerance, decision making ability, and self reliance. How can schools teach these values? Kagan supports using cooperative learning and teaching kids strategies basic to cooperative methodology: positive interdependence, group decision-making skills, individual accountability, skill in collaborating, and social skills.

David and Roger Johnson argue that all young people need to also be taught how to manage conflicts constructively. They suggest three steps for this process:

1. Establish a cooperative context, primarily through the use of cooperative learning.
2. Create intellectual conflicts through the use of structured academic controversies which increase student achievement, critical thinking, higher level reasoning, and intrinsic motivation to learn.
3. Establish a peer mediation program to give students experience in negotiating and mediating.

During collaborative learning, students acquire knowledge and social skills. To be truly effective, however, collaborative learning requires that students also develop communication skills. Good performance requires including all members of the group; the group often "sinks or swims" on the degree and quality of their interaction and communication. Collaborative learning activities teach the kinds of skills and attitudes required for minimizing rejection of one student by others and for increasing the ability of all students to deal with conflict and aggression in peaceful ways. In fact, in Johnson & Johnson's review of research on cooperative, competitive and individualistic efforts, they reported that cooperative learning produced more positive relationships among students regardless of ethnicity, gender, culture, or achievement. Cooperative learning also was shown to promote greater psychological adjustment—including psychological health, self-esteem, and social competence.

A meta-analysis of kinds of learning revealed that cooperative learning experiences promoted greater acceptance of differences among young people. They found that placing students who might not ordinarily have sought the contact afforded by cooperative learning into cooperative interactions moved them beyond initial prejudices toward other students and towards more multidimensional views.

Furthermore, in well-planned collaborative instruction, teachers assign students roles which enhance the functioning and cohesiveness of the groups. These roles give students practice in listening, presenting, recording, questioning, clarifying, encouraging and researching. These skills form the foundations of successful democracy which is itself a form of government which emphasizes peaceful conflict resolutions and the inclusion of all.

In a recent focus group session on school violence with parents from a large two county area in upstate New York, the group emphasized the need for more social skills training. "The earlier, the better!" was their response. In that same focus group study, school administrators reported that few of the schools had offered training to their teachers in defusing hostilities between students, in teaching social skills and values, or in cooperative learning techniques. Even in schools where some awareness had been raised, little real implementation had occurred. Their situation seems to be more the norm than the exception in schools across the country.

Conclusions

1. Youngsters who commit violent acts often express prejudice toward particular groups in school—athletes, minorities, serious students. Face-to-face interactions, promoted by cooperative learning, encourage students to listen to others and to play an active role in group responsibilities and decision-making.
2. Young people who commit violent acts have learned few skills for coping with frustration or negotiating with others. Group collaboration, a centerpiece of cooperative learning, has the power to awaken youngsters to the views of others and the need to talk through disagreements and to come to consensus—for the good of the group.
3. Violent teens seek out other troubled teens who reinforce negative social attitudes, provide a receptive audience for pent-up anger and spur more and more daring expressions of their hatreds. Cooperative

learning emphasizes the importance of positive interdependence in human culture. Positive interdependence shows troubled kids that the group can help them and that they can be useful and important in helping the group make decisions.

4. Troubled teens often report that they feel rejected and powerless. Their need for power combined with their anger at not belonging frequently lead them from finding vicarious satisfaction through television, music, video games and the Internet to actual practicing of aggression. Talk is a central activity in cooperative learning activities. Young people are taught to articulate their ideas, listen to others, respect ideas that are brought forth and talk through a variety of options.

How a School-Wide Effort Might Be Approached

Ideally, the first stages of school-wide change would involve a number of informational meetings about the reasons for change and the kinds of change that are desired. Training would follow for all shareholders in the school system. Experts in school violence, conflict resolution, and cooperative learning methods could work with school personnel to increase their awareness and their abilities in the use of a variety of new methods for dealing with students. Generally, new initiatives which involve changes in teaching fare best when a few key teacher-leaders are involved in the earliest stages—perhaps at a weekend summer retreat where they could be trained as turnkeys to serve as building level "experts" in their schools.

Teachers will need time to design or revise lessons to include cooperative activities and approaches. Such designs and revisions will be most successful if done in teams, with team members supporting one another in constructing curricula and talking about the efficacy and appropriateness of their plans. Building level administrators need to make it possible for teachers to meet often during the school year to discuss problems and assess their work. Three or four conference days should be scheduled throughout the year with the focus on follow-up sessions with the teachers and staff either by returning experts or by those who are locally trained.

Throughout the planning and implementing of the new system, parents and students need to be kept informed about the kinds of changes they should expect in their schools' classrooms. Their support should be gained; this can often be accomplished PTA- sponsored town meetings and through carefully planned "Meet the Teacher" evenings. In fact, "Meet the Teacher" should become "Meet the School," with a heavy emphasis on the teamwork among teachers themselves and among teachers, staff and administrators as well as on their school's mission, based on the new changes. Posters generated by the students or student clubs could highlight the goals of the school. Newcomers to the school should be able to identify the school's new goals as they enter the lobby.

Schools stand a better chance of improving their students' social skills and behavior by using the classroom as their forum. Young people must be in the classroom every day during the school year; they are in the presence of their teachers more than that of any other adult. Anonymity, so easily attained in school hallways, lobbies and auditoriums, is impossible in a well-planned classroom setting—especially when cooperative learning is introduced. It is in the classroom, then, that we have the time and ability to build new routines and new habits, and improve ways of interacting with one another. It is in the classroom that we can turn the tide for our troubled students.

POSTSCRIPT

Does Zero Tolerance Work?

Another issue for discussion regarding zero-tolerance policies is whether or not they contribute to disproportional punitive measures for minorities and low-income students. Various studies have pointed to the unequal amount of suspensions and expulsions of minority students, as well as those of lower socioeconomic status. Administrators need to be aware of these statistics as well as how objectively they are enforcing punitive measures.

This issue again opens the debate as to what stance schools should take regarding the safety of the learning environment. Is there a place for more extreme policies that send a clear message to students and families about specific behaviors? After all, aren't policies rendered ineffective if given various levels of consideration and exemptions? Why even try to implement a policy if it will not be enforced as written? Isn't it most clearly communicated when the bottom line is non-negotiable?

Should there be a limit on zero-tolerance policies? There are various cases or incidents that seem to be more extreme for these policies. For example, one student was suspended for taking Tylenol, one for carrying a pocket knife to fix a car window, and a third was expelled for shooting a paper clip with a rubber band at a classmate, missed, and broke the skin of a cafeteria worker. Is this a reasonable use of such a policy, or is it going too far? Are schools at a place where the enforcement of rules has to be black and white? If not, where do educators draw the line for rule-breaking behavior?

Suggested readings include K.T. Bucher and M.L. Manning, "Challenges and Suggestions for Safe Schools," *The Clearing House* (vol. 76, no. 3, 2003), N.L. Essex, "Zero Tolerance Approach to School Violence: Is It Going Too Far?" *American Secondary Education* (vol. 29, no. 2, 2000, pp. 37–40), R.C. Hunter and D.G. Williams, "Zero-Tolerance Policies: Are They Effective?" *School Business Affairs* (vol. 69, no. 7, 2003, pp. 6–10), and J.A. Sughrue, "Zero Tolerance for Children: Two Wrongs Do not Make a Right," *Educational Administration Quarterly* (vol. 39, no. 2, 2003, pp. 238–258).

ISSUE 17

Can Schools Provide Effective Intervention for Adolescents with Conduct Disorders?

YES: Monica M. Garcia, Daniel S. Shaw, Emily B. Winslow, and Kirsten E. Yaggi, from "Destructive Sibling Conflict and the Development of Conduct Problems in Young Boys," *Developmental Psychology* (vol. 36, no. 1, 2000)

NO: Leihua Van Schoiack-Edstrom, Karin S. Frey, and Kathy Beland, from "Changing Adolescents' Attitudes about Relational and Physical Aggression: An Early Evaluation of a School-Based Intervention," *School Psychology Review* (Spring 2002)

ISSUE SUMMARY

YES: Monica Garcia, et al. are professors in the department of psychology at the University of Pittsburgh. These colleagues present research to show that early destructive sibling conflicts and rejecting parenting are predictive of later aggressive behavior problems, thus suggesting that adolescence may be too late to change this aggressive pattern of social interactions.

NO: Leihua Van Schoiack-Edstrom is a research scientist at the Committee for Children. Van Schoiack-Edstrom and colleagues have shown that adolescent students enrolled in their second year in the Second Step Program decreased in their overall endorsement of aggression and perceived difficulty of performing social skills, thus discounting the contention that adolescence is too late for students to improve conduct disorders.

Conduct disorder is a clinical diagnosis used by mental health professionals to describe the population of children and adolescents who display significant rule-breaking behaviors that are typically aggressive and harmful to other people and sometimes animals. Many of the exhibited behaviors can also be defined as illegal. The diagnostic criterion for conduct disorder is as follows:

> "A repetitive and persistent pattern of behavior in which the basic rights of others or major age-appropriate societal norms or rules are violated, as

manifested by the presence of three (or more) of the following criteria in the past 12 months, with at least one criterion present in the past 6 months:"

1. Aggression to people and animals (i.e., bullying and threatening behavior, initiating fights, physically cruel to people or animals)
2. Destruction of property (i.e., fire setting)
3. Deceitfulness or theft (i.e., stealing, "cons" others)
4. Serious violations of rules (i.e., truant from school)

The population of youth diagnosed with this type of behavioral pattern has typically been difficult to treat effectively. It is challenging for school personnel and other community agencies to implement intervention plans that will create significant change in behavior and overall functioning for the individual. Research indicates that there may be some genetic component to conduct disorders and that children and adolescents with conduct disorders typically come from homes that have coercive interaction patterns, especially between the parent(s) and child. Coercive parenting can be defined as parents who establish negative and punitive discipline procedures and who are inconsistent in applying discipline. It appears that a coercive parenting style is frequently a fairly consistent factor in the lives of children and adolescence with significant behavioral difficulties.

Of course, this type of behavioral pattern is not conducive to healthy growth for a young person. When this profile is apparent, there are many risk factors. The first and foremost concern includes the consequences of law-breaking behaviors, such as the harm inflicted on other individuals and the consequences that occur as a result of breaking the law. Secondly, a young person's education is typically compromised because he or she is not focused on learning. In addition, difficulties in maintaining various healthy interpersonal relationships are present.

Garcia, Shaw, Winslow, and Yaggi describe the difficulties of a coercive familial interaction pattern and provide evidence that negative, aggressive, and stressful sibling relationships can also contribute to the conduct disorder profile. Typically, highly coercive sibling relationships are reflective of difficult parent-child relationships as well. The authors appear skeptical about intervention at this level, but in a final statement conclude that intensive family intervention should be a part of the treatment plan for these individuals. This paints the picture that effective intervention falls into the hands of mental health professionals and out of the school arena.

However, Van Schoiack-Edstrom, Frey, and Beland provided program-effectiveness data on a program established for schools that target the types of skills students with conduct disorders are typically missing. This program provided education in the area of reducing aggressive behaviors, increasing emotional intelligence, and improving social interaction skills. Results indicated program effectiveness evidenced by a decrease in aggression by the participating students, which may mean that school intervention with students at a secondary level can be effective.

YES ↵

Monica M. Garcia, et al.

Destructive Sibling Conflict and the Development of Conduct Problems in Young Boys

Many researchers have shown the importance of sibling relationships in child development. Research suggests that siblings can be important contributors to each others' acquisition of prosocial skills and to the development of social understanding. Siblings are often each others' first playmates, and this early play may be the medium through which they influence each other in these areas. Theorists also believe that siblings play a role in shaping the development of antisocial behavior from early to middle childhood. For example, Patterson has hypothesized that coercive cycles may be a mechanism through which sibling interactions contribute to the development of externalizing behavior problems.

Much of the research on siblings and development focuses on sibling conflict, its causes, and its antecedents. Implicit in this research is the idea that extreme sibling conflict and aggression have implications for children's adjustment; however, a connection between sibling conflict and conduct problems has yet to be demonstrated. It is probable that most sibling conflict is normal and harmless. However, prolonged aggressive and aversive conflict between siblings (i.e., destructive sibling conflict) may play a role in the development of conduct problems or may be an indicator of coercive family processes associated with the development of conduct problems. Because antisocial behavior is relatively stable, difficult to treat, and resistant to change, it is important to explore its early markers and signs. Aversive and prolonged (i.e., destructive) sibling conflict may prove to be one such marker that will increase psychologists' ability to identify and treat antisocial behavior.

The Influence of Siblings

Research has confirmed that siblings imitate each other and that most often younger children imitate their older siblings rather than the reverse. Because siblings often spend large amounts of time together, especially during early childhood, it makes sense that the behavior of an older sibling will affect the

From *Developmental Psychology*, vol. 36, no. 1, 2000, pp. 44–53. Copyright © 2000 by American Psychological Association. Reprinted by permission of the Author. References omitted.

younger child's acquisition of certain behaviors, such as cooperating, sharing, and acting aggressively. For example, in the area of prosocial behavior, older siblings' prosocial behavior during sibling interaction is predictive of helping, sharing, and cooperating in younger siblings. Sibling interaction is also predictive of the development of later social and emotional understanding in younger children. Dunn and Munn found that children whose older siblings showed high levels of prosocial behavior during sibling interaction demonstrated more conciliating behavior and cooperating 6 months later than did children whose older siblings did not behave as prosocially. Dunn and Munn also found that teasing or justifying by older siblings in a high proportion of sibling conflicts was associated with the younger siblings' justifying their own behavior and referring to rules at the 6-month follow-up. These findings show that sibling interaction is related to the development of prosocial behaviors and mature conflict-resolution tactics in younger siblings.

A logical hypothesis that follows from this research is that if siblings can influence the development of prosocial behavior, they can also influence the course of disruptive and aggressive behavior. However, few researchers have examined whether sibling interaction is related to children's conduct problems and, if this relation exists, whether it is simply a marker for other processes (e.g., parenting) or contributes uniquely to the prediction of conduct problems.

Coercion, Sibling Interaction, and Disruptive Behavior

G. R. Patterson, whose work links sibling interaction to the development of aggressive behavior, approached the subject from a transactional perspective. In Patterson's model, parents unwittingly reinforce children's oppositional and aggressive behavior through inconsistent and/or punitive discipline practices, which in turn are exacerbated by the child's increasingly aversive responses. Patterson dubbed these interactions *coercive cycles;* these cycles maintain and are reinforcing to the target child's problem behavior. In his work with families of clinically referred boys, Patterson found that siblings were also aversive in their initiation of interactions and that they were the family members most likely to become involved in coercive cycles with the target child. In his 1984 study, he analyzed these coercive family interactions to examine the role siblings played in the identified child's deviant behavior. Patterson's hypothesis was that in homes where family management practices had been disrupted, both children would exhibit problem behavior, and the additional stress of a coercive older sibling would make the younger child even more coercive. The results of the study supported this hypothesis to some extent. Older siblings from abusive families and from families with a clinically referred child were more coercive than siblings from typical families and were only slightly less coercive than the younger (referred) child. Siblings, both older and younger, were involved in 80% of the coercive exchanges with the target child that began as neutral events (e.g., fighting out of boredom). Patterson concluded from these data and previous studies that siblings can train younger children to be coercive by modeling and then reinforcing aversive behavior. . . .

Dunn and Munn examined a similar question with a longitudinal study of a nonclinical sample of siblings. Their study examined the relations between sibling conflict, physical aggression, and other conflict-resolution strategies. They found that physical aggression by the sibling was negatively related to conciliation in the target child and positively related to physical aggression by the target child 6 months later. This study was one of only a few to associate aggressive behavior by a target child's sibling with later aggressive behavior by the target child. Another interesting finding from this work is that a high level of maternal intervention in sibling conflicts was associated with physical aggression in the target child at follow-up. From the analyses performed, it is difficult to tell if it was the sibling's behavior, the mother's behavior, or both that accounted for increased levels of physical aggression in the target child. Dunn and Munn pointed to these results as suggestive evidence for Patterson's model showing siblings to be "shapers" of physical aggression.

Longitudinal analyses that examine families whose children are at risk for conduct problems would permit more extensive tests of Patterson's sibling-training model. Beginning at school age with a clinical sample, as Patterson did, makes it difficult to determine how the antisocial behavior developed initially. In addition, Patterson did not allow for alternate pathways in his model. A child who shows oppositional behavior in late infancy, possibly from genetic sources, may stress parenting resources, precipitating the breakdown of family management techniques. Bidirectional, transactional models have the potential to account for the individual and interactional contributions of each family member. Patterson's data do suggest that coercive cycles may be a key component in the development of antisocial behavior and that siblings are an important part of this process.

Although the work of Patterson and Dunn and Munn suggests that sibling interactions may contribute to the development of antisocial behavior, important questions remain. There has been little work specifically linking qualitatively destructive sibling conflict with conduct problems. This link would be important not only for Patterson's model but also for research that has examined gene–environment interactions and hypothesized sibling interaction to be a factor in the development of antisocial behavior. Whereas sibling conflict may be statistically related to conduct problems in children, it is also important to examine factors that may account for its association with these problems. Problem behavior in early childhood and parenting are two variables that could potentially account for this relation. Early conduct problems frequently remain relatively stable throughout childhood, and early problem behavior often predicts later behavior problems. Rejecting parenting, which is characterized by hostility and a lack of warmth, is also associated with the development of conduct problems in children. It is especially important to test whether rejecting parenting accounts for the relation between destructive sibling conflict and conduct problems, because in Patterson's model, disrupted parenting practices are one of the chief mechanisms responsible for the initiation of coercive cycles and their spread to sibling interactions. It is important to measure parenting and children's behavior at an early age (e.g., 2 years) in order to account for the effects of these variables on children's later behavior—before siblings are playing together extensively and influencing each other both behaviorally and cognitively as well as receiving increasingly less adult supervision.

It is unclear from Patterson's model whether parenting, children's previous behavior, and sibling interaction each contribute unique variance to the development of conduct problems or whether variance contributed by sibling interaction is actually accounted for by one or both of these other variables. Therefore, it is important to determine whether sibling conflict continues to contribute unique variance in explaining conduct problems once the effects of earlier externalizing behavior and parenting have been taken into account. Another possibility is that the interaction of destructive (aggressive and prolonged) sibling conflict and rejecting parenting contributes unique variance beyond that accounted for by the main effects of these three variables. In his model, Patterson posited that destructive sibling conflict and rejecting parenting help to create and exacerbate coercive cycles of interaction in families and subsequent behavior problems in young children. Another possibility is that sibling conflict takes on a different meaning in the presence of parental rejection. In this context, siblings may be aggressive toward each other because of rivalrous competition for scarce parental affection.

In the present study, two hypotheses involving the relation between sibling conflict and conduct problems were tested. First, we hypothesized that destructive sibling conflict would contribute unique variance to the prediction of conduct problems after we controlled for early behavior problems and rejecting parenting. On the basis of Patterson's and Dunn and Munn's work, we expected that destructive sibling conflict would be directly related to aggressive and delinquent behavior at the ages of 5 and 6 years. We examined these two types of antisocial behavior separately to explore the specific types of behaviors that would be related to destructive sibling conflict. There was reason to believe that both aggressive behavior, which is primarily reactive, and delinquent behavior, which is primarily proactive, would be related to sibling conflict through modeling but that rejecting parenting would be more implicated in reactive types of aggression. Second, following Patterson's model, in which children learn anger control and social (or antisocial) behaviors from their parents that are then reinforced through sibling interaction, we hypothesized that the interaction between destructive sibling conflict and rejecting parenting would contribute unique variance to the prediction of conduct problems over and above that contributed by these factors' main effects.

Method

Participants

Participants in this study were 180 families from a larger study of 310 low-income families that focused on the developmental precursors of antisocial behavior in boys. Boys were chosen because of their higher risk of developing conduct problems. The larger sample was recruited from the Women, Infant, and Children Nutritional Supplement Program (WIC) in the Pittsburgh metropolitan area, which provides nutritional resources to low-income families. At the time of recruitment, mothers were required to have at least two children at home, with the male target child approaching 1.5 years of age. For the present sample, the average educational level of mothers and fathers at recruitment was 12.5 years, and yearly family income was $12,816 (mean per capita income was $2,810 per year). The majority of the mothers, 58%, identified themselves as married or living together; 27% stated they were single (never married); and 14% were separated, divorced, or widowed. This sample consisted of European American (57%), African American (37%), and mixed or Hispanic (6%) families. None of these demographic statistics were statistically different from those of the larger sample.

Observational and maternal report data for this study were collected at the laboratory or at home when the target children were 2, 5, and 6 years old. At each visit, families were reimbursed for their participation. Because of strict criteria for inclusion in the study, sample sizes ranged from 115 to 180. The inclusion criteria were that the target child have a close-age sibling (a) who was between 1 year younger and 4 years older and (b) who was able to participate in the study at the 5-year visit. Of the 180 siblings, 28 were 1 year younger than the target child, 48 were 1 year older, 48 were 2 years older, 39 were 3 years older, and 17 were 4 years older. This age range was chosen so that the siblings would be close enough in age to the target children to be playmates, less likely to be in caretaker roles (as may happen with much older siblings), and in a developmental range similar to that of the target children. . . .

Procedure

The families were visited in their homes when the target children were 5 years old. Each target child and his sibling were videotaped playing with sets of toys while the examiner and the mother completed questionnaires in the same room. The sibling dyad was videotaped for 1 hour, during which the siblings played with up to three sets of toys brought by the examiner. The toys were (a) a castle with a shooting cannon and knights, (b) a *Lion King* set with movable animal figures, and (c) Bendits bendable building materials. The children were allowed to change toys every 20 min, or they could continue playing with the same toy for the whole hour. However, they both had to agree to change before the assistant could introduce the next toy (a procedure based on the work of Volling & Belsky). The mother was told that neither the examiner nor the assistant would intervene in the children's play and that she should interact with them as she normally would. We coded sibling conflict from these videotapes using the system described in the *Behavioral Observation Measures* section below.

Also as part of the Age 5 assessment, mothers completed the Child Behavior Checklist (CBCL). Follow-up reports of child behavior were also available from mothers (CBCL) and teachers (Teacher's Report Form, TRF) when the target children were Age 6.

In addition, we used data from an observed parenting task and maternal-report CBCL data that had been obtained at the Age 2 laboratory visit. The Age 2 assessment had involved a combined home–laboratory visit that lasted approximately 3.5 hours. Parenting data were collected during the second half of the assessment in the laboratory (see description in *Behavioral Observation Measures* section).

Maternal and Teacher Report Measures

The CBCL and the TRF are the most widely used reports of childhood behavior problems. In the present study, data from the Ages 2–3 version of the CBCL collected at the Age 2 assessment and data from the Ages 4–16 parent version completed by mothers at the Age 5 assessment ($N = 180$) and the Age 6 assessment ($N = 156$) were used. Teachers also completed the TRF when the target children were 6 years old ($N = 117$). This enabled the use of comparable factors across settings and times for each child. After Age 3, scales are normalized by sex and age of the child. . . .

For the present study, the narrowband Aggression and Delinquency factors were used instead of the broadband Externalizing scale because of our interest in their potential differential relations to sibling conflict. Whereas the Aggression factor focuses on symptoms related to reactive aggression and impulse control (e.g., "temper tantrums or hot temper," "screams a lot"), the Delinquency scale focuses on proactive antisocial behavior (e.g., "stealing," "swearing"). . . .

Behavioral Observation Measures

Rejecting parenting.   Maternal rejecting parenting was measured at the Age 2 assessment with the Early Parenting Coding System (EPCS), which was designed to measure a range of parenting behaviors typically exhibited in interactions with young children. The EPCS is an observational coding system consisting of nine categories of parenting strategies coded molecularly, per behavior, as well as six global ratings. Molecular and global ratings were made from videotaped mother–child interactions during a 5-min structured cleanup task at the Age 2 laboratory assessment. For the purposes of the present study, we used only molecular and global ratings relevant to hostile or rejecting parenting. These included two molecular ratings—verbal or physical approval and critical statements—as well as three global ratings—hostility, warmth, and punitiveness. Verbal or physical approval included praising, verbal affirmations (e.g., "good," "yes"), nodding the head affirmatively, smiling at the child, and physical affection. Critical statements were verbal statements that prohibited the child from doing something or showed disapproval of his behavior or character. Hostility was defined as the mother's emotional expression of anger toward the child as indicated by the tone of voice and mannerisms. The warmth rating was an evaluation of the amount of positive affect expressed toward the child. Punitiveness was defined as the extent to which, considering the child's behavior, the mother was too strict, demanding, or harsh. Originally, global ratings were made on a 4-point scale; however, punitiveness and warmth were converted to 3-point scales (1 = *none to a little*, 2 = *a little to some*, 3 = *some to a lot*) to improve interrater agreement. . . .

Sibling Conflict Coding System (SCCS).   We coded destructive sibling conflict using the SCCS, an observational coding system for sibling interaction based on a coding system developed by Volling and Belsky (1992). The system was designed to capture the amount and quality of sibling conflict during a 1-hour videotaped sibling interaction. . . . Four coders were instructed to record several aspects of each instance of conflict between the siblings: total number of utterances, number of seconds spent in each conflict sequence, intensity level of the affect (low, moderate, or extreme), whether physical aggression was involved (yes or no), and which sibling's action or utterance initiated the conflict sequence (target or sibling). We created an intensity-of-conflict score for each conflict sequence by combining the number of utterances and the affect rating. Intensity was scored as follows: 1 = one unreciprocated utterance with low or moderate affect; 2 = two utterances with low or moderate affect *or* one unreciprocated utterance with extreme affect (i.e., yelling); 3 = any conflict with three or more utterances that had low affect *or* any conflict with moderate affect and three to six utterances *or* any one-step physical aggression that was unreciprocated (i.e., slap or hit); 4 = any conflict with seven or more utterances with moderate or extreme affect *or* any conflict sequence with three or more utterances that included extreme affect and physical aggression; 5 = any conflict with reciprocated physical aggression. Level 4 and Level 5 conflicts represent the most prolonged and aversive types of conflict.

Global ratings were added to the coding system to account for characteristics of the sibling interaction that might enhance or mitigate the effect of the conflict on the target child's behavior. The global rating of destructive conflict (a 4-point scale measuring the overall severity of the destructiveness of the sibling conflict sequences) was used for this study. The definition of destructive conflict encompassed the extreme behaviors in the negative conflict sequences, such as aggression, yelling in anger, swearing, and especially denigrating comments. Our aim in using this rating was to identify conflict that would be actually destructive to objects, people, and the sibling relationship. The 4-point scale included the following codes: *no destructive conflict* (1), *occasional destructiveness* (2), *some* (3), and *several instances/very destructive* (4). . . .

Examining the Relation Between Sibling Conflict and Conduct Problems While Controlling for Early Predictors of Conduct Problems

. . . These results show that destructive sibling conflict added unique variance to Ages 5 and 6 conduct problems, both Aggression and Delinquency, after the entry of SES, Age 2 externalizing behavior, and Age 2 rejecting parenting. . . .

Discussion

The present study yielded several interesting findings. First, destructive sibling conflict was directly related to maternal report of delinquent behavior but not to teacher-reported outcomes. Second, sibling conflict accounted for unique variance in the prediction of delinquent behavior once SES, early child behavior, and parenting were accounted for; again, this was found only for maternal report. Third, and most important, the interaction between destructive sibling conflict and rejecting parenting accounted for unique variance in the prediction of aggressive behavior as reported by both mothers and teachers after these predictors' main effects and SES were accounted for.

These findings suggest that the pathways toward the development of aggressive and delinquent behaviors are somewhat different. The results were strongest for the Aggression factor; children who experienced high levels of aversive sibling conflict and high levels of parental rejection were rated as having higher levels of aggressive behavior by both mothers and teachers than were children who experienced only one of these predictors. It is possible that these results were consistent only for the Aggression factor because of the types of behaviors measured in that scale. It consists of items involving reactive dysregulation, including temper tantrums, destruction of objects, fighting, and screaming. These aversive behaviors are also likely to elicit parents' use of aversive control strategies, as described in Patterson's coercion theory of dyadic family interaction. It is also probable that teachers would observe these kinds of self-regulatory problems in classroom situations. This finding challenges the validity of direct relations between sibling conflict and aggressive behavior problems, because it is only in conjunction with rejecting parenting that sibling conflict appears to influence child aggressive behavior.

This result is also consistent with an additive risk model in suggesting that children who experience conflictual relationships with both parents and siblings in the home are more likely to demonstrate aggressive behavior at home and in school. The significant interaction between sibling conflict and early externalizing behavior contributes additional support to the additive risk hypothesis in that children who experienced high levels of both were more likely to be seen by their mothers as aggressive at school entry.

The interaction between rejecting parenting and sibling conflict adds depth to our understanding of Patterson's "coercive family processes." It describes a process in which family interactions take on a hostile and angry tone, a tone that may be initiated during infancy by parents, infants, or both. The hostility exhibited by a rejecting parent may spread to the sibling relationship via modeling as children adopt the parent's negative relational style and fail to learn more prosocial ways of negotiating conflict. Although the precise pathways linking rejecting parenting and destructive sibling conflict to conduct problems require further study, it seems clear that a boy who has experienced coercion and hostility with both his mother and his sibling is at a greater risk for aggressive problems than is a boy who has experienced coercion and hostility in only one relationship. . . .

Prediction of the Delinquency factor was not as clear. Although there was a main effect for destructive sibling conflict predicting maternal report of delinquent behavior after other predictors were controlled for, this relation was not found for teacher-reported outcomes. The nature of the Delinquency factor items may be informative as to both why there was no effect for teacher report of these behaviors and why there was a main effect instead of an interactive effect. First, the Delinquency factor items include more proactive, discrete acts such as stealing, lying, and associating with deviant peers, which teachers may not be witnessing as much as aggressive and dysregulated behavior. Second, these items are comparable to the theoretical construct of proactive aggression proposed by Dodge et al. In their model, proactive aggression is driven by the expectation of reward or enjoyment and is more likely to be influenced by exposure to aggressive role models (such as siblings). Alternatively, reactive aggression is more driven by frustration and is influenced by rejecting parenting and maltreatment. The relations between sibling conflict and delinquent behavior also support Patterson's sibling-training hypothesis for children with close-age siblings. Our results are consistent with the notion that aversive and aggressive exchanges with a close-age sibling may promote more serious types of problem behaviors in the target child, as spending time with a deviant peer group has been shown to do.

Two other issues from the pattern of results are worth noting. First, maternal rejection appears to be more significant to the development of aggression than to the development of delinquent behavior. This makes sense from a modeling perspective in that mothers would be more likely to display aggressive behavior (e.g., hostility, physical aggression) than to commit delinquent acts (e.g., stealing, vandalism). It is also possible that maternal rejection may promote hostile expectations toward others in the child (a hostile attributional bias) and increase the likelihood that she or he would act aggressively toward others regardless of the actual level of hostility they displayed. Second, the presence of only one significant finding with regard to teacher-reported outcomes is worth consideration. Such a result is in line with previous work showing that parents and teachers disagree more often than not when rating problem behaviors in children. We can also see from the differences in the mean *t* scores for maternal and teacher reports that the teachers in general rated the children as having fewer problem behaviors. This result highlights the importance of analyzing data from multiple informants separately to account for the various contexts of the child's environment.

This study was limited by the lack of earlier data about the siblings involved in the interactions. Because data were not available on siblings' conduct problems, questions could not be answered about which children (targets or siblings) were driving the interactions. Patterson's sibling-training hypothesis would postulate that it is the older siblings who are shaping the younger children's behavior, and other researchers have also assumed an older-to-younger sibling influence. However, it is also possible that close-age siblings have mutual influence on each other. Another limitation of the study was that only target children and their closest-age siblings were observed. This meant that for families with multiple children, the interactions with other siblings were not taken into account. Finally, the target children in this study were all low-income boys, which limits the generalizability of these findings to brother–brother and brother–sister pairs of siblings and to the predictive validity of sibling conflict for conduct problems in boys living in low-income families. Further studies should address these relations for girls and sister–sister sibling pairs and in other diverse SES samples.

Despite these caveats, the results offer support to the idea that sibling relations play an important role in children's social development, specifically in the development of early school-age conduct problems. They show that just as there are associations among sibling relationships, prosocial behavior, and social and emotional understanding, there are also similar connections between destructive sibling conflict and conduct problems. The results also suggest areas for future research, such as the linkages between sibling and peer relationships. Because the interaction between rejecting parenting and sibling conflict has been shown to be related to teachers' reports of conduct problems, it is possible that sibling conflict is related to peer interaction in school. If children are learning aggressive conflict-resolution strategies through interactions with their siblings, then they also may be adopting these strategies with peers. Further areas for research include taking into account child genetic and biological vulnerabilities and the effects of marital conflict on parenting, sibling interaction, and conduct problems.

The results of the present study may have implications for the assessment and treatment of conduct problems. Sibling conflict appears to be related to externalizing problems in the same way that other family process variables such as parental conflict are. Knowledge of the child's behavior in the context of the sibling relationship may be an important indicator of the pervasiveness of coercive relationships in the family. The results also indicate that sibling interaction is especially important to consider in conjunction with early rejecting parenting, because their interaction was associated with an increased risk of conduct problems over time and across settings. The results argue for a family approach to the assessment and possibly to the treatment of conduct problems in boys.

NO ↰

Leihua Van Schoiack-Edstrom, Karin S. Frey, and Kathy Beland

Changing Adolescents' Attitudes About Relational and Physical Aggression: An Early Evaluation of a School-Based Intervention

The long-term sequelae of childhood aggressive behavior have been extensively studied. They include delinquency, substance abuse, depression, school drop out, and early parenthood. In most of these studies, aggression is synonymous with physical aggression, much less common among girls than boys. Recent work has also associated negative consequences with relational aggression, more typical of girls than physical aggression.

Relational aggression refers to covertly inflicted damage that compromises the victim's peer relationships and social standing (e.g., ostracism, malicious gossip). Like physical aggression, relational aggression is stable over time, predicts peer rejection, and is associated with maladaptive friendship patterns.

Given the poor trajectory for aggressive children, there has been considerable interest in prevention efforts, although these have also tended to focus primarily on reducing physical aggression. Crick and Dodge's model of social interaction suggests that similar processes underlie physical and relational aggression and that promoting prosocial skill development may help reduce reliance on both types of aggression. According to the model, potential for aggression is higher when individuals have (a) deficits in social information-processing, and (b) attitudes that support the use of aggression or undermine the use of constructive alternatives.

Attitudes Associated With Aggression

Initial research in this area indicates that hostile attribution biases (the tendency to presume another's malicious intent in an ambiguous social situation) are characteristic of relationally aggressive as well as physically aggressive children. More information is particularly needed on the social cognitions of relationally aggressive children.

Attitudes characteristic of physically aggressive children appear to affect an individual's choice of goals and evaluation of possible responses in a given

From *School Psychology Review*, vol. 31, Spring 2002, pp. 210–216. Copyright © 2002 by National Association of School Psychologists. Reprinted by permission. References and notes omitted.

situation. Thus, beliefs that aggression is an effective way to avoid a bad image or that there are no real alternatives to aggression can legitimize the use of physical aggression. Aggressive youths' self-appraisal also contributes to their inappropriate behavior. They see themselves as relatively inept at managing their anger and aggression, yet more effective than their nonaggressive peers at using physical aggression to achieve goals. Attitudes such as these have yet to be explored with respect to relational aggression.

Prevention Efforts

The literature documenting the effects of prevention efforts offers some promising results, particularly when social competence promotion is part of a larger systemic, multicomponent effort within the school and programming is coordinated and long-term. The most common foci for prevention programs are broad social competencies and social interaction skills, and coping or stress management.

Several large-scale prevention projects undertaken in recent years have demonstrated effectiveness in increasing children's social competencies and decreasing antisocial behaviors and social cognitive attitudes. One of the largest multisite studies involving some 50 elementary schools in four geographical sites across the country is being conducted by the Conduct Problems Prevention Research Group (CPPRG). The intervention model used by these researchers involves a long-term program with multiple components targeting both universal and indicated (i.e., at-risk) student populations. The Promoting Alternative Thinking Strategies Curriculum (PATHS) is used as the universal prevention program for Grades 1 through 5, and offers a comprehensive treatment of social awareness and interaction skill, inhibition of inappropriate behavior, and social problem solving. In a randomized trial, first-grade intervention students demonstrated less aggression and more compliance with rules across self, peer, and unbiased observer ratings compared to controls.

The Resolving Conflict Creatively Program is a longitudinal program spanning Grades K-12 with a similar focus on effective interpersonal problem solving, but less broad than PATHS in its overall scope. Aber and his colleagues studied over 5,000 New York City students in Grades 2 through 6 and their teachers during the first year of implementation across varying levels of program implementation. Students receiving a high level of program intervention (i.e., moderate degree of teacher training, the majority of curriculum lessons taught, but few peer mediators in the classroom, as defined by cluster analyses) exhibited the slowest growth of aggressive cognitions, such as hostile attribution bias and use of aggressive problem-solving strategies, compared to other intervention conditions and controls.

The Social Problem Solving (SPS) Program initiated by Weissberg and his colleagues focuses specifically on middle school students. The 45-session program is similarly classroom-based and teaches the affective, cognitive, and behavioral skills necessary for social problem solving, decision making, and stress management. Study results indicated that students receiving the program demonstrated more effective and prosocial problem-solving strategies and better coping as reported by self and teachers. Moreover, program students' self-reported delinquent behavior remained stable from pre- to posttest, whereas controls' delinquency increased.

The Second Step program, the curriculum in the current study, is a classroom-based social emotional learning program that attempts to prevent aggression by fostering empathy and perspective-taking, problem solving, and anger management skills. (See Method section for a detailed description.) The Second Step curriculum is similar to the previously described programs (e.g., PATHS, SPS) in the competencies taught, such as emotion regulation, stress management, and problem solving. In addition, the Second Step program addresses aggression in a broad sense by devoting a significant proportion of lessons to relational aggression topics and the application of skills to reduce or inhibit such behaviors.

A review of research on the Second Step program documents a series of formative and outcome evaluation studies demonstrating its efficacy with students across grades. The most convincing results of the program's effectiveness to date come from an experimental study by Grossman and his colleagues employing systematic classroom and playground observations by unbiased observers as the outcome measures. Second- and third-grade participants in the Second Step program showed decreased physical and verbal aggression, and increased prosocial behavior relative to nonparticipating students.

Less information is available regarding secondary students' response to the Second Step program. A preliminary program evaluation with students in their first year of secondary school (i.e., junior high or middle school) assessed social skill knowledge only. Students were found to have greater understanding of perspective-taking, problem-solving, and anger management strategies after completing participation in the program. Since then, the program was extended for students in their second or third year of secondary school. The current research was part of a pilot study of the expanded program, examining program effects on adolescents' beliefs about the legitimacy of aggression and the perceived difficulty of performing prosocial behaviors.

Although intervention research has largely been limited to physical aggression, the present study was designed to overcome this limitation by intervening in and measuring attitudes that support the use of both physical and relational aggression. The Second Step program strongly emphasizes the negative consequences of both. Thus, participants were predicted to decrease their endorsement of physical and relational aggression relative to nonparticipants. In line with previous research, boys were predicted to endorse physical aggression more than girls. However, girls were expected to endorse relational aggression at levels equal to or higher than those of boys. Gender differences in response to the program were not predicted.

In addition to establishing norms counter to aggression, the program was designed to provide opportunities to practice positive solutions to social problems. It was predicted that the role-playing during lessons and skill application opportunities throughout the school day would decrease students' perceived difficulty of performing social skills. After participating, students were predicted to view prosocial alternatives as less difficult to perform, relative to nonparticipating students.

Method

Participants

Participants were 714 students in sixth (n = 179), seventh (n = 382), and eighth grade (n = 153), evenly divided by gender (51% girls). Students were drawn from five schools in the United States and Canada (with school sample sizes as follows). Two of the schools were a junior high (n = 273) and a middle school (n = 85) in neighboring Pacific Northwestern cities. Another middle school (n = 268) was in a large Southwestern city. The two remaining schools were junior high schools (ns = 54 and 34) located in an eastern Canadian city. Schools ranged in overall ethnic diversity (4% to 89% Caucasian), and proportion of students receiving free/reduced lunch (0% to 83%).

Intervention and control classrooms were both drawn from four of the five schools, thereby ensuring equivalence in ethnicity and proportion receiving free/reduced lunch. The one exception was the Pacific Northwestern middle school from which only intervention classrooms were drawn; the two demographic indices for this school were in the mid-range compared to the other schools in the study. . . . Classrooms were grouped according to their year in secondary school. Hence, the Year 1 group consisted of sixth and seventh grade students (n = 387) in their first year of middle/junior high school, and the Year 2 group were seventh and eighth grade students (n = 327) in their second year.

Sixteen educators (11 female) from the five schools participated in the study. All were teachers, with the exception of one principal.

Program Description

The Second Step, Middle School/Junior High program is commercially available and published by the Committee for Children. The stated goals of the program are to foster student learning of prosocial skills and to reduce impulsive-aggressive behavior. Prosocial learning objectives include: identifying feelings in oneself and others, responding empathically to others, and improving social interaction skills. Specific objectives related to reducing aggression include: recognizing anger warning signs and thoughts that fuel anger, using anger management techniques, applying a problem-solving strategy to social conflicts, and practicing behavioral skills to deal with challenging social situations.

The Second Step, Middle School/Junior High program was expanded from the original 1-year curriculum to a 3-year program, designed to begin with the first year in middle school or junior high school. Classroom teachers in health, English, or social studies are the most frequent presenters of the program. However, school psychologists or counselors sometimes perform this role themselves or in collaboration with the classroom teachers. In some schools, teachers present the material to the class, and psychologists provide additional lessons for specially targeted students. A model used in some schools employs school psychologists as trainers and coaches to classroom teachers. A 3-day training for trainers offered by the Committee for Children provides guidance for presenting the program to teachers and supporting implementation, using a variety of instructional strategies and extensive videotaped examples.

The program is composed of scripted lessons, each with clear objectives and preparatory activities that introduce the key concepts. Using the suggested lesson scripts, program implementers lead class discussions stimulated by videotaped vignettes, newspaper events, or stories. Discussion questions are designed to promote perspective-taking and, as the discussion progresses, specific strategies for dealing with the illustrated situation. Videotaped vignettes present students with opportunities to observe skills. Students practice the specific skills in small groups with role-playing and other classroom activities. Individual extension activities include tasks such as goal setting and self-monitoring of behavior and skill use. Homework assignments attempt to involve students in a larger social milieu by interviewing relatives or working with mentors. Activities for parents and teachers are intended to encourage skill use every day.

The first module in the program, Level 1, introduces basic emotional skills and problem-solving strategies, emphasizing perspective-taking and responding to the emotions and needs of oneself and others. The Level 2 module reviews the concepts and skills presented in the previous unit, and also focuses on factors related to aggression, including hostile attributions and beliefs about its use. . . . Each lesson is designed to be taught over one to two class periods.

Teacher Training and Implementation

In the current study, teachers received a 1-day training by one of two experienced Committee for Children trainers. The training began with a rationale and conceptual framework for the program, followed by a dual focus on conducting lessons and providing environmental classroom support for student skill use. Trainers modeled effective teaching strategies as part of the workshop presentation using a variety of formats (e.g., lecture, discussion, reflection, both live modeling and videotape examples). The interactive training workshop also gave opportunities for teachers to practice teaching lessons and specific instructional strategies.

Over the course of a semester within the intervention classrooms, teachers implemented the program as part of a class (health, life skills, social studies, or English) that students completed for credit (pass/fail). Teachers in both groups (intervention and control) sent home letters with students inviting parents to allow their children to participate in the study. The consent rate by class was high (M = 83%). Students whose parents withheld consent participated in regular classroom activities (including the Second Step program) but not study activities (i.e., surveys).

The Level 1 module was implemented with students in their first year of secondary school (Year 1 group), and Level 2 with students in their second year (Year 2 group). Thus, this pilot evaluation study examined students' responses to the second module without systematic exposure to the previous unit, although the intended practice is that the modules are taught in sequence. The study design allowed a preliminary and expeditious evaluation of the first two modules at the grades for which they were developed.

The curriculum developer regularly consulted with teachers and observed lessons. Assistance and coaching were given to teachers as necessary to ensure implementation integrity. Teachers completed written evaluation of each lesson, enabling a determination of the rate of lesson completion. Individual exit interviews with the curriculum developer also established evidence of program completion.

Measures

. . . For the current study, skills specifically targeted by the Second Step program were identified. Students rated the difficulty they would have performing skills such as managing anger, understanding another's point of view, standing up for oneself, and generating solutions to problems. The response format was a 4-point Likert scale (1 = EASY!, 2 = easy, 3 = hard, 4 = HARD!). Possible range of pre- and posttest scores was 8 to 32.

Procedure

The confidential surveys were given to the intervention and control students at the beginning (Time 1) and end (Time 2) of the semester. Each teacher appointed a student who would collect the surveys, place them in an envelope, and deliver to the school office for mailing. Thus, responses were never viewed by the classroom teacher.

Because teachers differed in their pacing of lessons over the semester, the interval between program completion and posttest varied between 1 and 5 weeks across classrooms.

Study Design and Analysis

Although the design of the study called for random assignment of classrooms to the experimental and control groups, only the Canadian sample met this criterion. Each of the Canadian teachers had two participating classrooms, one of which was assigned at random to the intervention and the other to the control condition. Some of the other teachers in the study were unwilling to be in one group or the other. For example, several teachers who had previously taught the program indicated they would participate in the study only if they were allowed to teach the program to their students. Intervention and control groups, therefore, may not be equivalent due to the lack of randomization of classrooms. . . .

Discussion

The current study is the first to suggest that a school-based intervention can change attitudes about relational, as well as physical aggression. By the end of the school term, students in their second year of middle/junior high school who participated in Level 2 of the Second Step program were less likely to endorse the use of aggression compared to control students. The Level 2 participants were less tolerant of physical aggression, verbal aggression, and social exclusion than were controls, and were also less likely to view prosocial skills as difficult to perform. Effects of the Level I module on students in their first year of middle/junior high school were less consistent. Level 1 participants significantly differed from controls only in their lower endorsement of social exclusion. However, a higher concentration of lessons (i.e., more than two lessons per week) was related to reductions in endorsement of physical aggression for Level 1 participants.

It cannot be determined whether differences m response to the Year 1 and Year 2 programs are due to differences in the samples, variations in program content, or in lesson concentration, because the three factors are confounded in the current design. Whereas the Year 1 program concentrates on acquiring basic social skills, the Year 2 lessons were specifically designed to increase motivation to perform the skills. An alternative explanation of the outcome differences by year is the greater emphasis on physical and relational aggression in Year 2 lessons. For example, the Year 2 program included a lesson on blocking the spread of rumors, a technique that elicited the most appreciative comments on student evaluation forms.

Another possible explanation is that the more robust findings for the Year 2 curriculum were due to the more concentrated implementation in those classrooms. Year 1 students who were taught the lessons more frequently during the week showed significant declines in the endorsement of physical aggression, relative to those receiving less frequent lessons. This finding lends support to informal educator assessments that the program has more impact if concentrated. The current results must be viewed cautiously, however, because the number of lessons taught per week was not a controlled variable.

Gender Differences

Male and female program participants exhibited few differences in the degree of attitude change. Gender differences, when present, generally appeared in the pretest scores. As predicted, girls in this study showed less initial tolerance of physical aggression than boys. Girls in their second year of middle/junior high school were also less tolerant of verbal aggression and rumor-spreading than their male counterparts. However, social exclusion of peers was endorsed equally at pretest by boys and girls. . . .

Differentiation of Physical and Relational Aggression

Consistent with research by Crick and Grotpeter, adolescents' beliefs about physical aggression were differentiated from beliefs about social exclusion. It was anticipated that items related to social exclusion and rumor-spreading would group together on a "relational aggression" factor. The rumor items, however, formed a factor with more direct forms of verbal aggression. . . . The current students were older than those studied by Crick and colleagues, which may account for the differences. The relatively small number of items in the two studies may also have contributed to unreliability in the factor structure.

Reliability is a particular issue for the social exclusion factor, which consisted of only two items. Future research should expand the number of items related to direct and indirect physical, verbal, and exclusionary aggression for a more accurate view of the factor structure. Differentiating more precisely between subtypes of aggression endorsement would also enable further investigation of apparent gender differences.

Future Directions

A limitation of the present study was our inability to randomly assign intervention condition and thus infer causality. Some of the teachers' reluctance to be in the control group is most likely indicative of the importance they placed on teaching social-emotional skills. Thus, the differences found between the Second Step and control groups may be due to dissimilarities in general teaching practices or teacher attitudes rather than to program implementation. An experimental design that counterbalances grade, program content, and secondary school entry would help disentangle developmental, curriculum, and contextual effects.

Further research is particularly needed to look at the impact of program participation under varying conditions of implementation. The present results suggest that concentration of lessons may be influential in program success. However, this study was limited in its measurement of other aspects of implementation, such as lesson quality and extra-lesson support of students' skill use. Indeed, the importance of examining the implementation process has been increasingly recognized by prevention researchers.

Long-term, sequential exposure would also be expected to strengthen program effects. The curriculum investigated here is designed to be implemented over the first 2 years of secondary school. Although students receiving the Level 2 module in this study did not receive the preceding Level 1 unit, these students evinced more extensive social-cognitive changes compared to controls than did students receiving the Level 1 unit. A more comprehensive and sequenced program implemented school-wide would likely have been more effective, a design recommended for social emotional learning programs. The Level 3 module in conjunction with Levels 1 and 2 allows for such an implementation throughout 3 years of secondary school, but has yet to be empirically tested.

The current study used only self-report data, which can suffer from significant biases including the desire to present oneself in a socially desirable manner. It is possible that a program-related change in what behavior students consider socially desirable may itself have positive implications for behavior. Nevertheless, it is unknown whether the social-cognitive changes noted in the Second Step group were accompanied by parallel behavioral changes.

A more extensive battery of outcome measures should be used in future research, including behavioral ratings (e.g., self, peer, or teacher reports) and/or direct observation of behavior. A multimethod, multi-informant approach is particularly important when assessing aggression, for several reasons. First, informant information will be limited by the respondents' direct experience and awareness of the behavior. Adult informants, for example, are likely to be most accurate when they assess aggression that is associated with visibly disruptive behavior. In contrast, adults appear to have a quite limited awareness of bullying, which tends to be more covert in nature. Peers may therefore be more accurate informants than teachers in such cases. Peer reports have been used extensively in studies of relational and physical aggression and have demonstrated both concurrent and predictive validity. . . .

The social-cognitive self-report measures utilized here need to be cross-validated with behavioral measures to determine their concurrent and predictive validity. Although many measures relating to physical aggression are available, relational aggression measures are few. Development of basic measurement capabilities is needed to assist with evaluation research in the area of relational aggression and its intervention.

Perhaps the greatest need is for additional information about effective ways to reduce relational aggression. To our knowledge, this is the first attempt to assess the impact of a school-based intervention on attitudes about social exclusion and gossip. The current findings offer some encouragement that an approach shown to be effective at reducing physical aggression might also influence student use of relational aggression.

POSTSCRIPT

Can Schools Provide Effective Intervention for Adolescents with Conduct Disorders?

Most experts would agree that early identification and treatment of children with conduct disorders is important to effectively intervening. Several forms of treatment approaches have been tried with varying degrees of success. At this point, not one specific program or approach has shown itself to be the best. However, specific areas to be addressed are commonly agreed upon by professionals. These would include behavioral intervention, such as setting up contingencies within the environment to encourage and reinforce specific desirable behaviors. Providing a high level of structure is also important. Secondly, family intervention is key. Therapeutic interventions related to familial relationships and interaction patterns should be addressed. Third, other areas of difficulty should be identified and addressed. For example, if the child has difficulties with learning or attention, these issues need to be treated at the same time in order to provide the student with the maximum chance for success in all areas of his or her life. Lastly, providing a comprehensive plan for these youngsters is in all probability an important component of the intervention. With all individuals involved in major aspects of a child's life working toward the same goal, the child is more likely to experience a positive behavior change.

Individuals with conduct disorders display some of the most difficult and concerning behaviors to society as well as to educational institutions. Because schools are a significant part of children's lives and educators frequently engage in teaching behavioral and pro-social skills, schools are a logical place for intervention when it comes to children with varying types of problems. Again, the logical question is whether or not schools can provide this type of intervention in an effective manner because if the time, money, and energy spent on intervening produce minimal results, should schools engage in this type of intervention?

Suggested readings include Stephen S. Leff, Thomas J. Power, Patricia H. Manz, Tracy E. Costigan, and Laura A. Nabors, "School-Based Aggression Prevention Programs for Young Children: Current Status and Implications for Violence Prevention," *School Psychology Review* (vol. 30, no. 3, 2001, pp. 344–362), M. Mowder, "Juvenile Offenders and School Psychology: Implications for Psychological Services," *The School Psychologist* (vol. 57, no. 4, 2003, pp. 155–157), A. Gerten, "Guidelines for Intervention with Children and Adolescents Diagnosed with Conduct Disorder," *Social Work in Education* (vol. 22, no. 3, 2000 pp. 132–144), and R. W. Greene, *The Explosive Child* (Harper Collins, 2001).

ISSUE 18

Should Schools Treat the Mental Health Needs of Students?

YES: Marc S. Atkins, Patricia A. Graczyk, Stacy L. Frazier, and Jaleel Abdul-Adil, from "Toward a New Model for Promoting Urban Children's Mental Health: Accessible, Effective, and Sustainable School-Based Mental Health Services," *School Psychology Review* (Spring 2003)

NO: Heather Ringeisen, Kelly Henderson, and Kimberly Hoagwood, from "Context Matters: Schools and the 'Research to Practice Gap' in Children's Mental Health," *School Psychology Review* (Spring 2003)

ISSUE SUMMARY

YES: Marc S. Atkins, Patricia A. Graczyk, Stacy L. Frazier, and Jaleel Abdul-Adil are professors at the University of Illinois at Chicago. They take the position that schools should take the lead in providing mental health services to needy students by encouraging greater involvement of families in children's mental health services, by creating teacher key opinion leaders as on-site experts on topics related to children's mental health, and by implementing the PALS (Positive Attitude toward Learning in School) program to foster and maintain parents and children in treatment.

NO: Heather Ringeisen is chief of the child and adolescent services research program at the National Institute of Mental Health. Researchers Ringeisen, Henderson, and Hoagwood contest that while students and their families might well benefit from mental health services in other contexts, current research has paid insufficient attention to the school context and has not offered means by which school organizations and the behaviors of professionals within those schools might need to be modified to support school-based mental health programs.

$\mathbf{A}$ range of mental illnesses can be diagnosed in childhood, including disorders that are anxiety-based such as obsessive-compulsive disorder, posttraumatic stress disorder, and generalized anxiety disorder. They also include mood disorders (such as depression and bipolar disorder), and eating disorders, tic disorders, and attention and behavioral disorders.

National statistics estimate that 10 percent of children have mental health illness, and one-third to one-fifth of those attain treatment. This means that much fewer than half of our children who need mental health treatment receive it, which is a significant gap. One key concern with the paucity of childhood mental health treatment is the developmental consequences for our young people. Without treatment, the consequences of mental health illnesses can take a large toll. For instance, childhood depression impacts social development, learning, and overall psychological functioning. If left untreated, the symptoms of depression can lead to delays in a child's education and socialization, and increase the risk of suicide and future bouts with depression. Another issue is the timeliness of treatment. If treatment is in fact received, but only after a significant period of time has passed since the symptoms began, the level and cost of treatment may be magnified because more issues have developed over time, the issues are more severe, and/or developmental skills have been delayed.

Questions related to providing comprehensive effective services to children and adolescents have been raised at the national level. Governmental agencies and national organizations have voiced concern regarding the state of children's mental health. There are many questions surrounding the identification and treatment of mental health needs in children, but one of the chief questions is how do we as a society effectively address the mental health needs of children? Subsequent to that, how do educators and schools, those who play a chief role in the development of our youth, address the mental health needs of children and adolescents? How involved should schools be or become?

Much has been written on mental health service models in the schools. These models provide for various levels of treatment for children. For example, Atkins, Graczyk, Frazier, and Abdul-Adil review three different program interventions that provide some varying levels of mental health services to children living in low-income areas. They argue that schools are a logical place to provide these services due to easy access to children and the opportunity to assess the effect of these services at varying levels, such as academic progress, peer interactions, and overall behavior. They conclude that positive effects were attained from the studies and advocate for continuing and improving mental health services for children within the school setting.

Contrary to this, Ringeisen, Henderson, and Hoagwood point out that the school context is quite different than a clinical context, and research-based mental health interventions have not been researched or developed for the educational environment and school organizational structures. Therefore, one cannot expect to transfer specific mental health services that have been successful in one context to the school context and anticipate the same outcome. In addition, the organizational structure of a school and district must be addressed in order to bring about organizational change that will truly support effective prevention and intervention of mental health needs. Otherwise, the level and effectiveness of mental health services remain somewhat minimal. Are schools prepared to make the types of changes? Or, is it a central role of schools to invest in more intensive mental health treatment for children and adolescents?

YES

Marc S. Atkins, et al.

Toward A New Model for Promoting Urban Children's Mental Health: Accessible, Effective, and Sustainable School-Based Mental Health Services

In this article three studies are described that are part of an ongoing program of research focused on the development of school-based models for mental health service delivery to inner-city children and families. These models are specifically designed in response to three concerns: (a) limited access for children and families in need, (b) limited effectiveness on children's real-world functioning, and (c) limited consideration of indigenous community resources as a means to foster sustainability. These foci have provided a framework to consider alternative mechanisms by which to engage families in services, to influence teachers towards accommodating children with ADHD, and to collaborate with policy officials at the Illinois Office of Mental Health and the Chicago Public Schools to develop a model with long-term sustainability.

The historic Surgeon General's report on mental health has, among many things, brought attention to the urgent call for a new understanding of children's mental health needs and for a broadening perspective on ways to address these needs. As noted in the report, and first noted by Weisz and colleagues, there is a critical gap between university-based clinical trials and community-based mental health practice. A highly influential task force report by the National Institute of Mental Health also concluded that practice-oriented research was a high priority for future funding. Since the publication of these reports, closing the gap between university-based clinical trials and community practice has become a national concern.

For children and youth, this movement has focused primarily on improving the effectiveness of mental health services offered in community practice, largely through the dissemination of evidence-based practices. However, perhaps even more urgent is the need to improve access to services. A recent analysis of

From *School Psychology Review*, vol. 32, no. 4, Spring 2003, pp. 503–514. Copyright © 2003 by National Association of School Psychologists. Reprinted by permission. References omitted.

three national surveys indicated that nearly 80% of youth ages 6–17 who were in need of mental health services did not receive services within the preceding 12 months, with rates approaching 90% for uninsured families. Furthermore, the assumption that there is sufficient knowledge regarding intervention effectiveness to transport evidence-based strategies to community settings is questionable. In fact, in many ways, recent efforts to transport evidence-based practices for children and youth are revealing as much about gaps in *knowledge* as about gaps in *services* offered in clinical practice with children and youth.

An additional shortcoming of children's mental health services research is the lack of consideration for how programs will be sustained. To improve services provided in community settings, research programs need to consider who will provide services, under what conditions, and how these services will be funded. A focus on sustainability also requires consideration of ecological factors that either mediate or moderate positive functioning, and those factors that have been shown to impact on these mechanisms. Therefore, a major goal of mental health programs should be to ensure that effective services rely on indigenous resources as a mechanism toward sustainability. This focus addresses the problem common to many, if not most, urban schools and community-based social service agencies that find they do not have the resources to sustain services and programs once implemented.

Schools are a logical site in which to base children's mental health services. In regard to access to mental health services, schools offer the advantage of having relatively easy access to children, especially as compared to community mental health clinics where no-show rates are 50% or greater. However, there continues to be a reliance on individual counseling in most school-based programs, which is generally inappropriate for many childhood externalizing disorders. Alternatively, school-based programs that focus on consultation with teachers and efforts to reduce barriers to parent involvement in their children's schooling have been proposed more recently.

A second reason for mental health services to focus on children's schooling is the opportunity to assess the effect of services on multiple indicators of children's functioning such as academic performance, peer relations, and classroom behavior. Hoagwood, Jensen, Petti, and Burns called attention to the overemphasis of children's mental health services research on the reduction of symptoms to the exclusion of improved functioning. They noted that, although often correlated, the two are not the same. They proposed that a successful intervention should be assessed not with symptom checklists but with measures of daily life functioning such as homework completion, participation in classroom discussions, problem-solving disputes with peers, and so forth. This requires involvement from key stakeholders in children's mental health, principally parents and teachers, to define appropriate program goals—a relatively rare occurrence in children's mental health research.

We will describe results from three recent studies in Chicago focused on improving access to services, enhancing children's functioning at school, and planning for sustainability. These studies represent a program of research designed to improve mental health service delivery in inner-city schools and communities by attending to the unique needs and characteristics of teachers, children, and families. In the first study, we attempted to engage more families in mental health services by including parents from the community in the design and delivery of our program. For the second study, we trained peer-identified teacher leaders in evidence-based classroom practices for students with ADHD, and we examined the diffusion of information about these practices to other classroom teachers. Finally, a third, planned study with the Illinois Office of Mental Health and the Chicago Public Schools is described that involves a multitiered service delivery model that builds on the skills and strengths of influential parents *and* teachers. We present these studies as steps towards the development of comprehensive, effective, and sustainable mental health services for schools and families in underserved, low-income communities.

Accessibility Through Community Collaboration: Positive Attitudes Toward Learning in School (PALS)

Recognizing the importance of schooling to children's healthy development, we designed a service that integrated mental health goals into ongoing school routines and resources. The research was funded through a 3-year federal grant but the services were supported through Medicaid billing and, therefore, were applicable to community-based mental health programs serving low-income families. Positive Attitudes Toward Learning in School (PALS) was designed to (a) minimize barriers and maximize service accessibility; (b) improve children's academic, behavioral, and social functioning; and (c) develop the capacity of classrooms, schools, and families to sustain positive change. . . . For the purposes of this article, a brief review of the methods and results will be presented.

Research Design

PALS participants were drawn from three low-income, inner-city schools on the Near Westside of Chicago, an economically disadvantaged community. Kindergarten through sixth grade students identified by teachers as evidencing disruptive behavior in school were randomly assigned by classroom to receive services through our school-based PALS program or at a university-based mental health clinic. Families assigned to clinic-based services received an extensive telephone-based engagement interview that had been shown to be successful with inner-city families. Across the 3 years of the study, a total of 75 children were enrolled in PALS (41% female, 97% African American) and 36 children were enrolled into clinic-based services (55% female, 97% African American).

PALS was developed specifically in response to the urgent need to engage more families in effective services and, therefore, was based on an engagement framework. The goal was to approach families in ways that encouraged the development of an ongoing working relationship, and to identify treatment goals consistent with family priorities. We enlisted parents in the community as partners in the design and delivery of services to provide a perspective that reflected the daily experiences of families and to offer clinicians a window into the cultural world of families. Community consultants also provided parents with a community-based contact to enhance communication between families and mental health service providers.

Staff clinicians and community consultants worked collaboratively on school-based teams. The community consultants played an increasingly larger role over time. Early in the project, they educated staff about the resources and needs of the community, and accompanied staff on school and home visits. They participated in the development of clinical resources, and assisted with the initial and ongoing engagement of identified families in services, principally via home visits, phone calls, flyers, and informal contacts on the streets. However, given the extensive distrust of social services within these communities due to a history of discrimination and neglectful services, their role gradually expanded to capitalize on their unique strengths and expertise. By project's end, they were participating in curriculum planning for parent groups, and ultimately, they became group facilitators with clinicians in a supportive role.

Once families had enrolled their child in PALS, we proceeded with a flexible service delivery model that included family services and classroom services. The family services emphasized support for children's academic and behavioral progress at school, as well as social support and skill development for parents, and offered multiple opportunities for parent involvement in their child's schooling. These included biweekly parent groups (which were facilitated by our community consultants and referred to as "parent parties"), home visits, school-sponsored meetings, informal meetings at school or within the community, contacts with community consultants, and phone conversations. Classroom services incorporated multiple levels of intervention and evidence-based practices. They included opportunities for contingency-based, classwide, behavior management strategies such as the Good Behavior Game, academically oriented interventions such as peer tutoring, individualized programs such as school-home notes, small groups for reading and social skills building, and teacher support.

Our examination of the first 9 months of data from PALS suggests that the strong emphasis on engagement and our reliance on the community consultants were appropriate strategies for enrolling families in services. At recruitment, 60 of 64 families (93.8%) assigned to the 12 PALS classrooms agreed to enroll in the program, whereas only 24 of 35 families (68.6%) assigned to the 8 control classrooms agreed to enroll in clinic-based services. . . . At 3 months following enrollment, all PALS families remained in services, whereas no clinic families were receiving any mental health services for their children. In fact, only 2 of the 24 clinic families received any services at all during this time, and those 2 children received only one session of medication management with no follow-up. By 9 months following enrollment, 86% of the 64 PALS families still remained involved in services. The only families who withdrew from the program by that time did so because their children changed schools.

Several unforeseen events during the second year of the project disrupted our clinical service and research design and limited the involvement of additional families. Specifically, a university-wide shutdown of all human subject research during an institutional review board investigation led to the curtailment of recruitment for an entire year. By the time research was reinitiated, a shortage of funds resulted in a need to withdraw from one of the three schools. Nevertheless, approximately two-thirds of PALS families agreed to re-enroll in PALS services for our third and final project year, compared to approximately one-quarter of control families who re-enrolled in clinic-based services. Unfortunately, these results also resulted in a very low sample size in the third and last year of the project and a control group too small to compare child outcomes.

PALS results suggest that our flexible model coupled with the intensive parent outreach efforts may have increased access to services for families historically underserved by the mental health system. Our next research objective was to explore how indigenous resources in urban schools could provide support to classroom teachers to implement effective strategies for children with mental health needs, such as students with Attention Deficit/Hyperactivity Disorder (ADHD).

Sustainability Through Indigenous Resources: Teacher Key Opinion Leaders (KOL)

The Teacher Key Opinion Leader (KOL) project applies social diffusion theory to enhance implementation of school-based mental health services for students with ADHD in low-income urban schools. Specifically, we were interested to see if highly regarded teachers would be more influential with their peers than would community mental health providers. We received funding for a 3-year study of this model in 10 inner city Chicago Public Schools. The study is in its final year and, therefore, for this article, we will describe the rationale of the project and present a brief review of the study, including preliminary data on the program's effectiveness at impacting teachers' willingness to use evidence-based accommodations for children with ADHD.

Social Diffusion Theory

Social diffusion theory posits that innovations become disseminated throughout a social network through the persuasion of key opinion leaders (KOL) within that network. Valente showed that influential peers who are early adopters of an innovation effect change within their social networks which, in turn, impacts other social networks in ways that are highly specific to settings and systems. Rogers noted that professional change agents are individuals who have knowledge to help a client but may have difficulty communicating that knowledge directly. If the change agent has access to a key opinion leader, Rogers proposed, the change agent could more effectively transfer information or knowledge to the network members through the persuasive influence of opinion leaders. Thus, by working in conjunction, opinion leaders and change agents can introduce new innovations and increase the adoption of those innovations in a social system. This is highly relevant to mental health consultation to schools and to the efforts of mental health providers to affect teachers' classroom practices for students with ADHD. Therefore, the goal for this study was to test whether diffusion theory may be a useful and potentially important model to improve collaboration between mental health providers and teachers.

The *networks* targeted for this project were first through fourth grade classroom teachers in predominantly low-income African American urban communities. The *innovations* we targeted for adoption by teachers were selected evidence-based educational practices for children with ADHD. The *mechanism* by which we intended to influence classroom teachers to adopt these practices was the endorsement of key opinion leader (KOL) teachers in their buildings.

Sustainability was a key consideration in the design of the KOL project and it was addressed in two ways. First, the "active ingredient" that distinguished treatment from comparison schools was the inclusion of KOL teachers as disseminators of selected classroom practices among their fellow teachers. By definition, KOL teachers were highly regarded members of their school's teaching faculty and as such represented key indigenous resources in their schools.

Second, sustainability issues were addressed by the project's focus on developing the necessary infrastructure for mental health agencies and schools to partner in providing services to children with ADHD. The complexity of this task cannot be overstated. In spite of the fact that the schools and the agencies were eager to form these partnerships, interorganizational collaboration required a meshing of procedures between institutions operating from different models of service delivery. For example, schools had to develop a referral process that would work best for their staff and families, at times adding more work to an already very full school day. Community mental health agencies needed to free staff to learn billing procedures for school-based work and to spend time in the school to learn the school's norms and practices. Nonetheless, most schools and agencies were able to vault the many obstacles they faced in establishing their collaborations and now have procedures in place for the next school year.

Research Design

Participants in this ongoing project included first through fourth grade children with ADHD and their teachers in 10 Chicago public schools serving predominantly low-income African American communities. Participating schools were randomly selected from a set of 64 schools of similar size, SES, ethnic composition, and achievement level. Six schools were assigned to the KOL condition and 4 schools to a control condition consisting of mental health consultation with no KOL support. Children with ADHD in Grades 1–4 were identified by teacher screening, parent interviews, and clinician diagnosis.

In the six experimental condition schools, KOL teachers were identified through nomination procedures with the targeted classroom teachers. Classroom teachers were asked to name the other teachers at their school to whom they go for advice on a variety of classroom issues. Teachers who received the highest number of nominations were identified as the KOL teachers in their respective buildings. Two or 3 teachers were identified at each school to reach an exposure rate of 70% of teachers in each school (i.e., 70% or more teachers identified one of the KOL teachers as someone to whom they go for advice). All 13 identified KOL teachers agreed to serve as teacher consultants for the project at their schools. Three groups of classroom teachers were followed: those who reported receiving support from a KOL teacher (KOL-support), those who taught in KOL schools but did not report receiving KOL support (KOL-no support), and teachers in comparison schools (controls).

KOL teachers and mental health staff from local community agencies received training on 11 classroom practices derived from the Chicago Public Schools ADHD policy manual (http://www.cps.k12.il.us/AboutCPS/Departments/OSS/Publications/adhd_manual.pdf) via a web-based course. The practices included individual behavior plans using positive reinforcement and response cost procedures, the Good Behavior Game, home-school notes, and peer tutoring. In the four comparison schools, mental health staff underwent the same training as the KOL teachers and mental health providers in the experimental condition schools, and provided support to classroom teachers who had one or more student with ADHD in their classroom.

A primary goal of the project was to determine whether teachers in KOL schools used more recommended strategies compared to teachers in comparison schools as would be suggested by the diffusion of innovation literature. Teachers reported on their use of strategies, the effectiveness of each strategy used, and the support they received during the prior month from mental health providers (both conditions) and KOL teachers (KOL condition only). Preliminary results from Year 2 and the first time point of Year 3 are encouraging. KOL-supported teachers reported using significantly more of the 11 recommended strategies compared to the other two groups of teachers . . . and significant between-group differences were found on 7 of the strategies. . . . In contrast, support from mental health providers was not significantly associated with either overall use of strategies or with the use of any specific strategy in either condition. Ongoing use of these practices is being studied across the current school year to determine the extent of KOL influence over time and the differential effect on different types of classroom practices on student outcomes.

Service Integration and Sustainability: System of Care—Chicago (SOC-C)

In collaboration with the Illinois Office of Mental Health (OMH), the Chicago Public Schools (CPS), and the Illinois State Board of Education (ISBE), we have recently begun to develop a model for school-based mental health services specific to the needs of inner-city children and families. Considering the limited knowledge regarding sustainability of mental health programs for urban children, this collaboration provided a unique opportunity to consider the public policy implications of school-based mental health services.

ISBE had several years of experience with Positive Behavioral Interventions and Supports (PBIS), a popular program for improving school discipline and enhancing learning. Although the program was adopted throughout the state, it previously had been largely unsuccessful in the Chicago schools. In fact, ISBE staff reported that in the prior 3 years, 18 of 19 CPS schools that expressed interest in implementing PBIS withdrew from training within the first year. The consensus was that this was due to the schools' inability to accommodate the apparent high resource needs of the program.

Therefore, to provide schools with additional implementation support, CPS reassigned existing resources, through a school-based pre-intervention referral program implemented district-wide, to help teachers develop behavioral or academic interventions for high-risk students. In addition, given the high social service needs of children in CPS schools, each school was additionally linked with a neighboring community mental health agency. However, instead of being primarily a referral source for the schools, social service agency resources were allocated toward implementing and sustaining PBIS. The rationale was that well-organized and successful schools have considerable mental health benefits for all students, and additional social services could then be targeted to children and families with the greatest needs. To date, this is one of the largest implementations of PBIS in urban schools in the country, and the first to propose extensive collaboration with community-based social service agencies.

As described in Sugai and Horner and Crone and Horner, PBIS uses a multi-tiered model to reduce disruptive school behavior. The first tier is a *universal intervention* that is available to all students, teachers, and families regardless of student risk status. Each school forms a team composed of administrators and teachers and uses disciplinary record data to determine the source and function of disruptive student behavior. Based on their review of these records, the team decides on specific activities and interventions appropriate for their school. As the title of the program implies, the emphasis is on providing positive alternatives to disruptive behavior. In SOC-C, a representative of the assigned community social service agency participates on this team. Examples of universal activities include organization of supervised activities before or after school, organizing school-wide events to support learning, and parent involvement activities.

The second tier is a *targeted intervention* team that identifies students who need support beyond the school-wide universal strategies, and have elevated risk for social-emotional difficulties (e.g., disruptive behavior, anxiety and depression). As with the universal tier, each school forms a team with similar composition to the universal team, including membership by a representative of the participating social service agency, to decide upon needs and programs for that school. Examples of activities at this level are consultation with teachers for classroom behavior management strategies, student peer social support activities, peer tutoring, and group social skills instruction.

The third tier is an *intensive intervention approach* for those students who have not responded sufficiently to targeted interventions. Intensive services are based on the *wraparound process,* which is a strength-based approach for identifying and allocating indigenous resources in school and community settings to meet the individual needs of children and their families. An individualized wraparound team is formed for each referred child, composed of that child's parent and teacher, a member of the school mental health team, and, in SOC-C, a representative of the community mental health agency. These school-based wraparound teams may blend supportive services for families and students (e.g., respite care) with traditional behavioral, clinical, and academic interventions at school or home. In addition, community-based mental health providers may provide access to a variety of community-based services, including case management, in-home supports, medical interventions, and home-based or clinic-based family therapy.

SOC-C offers several key policy implications for the advancement of school-based mental health. First, SOC-C provides a structure to enable an array of child-serving agencies to coordinate the delivery of multiple services to inner-city children and families. For example, through this collaboration, efforts have been initiated to provide waivers for Medicaid funding that will allow agencies and schools to bill Medicaid for universal prevention programming based on the likely benefit to special need children and families. Second, SOC-C provides a formal interface between school-based and community-based mental health providers to promote the positive academic and behavioral development of inner-city children. This shared vision for school-based and community-based providers can avoid fragmentation of services and marginalization of mental health goals within schools. The participation of community-based social service staff at all three tiers of PBIS is intended to encourage a systemic awareness of resources and needs of the school, and to avoid overidentification of child or family characteristics as responsible for child difficulties. Third, SOC-C uses a data-driven approach to provide effective school-based interventions at the universal, targeted, and intensive intervention levels. This approach is consistent with the increasing calls for the adoption of evidence-based practices to guide service provision and agency reimbursement.

Toward the goal of sustainability, SOC-C focuses on the identification and support of indigenous school and community resources to sustain programs and services. The use of school teams to consider how to realign school resources to support positive behavior at all three levels (i.e., universal, targeted, intensive) avoids the problem of overloading schools with services and programs that they are unable to maintain and support. In addition, the linkage between schools and community social service agencies encourages a consideration of the best use of social service resources on behalf of children's mental health. The ultimate goal is to develop a new standard of care for the delivery of effective services for children and families living in inner-city communities.

Summary and Conclusions

This article describes three studies of school-based mental health services for urban children. The studies are part of an ongoing program of research focused on improving families' access to services, enhancing children's functioning, and providing for long-term sustainability through reliance on indigenous community resources. As noted throughout, we view these studies as part of a programmatic effort to develop a service delivery model sensitive to the unique needs and competencies of inner-city communities. . . .

Although numerous avenues of inquiry remain unexplored, it seems clear from this work that in the communities we serve, mental health services are enhanced by collaboration with influential community members. From PALS, our data suggest that without an extensive outreach effort in which community consultants played a large role, many families would never have entered services and others would have been lost to services over time. This is not to discount the considerable effort of the PALS clinical staff. However, it was clear that the community consultants enhanced the program's credibility in a community that has historically been distrustful of university-based researchers and mental health providers. The dismal show rates for our clinic-based control group conforms to a larger literature and testifies to the inaccessibility of these services to a vast majority of families in these communities, and the powerful effect of the focus on engaging families in PALS services.

The KOL study has been an exciting and energizing demonstration of the activation of experienced teachers on behalf of their colleagues. They are, perhaps, an ideal example of an indigenous resource with unique and powerful influences on their colleagues, although we have much to learn regarding the extent of their influence and the ideal use of their time and resources. Among the many questions that remain unresolved are the specific types of mental health programs that are most appropriate for dissemination in these schools, and the extent to which other forms of educational innovations can be accommodated by the KOL method.

Although the SOC-C program is in a preliminary phase of development and implementation, it appears to be a promising vehicle for effective school and mental health collaboration for inner-city children. The interagency framework links educators, community-based mental health providers, and child welfare systems in collaborative efforts to promote positive development in inner-city children and their families. This framework appears particularly important for urban school settings where children often have multiple needs that require coordinated efforts between multiple agencies. Moreover, SOC-C provides a multitiered model for designing and delivering mental health interventions to meet the range of needs of urban children. This is an often overlooked element of effective mental health programs and especially difficult for community mental health agencies to manage independently, given the overwhelming need in the inner city and the considerable lack of resources to meet this need.

Future research needs to address the large discrepancy between a public sector mental health system that is unable to address the needs of the vast majority of children and families and a university-dominated research model that has neglected the major systemic issues that undermine the use of effective services. In this regard, the movement to advance evidence-based practice is an important start but requires an additional focus and direction. Specifically, we propose that issues of access and sustainability emerge into the forefront of a research agenda, leading to a new definition of effective services defined in part by the degree to which these issues are addressed. This may require a new set of research standards and techniques that highlight barriers to initial and long-term utilization and that include consumer perspectives.

This is not to downplay the substantial challenges to such work. How best to overcome systemic barriers to effective practice is neither obvious nor certain, although we are encouraged that such a focus can lead to new insights. For example, in our own work, our commitment to engage all families in services, and to sustain this engagement through active outreach, substantially changed the nature and focus of our services to accommodate the input and perspectives of our families and community consultants. Similarly, in regard to consultation with teachers, our goal was to provide services that addressed the needs of their students, which in some cases required sustained dialogue to accommodate different perspectives of parents, teachers, and mental health providers. This ultimately led to our interest in studying a teacher key opinion leader model, which as we further this work, will likely lead to an everwidening appreciation for other indigenous supports in urban schools.

Finally, it is important to highlight that both PALS and KOL demonstrated that, under the right set of conditions, parents and teachers in impoverished, urban communities are eager to become involved in efforts to promote the mental health of their children and students. Our experiences on PALS and KOL also led us to appreciate the stresses and frustrations of teachers at these inner-city schools. Ultimately, we will continue to learn through iteration and trial and error. In many ways, we realize that we are confronting the residual and overwhelming influence of poverty. Indeed, the name for PALS, Positive Attitudes for Learning in School, evolved from discussions with parents, teachers, and children that highlighted the need to combat the negativism that often permeates inner-city schools and communities. Nevertheless, it is not difficult to see that mental health resources can make a real difference when applied to the enhancement of children's schooling. Effective collaboration towards the goal of effective services may be the key building blocks for the next generation of children's mental health services research.

Heather Ringeisen, Kelly Henderson, and Kimberly Hoagwood

NO

Context Matters: Schools and the "Research to Practice Gap" in Children's Mental Health

In language, a word's content may be less important than the context in which it is embedded. For instance, request a "pop" across most of the United States and you will receive some form of carbonated beverage. Request a "pop" in southern Georgia and you will likely be met with a strange look or possibly a jab to the jaw. Even beyond language, context must be understood prior to interpretation. The public education and mental health systems have unique histories, distinct value sets, principles, and beliefs, as do the traditions of academic research and community practice. When these worlds are brought together, contextual differences become especially important.

In the last 20 years there has been tremendous growth in knowledge about how best to identify and treat behavioral and emotional disorders of childhood. In addition, available service models for children diagnosed with emotional disturbances have shifted from those predominantly available in inpatient hospitals, residential centers, or outpatient centers to alternative service delivery approaches available in community settings. This growth in empirical knowledge and focus on community-based care has resulted in increased attention to the different worlds of research and practice. In fact, research has demonstrated that child mental health interventions used in everyday clinical practice are not only different from those studied in academic settings, but also potentially less effective. Spurred by the release of the Institute of Medicine Report, Surgeon General's Report on Mental Health, and the Surgeon General's Conference on Children's Mental Health, overcoming this gap between research and practice in children's mental health has become a national priority.

The mental health research literature describes multiple interventions with potential school application; these interventions range from those targeting select students to broad school-wide prevention programs. Recent reviews have documented efficacious psychopharmacologic; psychosocial; integrated community and preventive services; and school-based interventions. Certain approaches appear helpful for individual children with Serious Emotional Disturbances (or SED) (e.g., cognitive problem solving, social skills training, classroom behavior

From *School Psychology Review*, vol. 32, Spring 2003, pp. 153–168. Copyright © 2003 by National Association of School Psychologists. Reprinted by permission. References omitted.

management) and other school-wide programs reduce child disruptive behaviors and/or improve social/emotional health. Unfortunately, the literature on "evidence-based practices" in children's mental health pays insufficient attention to features of the school context that might influence intervention delivery. This literature also tends to neglect outcomes of relevance to schools, such as academic achievement or special education referral patterns. Meanwhile, a growing research base demonstrates the influence of setting-specific factors (e.g., organizational climate) on the delivery of effective interventions.

Given the different natures of education and mental health systems and the known influence of setting context on care delivery, factors within the school environment are likely relevant in narrowing the gap between research and practice in school mental health. In this article, we argue that there are several aspects of school context that likely influence the ability of schools to change current practices or adopt new ones. These factors should be addressed when integrating mental health interventions into school settings. Relying on a contextual organizational framework, we describe a three-level model of school context that we believe is particularly relevant to the delivery of mental health interventions. This model includes factors broken down into: (a) individual, (b) organizational, and (c) state/national levels. Each level of the model is described by highlighting factors uniquely relevant at a particular level of setting context. For instance, pertinent individual-level contextual factors include those related directly to child (i.e., academic achievement, peer relationships) and teacher outcomes (i.e., training, stress, support). . . . Relevant research findings related to the three levels are discussed in an effort to highlight opportunities for greater connection between mental health research and school mental health service delivery.

The Changing Context of Schools

Schools play a critical role in the delivery of children's mental health services. Seventy percent to 80% of children who receive any mental health services receive them in school. In addition, children with mental health needs identified in school are more likely to enter and receive treatment when mental health services are offered in school rather than when services are offered within the community. Despite the importance of school mental health services, the U.S. Department of Education estimates that less than 1% of all children are identified as having an emotional disturbance and receive special education or related services under IDEA. Logistical accessibility makes schools a logical and important point of intervention for children with emotional or behavior problems; however, creating access to such mental health services is not a simple process.

Schools today represent systems with multiple, and often competing, pressures. A rising number of children across the U.S. are being identified as having emotional, behavioral, or learning problems, which places increasing demands upon education systems. Special education programs currently serve 5.68 million children and youth ages 6–21 years nationally at an estimated cost of about $50 billion. As special education demands rise, education reforms have focused on improving student outcomes by increasing accountability for results. Education systems have fixed resources that must be allocated across multiple needs with a necessitated priority on student achievement. Population changes, increasing student special needs, and mounting federal/state performance standards have clear implications for schoolbased delivery of mental health interventions.

Mental health interventions could easily be seen as additional burdens to education systems unless they are naturally integrated into school settings. As Adelman and Taylor point out, "schools are not in the mental health business. Their mandate is to educate. Thus, they tend to see any activity not directly related to instruction as taking resources away from their primary mission." Given the dynamic nature of schools and the significant differences between the school environment and traditional outpatient mental health clinics, how does one know if mental health interventions developed for clinic-based delivery systems will be relevant or transferable to a school environment? We believe that the upfront consideration of school-specific contextual factors in both the design and implementation of mental health interventions is critical in closing the gap between mental health research and school mental health practice.

Contextual Influences on Intervention Outcomes

The discovery of efficacious child interventions raises interest in why certain interventions work and how such interventions can be integrated into "real world" service settings. Emerging research has demonstrated the importance of both content-specific and contextual factors. For instance, one study attempted to tease apart specific mechanisms of action within a cognitive-behavioral intervention for childhood anxiety disorders; this study demonstrated the potential importance of a particular technique called "exposure." This intervention component or "content" appears to be especially critical in reducing reported childhood fears and anxiety responses. Other research demonstrates the importance of factors beyond a particular intervention technique that similarly influence intervention outcomes. Such factors might include clinical supervision, therapeutic processes, or an organization's support for employees. These factors could be considered a part of intervention setting, or context. . . . In addition, child mental health services researchers are beginning to understand that systemic features, such as organizational leadership or morale, may explain variance in the quality of provided services.

The importance of setting context on intervention outcomes has been demonstrated in schools as well as within traditional mental health programs. A recent review of effective school-delivered mental health interventions identified several features of implementation that facilitate program sustainability. Identified factors include both intervention-specific and implementation-specific influences: consistency of program implementation; inclusion of parents, teachers or peers; use of multiple intervention modalities; the integration of program content into general classroom curriculum; and the use of developmentally appropriate program components. Other research points to the importance of integrating mental health interventions into classroom curricula. Efforts to integrate interventions in an integrated, as opposed to adjunctive, manner are associated with more positive child outcomes and long-term sustainability. Clearly, an intervention's core content (principles, treatment strategies) is only one piece of an overarching systemic structure that adapts to facilitate successful program implementation.

Factors associated with a school setting also directly affect child academic outcomes. Research on school organization, systems change, and restructuring reinforces the importance of school characteristics on child outcomes. For example, small school size, the adoption of a teacher pedagogy emphasizing academic skills, adaptive learning strategies, and flexible supports are associated with attendance rates, achievement test scores, graduation rates, and college entrance among students in urban high schools. Reihl reviewed the literature on administrative characteristics that support inclusive school cultures, or academic environments deemed highly responsive to ethnic, socioeconomic, or disability diversity. Dimensions associated with such academic cultures included the ability to create a caring environment with a high level of cooperation among students, teachers, and families; the ability to focus on academic achievement and provide appropriate supports; and the ability to hold high expectations for all students. School structures, principles, cultures, and values affect the promotion of student learning and mental health.

The context in which a particular intervention is delivered, whether targeting educational or mental health outcomes, may have key features that affect intervention success. Because many promising mental health interventions were not developed or tested within school settings, it becomes critical for researchers to examine the effect of school contextual factors as these interventions are incorporated into school environments.

A Context Map for Schools

What theories should researchers use to guide hypotheses about the integration of novel interventions into service delivery settings? Two possibilities include theories of organizational change or context. In speaking about health care settings, Ferlie and Shortell suggest that four levels of change be considered to improve the quality of healthcare: individual, group or team, the overall organization, and the larger system in which individual organizations are embedded. Successful change efforts are hypothesized to happen when they target multiple levels of a particular organization. These levels represent integrated pieces of an organizational system or context. Ferlie and Shortell's levels of change are consistent with other conceptualizations of context that describe individuals as embedded within organizations that are in turn embedded within larger systems. If levels of organizational context are important to strategic organizational change, it is likely that they are equally influential in the delivery of mental health interventions within novel service delivery systems.

Although Ferlie and Shortell discuss generic levels of organizational context, specific "real-world" mental health setting contextual factors are increasingly cited as important in intervention development and deployment. For instance, a model described in the recent National Institute of Mental Health (or NIMH) report entitled Blueprint for Change: Research on Child and Adolescent Mental Health is grounded by the belief that high quality practices in mental health need connections between the best available science and ongoing feedback from the real-world context. The model proposes a cyclical feedback process to address the relationship between basic science and child mental health services. Here described, basic research informs intervention development, which then informs intervention testing in an effort to identify what works best for children with emotional or behavior problems. A key feature of this model involves intervention deployment, described as "efforts to take evidence-based interventions into the field and encourage their use by providers." The model proposes that information gained via research on deployment inform all other pieces of the model. Contextual factors relevant for intervention deployment (e.g., provider acceptability) are seen as critical across all stages of the research process. . . .

Individual Level Factors

Individual and group level factors are described at the core of the Ferlie and Shortell model. Here, individual level factors include personal characteristics, beliefs, and behaviors that may affect organizational change. This section includes a discussion of potential individual level factors that might play a role in school mental health intervention development, testing, or implementation. We choose to discuss primarily child- and teacher-specific factors, but realize other relevant education stakeholders might include parents, principals, school social workers, superintendents, or others. Individual level factors for consideration include primary intervention outcomes of interest as well as key factors for intervention implementation, such as professional training or support.

Child level   One very obvious way to increase the relevance of mental health interventions for schools is to focus upon education-relevant outcomes. Mental health treatments have traditionally tailored interventions to address individual level risk factors, diagnostic profiles, or family characteristics. In fact, this individual level tailoring of interventions could well be considered a major strength of mental health intervention research. Primary individual level outcomes of interest, however, have tended to focus on child diagnostic-specific variables (e.g., aggression, inattention, anxiety) with less of an emphasis on child functioning in school (e.g., peer relationships). Furthermore, Rones and Hoagwood concluded that research on school-based mental health services has typically downplayed or ignored school-relevant outcomes. They found that studies of school-based mental health interventions only minimally examined the effects of mental health services on student achievement, attendance, and school-related behavior. (e.g., disciplinary referrals, suspensions, retention). Meanwhile, research suggests that childhood mental health difficulties are associated with academic underachievement and other school-relevant functional outcomes. Several childhood disorders (i.e., Attention-deficit/Hyperactivity Disorder) are associated with poor academic performance, learning disabilities, peer difficulties, or language delays. Furthermore, almost 78% of children with emotional disorders never receive a standard high school diploma. Research also suggests children who fail to reach age-appropriate social and emotional milestones face a far greater risk for early school failure than their peers. With increasing emphasis being placed on education systems for academic accountability in spite of limited school resources, it will be critical for researchers to examine the impact of mental health interventions upon factors such as academic performance and intensive service placements (e.g., special education).

Provider level   Due to the typical focus on child behavior change, mental health intervention research has frequently failed to examine provider level variables. Such variables might be primary intervention outcomes of interest (e.g., reductions in teacher stress or burden) or key factors in intervention implementation or feasibility (e.g., professional training). Furthermore, despite their critical role in program sustainability, school professional perspectives are not typically considered during the development of interventions. Without such consultation, teachers may appear resistant or uncooperative to mental health staff or researchers when, in fact, such responses might be a reaction to interventions that are too complex for current levels of training or too far removed from standard educational practices. Active collaboration with school staff, attention to provider-level outcomes of interest, and professional supports for program implementation will aid in successful mental health program integration.

School personnel operate within a system of multiple, and sometimes competing, demands. Opportunities for general education teachers to have training and support for dealing with child behavioral problems are rare; and there is a general shortage of school personnel who focus specifically on student behavioral health. Findings from the recent School Health Policies and Programs Study revealed that more than 75% of schools indicate having school guidance counselors available to students, 66% have a school psychologist on staff, and less than 50% have a school social worker. Only one in five states require a maximum student-to-staff ratio for guidance counselors (even less for school psychologists and social workers). So, it is estimated that the ratio of school psychologists or school social workers averages 1 to 2,500 students; for school counselors the ratio is 1 to 1,000. Although the mental health literature does not point to an ideal mental health personnel-to-student ratio, current ratios suggest that time to devote to individual students with behavioral or emotional problems may be limited.

With limited time availability, opportunities for staff training, support, and communication are vitally important for general education efficacy, but also for successful mental health program implementation. Traditional inservice-type training opportunities are even more helpful when supplemented with increased access to informal or even formal professional networks. Formal and informal networking opportunities are likely important to facilitate school staff communication and increase morale. And teacher morale seems linked to general classroom efficacy. Training, communication, and staff support are equally important factors for successful school-based program implementation. . . .

Organizational Level Factors

Children, teachers, counselors, and other school staff are all embedded within an organizational context. Organizational level influences may act directly upon individuals within these systems (e.g., affecting professional stress or morale) and upon intervention strategy success (e.g., program fidelity). Organizational characteristics have been found to influence the effectiveness of delivered social services as well as student outcomes in schools. Increasing knowledge about the influence of organizational factors on the ability to provide mental health care in schools is critical in improving the quality and sustainability of services. Although there are multiple forms of organizational level influence, for illustration purposes, we will specifically discuss resource availability and organizational climate.

Resource availability   One source of funding for mental health services delivered individually to children in need comes from special education; however, schools may also set aside resources for the provision of school-wide or classroom-based preventive interventions. Because many of these programs are unevaluated, school resources may be expended with unknown results. For instance, more than 75% of schools report providing alcohol and other drug use prevention, suicide prevention, and violence prevention in one-on-one or small group discussions. In addition, the Surgeon General's Report on Youth Violence indicated that hundreds of youth violence prevention programs are used in U.S. schools and communities; however, the effect of many such programs is relatively unknown. Through knowledge of empirically supported interventions, mental health professionals could assist schools in utilizing existing resource allocations to maximize mental health impact.

As described previously, staff resources to address student mental health needs are often limited. Despite such staffing shortages, school-based mental health services are available in most systems, primarily for individual students. Findings from the recent School Health Policies and Programs Study indicated that the three most common forms of mental health service delivery were individual counseling, case management, and evaluation/testing. Growing child mental health needs and an inadequate supply of school-based specialty mental health personnel have led some to suggest that an individually driven school mental health service delivery model may be inadequate. With finite available resources for school mental health, others have argued for moving away from a model of one-to-one service provision into an integrated model that incorporates classroom-wide interventions, group approaches, and professional consultation to maximize existing school capacity. School mental health delivery models such as the ecological model or the expanded school mental health programs model offer ways of conceptualizing how mental health service providers can work in collaboration with existing school resources and personnel. Such approaches might include prevention, assessment, treatment, and/or case management to students in both special education and general education. Mental health professionals should be aware of existing interventions within local schools and consider the impact of such programs on current additional efforts. Clearly education systems value the presence of behavioral interventions;

mental health professionals might aid schools in maximizing the use of potentially scarce resources.

Organizational climate   One of the most significant challenges to implementing evidence-informed interventions into schools may involve problems of organizational fit. Research-based interventions targeted towards improving mental health functioning of children have been developed largely in isolation from schools. Assumptions that such interventions can be readily transferred to school contexts are probably naive. Glisson and colleagues have undertaken studies of organizational culture, climate, and structure within social service agencies. Within these studies "organizational climate" is defined as those attitudes shared by employees about their work environment. These researchers found organizational climate factors (including low conflict, high cooperation, role clarity) to be strong predictors of positive service outcomes (improved psychosocial functioning in children and adolescents) and service quality. Within the field of educational practices, studies of school organizational climate have also been a major focus of efforts for many years. . . .

The term "school climate" appears to have first been coined by Halpin and Croft but has been refined by Kelley et al. into a measurable construct typically involving five domains: teacher-student relationships, administrative leadership, security/maintenance, student academic orientation, and parent/community-school relationships. . . . In general, the construct of school climate refers to perceptions of the physical and psychological school environment by teachers, students, parents, and principals.

Few studies have assessed the effect of school climate on social, emotional, or behavioral problems in students. One exception is Esposito, who assessed the impact of school climate on low-income K-2nd grade children's social and emotional development, and found that parental perceptions of school climate, especially teacher-student relationships, predicted school adjustment. In addition, parental perceptions of the student/teacher relationship changed with time and increased in importance from kindergarten through second grade. A larger body of work has been undertaken examining the relationship between climate and school achievement; characteristics of school climate that appear to affect school achievement include teachers' perceptions of schools as work environments, teacher expectations of the students and resources available in the schools, and faculty trust. In a meta-analysis of several hundred studies, Wang, Jaertel, and Walberg found that teacher instruction strategies—in particular, classroom management—had nearly as much effect as student aptitude on learning. Given that existing data demonstrate the influence of organizational and school climate on social service provision, student achievement, and teachers, these are factors important for consideration in the implementation of school mental health interventions. . . .

State/Federal Level Factors

Just as individuals are embedded within organizations, organizations are embedded within their broader regulatory systems. Hence, the local school context is intrinsically embedded within a state and federal education system. Over the past two decades there have been a number of education reforms related to school service eligibility, financing, and structure. The effect of such regulatory actions upon the delivery and outcomes of mental health interventions has not been measured; however, these factors will likely have a very important impact upon the long-term sustainability of such interventions within education systems. Sustainable mental health interventions will be those that are consistent with current mandates, can be financially supported through existing sources, and serve eligible students. In this section, the focus is specifically upon the accountability movement, recent changes in school financing, and special education service eligibility criteria.

Accountability   Education reforms over the past two decades have focused on improving student outcomes by increasing accountability for results. Testing programs are now in place in all states, most of which are driven by one or more standardized statewide assessments, the performance results of which are reported publicly. Generally, performance deficits can result in varying, but significant, consequences to school, school personnel, districts, and students directly.

Although state reforms play a large role in shaping accountability policies, federal legislation is a driving force. In 1994, the Improving America's School Act reauthorized the Elementary and Secondary Education Act, including Title I. Legislative provisions required states to perform assessments for at least three separate grade levels and to provide student assessment performance reports at the school level by race, gender, English proficiency, migrant status, disability, and economic status. The 2002 passage of the No Child Left Behind Act raised the bar even higher by requiring states to set standards for student achievement, to test all students in Grades 3 through 8, and to publish state and school district report cards on academic achievement. The No Child Left Behind Act requires the establishment of a minimum level of improvement that schools and school districts must achieve each year. If schools do not meet such standards or show improvement through technical assistance, sanctions can include implementing corrective actions, significant staff restructuring, and/or state takeover.

Although some have questioned the potential outcomes of these "top-down" accountability-driven reforms, there is little debate about the infusion of resources necessary to sustain such reforms. The effect of accountability reforms and resulting consequences for schools and districts increases attention and redirects resources to efforts to directly improve performance on assessment. A consideration of recent accountability education reforms clarifies the need to study both the direct and facilitating role of mental health interventions in promoting positive academic achievement within education systems. New resources directed solely at social, emotional, or behavioral functioning may be rare, but support may be found for these interventions if demonstrated to facilitate a school's ability to meet new accountability requirements.

Financing   Education funding for the provision of services for students with emotional or behavior problems is primarily drawn from support for special education. Because children with emotional disturbances represent a particularly costly group, state and federal incentives will be important for consideration by mental health professionals as they shape program implementation and outcomes of interest.

Through the Individuals with Disabilities Education Act (IDEA), federal dollars finance 10.2% of state special education services. Prior to the 1997 reauthorization of IDEA, federal funding was allocated to states based on the number of special education students identified. The formula by which federal funds are distributed to state education agencies is now more complex, and ends the reliance on child count data by substituting a population factor plus a poverty factor. States distribute the federal portion of their funds to local districts in a similar manner, but have significant flexibility in how state-generated funds are allocated to local districts. The majority of the financial burden of special education programs falls on individual states, which vary greatly in the formulas used to support students with disabilities. The way in which state funds are distributed to local districts appears to have the potential to affect special education enrollment and types of placements.

Tension exists between federal policy and state funding methods regarding special education services. On one hand, IDEA mandates that a full continuum of placement settings be available to provide the range of services needed by children with disabilities within the least restrictive environment. On the other hand, states retain discretion over the distribution of much of the state special education funds; some state formulas provide financial incentives to place special education students in more restrictive, expensive settings. State differences in available financial resources and targeted purpose are clearly important factors in school mental health service delivery.

Definitions of service eligibility   Schools determine eligibility for special education and related services using definitions derived from the Individuals with Disabilities Education Act (IDEA). Under IDEA, a child may become eligible for special education and related services under the "emotional disturbance" (ED) category. The definition of ED has long been the source of contention. Several aspects of the ED definition are thought to inappropriately limit eligibility to those children whose education may adversely be affected by an emotional problem. For example, a clause in the federal ED definition excludes those children who are socially maladjusted, unless they have an emotional disturbance. Furthermore, factors such as gender, ethnicity, and communities' sociodemographic characteristics appear to affect the likelihood of being identified with an ED. It also appears that the definition lends itself to identify children only after aggressive externalizing or disturbing internalizing behaviors have reached the crisis level. Such definitional considerations are relevant as mental health interventionists consider the location of targeted services within special or general education classrooms.

Little national data are available about the prevalence of related services delivered under IDEA. Although states are required under IDEA to report specific counts of children receiving special education, the settings in which that education is provided, and the personnel employed and needed to deliver the special education, no similar mandate exists for related services. Until national and state data accurately represent utilized or available services, researchers should confirm services utilized at the local system and individual school level. . . .

Conclusion: Expanding Mental Health Intervention "Evidence" to School Practice

Mental health intervention research, albeit limited, has developed both targeted and preventive interventions that have implications for the delivery of child mental health services within school settings. Many such "evidence-based" interventions are not embedded in school systems. A deeper consideration of factors relevant to school context will facilitate the transition from mental health intervention research to school practice. Such consideration will consist of stronger collaborative relationships between mental health and educational professionals, a focus on both intervention development and infrastructure building, as well as increased attention to school-relevant variables in research designs.

Many have written about the importance of collaboration between mental health and school professionals as well as researchers and practitioners. We too argue that collaboration is essential and that it is particularly critical at the outset of intervention development and testing. Unfortunately, when collaboration exists between community care systems or providers and academic researchers, it all too often happens in the context of program implementation, and not program development. Consistent with the Blueprint report and with Hoagwood, Burns, and Weisz, we argue that factors related to intervention deployment (such as provider training, fit with provider context) be considered not only when an intervention has been found efficacious and ready for deployment, but at the outset as a particular intervention is being developed. Such collaboration should focus on provider attitudes/roles, organizational factors and governance issues that might influence the type of intervention developed, the feasibility of implementation, and factors critical to sustainability.

Mental health research should move beyond the development and testing of efficacious interventions; such investigations in and of themselves will not change school-based practices for children with emotional or behavior problems. As McLaughlin et al. rightly argue, the establishment of an array of interventions alone will be insufficient to promote capacity building within local schools and school districts. Such an intervention-driven focus could leave schools in the position of expending precious resources in "collecting" interventions without modifying the necessary organizational structures to support such interventions or without paying adequate attention to promoting changes in professional behavior. Similarly, school policy cannot focus solely on system reform and/or infrastructure development. Mental health services research has demonstrated that systemic reforms without concordant attention to the integration of high-quality services may not improve child mental health outcomes. Mental health services researchers have argued that the integration of systemic reforms with efficacious interventions will best promote access to services and improve the quality of child mental health care. We argue that school mental health service improvement will follow a similar model. Positive changes in the provision of school-based mental health care will result from the marriage of system reform efforts, capacity building, and delivery of empirically driven intervention strategies.

A thorough consideration of school context offers an expanding role for mental health research and practice in education. Interventions targeted at the individual child level only may be inadequate to the task. Even though individual counseling and case management are the typical school-based mental health models, such approaches are resource-intensive and have limited impact. To be most helpful to schools, it is important for mental health professionals to move beyond the development and testing of clinically focused treatments and move into the study of interventions relevant to the contextual needs of a dynamic education system. Such arguments have been made by others within education and mental health and are supported here. Mental health research could make an even greater contribution by adding emphasis to nontraditional interventions such as targeting the health of school personnel (e.g., decreasing burden, increasing morale), global prevention efforts to reduce truancy, or systemic interventions that aid in the reduction of disciplinary referrals or unnecessary special education placements. Mental health research has the tools to create such interventions; however, these mental health resources have gone largely untapped.

In summary, the school context is a particularly critical one in a child's development; this is particularly true for children with emotional disturbances. Research demonstrates that contextual factors are critical in the successful, sustainable implementation of school-based mental health interventions. Nevertheless, these factors are all too often ignored. Time and resource investments only in mental health intervention content development will be insufficient. Because intervention content is likely shaped by the ultimate care context, efforts should be made to understand this interaction. Future successful attempts to truly integrate mental health interventions in a school environment will depend upon a deeper consideration of individual, school, and state or federal governance factors. Mental health interventions will not be successful if they are seen as totally distinct from academics or as additional burdens to the system. Decisions regarding intervention type, focus, placement, and fundamental integration should be grounded by a consideration of factors relevant to the school environment. Simply stated, context matters.

POSTSCRIPT

Should Schools Treat the Mental Health Needs of Students?

In 2000, David Satcher, the assistant secretary for health and the surgeon general, released the National Action Agenda, which identified eight goals and multiple action steps, to address the mental health needs of children, adolescents, and their families in this country. It includes areas such as promoting public awareness of children's mental health issues, reducing the stigma associated with mental illness, and improving the assessment and recognition of mental health needs in children. Dr. Satcher discussed the need to educate persons involved with children to identify symptoms of mental health issues. Within this list, he included educators because teachers and support personnel play a significant role in the lives of children. Dr. Satcher also addressed the need to learn and understand research-based approaches for intervention and treatment. The concern for the mental health of children and adolescents is clearly at the national forefront.

Dr. Satcher also addressed the need for our country to create a comprehensive infrastructure that will provide mental health services to children and families. This would be the most effective way to begin to systematically treat our youth. However, how this should be done is an open question. Considering that schools are a significant institution in the lives of children and families, it would stand to reason that schools would play a role in such a comprehensive infrastructure. However, to what capacity? Should educators engage in the prevention, diagnosis, and treatment of mental health services? Do schools have the resources to do so, and is it in the best interest of education?

Suggested readings include U.S. Public Health Service, *Report of the Surgeon General's Conference on Children's Mental Health: A National Agenda* (Department of Health and Human Services, 2000), S. Gowers, S. Thomas, and S. Deeley, "Can Primary Schools Contribute Effectively to Tier I Child Mental Health Services?" *Clinical Child Psychology and Psychiatry* (vol. 9, no. 3, 2004, pp. 419–425), G. Baruch, "Mental Health Services in the Schools: The Challenge of Locating a Psychotherapy Service for Troubled Adolescent Pupils in Mainstream and Special Schools," *Journal of Adolescence* (vol. 24, no. 4, 2001, pp. 549–570), S.C. Scholzman, "The Shrink in the Classroom," *Educational Leadership* (vol. 60, no. 5, 2003, pp. 80–83), Ann S. Masten, "Commentary: Developmental Psychopathology as a Unifying Context for Mental Health and Education Models, Research, and Practice in Schools," *School Psychology Review* (vol. 32, no. 2, 2003, pp. 169–173), and *Diagnostic and Statistical Manual of Mental Disorders*, 4th ed., text revision (American Psychiatric Assocation, 2000).

ISSUE 19

Are Antidepressant Medications an Appropriate Treatment for Students?

YES: David A. Brent, from "Treating Depression in Children: Antidepressants and Pediatric Depression—The Risk of Doing Nothing," *The New England Journal of Medicine* (October 14, 2004)

NO: Jennifer Couzin, from "Volatile Chemistry: Children and Antidepressants," *Science* (July 23, 2004)

ISSUE SUMMARY

YES: David A. Brent is a professor of psychiatry at the University of Pittsburgh School of Medicine. Professor Brent discusses the historical concern of child and adolescent suicide as well as the factors that have contributed to the drop in suicide rates in recent years. He concludes that specific antidepressants (SSRIs) are a viable treatment for pediatric depression, and discontinuing their usage would put treatment for depression back 25 years.

NO: Jennifer Couzin is a contributing author to *Science*. Couzin offers evidence that when school-age children use SSRIs to treat anxiety and depressive disorders, they are at increased risk of suicidal ideations and suicide. The medications may prove to have little value in treating their depression.

Suicide rates are holding steady, but they were on the rise for many years, especially in the early 1990s. Suicide is ranked as the third-leading cause of death among adolescents ages 15 through 19, comprising approximately 13 percent of all adolescent deaths in this age group. Equally concerning is the fact that the rise in suicide rates among children ages 10 to 14 has increased 99 percent from 1980 to 1997. However, a bit of good news is that in the past few years, suicide rates among youth have declined slightly. The Center for Disease Control and Prevention has estimated the suicide rates for the age group of 15- to 19-year-olds is approximately 8 in every 100,000.

One of the hallmark signs that a child or adolescent may commit suicide is the presence of a psychiatric disorder such as depression. Professionals in the mental health field have continued to develop more accurate methods of diagnosis and treatment for depression. One of the major contributions to treatment has been medication. The field of psychopharmacology has made numerous contributions in recent years when considering the options that physicians have to chemically treat children and adolescents suffering from various types of mental health illnesses.

One of the most utilized and well-known types of medications are selective serotonin reuptake inhibitors (SSRIs). These medications work at a chemical level between the neuron receptor sites. SSRIs have been much more widely used with children and adolescents, as well as adults, for different forms of mood and anxiety disorders. Many individuals have found relief and assistance with their ailments from using these medications. Physicians and mental health professionals have been prescribing these medications in greater numbers, anticipating positive changes for suffering youth.

However, various stories have also flourished in the media regarding the dangers of children and adolescents using SSRIs, including increased risk of suicide, suicidal thoughts, and psychotic behaviors. A number of families have claimed that the use of SSRIs are dangerous and that their lives and the lives of their children have been significantly impacted by the effects of these medications. Whether these medications are a safe intervention for children and adolescents is controversial.

Couzin presents specific cases of children who experienced significant and negative side effects, including suicidal and homicidal thoughts. She asserts that the quick rise in use and rate of prescribing antidepressant medications have superseded the level of research that is needed to support its effectiveness with young people. Has the mental health field jumped the gun, so to speak, with the distribution of SSRIs to children and adolescents?

On the other hand, Brent argues that taking SSRIs off the market would be a major step back in the field of pediatric psychopharmacology. Doctors and mental health professionals have been waiting a long time for more effective treatment for mood disorders and for individuals who at risk for suicide due to their mental illness. He acknowledges that these medications should be closely monitored, and if done so correctly, negative side effects can be caught soon. Even though a minority of individuals have suffered negative and severe consequences, is it prudent to discontinue a treatment that has the potential to help many others?

YES ↰

David A. Brent

Treating Depression in Children: Antidepressants and Pediatric Depression—The Risk of Doing Nothing

There is great concern that antidepressants used in children and adolescents may paradoxically increase their risk of suicidal thoughts and behavior. Is this concern valid, and if so, how should it modify our clinical approach to pediatric depression?

Twenty-five years ago, long before the introduction of selective serotonin-reuptake inhibitors (SSRJs), the adolescent suicide rate was increasing rapidly, having tripled over the previous two decades, but the risk factors involved were unknown. Adolescents who committed suicide were regarded as misunderstood teenagers who had been under too much stress. There was debate about whether depression could occur in children, and the prevailing view was that moodiness was normal in adolescents. Furthermore, even if we could have diagnosed depression and recognized young people who were at risk for suicide, there were no empirically validated treatments to offer.

Eventually, we learned that depression did indeed affect children and adolescents. Through retrospective interviews with family members and friends, this disorder emerged as the single most important risk factor for adolescent suicide, although it often acted in concert with substance abuse and impulsive aggression. Adolescents who committed suicide frequently had a history of suicidal thoughts or behavior, disclosed only to a friend who was sworn to secrecy. Most commonly, adolescents killed themselves with a gun, and guns were much more frequently available to those who had died by suicide than to those who had attempted suicide but lived.

These findings suggested some straightforward approaches to prevention. Although it had been thought that people who talk about suicide don't kill themselves, these results showed that previous suicidal behavior and current suicidal thoughts are potent risk factors for suicide and must be taken seriously. The association between the availability of guns and their use in suicides suggested that guns should be removed, or at least secured. Finally, the development and testing of treatments for pediatric depression should be given high priority.

From *New England Journal of Medicine*, vol. 351(16). October 14, 2004, pp. 1598–1601. Copyright © 2004 by Massachusetts Medical Society. Reprinted by permission.

Today, we are able to identify young people who are at high risk for suicide and to offer empirically validated treatments for depression. It is ironic
that concern about the risks posed by antidepressants has arisen now, when
the adolescent suicide rate has been decreasing for a decade, for the first time in
more than half a century. This trend is accounted for primarily by a drop in the
rate of suicide by means of firearms, suggesting that more restrictive gun-control
laws may be partially responsible. A portion of the decrease may be related to
better detection of depression and suicidality (suicidal ideation, behavior, or
both) and the dissemination of validated treatments. There is some ecologic
evidence that increases in the number of prescriptions for SSRIs for adolescents
are associated with a decrease in adolescent suicide.

Nevertheless, given findings showing a relationship between suicidality
and completed suicide, one must take seriously the possibility that antidepressants might increase the risk of suicidality. And yet the concern about SSRIs in
pediatric depression that has been aroused by the British Medicines and Healthcare Products Regulatory Agency (MHRA) (http://www.mhra.gov.uk/our-
work/monitorsafequalmed/safetymessages) is based, in my opinion, on
an overestimation of risk and an underestimation of benefit.

Current clinical practice with regard to SSRI use for pediatric depression is
based on six published studies, although five unpublished studies were much
less favorable. There is the most incontrovertible evidence of efficacy for fluoxetine, which had positive results in three clinical trails. For sertraline, the results
were positive but modest, with a 10 percent difference in response between
drug and placebo. One study of citalopram was positive and one negative, but
the latter involved both inpatients and outpatients and had a very high dropout rate. There were two negative trials of venlafaxine, but the doses used were
often well below the minimal therapeutic dose for adults, and when the results
were stratified according to age, venlafaxine was superior to placebo among
adolescents. There have been three clinical trials of paroxetine, of which only
one was positive.

In addition to questioning the benefit of these drugs, the MHRA and the
Food and Drug Administration (FDA) focused attention on a possible increase
in the likelihood of suicidality. In response, the MHRA declared that all antidepressants except fluoxetine were contraindicated in pediatric depression.
The FDA initially advised against the use of paroxetine only, since there was
some evidence of efficacy for sertraline and citalopram. More recently, the
FDA labeled all antidepressants with a warning about their possible potential
for inducing suicidal thoughts or behavior. The FDA also recently commissioned a blind independent review of these adverse events by a consensus
panel of international experts.

With regard to the main outcome, suicidality (the combination of new
suicide attempts, new-onset suicidal ideation, and worsening of existing suicidal
ideation), the FDA analysis, presented to an advisory committee in a public
hearing September 13 and 14, 2004, found an increase by a factor of 1.8 associated with drug treatment, which translates to a difference of 1.7 percentage
points between drug and placebo (3.8 percent vs. 2.1 percent). Although the
difference is small, it seems likely that the effect is real, because the findings

were statistically significant in aggregate and are consistent across multiple studies of various agents.

Although the initial MHRA report and the FDA analysis found that fluoxetine treatment was not associated with suicidality, an FDA analysis of a new clinical trial found otherwise—but the results help to put the benefits and risks into perspective. In this study, cognitive-behavioral therapy and fluoxetine treatment, alone and in combination, were compared with each other and with placebo. Fluoxetine was much more likely than placebo to result in a significant clinical improvement (in 61 percent of cases vs. 35 percent) but, according to the FDA analysis, was associated with a significant increase by a factor of 4.6 in the rate of suicidal events (8.3 percent vs. 1.8 percent). Once a suicidal event was detected, the patient was withdrawn from the trial. Although depression and suicidality are both significant risk factors for suicide, depression improved in these patients four times as frequently as suicidality developed, which seems to represent an acceptable risk-benefit ratio. Fluoxetine plus cognitive therapy was not superior to fluoxetine alone according to most measures of depression, but the combination was superior to all other treatments in reducing the intensity of suicidal thoughts. This finding suggests that the optimal treatment for suicidality in a depressed patient may be multimodal—a logical approach, given the multiple risk factors for suicide.

In light of these concerns, why use SSRIs at all? Although cognitive-behavioral therapy appears to be more effective than other psychosocial treatments for depression, this comparison between it and medication found it inferior to fluoxetine therapy. And although the risk-benefit ratio is best for fluoxetine, nearly 40 percent of depressed adolescents do not have a response to this drug, and others cannot tolerate it. Other agents with some evidence of efficacy should be considered for these patients.

In addition to increasing the risk of suicidality, SSRIs are twice as likely as placebo to result in agitation and hostility. The FDA could not test whether hostility and suicidality were linked, but the drugs most closely associated with one were also most closely associated with the other. In addition, treatment with antidepressants is much more likely to unmask an underlying bipolar disorder in children or adolescents than it is in adults, which can result in the induction of a mixed manic and depressive state—a condition that carries a very high risk of suicidal behavior.

As SSRIs have gained in popularity, their ease of use and relatively favorable side-effect profile may have led to an overly casual approach to the treatment of depression. All depressed patients who are treated with antidepressants must be closely monitored for emergent suicidality, hostility, agitation, and mania. Families and patients must be informed about the benefits and risks of these drugs and should be educated about monitoring for emergent side effects, as recommended in recent public statements and labeling changes made by the FDA. Because children and adolescents generally metabolize antidepressants more rapidly than adults, they must receive doses adequate to achieve a clinical response. Suicidality in depressed patients may be best treated by a combination of psychotherapy and medication.

The FDA's recent analysis suggests that the risk of emergent suicidality in children and adolescents receiving SSRIs is real—but small. The FDA's advisors recommended stronger warnings in labeling and better information for patients and caregivers, but they stopped short of recommending contraindications for these drugs. However, many participants in the public hearing seemed convinced that the pharmacologic treatment of pediatric depression should be banned or severely curtailed. That would turn the clock back 25 years, to a time when the only thing we could offer the families of suicide victims was the hope that someday we would have effective treatments. Ideally, the FDA, families, and clinicians will find the right balance between the risk of suicidality and another, greater risk; the risk that lies in doing nothing.

NO ↵

Jennifer Couzin

Volatile Chemistry: Children and Antidepressants

Even in the earliest studies, there were troubling hints: Some children seemed to fare poorly on a type of drug now widely used to treat depression. Take the case of F., a chronically anxious 12-year-old boy with obsessive-compulsive disorder (OCD). More than 13 years ago, F. received Prozac—which boosts levels of serotonin, a signaling protein in the brain—as part of a study at Yale University. In the weeks that followed, he told doctors he was wracked by nightmares of killing his classmates and himself. He went off the drug and spent a month in a psychiatric unit before recovering.

F. wasn't the only one. Five other young people among 42 receiving Prozac for OCD at Yale experienced similar symptoms, according to a published account. The drug, a selective serotonin reuptake inhibitor (SSRI), made them feel "like they were jumping out of their skin," recalls Yale child psychiatrist Robert King, who helped run the study and write the report.

Today, King looks back on those six patients, three girls and three boys, as harbingers of what has become a badly muddled debate in psychiatric medicine. After 16 years during which SSRIs have been viewed as life-saving and have been widely prescribed for depression, experts face an unsettling possibility—that in a small number of young people, some of these drugs may trigger suicidal thinking or behavior. Recently released clinical trial data, moreover, reveal flaws in the evidence that SSRIs ease depression in children and adolescents.

Although doctors have been giving SSRIs to children for more than a decade, the controversy over risks and benefits erupted a year ago, after a manufacturer sought approval for use of one such drug, Paxil, in children. Not only was the request denied, but it triggered new inquiries into an alleged association between SSRIs and suicidal thinking or behavior. The U.S. Food and Drug Administration (FDA) has commissioned an outside review (*Science*, 6 February, p. 745) and aims to issue a report by September.

In contrast, many psychiatric researchers credit SSRIs for a drop in youth suicides in the last decade. They doubt that the FDA review will settle the matter, partly because it lacks reliable information. Only a handful of large studies have been conducted on SSRI use in youngsters, and none was designed to assess suicidality.

Nor is mining data likely to address another troubling issue, psychiatrists say: If SSRIs can induce suicidality, who is at risk, and why? Scientists have suggested that SSRIs may unleash dangerous behaviors in patients with bipolar disorder, and that some individuals may be acutely sensitive to these drugs.

Companies that make SSRIs and the doctors who prescribe them are now on the defensive. In June, New York State Attorney General Eliot Spitzer accused U.K.-based GlaxoSmithKline (GSK) of concealing negative data on Paxil (*Science*, 11 June, p. 1576), and Congress is planning an inquiry. Psychiatrists worry, meanwhile, that the studies needed to resolve this issue may never be done. "Something is occurring with the medications," says Timothy Wilens, a child psychiatrist and pharmacologist at Massachusetts General Hospital in Boston. But researchers say they don't know enough about SSRIs to explain why they work—or fail—in young patients.

Guilt by Association?

In his Riverside Drive office overlooking the Hudson River, Donald Klein, director of the New York State Psychiatric Institute, dismisses the SSRI fuss as "a tempest in a teapot." Like most others in his field, Klein says that SSRIs transformed the treatment of depression. An earlier type of antidepressant, the tricyclics, sometimes caused cardiac arrhythmias or fatal overdoses—a serious concern for potentially suicidal patients. And these drugs were never shown to work in children.

Prozac was the first SSRI to hit the market, in 1988. Child psychiatrists began prescribing it. The first large study of Prozac in children appeared in 1997: Ninety-six volunteers received the drug or a placebo for 8 weeks. Fifty-six percent of those on Prozac improved, compared to 33% on placebo.

"Quickly, practice patterns began to shift across the country," recalls David Fassler, a child and adolescent psychiatrist in Burlington, Vermont. The use of SSRIs in young people took off, he says, "despite the fact that we had limited research."

Drug companies followed up with a handful of published SSRI studies in youngsters. Although few drugs on the market have been tested in children, physicians may prescribe them to youngsters "off label." But companies were drawn to pediatric testing by the 1997 FDA Modernization Act, which promised a 6-month patent extension for any drug tested in children. Annual sales of Prozac reached $2.5 billion at the time. For some companies, the carrot was irresistible.

In 2002, GSK submitted data to FDA on trials of Paxil in children. An FDA reviewer asked for more information about patients who suffered from what Glaxo called "emotional lability." Many of these cases, GSK explained, involved self-harm or thoughts of self-harm that might be suicide-related. In one pediatric Paxil study, six depressed youngsters exhibited "possibly suicide-related events" compared to one on placebo; five attempted suicide, compared to none on placebo. Two other pediatric Paxil studies of depression, though, reported no difference in suicidality between drug and placebo patients.

Reaction was swift. Both the U.K.'s drug regulatory arm, the Medicines and Healthcare Products Regulatory Agency, and FDA issued warnings against

Paxil's use in children. Both agencies also launched reviews of other antidepressants to determine whether they, too, might cause suicidal thinking or behavior.

Although such effects have been seen in adults taking SSRIs, it is unclear whether they occur more frequently in children, and no similar review is being undertaken—in part because many clinical trials have found that SSRIs work in adults, shifting the risk-benefit calculus. The ongoing pediatric reviews include Prozac, the only SSRI approved for use in depressed youngsters.

Many observers, meanwhile, hope that a $17 million National Institutes of Health study, the Treatment for Adolescents With Depression Study, will provide insight. It compares the effectiveness of Prozac and psychotherapy in depressed teenagers over 9 months and assesses suicidality. Preliminary results are expected later this summer.

Unbottled Emotion

Psychiatrists have long spoken of "over-responders," children whose thoughts or behavior seem to surge in strange directions on SSRIs. Child psychiatrist David Shaffer of Columbia University in New York City says he encountered one this summer. He was treating a 15-year-old girl who had been profoundly depressed since the death of a friend. Several days after starting on a low dose of Prozac, she burst into Shaffer's office for an appointment, announcing that the hatred she'd long bottled up was coming out and that she'd been mean to her mother. "She had overresponded," says Shaffer, who quickly halved her dose. The symptoms soon receded.

In a study Mass General's Wilens published last year, one in five children on an SSRI had an adverse event, including disinhibition, agitation, and sleep disturbance. But Wilens and his colleagues didn't see any hints of suicidality.

Only a handful of published reports have. The first to find it among adults appeared in 1990; a year later, King and his colleagues detailed cases among children on Prozac for OCD. The adult finding prompted FDA hearings in 1991 at which Prozac's maker—Eli Lilly of Indianapolis, Indiana—presented data that convinced the agency and its advisory panel that Prozac was safe in adults. (The company hadn't yet tested the drug in children.)

But the concerns never completely disappeared. "Things can go very sourly wrong in the first few weeks" on an SSRI, says Martin Teicher, director of the developmental biopsychiatry research program at McLean Hospital in Boston and the lead author of the 1990 study in adults.

Even the staunchest advocates of SSRIs agree that a small minority of pediatric patients do poorly on them. "Everybody, myself included, said it's clear there are patients who are put on these meds who get worse," says John March, chief of child and adolescent psychiatry at Duke University Medical Center. How many—if any—of those patients become suicidal as a result of taking the drugs isn't known. It's possible, March and others say, that many of these patients are already suicidal; the SSRIs may supply them with the impulsivity to act.

King doubts that this explanation covers all cases, however. In youngsters with OCD, suicidality is not pervasive. In his study, "the notion that these were just depressed kids" who were disinhibited by the drug "doesn't make a lot of sense," he says.

Researchers have sought a biological explanation for the adverse effects in children, but so far with little success. SSRIs boost serotonin levels, but how this affects the developing brain isn't well understood. Serotonin facilitates nerve signal transmission, modulating mood, sleep, appetite, and a variety of brain functions. Depression may occur when too little serotonin is available in nerve synapses. SSRIs block "reuptake" or absorption of serotonin after it has been released, making more of it available.

In chemical structure, SSRIs differ subtly, but the clinical implications are poorly understood. Paxil has a short half-life in the body, for example, just 8 or 9 hours compared with 2 to 7 days for Prozac. It's not clear how that affects young patients, says Wilens, or whether SSRIs differ in the regions of the brain they affect: "We're just now developing the technology to look at that." David Rosenberg, chief of child psychiatry at Wayne State University in Detroit, Michigan, is conducting some of the first imaging studies to see how Paxil, Prozac, and Zoloft each affect certain brain structures in children and adolescents—and whether youngsters with specific brain patterns to begin with fare better on the drugs.

The biological picture is even murkier when it comes to explaining why SSRIs might cause suicidality. Teicher believes that the doses used in some studies—including the pediatric studies of Paxil that have come under scrutiny—were too high and may, paradoxically, have had the opposite of their intended effect. High doses, he suggests, may desensitize serotonin receptors, diminishing serotonin neurotransmission and worsening depression. Teicher and others also think that many children who react badly to SSRIs are suffering from bipolar disorder rather than depression. In patients like these—who are notoriously hard to diagnose because they often experience several depressive episodes before a manic one—SSRIs can precipitate mania. And this may lead to suicidal behavior, says Vermont's Fassler. Many child psychiatrists favor an extended evaluation of patients before prescribing an SSRI to try to make sure they're not bipolar and starting at very low doses.

"Do we really know how to diagnose depression in kids?" asks Bill Potter, vice president of clinical neuroscience at Merck Research Labs outside Philadelphia. "The truth is, no. We don't even know that the people we are treating with childhood depression have the same illness as the people we are treating with adult depression."

Balancing Risks

Psychiatrists say they must weigh the risks and benefits of SSRIs in treating very sick children and adolescents and choose the course that seems most likely to help. The threat of suicide is ever-present: Two thousand teenagers take their lives every year in the United States, and 2 million make attempts. Many psychiatrists are convinced that drug therapy offers the best hope of reducing that toll, despite a small associated risk that some patients may respond poorly. If this were childhood cancer, says John Mann, a psychiatrist at Columbia University, the public wouldn't think twice about giving a drug that may have a small chance of causing suicidal thinking and behavior.

But as the SSRI controversy has ballooned over the last year, the risk-benefit calculus has become knottier. First, unpublished studies of Paxil released by GSK suggest that this therapy didn't consistently help depressed children any more than a placebo did. The one published pediatric study of Paxil had shown the opposite.

The concerns have also prompted regulators to reanalyze unpublished data for other SSRIs. In April, a set of experts commissioned to advise the U.K. government found that unpublished data suggested that four of five SSRIs were unlikely to benefit children—sometimes in contrast to what published data implied. The British team expects to publish its final recommendations in May 2005.

FDA, meanwhile, has asked a team at Columbia to reclassify more than 400 adverse events from 25 pediatric trials of nine different drugs. Columbia received a mishmash of reports describing children who slapped themselves, stabbed themselves with pencils, held pocketknives to their necks, or otherwise behaved adversely. They're charged with assessing which are suicidal as opposed to self-destructive.

Shaffer, who recused himself from the review effort in February after being criticized at an FDA hearing for his support of antidepressants, is pessimistic: "I don't know that [the review] will clarify anything," he says.

Indeed, this may be the one point on which SSRI supporters and antagonists agree. "The material that's gone to Columbia is worthless," says David Healy, a psychiatrist at the University of Wales College of Medicine in the U.K., who has long warned about the suicide risk he believes is associated with SSRIs. FDA officials say they're convinced that the reclassification will help settle this issue once and for all.

POSTSCRIPT

Are Antidepressant Medications an Appropriate Treatment for Students?

The question has certainly been raised regarding the extent of our knowledge about the long-term effects of SSRIs in children, as well as whether or not all information about the possible and potential negative side effects have been made public. In the effort to find more effective ways to treat debilitating and potentially fatal mental illnesses, have medications been dispensed too liberally to youth? That can be a difficult question, considering that suicidal thoughts and suicide is elevated with the depressed population. Does the fact that suicide rates have slightly decreased in the past few years for adolescents provide some evidence to the effectiveness of pharmaceutical treatment?

In October 2004, the Food and Drug Administration required that pharmaceutical companies post warnings with the distribution of antidepressant medications. This sends a clear message that our society is concerned about potential harmful outcomes for children and adolescents. Physicians, mental health workers and families must certainly work together in order to provide the most effective treatment plan for youth who are experiencing symptoms of depression and signs of suicidal tendencies. Educators can also assist in being a part of the intervention team by monitoring behaviors of students, communicating with families and physicians, and learning more about the responses to antidepressant medications.

Suggested readings include K. Brown, "The Medication Merry-Go-Round," *Science* (March 14, 2003, pp. 1646–1649), K.M. Sibley and D.A. Kramer, "Reframing the SSRI Issue," *Journal of the American Academy of Child and Adolescent Psychiatry* (vol. 43, no. 10, 2004, pp. 1188–1189), A.L. Bauer, E. Ingersoll, and L. Burns, "School Counselors and Psychotropic Medication: Assessing, Training, Experience, and School Policy Issues," *Professional School Counseling* (vol. 7, no. 3, 2004, pp. 202–211), and J.F. Luebbert, R.P. Malone, and L. Rieser, "Disability Law and the Administration of Psychotropic Medication in the School Setting," *Psychiatric Services* (vol. 51, no. 11, 2000, pp. 1369–1370).

ISSUE 20

Are Suspensions and Expulsions Viable Responses to Violent Behaviors?

YES: Douglas C. Breunlin, Rocco A. Cimmarusti, Tara L. Bryant-Edwards, and Joshua S. Hetherington, from "Conflict Resolution Training as an Alternative to Suspension for Violent Behavior," *The Journal of Educational Research* (July/August 2002)

NO: Perry A. Zirkel, from "A Web of Disruption?" *Phi Delta Kappan* (May 2001)

ISSUE SUMMARY

YES: Douglas C. Breunlin is a research professor at the Family Institute at Northwestern University along with researchers Rocco A. Cimmarusti, Tara L. Bryant-Edwards, and Joshua S. Hetherington. These researchers think that schools over-rely on suspensions and expulsions and alternatively should consider utilizing a conflict-resolution training program as a means to prevent and manage violent behaviors in schools.

NO: Perry Zirkel is Iacocca Professor of Education at Lehigh University. Zirkel insists that schools have the right to keep their schools safe through suspensions and expulsions even if it means limiting the rights of students to say whatever they might like to of an offensive, derogatory, salacious, or threatening nature on the Internet.

What should school administrators do to keep learning environments safe? How should school officials respond to the aggressive actions of students? One long-standing response to aggressive or rule-breaking behavior has been suspending students from school for a short amount of time or expelling students from school when severe incidents have occurred.

Utilizing suspensions and expulsions as a response to aggressive student behavior is not without its criticisms. For example, in regard to the No Child Left Behind Act, *all* students are to make progress toward state-outlined standards. Logically, it is difficult to make educational progress when you are not in school. So, while being suspended or expelled may work toward solving one problem, it inadvertently creates another. Second, suspending or expelling a student does not often address the root of the problem, such as weak social problem-solving skills, family issues, significant behavior or adjustment problems, or mental health problems. Relying on suspension or expulsion only temporarily addresses an issue, but typically does not solve a larger issue with a student. Lastly, studies have indicated that there is a disparity between the number of minorities who are suspended and expelled versus Caucasian students. This calls into question a separate issue of whether administrators are managing behaviors in an equitable manner.

Many books about violence prevention discuss addressing various behavioral needs, school climate, and positive discipline. In line with implementing proactive approaches to school violence and students who engage in rule-breaking behaviors, Breunlin, Cimmarusti, Bryant-Edwards, and Hetherington implemented a program that is an alternative to suspension and expulsion. This program was based upon research findings that suggest that aggressive behavior is learned and can be prevented through teaching alternative methods. Their program utilized components that identified family issues and engaged the family educationally, utilized conflict-resolution strategies, skill building such as perspective taking, active listening, and problem solving. Results were positive for the students and families who completed the program. The targeted students were subsequently suspended less frequently for violent or aggressive behaviors.

Conversely, school administrators are responsible for maintaining the safety of the school environment as well as the rights and safety of the students and staff. If a person is threatened or is experiencing justifiable fear because another person is threatening harm, should the perpetrator lose his or her right to attend the public institution? Isn't it the school administrator's job to ensure safety for all? An administrator certainly cannot monitor every interaction and behavior that happens within a school building. So, while there may be negative educational consequences to suspensions and expulsions, the consequences of a person being seriously harmed, harassed, or worst of all, murdered, maybe a worse consequence. After all, maybe students surrender their right to a free education when they trample on the basic constitutional rights of others.

Zirkel discusses a case in which a student was utilizing the Internet to post disparaging and threatening statements of the most appalling nature about a teacher. The teacher experienced significant psychological difficulties because of these statements. Therefore, the student was suspended and later expelled from school. The parents of the student brought the case to court saying that their child's constitutional rights were violated. The court upheld the school district's right to discipline the student through the use of expulsion.

The debate becomes, when and how do schools utilize suspensions and expulsions? Are they an appropriate response to violent or threatening behaviors, or should schools create alternative programs for these students?

YES

Douglas C. Breunlin, et al.

Conflict Resolution Training as an Alternative to Suspension for Violent Behavior

Everyone knows that it is virtually impossible to prove a negative. Sadly, high school administrators throughout the country know that they cannot prove that a Columbine-style tragedy will not occur in their schools. Confronted with this stark reality, administrators are searching for proven approaches to violence prevention. These approaches fall into three categories: security, punishment, and school-based programs. Security approaches keep violence at bay. Punishment deters violence by sending a strong message that it will not be tolerated. School-based programs provide alternatives to violence and reduce the risk factors for violence.

The first category, security approaches, is designed to keep violence out of schools by using security guards, metal detectors, identification badges, locked campuses, and locker and book bag checks. These approaches are highly visible and immediate and certainly do prevent some incidents of violence. On the down side, however, they are expensive, and there is a risk that they will make the school feel like a fortress. Another security approach is profiling, which establishes the characteristics of potentially violent youths to identify and help them before they erupt with violence. Profiling has increasingly been questioned because it may injure innocent students and because it has yet to be proven that there is a profile.

The second category, punishment, has long been used as a deterrent for violence. The most common form of punishment has been out-of-school suspension. There are, however, significant concerns about its effectiveness. First, suspension often does not deter future violence because many students are repeatedly suspended for fighting. Second, the objectivity and fairness of out-of-school suspensions has been questioned as some groups of students, including male, minority, and academically and behaviorally challenged students, are suspended in disproportionate numbers. Third, suspension creates serious negative consequences for suspended students. They often perform poorly academically and cannot afford to be away from the classroom. Suspension further disempowers and isolates already marginalized students and their parents from the school. The cycle of fighting, suspension, and failure can culminate in a student's dropping out of school or being expelled.

From *Journal of Educational Research*, July/August 2002, pp. 349–357. Copyright © 2002 by Heldref Publications. Reprinted by permission. References omitted.

In an effort to take an even tougher stand against violence, President Clinton signed the Gun-Free Schools Act into law in 1994. The law mandates a 1-year expulsion for any student caught with a gun at schools receiving federal aid. This law set the tone for many schools to adopt zero-tolerance policies, which state that any form of violence results in expulsion. Although the majority of schools have zero-tolerance policies, those policies are increasingly being questioned. Expulsion can ultimately put violent students at even greater risk for careers of violence. Moreover, adopting more extreme forms of punishment may not actually make the school safer. For example, one national study that compared zero- and non-zero-tolerance schools found that more of the former had had a violent episode that required police involvement.

The third category, violence prevention programs, encompasses a vast array of programs ranging from climate improvement strategies to programs that provide skills-based training, which is generally designed for all students. Unfortunately for high school administrators, most of these programs target elementary schools, leaving only limited choices for high schools. Moreover, very few of those high school options have been tested empirically. Some commonly used programs, particularly peer mediation, have even been shown to be ineffective.

So, how are administrators going to develop comprehensive violence prevention efforts? They could simply use all three approaches; however, such an effort would not be practical because the approaches work in different and not necessarily complementary ways. Moreover, a comprehensive violence-prevention program must attack the spectrum of school violence that includes murder, physical fighting, and bullying. Finally, the individual students who commit these acts of violence vary greatly and, therefore, should be handled differently.

The emphasis on early intervention is predicated on the belief that the precursors to violence, particularly aggression, appear early in childhood and need to be addressed as soon as possible. Not acknowledged in this hypothesis is the fact that, although most seriously violent acts are committed by so-called early-onset offenders, still 40% of violent youths are so-called late-onset offenders. They show no precursors to violence and do not commit their first violent act until adolescence. There is a serious dearth of violence prevention programs for these late-onset offenders.

A comprehensive violence prevention effort must also take into account the fact that adolescent violence exists in several forms and has several causes. Tolan and Guerra defined four patterns of adolescent violence: psychopathological, predatory, situational, and relationship. Psychopathological violence, which is rare, is committed by seriously disturbed and perhaps chemically imbalanced adolescents. It is often lethal and represents the violence that administrators most want to keep out of schools. Predatory violence is perpetrated to obtain some gain. It can involve assault with bodily injury, armed robbery, and rape. Although estimates suggest that 20% of adolescents will commit an act of predatory violence, most of this violence is perpetrated by 5–8% of male and 3–6% of female adolescents. Predatory violence involves early-onset offenders who have multiple risk factors. To be treated effectively, predatory violence requires early and intensive intervention. As such, rates of predatory violence are not likely to respond to school-based violence prevention programs.

More than half of all violence is situational or relationship violence. Situational violence occurs in response to a set of unusual circumstances, and relationship violence arises from interpersonal disputes. Both types fit the pattern that is frequently found in schools: An adolescent finds him- or herself backed into a situation in which violence seems like the only alternative, or a conflict between students who know each other escalates until violence becomes the attempted solution. The first act of violence for many students in high school is an episode of situational or relationship violence, which would make them late-onset offenders. A survey of principles listed these types of physical conflicts as the third most pressing problem in schools.

A comprehensive violence prevention effort must address the question of which approaches work for which violent acts and which violent students. Security approaches target all students but are really designed to avert lethal acts of psychopathological and predatory violence. Punitive approaches, particularly zero tolerance, target all students. These approaches can remove a predator from school, but they also remove late-onset offenders who get into fights while engaging in situational and or relationship violence. Increasingly, the negative consequences of zero tolerance for these students are being questioned. However, administrators face a dilemma because they have few options for dealing with this sort of violence. Universal programs such as climate improvements and conflict skills training, which target all students, have not been shown to reduce violence among at-risk students. Secondary prevention programs that target at-risk students who are violent are critically needed. The group that is most likely to be helped by such programs is that of the late-onset offenders who engage in acts of situational or relationship violence. The question is, how?

When a student is caught fighting at school and some disciplinary action must be taken, there is a major opportunity for intervention with late-onset offenders. Rather than using punishment, schools could modify the disciplinary code to offer these students a violence prevention program in lieu of suspension or in addition to some part of it. The program and the findings reported in this article provide a secondary prevention program for violent adolescents who are at the point of suspension. Because reduced suspension is an incentive to enroll in the program, it was named the Alternative to Suspension for Violent Behavior (ASVB). This intervention was designed to provide violent adolescents and their parents with skills to reduce the risk of further violence. The hope is that intervening at the point of suspension will halt the downward spiral of disciplinary problems that can contribute to two risk factors for violence: academic failure and a poor attitude toward school. Surprisingly, no program like this has been previously reported in the literature.

Alternative to Suspension for Violent Behavior

The structure and format of the Alternative to Suspension for Violent Behavior (ASVB) is predicated on research findings that have provided substantial evidence that violence is largely learned and consequently can be prevented through teaching alternatives to violence. This theory does not deny that the factors contributing to violence are varied and that no one factor is the sole cause of violence. For example, although it is true that some acts of violence do result from extreme anger or lack of impulse control, still, "Inadequate impulse control puts an individual at risk for violence only if violent acts are that person's preferred response choice because of previous learning experiences."

The program components at the secondary prevention level that have been empirically proven to reduce violence or the risk factors for it include teaching social problem-solving and thinking skills. These skills are taught in recognition of the fact that violence often occurs when young people lack behavioral alternatives.

Several model programs also include parent training. Because research has shown that some of the most significant risk factors for violence originate in the family, it is critical to make the ASVB a family intervention. Reed found that the family affected students' attitudes and beliefs about conflict, and he identified lack of parental supervision, responsibility, and involvement as the most influential family issues. Weissberg and Greenberg linked poor parenting skills and family disharmony with adolescent problems. Engaging the family and changing its beliefs and practices about conflict and violence can contribute to changing a student's use of violence.

Because there was no program in existence at the secondary level that could be readily adapted for the ASVB, we created our own, incorporating the practices just described. The skill-building and thinking-skills components are grounded in conflict resolution theory.

The ASVB was developed at the Family Institute at Northwestern University and is offered through one of its satellite offices near the participating high school. Each family is assigned a trainer. Although this individual format is labor intensive, the special attention that alienated youths receive seems to be a factor in its success. For agencies that have insufficient resources to offer an individual format, a group format is available.

In the setting in which this research occurred, when a student is suspended, he or she meets with the assistant principal, who describes the ASVB and invites the family to enroll. In return, the student's suspension is reduced (10 to 5, 5 to 2, or 3 to 1 day[s]). If the family agrees to participate, the student and a parent must sign a contract and contact the Family Institute within 48 hr to arrange a first meeting with a trainer. The student is allowed to return to school immediately after the reduced suspension is served. If a student fails to complete the program, the balance of the suspension must be served.

The ASVB uses a 36-page skills manual titled "Making the Smart Choice: Tools for Resolving Conflict." The manual is covered in 6 hr, generally spread over four 90-min sessions. Our assessment of how much effort families would invest in return for a reduced suspension dictated the 6-hr time frame of the program.

The core premises and skills of conflict resolution are derived from the principles and practices of mediation. Mediation begins with the premise that conflict is inevitable and destructive only when it is handled inappropriately. Further, the mediator assumes that the parties in a conflict are deadlocked, because the positions they adopt are irreconcilable. In other words, the only allowable outcome results in one person winning and the other person losing. Violence enters into a conflict either when the winner uses violence to get his or her way or when the loser reacts to defeat with violence.

The goal of conflict resolution strategies is to find a solution to the conflict whereby both parties get what they want and avoid violence in the process. Attempting to do this by reconciling opposing positions usually leads to further polarization; therefore, the parties must learn to articulate the needs that underlie their positions. Negotiation can then take place around the respective needs of the parties. As long as the needs of both sides are met, they can drop their positions, and both can have a satisfying outcome.

These premises of conflict resolution are easy to articulate and to accept, but implementing them requires considerable cognitive and emotional skill. The cognitive skills that are required are perspective taking and active listening. One section of the manual is devoted to these skills. In addition, for many adolescents, excessive emotion is a major stumbling block to understanding and communicating their needs. In particular, anger can trigger physiological flooding, which impairs rational thought. The manual contains a section on the skills of anger management. Finally, these skills are tied together with a section on problem solving.

Although the ASVB was originally designed for students suspended for physical violence, it can be used with students who are suspended for other reasons. Accordingly, assistant principals at the host high school had the discretion to refer to the program any student whom they believed might benefit.

Method

Participants

The host high school for this study was a public high school with a student population of over 3,000, located in the western suburbs of Chicago. The school has a two-campus system, with freshman and sophomores attending one campus and juniors and seniors the other. Drawn from 10 surrounding communities, the student body is predominantly White and middle class. There is, however, a range of socio-economic levels and some minority representation. Some of the 10 communities are of lower or lower middle-class socioeconomic status, and African American and Hispanic students constitute about 3% and 4% of the population, respectively.

The sample included students who were suspended between August 1997 and December 1998 ($N = 165$). The bulk of the suspensions for the 1st school year were from the freshman/sophomore campus, because the assistant principals at this campus were more closely aligned with the goals of this new program. The sample from the 2nd school year included all suspended students.

Research Hypotheses

The ASVB program has four target outcomes. The first and most salient outcome is a reduced rate of resuspension for acts of physical violence. The second is a reduced rate of resuspension for nonphysical violence. Because the ASVB teaches conflict resolution and problem-solving skills, the third target outcome is a lower rate of resuspension for any reason for students who complete the program compared to the rate for those who do not. Finally, the impact of the program might extend to other disciplinary acts, so a fourth outcome is a lower rate of disciplinary acts for students who complete the program compared with those who do not. Accordingly, we examined one 4-part hypothesis in this pilot study: Compared with students who did not complete the program, those who did would have fewer resuspensions for physical violence, fewer resuspensions for nonphysical violence, fewer total resuspensions, and fewer disciplinary acts.

Design

. . . For all suspended students, archival data on disciplinary records were gathered during the summer after each year of the study. All out-of-school suspensions as well as other types of disciplinary acts (i.e., after-school detentions, Saturday detentions, and in-school suspensions) were included in the collection of data.

Data were gathered for all students who received out-of-school suspensions during the entire 1997–1998 school year and during the first semester of the 1998–1999 school year. A 3-year funded study commenced in the second semester of that year, and all additional data and refinements to it were made part of that study, which will be reported on in another article.

There were 35 reasons for which a student could receive an out-of-school suspension at the host high school. These were divided into three categories: acts of physical violence (physical confrontation), acts of violence that are nonphysical (e.g., intimidation, verbal confrontation), and nonviolent acts (e.g., smoking, drug use).

Data Analyses

Pre- and postintervention disciplinary data were examined for students who did and did not participate in the program. For a further examination of the data, we aggregated students into six groups: three groups of students who completed the ASVB program and another three groups who did not. Group 1 consisted of students who were suspended for fighting who attended the ASVB ($n = 25$). Group 2 consisted of students who were suspended for fighting who did not attend the ASVB ($n = 41$). Group 3 consisted of students who were suspended for other acts of violence who attended the ASVB ($n = 7$). Group 4 consisted of students who were suspended for other acts of violence who did not attend the ASVB ($n = 36$). Group 5 consisted of students who were suspended for nonviolent acts who attended the ASVB ($n = 10$). Group 6 consisted of students who were suspended for nonviolent acts who did not attend the ASVB ($n = 46$). Groups 3 and 5 had small sample sizes because these students were not suspended for fighting, and, therefore, there was no mandate to refer them to the program. Assistant principals had the discretion to refer these students and did so only sporadically. . . .

Results

In this section, we identified demographic information for the entire sample to allow the reader to explore who gets suspended, when, and for what reasons. These demographics favorably compare with other samples from previous research on school suspension. We then explore the data from Groups 1 and 2, both suspended for physical confrontation, with Group 1 participating in the program and Group 2 not. From there, we examine the remaining sample of suspended students. The other four groups are examined, as are a treatment and no-treatment aggregation, and findings are reported.

Demographics

During the year and a half of school included in the pilot study, 165 students were suspended from the host high school. Eighty-two percent (n = 136) of the participants were men and 18% were women (n = 29). Of these 165 students, 10% were African American (n = 16) and 12% were Hispanic (n = 20). The data indicate that African American and Hispanic youths were disproportionately represented among suspended students. African American students were twice as likely as, and Hispanic students were three times more likely than, White students to be represented in the sample of suspended students.

This trend of disproportionate representation by minority students was even more evident when we examined the distribution by race among students suspended for physical violence and among students suspended for violence other than fighting. Suspension rates increased to a high of 22% for African Americans students, or seven times the school population rate, and 20% for Hispanic students, or five times their representation in the student body. Eighty-four percent of the participants were from the freshman/sophomore campus. Although these numbers are not representative of a pattern because of the underuse of the program on the junior/senior campus during the 1st year, underclassmen are still much more likely to be suspended than are upperclassmen.

The evidence indicated that fights occurred between students who knew each other. Fifty-three percent of participants got into fights with students they knew. For Groups 1 and 2, this percentage jumped to 76% and 68%, respectively. By contrast, the students in Groups 3 and 4 were less involved with other students but instead were involved in an altercation with a teacher 42% and 50% of the time, respectively. These incidents were not fights but were acts such as insubordination, verbal confrontation, or gross insubordination. When the same incidents involved another student, they were acts of intimidation or threats of bodily harm.

On average, students received their "index" out-of-school suspension within the first 16 weeks of school. For students who were suspended for fighting and who did not complete the ASVB, their index suspension happened an average of 4 weeks earlier. This difference was also found with those students who were suspended for other violent acts besides fighting. Students suspended for nonviolent acts (Groups 5 and 6) on average were suspended later in the school year than the sample average. . . .

Discussion

On most measures reported, students who participated in the ASVB fared better than those who did not. They were resuspended less frequently for physical and nonphysical violence, their DAI scores were lower, and they were not expelled, whereas 7 students from the pooled nontreatment group were expelled. The goals of the ASVB—to reduce violence by providing a secondary prevention program for at-risk, late-onset offenders—appear to have been modestly met.

Yet, the findings must be held in perspective. Although the study contained comparison groups consisting of students who were suspended for similar reasons (who either refused or were not offered participation in the program), the assignment of the groups was not random, leaving the possibility that some difference between the accepters and refusers explains the results. Because we used archival data for this pilot study, we gathered no data that enabled us to compare students. In an ongoing study funded by the Illinois Violence Prevention Authority (IVPA) to further evaluate the ASVB, Masse conducted a qualitative study to determine why families accept or refuse the program. She found that the decision to refuse was primarily related to a defensive posture that the student and parent took toward the school over the fight. Accepters also seemed to have clear educational goals and valued the reduced suspension rates, whereas refusers did not see this connection or let the student decide whether to participate in the program. In the IVPA study, randomization is addressed by the designation of two treatment conditions: one in which the standard ASVB program is delivered to the student and his or her family and another in which a modified version is delivered to the individual student only. A random sample of students from the general population also serves as another comparison group.

If the ASVB is responsible for the differences found between the treatment and nontreatment groups, several possibilities could account for the differences: the actual skills training, the way the family came together through the program to respond to the suspension, or the way the school responded to the accepters, which may have increased attachment to the school. The bottom line is that the ASVB is not simply a discrete intervention targeted at discrete violent youth. Rather, it is also a systemic intervention that affects the youth, their families, and the culture of the school. This multilevel approach is exactly what the violence prevention research defines as necessary for good outcome. It also makes outcomes in field research that much more difficult to evaluate.

A closer look at the data reveals some interesting findings. A comparison of physically violent and nonphysically violent students reveals that the latter are disciplined more frequently, perhaps putting them at higher risk for becoming disaffected about school. For physically violent students (Groups 1 and 2), the data suggest that the out-of-school suspension serves as a wake-up call and that both the treatment and the nontreatment groups are not often resuspended for physical violence (there were six resuspensions for physical violence). On the other hand, in Groups 3 and 4 (nonphysical violence) there were 32 resuspensions for nonphysical violence.

This result suggests that several hypotheses should be tested in future research. Perhaps nonphysically violent students constitute a different group of students. Alternatively, because their brand of violence is more often directed at adults in the school, they may be labeled differently and, therefore, targeted for discipline more often. Finally, their attachment to the school may be eroded by their disciplinary problems, making them more vulnerable to trouble. We suggest that schools should be equally concerned with both physical and nonphysical violence.

The finding that the rate of discipline increases as the year progresses is troublesome. It suggests that the most heavily disciplined students are on a negative trajectory toward leaving school because of the sheer accumulation of trouble. Identifying and slowing down this process should be a prime objective of problem-solving strategies directed at at-risk students.

The introduction of the ASVB—a program that modifies the disciplinary code—into a high school has had interesting effects. Its very presence challenges the assumptions that discipline is just a punishment and that it functions only as a deterrent. It introduces the concept of discipline as problem solving. In addition, establishing the ASVB heightened the realization that some risk factors to attachment were embedded in the climate of the school. This realization triggered the creation of a larger initiative to change school climate. Known as the Peaceable Schools Initiative, this effort includes in-service training for teachers on peaceable classroom practices, student-led programs to improve climate, and community intervention. The consequent shift in school climate may positively affect the marginalized students in the school, who are most likely to fight and get suspended.

The ASVB has several attractive features for schools. First, because it is an off-campus program, attendance does not result in any missed classes. Second, because of its fee-for-service arrangement, it costs the school very little. Local agencies wishing to strengthen their ties to a high school bear the cost to set up and deliver the program. This arrangement presupposes that most families have the means to pay a modest fee and that an agency can deliver the service for that cost. With lower income families, the school may have to provide scholarships for some students. These costs may well be offset by the lower administrative costs that result because students who complete the program are disciplined less frequently.

Perry A. Zirkel

A Web of Disruption?

In spring 1998, when he was an eighth-grader at Nitschmann Middle School in Bethlehem, Pennsylvania, J.S. created a website on his home computer, on his own time. Titled "Teacher Sux," the website made derogatory comments about J.S.' algebra teacher, Kathleen Fulmer, and about the school's principal, Thomas Kartsotis. A page on the site titled "Why Fulmer Should Be Fired" listed these reasons: "She shows off her fat f—legs," "The fat f—smokes," and "She's a b—!" Related material included similar statements under the heading "Why Should She Die?"; a diagram of Fulmer with her head cut off, blood dripping from her neck, and morphing into Adolf Hitler; and solicitation to "give me $20.00 to help pay for the hit man." A page titled "Why Does Kartsotis Suck?" stated: "He sees Mrs. Derrico [principal of a nearby school] naked," and "He f—Mrs. Derrico." Although not password-protected, the website contained a disclaimer that required agreement that the visitor was not a member of the school district's faculty or administration and that the visitor did not intend to disclose the identity of or cause trouble for the website creator.

On or about May 12, a Nitschmann teacher learned of the website through an anonymous e-mail and promptly reported it to Kartsotis. After viewing portions of the site, Kartsotis notified the superintendent and the school's technology specialist. He also convened a faculty meeting in which he announced that there was a problem in the school, but he did not disclose the nature of it. He separately informed Fulmer, who subsequently began to show stress, anxiety, and loss of well-being. She lost weight and sleep, feared going out of the house and mingling in crowds, and—despite getting a prescription for an antidepressant—was unable to return to school at the end of the year.

On May 13, Kartsotis and his staff questioned 17 students, who pointed to J.S. as the creator of the website. Kartsotis also immediately contacted the local police and the FBI. Both agencies conducted investigations and were able to identify J.S. as the website creator.

On May 16, after learning of the school investigations, J.S. voluntarily removed the website. The website counter showed that it had been viewed approximately 234 times, and the website's contents revealed that other students had added their own derogatory comments.

On or about July 30, district officials sent J.S.' parents written notification of their intent to suspend him for three days based on his violation of three

From *Phi Delta Kappan*, vol. 82, no. 9, May 2001, pp. 717–718. Copyright © 2001 by Phi Delta Kappan. Reprinted by permission. References omitted.

rules in the district's student code of conduct: threat to a teacher, harassment of a teacher and a principal, and disrespect to a teacher and a principal. After an informal hearing on the suspension, the district opted to extend the period to 10 days, effective at the beginning of the 1998–99 school year. Shortly thereafter, the district commenced expulsion proceedings.

The hearing did not start until August 19 because of the schedule of the parents' attorney. Kartsotis testified that the effect of the website was worse than anything he had encountered in his 40 years of experience, including his 15 years as Nitschmann's principal. He also testified that Fulmer's inability to return to the classroom and the consequent use of substitutes disrupted the education of her students. When the hearing ran rather late into the evening, the school board offered to continue the testimony of its witnesses to the next date, but J.S.' father requested another day because he was unavailable the next day. The board scheduled the continuation for August 26, despite the parents' objection that they had enrolled their son in a private school out of state and that he would not be returning until Thanksgiving.

On August 31, after completing the hearing, the school board concluded that the statement about a "hit man" constituted a threat, the statements regarding Kartsotis and Fulmer constituted harassment of and disrespect to a teacher and a principal, and the effects on Fulmer and other members of the school community were harmful. Consequently, the board voted to permanently expel J.S.

On 1 October 1998, J.S.' parents filed suit on his behalf in state trial court, claiming that the district's decision violated his constitutional rights. On 17 August 1999, the trial court affirmed the school board's decision. Undaunted, the parents filed for appeal with the Commonwealth Court.

On 14 July 2000, the Commonwealth Court issued a 2-to-1 decision in favor of the school district. As for First Amendment speech, the majority concluded 1) that, in accordance with Tinker and its progeny, school officials may discipline students for off-campus expressive conduct that substantially interferes with the educational process; and 2) that the effect of the website, including Fulmer's continuing medical leave and the invitation to other students for their input, constituted such interference. Regarding the website statements as reasonably perceived as disturbing, the majority commented: "Regrettably, in this day and age where school violence is becoming more commonplace, school officials are justified in taking very seriously threats against faculty and other students."

The court found J.S.' procedural due process arguments to be flimsy. Specifically, the court concluded that, within the context of an expulsion hearing, 1) he had received adequate discovery; 2) the parents did not have the right to postpone the hearing to "counsel-shop" for an additional, specialized attorney; 3) similarly, they had no right to a three-month postponement based on J.S.' enrollment elsewhere; and 4) the initial delay in the expulsion decision was reasonable and nonprejudicial.

Next, the majority rejected J.S.' 14th Amendment equal protection claim, agreeing with the trial court that the contents of his website "do not constitute constitutionally protected speech and are, therefore, subject to a rational basis test" and dismissing the argument of differential treatment in light of "any evidence upon which we could conclude that other students were involved in the present situation or others like it."

Finally, the court rejected the family's various other arguments, including those concerning the website disclaimer and J.S.' common-law right to privacy. The court viewed the disclaimer as practically ineffective, because it does not limit access to the site and does not forewarn the viewer of its offensive nature, and as legally ineffective, because it "does not create a contract between [J.S.] and the viewer and does not create any rights thereunder that could be renounced." Similarly, the court concluded that J.S. had no expectation of privacy once he posted the website on the Internet, at least without effective password protection.

The dissenting judge expressed disagreement only with the majority's First Amendment analysis. Specifically, he viewed the proper test of an unprotected, true threat as "whether a reasonable person in Student's position would foresee that viewers of the web site would interpret it as a serious expression of intent to harm." Applying this test, he concluded that the student's age, his disclaimer, and the responses of the other students—which were typical of young people's reactions to the "sick humor . . . in some of today's popular television programs, such as South Park"—preponderantly proved that J.S. did not intend Fulmer, Kartsotis, or other school staff members to even view the site—much less to see it as a serious threat to harm them. Further, the dissenting judge pointed to the district officials' delay in charging J.S. with any offense (recall that they waited from mid-May, when they quickly found out that J.S. was responsible for the website, until late July, well after the local police and the FBI had completed their investigations and declined to initiate criminal proceedings) as confirming evidence that the district did not regard him as a true threat. Although recognizing the dangers of violence in schools, the judge suggested the need to "strike a delicate balance" with the constitutional circumstances, which included the inevitable naiveté of adolescent children and the belated overreaction of school authorities.

~◉~

Reporting that the family has sought review by the Pennsylvania Supreme Court, Attorney Robert Sletvold, who represented J.S. in this case, maintains that "the final chapter is not finished." Pointing out that the odds are slim that the court will take the case and reverse the lower court, Attorney Jeffrey Tucker, who represented the school district, counters: "Via the Internet or not, students cannot threaten, defame, or harass employees under the guise of First Amendment expression, and when such conduct is off-campus, it is subject to discipline where there is a nexus to school."

In any event, this decision is another illustration of the judicial view that subordinates students' rights to school safety. Paralleling the Ninth Circuit's 1996 "true threat" case, which involved an incident that took place in school, and the Seventh Circuit's 1998 "hacking article" case, which implicated the power of technology, this state appeals court decision in 2000 reflects the older generation's reaction to students' sick humor on the Web. Nevertheless, depending on the facts of the case and the judges on the court, other published court decisions concerning student websites are more in line with the dissenting judge in J.S.' case.

This decision also illustrates that a single set of facts can generate more than one case. Here, in addition to this suit, J.S. filed a separate civil rights suit against the district, principal Kartsotis counter-claimed for emotional distress, and teacher Fulmer separately sued J.S. and his family for defamation, invasion of privacy, and various other common-law torts. According to a recent news article, the trial court threw out the family's second suit, the family settled the suit with Kartsotis for an undisclosed amount, and a jury awarded Fulmer $500,000 based on invasion of privacy and negligent supervision.

Finally, this decision reveals the need for care in developing and applying policies relating to the use of the Internet. Given the burgeoning technology, new issues continue to arise. For example, in a recent case, a New Hampshire judge ruled that a parent has a right under the state's Right-to-Know Law to inspect logs of Internet sites visited via district computers as long as administrators remove any information that would identify student visitors.

For students, parents, teachers, and administrators, the message that accompanies the litigation arising from J.S.' semiprivate expression of frustration seems to be: "The Internet can be wonderful, but beware of being caught in the Web."

POSTSCRIPT

Are Suspensions and Expulsions Viable Responses to Violent Behaviors?

Are suspensions and expulsions a necessary response to violent or aggressive behaviors? Are they appropriate? If so, when are they appropriate? Most experts would agree that suspensions and expulsions do not generally produce significant changes in the attitudes, perceptions, and general behaviors of students.

Various national entities are raising awareness and seeking to provide funds and services to decrease the level of violence that school staff and students experience. For example, The U.S. Department of Health and Human Services, the U.S. Department of Justice, and the U.S. Department of Education have partnered to sponsor a federal grant that seeks to promote schools that are "safe, disciplined and drug free," The main components of the grant (Safe Schools/Healthy Students) are proactive, including violence, drug, and mental health prevention and intervention programs, safe school policies, and early childhood emotional and developmental services.

In a policy statement on school violence, the National Association of School Psychologists promote creating a safe school environment by forming school-community partnerships, promoting positive school climate and positive discipline, as well as seeking to intervene with students who are displaying behavioral difficulties.

As school administrators and the educational system as a whole continue to decrease school violence, the methods utilized will likely have an impact on the effectiveness of the interventions. It would be ideal to cease all school violence or aggressive acts within schools so that all students and staff experience a safe educational environment. However, if schools are a reflection of society and families, it is unlikely that all aggression will be eliminated in the near future. In light of this, what place do suspensions and expulsions have within our schools?

For further information on this issue, see B.L. Townsend, "The Disproportionate Discipline of African American Learners: Reducing School Suspensions and Expulsions," *Exceptional Children* (vol. 66, no. 3, 2000, pp. 381–391), T. Walker, "Catch Them Before They Fall: A Kentucky School District Bucks the Trend Toward Exclusionary Discipline," *Teaching Tolerance* (vol. 18, 2000, pp. 32–37), G.G. Bear, A.R. Cavalier, and M.A. Manning, "Best Practices in School Discipline." In A. Thomas and J. Grimes, eds., *Best Practices in School Psychology*, 4th ed. (The National Association of School Psychologists, 2002), and S. Black, "Locked Out: Why Suspension and Expulsion Should Be Your Last Resort," *American School Board Journal* (vol. 16, no. 1, 1999, pp. 34–37).

ISSUE 21

Is Student Restraint Ever Justifiable?

YES: Joseph B. Ryan and Reece L. Peterson, from "Physical Restraint in School," *Behavioral Disorders* (February 2004)

NO: Sandy K. Magee and Janet Ellis, from "The Detrimental Effects of Physical Restraint as a Consequence for Inappropriate Classroom Behavior," *Journal of Applied Behavior Analysis* (Winter 2001)

ISSUE SUMMARY

YES: Joseph B. Ryan and Reece L. Peterson, professors at the University of Nebraska–Lincoln, support the use of physical restraint in the public schools with the proviso that schools ensure that teachers receive training in physical restraint, that they create standards for the use of restraint procedures, that they maintain records about who is restrained, and that they require notifying parents and administrators.

NO: Sandy K. Magee and Janet Ellis, professors at the University of North Texas, oppose the use of physical restraint in schools due to its detrimental effects, including the escalation of the very behavior it was designed to reduce.

Since the passage of the Individuals with Disabilities Education Act and the inclusion movement, educators in the regular classroom and in public school settings have had to utilize added techniques for managing individual students with significant emotional and behavioral difficulties. One such method that has become somewhat commonplace is the physical restraint of students. Physical restraint has traditionally been used in hospital, clinical, and law enforcement settings. However, it is now also more prevalent in public school settings.

Physical restraint can be defined as restricting a person's movements by the use of physical force. It is typically done for prevention or intervention when a person is upset or agitated and is in jeopardy of hurting him/herself or others. One common type of physical restraint is the basket hold. It is performed by an adult holding a child from behind, grasping the child's wrists and crossing their arms across the child's chest while bringing the child to a seated position by sliding the child down across the adult's thigh. A successful basket hold will maintain and control the child's physical activity.

One of the controversies regarding physical restraint is whether or not it is safe. Instances of physical restraint frequently involve students whose behavior has become aggressive. When an adult decides that restraint is needed, the adult is at risk of being hit, kicked, or bitten by a student while in the process of trying to restrain, especially if the adult is restraining without proper training. In addition, when trying to restrain a student who has become aggressive, the student could be injured because of the physical nature of the incident, especially when the student feels like he or she is trying to be controlled. In these instances it is often a natural inclination to fight back. Considering these risks, is restraining students worth the risk? Should educators place themselves in a situation where they and/or the student can be injured? What kind of liability is this for educators?

A second controversy is whether or not it is an effective practice. Magee and Ellis review data on students where physical restraint was used as a method in behavior management. The results indicated that physical restraint elevated unwanted behavior, but certainly did not have the desired effect. More positive behavior did not occur as a result of physical restraint.

On the other hand, what are educators to do when students are aggressive and destructive to themselves, others, and/or the environment? In an instance where a student is harming someone or something and his or her behavior is out of control, how do you stand back and not do anything? How can that be acceptable? Within their article, Ryan and Peterson discuss advocacy statements from various organizations in regard to physical restraint as well as their own recommendations toward the use of physical restraint in schools. They recognize the need for training in this area but also view physical restraint as a viable intervention in the schools. The authors also offer a handful of areas to be addressed by educators in order to utilize physical restraint and maintain the safety of all under these circumstances.

YES ↵

Joseph B. Ryan and
Reece L. Peterson

Physical Restraint in School

A headline of the Austin, Texas, *American-Statesman Staff* stated that a 14-year-old boy died after being restrained in a classroom by his teachers. According to a preliminary autopsy, the child succumbed to an intense amount of pressure to his chest (Rodriguez, 2002). Unfortunately, newspapers across the nation carry similar stories. The exact number of deaths caused by physical restraint remains in dispute. The *Hartford Courant,* a Connecticut newspaper, reported that 142 restraint-related deaths, 33% of which were caused by asphyxia, occurred in the United States over a 10-year period. The U.S. Government Accounting Office (GAO) stated in 1998 that an accurate estimate was impossible because only 15 states had established reporting procedures for such incidents. Based on the information available, the GAO estimated that there were 24 restraint-related deaths in the United States among children and adults in 1998. More recently, the Child Welfare League of America (CWLA) estimated that between 8 and 10 children in the United States die each year due to restraint, while numerous others suffer injuries such as bites, damaged joints, broken bones, and friction burns. There is no precise way to measure the number or extent of the injuries to children and also to staff as a result of the use of restraint.

In this article we review and provide a brief summary of research literature, legislation, and court decisions related to physical restraint used in school settings. We also identify position statements and recommended practices from nationally recognized professional organizations and advocacy groups. Finally, we make recommendations regarding needs for research, policy, and procedures for the use of physical restraint in schools.

Definition

As a professional term, *restraint* is defined as any physical method of restricting an individual's freedom of movement, physical activity, or normal access to his or her body. The term is sometimes used to address three different types of restraint procedures: mechanical, ambulatory, and chemical. *Mechanical restraint* entails the use of any device or object (e.g., tape, tiedowns, calming blanket, body carrier) to limit an individual's body movement to prevent or manage out-of-control behavior. *Ambulatory restraint* is also known as manual

From *Behavioral Disorders*, 29(2), excerpted February 2004, pp. 154–168. Copyright © 2004 by CCBD Publications. Reprinted by permission. References omitted.

restraint or "therapeutic holding." It involves one or more people using their bodies to restrict another individual's body movement as a means for reestablishing behavioral control and establishing and maintaining safety for the out-of-control client, other clients, and staff. Finally, *chemical restraint* uses medication to control behavior or restrict a patient's freedom of movement. This type of restraint is typically used only in institutional or hospital programs; it has evolved only in the past 40 years as a result of developments in psychotropic medications.

Today, physical restraint is used in numerous professional settings including medical and psychiatric facilities, law enforcement and correctional facilities, and schools. These different types of restraint can be used with both adults and children in the event of emergency situations stemming from aggressive, violent, or dangerous behavior or as a precaution against such behavior.

The primary focus of this article is on the use of ambulatory or manual restraint as an intervention by educators in schools. There are numerous instances in which mechanical restraint has been used in educational settings, but its use will be addressed only in the context of some court decisions and policies that relate to physical restraint. While some might include confinement, such as that which occurs in time-out rooms, as a form of mechanical restraint, it is beyond our scope to address that controversial issue here. Since chemical restraint is not typically used in schools, it is not addressed here.

History

The use of physical restraint originated in the psychiatric hospitals of France during the late 18th century. Restraint procedures were developed by Philippe Pinel and his assistant Jean Baptiste Pussin for the same intent it is used today, as a means of preventing patients from injuring themselves or others. From their initial usage, mechanical and manual restraint have been controversial procedures. Almost immediately after the procedures became popular, a non-restraint movement was started in England in an attempt to prevent physical and often brutally aversive mechanical restraint from being used on psychiatric patients in hospitals. In response, a Lunacy Commission was established in 1854 to monitor and regulate the use of seclusion and restraint in asylums. In contrast to England's decreased use of restraint during this time frame, the United States viewed physical restraint as a form of therapeutic treatment and adopted it as an accepted practice for dealing with violent patients.

For many years, law enforcement and correctional agencies have employed physical restraint and related conflict deescalation procedures as tools in apprehending and managing prisoners. Physical restraint also has a long history in hospitals and psychiatric institutions, particularly in the clinical treatment of violent persons. The use of physical restraint has been applied to children with emotional disturbance since the 1950s, and it was included in a list of "techniques for the antiseptic manipulation of surface behavior" compiled by Redl and Wineman. Redl and Wineman stated explicitly that physical restraint should not be used as, nor should it be associated with, physical punishment. They stated that a child's loss of control should be viewed as an emergency situation in which the educator or clinician should either remove the child from the scene or prevent the child from doing physical damage to himself or herself or others. The person performing the restraint should remain calm, friendly, and affectionate while attempting to maintain a positive relationship with the child, thereby providing the opportunity for therapeutic progress once the child's crisis subsides. . . .

Use of Restraint in Education

Once thought of as an exclusive tool of psychiatric institutions, physical restraint has been thrust into the mainstream of public education. This is, in part, due to the Individuals with Disabilities Education Act (IDEA), which established the principle of serving children with special needs in the least restrictive environment. Many students with emotional or behavioral problems, regardless of disability label, are now being included in public school environments, frequently in general education schools and classes. The physical restraint procedures have moved with the students to more typical school and classroom settings. In addition, because of high-profile media attention, schools are now challenged to demonstrate practices that prevent or contain challenging and sometimes violent behaviors. Physical restraint may be one element of these practices. . . .

Research on Restraint

We conducted an extensive search to identify articles related to physical restraint. We searched computer databases of the Education Resources Information Center (ERIC), LEGALTRAC, psychINFO, and FindArticles for relevant articles. Keywords used in the computer search included *restraint, physical restraint, therapeutic holding, ambulatory restraint,* and *mechanical restraint.* In addition, we conducted a hand search of studies published between 1970 and 2002 from the following journals: *Journal of Psychosocial Nursing, Journal of Special Education, Journal of Emotional and Behavioral Disorders, Behavioral Disorders,* and *Exceptional Children.* Finally, we performed an ancestral search by checking the citations from relevant studies to determine whether any of the articles cited would qualify for inclusion in this review. Literature related to restraint in the field of geriatrics was not reviewed.

After conducting an extensive search, we identified 26 articles. These included three articles that reviewed the legal aspects of restraint and five articles reviewing the use of physical restraint. While there were 15 experimental research studies investigating the use of restraint with children, only 3 were conducted in school settings. The majority of studies were conducted in either a psychiatric facility or a hospital.

The last five studies were conducted with children and adolescents suffering from severe autism or mental retardation and focused on attempting to reduce the use of mechanical restraint for the prevention of self-injurious behaviors. Finally, we found eight position papers offering guidelines for the proper use of restraint with children.

Prevalence of the Use of Physical Restraint

After an extensive search, we were unable to identify any research indicating how widespread the use of restraint in schools has become. Anecdotal information based on court cases and legislation seems to indicate that it has become common at least for larger school system to have some staff performing physical restraint in public school settings.

While studies regarding the prevalence of physical restraint procedures in more restrictive settings were also limited, Day (2002) asserted that the use of these procedures in residential settings has become commonplace. A survey of frontline child care workers from psychiatric facilities found that restraint was used frequently, with 34% of staff reporting to have used these procedures more than twice per week. Currently the accreditation of psychiatric hospital programs requires written procedures and training on these topics, presumably meaning that these procedures are commonplace in these settings as well. An early study conducted within an adolescent psychiatric unit found that 23% of the population experienced at least one restraint during an 18-month period. Additional findings of interest included higher occurrences of restraint on Mondays and Fridays due to what the authors called "weekend anxiety." Researchers also reported that restraint was more common among younger children, perhaps because they possess fewer mechanisms for coping with frustration. Male staff members were more likely to initiate restraint than females.

One study performed by Persi and Pasquali tracked the frequency of physical restraint used among 281 children ages 4 to 17 who were placed in four different types of segregated settings: psychiatric inpatient unit, residential group home, day treatment program, and day treatment program located in community schools. The study found that 107 restraints were performed throughout the year. The incidence of restraint varied among settings, with the group home and day treatment programs using the procedure more frequently than either the community day treatment program or inpatient unit. The study also found that males were slightly more likely to be restrained than females, and there was a mild significant relationship between age and restraint. Researchers did not find a linear relationship with age but noted that the onset of adolescence brought about an abrupt increase in the level of restraint administered. Surprisingly, in direct contrast to earlier findings, the study found that female staff initiated a larger number of restraints than their male counterparts. When comparing the use of restraint among placement settings, the study concluded that the pattern of physical restraint in actual settings is highly variable and difficult to explain, requiring additional studies.

Physical restraint has not been researched as an educational intervention. A review of literature found several journals that had published articles regarding restraint, but most articles focused on addressing the controversial nature of the procedure. One of the first studies on reducing restraint was performed by Swett, Michaels, and Cole, who investigated whether the passage of a Massachusetts state law addressing restraint effectively reduced the number of chemical restraints and seclusionary procedures used in a juvenile psychiatric facility. The researchers found that while the number of chemical restraints had decreased significantly, the number of physical restraints had actually increased. A later study, by Berrios and Jacobowitz, was conducted in a psychiatric inpatient unit with children ranging in age from 5 to 12 years being restrained with therapeutic holds (e.g., ambulatory restraints). The study claimed that therapeutic holding reduced the duration of a child's behavioral episode only slightly but was effective in reducing the number of other restraints performed by 15.9%.

Situations or Behaviors That Prompt Use of Restraint

We identified only one study that examined the circumstances when physical restraint was employed. Researchers debriefed both staff and clients following 81 incidents of restraint in a psychiatric hospital setting. Findings of interest included staff reporting that 65% of restraints were initiated due to a perceived safety threat, while 19% were the direct result of patient noncompliance. An interesting finding from patient interviews was that a staff member threatening time-outs was a causal factor for escalated levels of aggressive behavior. This may suggest that patients perceive time-outs as a coercive intervention.

Unfortunately, no similar studies were performed in a school environment. What is recognized by the professional community is that physical restraint is a widely used protective procedure, often implemented for a variety of reasons including prevention of violence, self-injurious behavior, and injury or property damage due to temper tantrums, as well as a response to noncompliance. However, physical restraint has long been considered to be a behavior management technique appropriate for teachers when crisis behavior occurs, and it may be used for a much wider set of student behaviors such as preventing children from leaving a classroom or school grounds or from destroying private or school property. One study conducted with teachers of students with emotional or behavioral disorders (E/BD) in public schools found that many had used restraint either as part of a planned behavioral intervention or as a spontaneous reaction to aggressive behavior. The study reported that 71% of these teachers used physical restraint with their students if they displayed aggression toward others, 40% to prevent self-abuse, and 34% to prevent destruction of property.

Efficacy of Restraint Procedures

Despite the belief that physical restraint is a commonly used procedure in schools serving children with E/BD, little is known about its efficacy, due to a lack of research. Few of the proponents of physical restraint have claimed that the procedure has any therapeutic value in and of itself. However, proponents of therapeutic holding justify restraint procedures through the attachment theory developed during the early to mid 1970s. Day reviewed these theories and for the most part concluded that there was very little empirical support for therapeutic benefits to children receiving restraint. Most of the studies located were of poor quality and relied upon "unverifiable, and hence questionable, anecdotal evidence and case reports." There was also no evidence for any potential side effects of restraint. While some might believe that children diagnosed with E/BD who are exposed to restraint on a daily basis could be humiliated by such highly aversive procedures, there is no scientific evidence of psychological damage or harm beyond the clear physical danger of injury or death. Instead, restraint is usually viewed as a physical safety mechanism that may permit continuation of other therapeutic interventions once the restraint is completed. Most educational textbooks dealing with aggressive or violent behavior of students with E/BD suggest that physical restraint might be warranted for purposes of safety despite a lack of empirical research supporting such claims.

Summary of Research

Very little research has been conducted on the prevalence, appropriate applications, or efficacy of physical restraint. Almost no research has been conducted on the use of restraint in school settings. We do not know how widely physical restraint is used in the schools, the extent or nature of injuries occurring when it has been used in the schools, or its effectiveness in achieving the desired outcomes.

Policy Related to Restraint

An extensive search was conducted to identify court or hearing officer decisions, as well as legislation related to physical restraint. To identify cases that have dealt with restraint, we conducted a search of legal databases (i.e., *Federal Supplement,* which lists all Federal Trial Court decisions; *Federal Reporter 3rd Series,* listing all Middle Appellate Court decisions; *United States Reports,* the official publication for all U.S. Supreme Court rulings; LEGALTRAC, a database that indexes law reviews and other legal periodicals; *Individuals with Disabilities Education Law Report* [IDELR], a specialty law reporter that publishes case law specific to special education, including some hearing officer reports). The results of this search are described in the following sections.

Legislation

The passage of the Children's Health Act of 2000 established national standards regarding the use of physical restraint with children in psychiatric facilities. Unfortunately, this legislation did not affect schools. Five states—Massachusetts, Colorado, Illinois, Connecticut, and Texas—have passed legislation over the past several years addressing the use of physical restraint with children in the school environment. Texas is the most recent state to do so (Amendments to 19 TAC Chapter 89, 2002), while one additional state, Maryland, has proposed legislation on this topic. Although state guidelines differ, the legislation typically contains many similar elements including (a) definitions of terms common to physical restraint, (b) required procedures and training for staff, (c) conditions when physical restraint can and cannot be used, (d) guidelines for the proper administration of physical restraint, and (e) reporting requirements when restraint is employed.

Court and Hearing Officer Decisions

Over the years, parents and advocacy groups have filed numerous lawsuits and/or grievances against school districts and psychiatric units regarding the use of restraint on children. Plaintiffs have typically argued that restraint violates an individual's rights under the Eighth Amendment, which prohibits administering cruel or unusual punishment, and the Fourteenth Amendment, which provides for an individual's liberty interests in freedom of movement and personal security. Cases resulting from these complaints have been lodged through state education agency hearings (e.g., under IDEA or state school disciplinary laws), with the Office for Civil Rights (OCR) in the U.S. Department of Education, and through state and federal court cases. . . .

Court rulings can be grouped into four general categories pertaining to the use of physical restraint: (a) decisions affecting the use of mechanical restraint; (b) decisions affecting the use of ambulatory or manual restraint; (c) professional training pertaining to staff who perform restraint; and (d) individual rights related to the Eighth and Fourteenth Amendments, Section 504, and ADA.

Mechanical and Ambulatory Restraint

The preponderance of rulings by the courts, SEAs, and OCR found the use of any type of mechanical restraint other than a time-out or tray chair to be unacceptable and in clear violation of a student's individual rights. . . . In contrast, the courts, SEAs, and OCR have consistently found that ambulatory restraint may be used without violating an individual's rights or threatening the individual's safety. . . .

Professional Training

In *Wyatt v. King*, the U.S. Circuit Court determined that staff working with individuals with mental illness required specific training regarding interventions germane to their unique care. The Court stated that training should include psychopharmacology, psychopathology, and psychotherapeutic interventions, as well as interviewing and assessment procedures for determining a patient's mental status. These findings have since been supported by national training prevention programs, which advertise that intensive staff training in schools has reduced assaultive incidences by 80% and resulted in a 77% reduction in disruptive incidents. Similarly, the states of Pennsylvania and Delaware experienced a 90% reduction in the use of physical restraint in their state mental health facilities after instituting intensive staff training programs. Training included crisis management and crisis prevention procedures for staff, as well as extensive training on methods for determining when and how to conduct physical restraint. Texas legislation now requires school personnel who use restraint to be trained; its supporting technical assistance materials have identified critical components for training programs. Courts, hearing officers, and legislation strongly support adequate training before these procedures are employed.

Individual Rights

Numerous court cases have addressed patient rights. This section provides a synopsis of all decisions pertaining to an individual's rights regarding the Eighth and Fourteenth Amendments, Section 504, and ADA. In essence, the courts have ruled that institutions must take into account a patient's rights at all times and that any restrictions to individual liberties must be in their best interest. . . . Perhaps the most influential decision regarding the use of restraint came from the Supreme Court decision *Youngberg v. Romeo* (1982). The court emphasized its concern that the judicial system should not invade the province of those whose job it is to make medical and custodial decisions. This case was critical in establishing a precedent for the establishment of procedures used to determine whether the use of physical restraint was considered reasonable and hinged on whether staff exercised professional judgment. Professional judgment, the court ruled, was to be considered presumptively valid. This presumption effectively shifted the burden of proof from the caretaker to the individual alleging that the imposition of restraint was unreasonable. However, to ensure the restraint was not being used improperly, the courts determined in *Converse v. Nelson* (1995) that inappropriate behavioral programs that constitute punishment disguised as treatment should be subject to analysis under Eighth Amendment standards. . . .

Summary

A review of state and federal policies regarding the use of physical restraint in schools has resulted in several findings: (a) limited forms of mechanical restraint are permitted; (b) ambulatory restraint performed with trained personnel is authorized; and (c) any agency, including schools, that uses restraint needs to provide professional training for staff who perform these procedures.

Advocacy Statements

While professional organizations and advocacy groups frequently hold differing opinions regarding specific issues, it is important to recognize areas of agreement to promote standardization and policy. Therefore, we reviewed and summarized position statements regarding the use of physical restraint from nationally recognized advocacy groups and professional organizations.

In 1998 the American Medical Association (AMA) reviewed existing restraint guidelines and attempted to coordinate the development of updated national guidelines for the safe and clinically appropriate use of restraint techniques for children and adolescents. In a 1999 report, the AMA supported the development and use of guidelines currently issued by the American Academy of Child and Adolescent Psychiatry (AACAP), the American Academy of Pediatrics, and the American Psychiatric Association regarding restraint, while encouraging future empirical studies on physical restraint with children and adolescents across all settings.

AACAP's policy statement suggests that institutions that use physical restraint establish procedures and policies addressing the circumstances in which restraint is permissible. AACAP also calls for documentation procedures, as well as inservice training requirements for all staff. They recommend that physical restraint be used only as an emergency intervention to maintain safety and that it be implemented in a manner sensitive to the child's particular developmental level, specific vulnerabilities, and overall treatment goals. The American Psychiatric Association policy statement is similar to AACAP's, but expresses concerns regarding Children's Health Act terminology, specifically that this legislation defines physical restraint so broadly that it essentially encompasses any unwanted touching that might reduce an individual's ability to move freely. This definition would classify commonly used escort procedures as a type of physical restraint.

Finally, the position statement by the International Society of Psychiatric and Mental Health Nurses (ISPN) claims that restraint should be used as a last resort and only when less restrictive alternatives have failed. ISPN recommends that family members be informed immediately after the use of a restraint and that the child receive a debriefing from the care-givers in clear words that the child can understand. The organization claims the debriefing process is necessary to minimize negative effects related to patients' experiences of being restrained. ISPN also advocates training all staff members on the cycle of aggression, verbal intervention skills, and critical thinking strategies designed to select the least restrictive intervention that is best suited to the presenting needs of the child.

Parents and advocacy groups have argued for the outright banishment of physical restraint, claiming its usage unfit for man, woman, or beast. Many nationally recognized advocacy groups have posted position statements regarding the use of physical restraint on their Web sites. The National Alliance for the Mentally Ill recently posted a position statement supporting the Children's Health Act of 2000 regarding the use of physical restraint and proposed similar standards be established for schools. Another group, the Child Welfare League of America, called for a minimum national standard of training in behavior management techniques, especially in the area of deescalation. In addition, it called for future research to develop a better understanding of what crisis prevention models work best for specific situations. More recently, the Autism National Committee has called upon Congress and state legislatures to limit the use of restraint on children with disabilities to brief, emergency situations involving serious threat of injury to the person with disabilities or to others. They are also asking for standardized reporting procedures following a restraint, with an investigation of circumstances leading to the incident to develop supports and accommodations for the prevention of future restraint.

Recommendations for Use of Physical Restraint in School Settings

After reviewing the compilation of research, legislation, case law, and position statements regarding the use of physical restraint, it appears that schools should use extreme caution when contemplating the use of physical restraint procedures. The following recommendations regarding restraint procedures, staff training, notification, and monitoring seem to combine the best practices emerging from our review and would be appropriate for any school that would employ physical restraint.

Restraint Procedures

Restraint should never be performed as a means of punishment or to force compliance from a student. In addition, physical restraint procedures should never be performed by untrained personnel. Through numerous rulings, the courts have established that very limited forms of mechanical restraint are permissible with students in a school setting and that physical or ambulatory restraint should be administered only when the safety of the student, peers, or staff members is at risk.

When physical restraint is administered, staff must use the safest method available, using the minimal amount of force necessary to protect the student and others from physical injury or harm. Once a restraint is used, it should be discontinued as soon as possible. In addition, no restraint should be administered in such a manner that prevents a student from breathing or speaking. The student's physical status, including respiration and skin color, should be monitored continuously throughout the restraint procedure.

Professional Training

All staff members who work with students with E/BD should be required to receive specialized training in conflict deescalation, crisis prevention, and behavior management techniques. Staff should receive specialized training and recurring updates in the use of physical restraint before any such procedures are used. Physical restraint should never be used unless the person doing it is trained specifically in the particular technique to be used. Training should include recognition of the various phases of the cycle of aggression, verbal deescalation strategies, and restraint and counseling procedures. Staff should also receive certification in first aid and cardiopulmonary resuscitation (CPR) in the event of an emergency related to restraint.

Reporting and Parent Notification

Procedures for reporting and notification should be in place. Following the administration of a physical restraint, a staff member who administered the restraint should verbally notify an administrator as soon as possible. Within 24 hours, a written report should be provided to the administrator responsible for maintaining an ongoing record of all physical restraint conducted by the school. In addition, the administrator should verbally inform the student's parents or guardians of the restraint as soon as possible. Written reports to the parents, including a description of the event and staff involved, should be postmarked no later than 3 working days following an incident.

Advocacy

Policies, procedures, and legislation, even if noble in intent, are all but meaningless if not enforced. The guidelines for schools regarding the use of physical restraint on children are the result of decades of professional practice, state and federal legislation, case law, and grassroots efforts by advocacy groups, all concerned with the safety of children. To ensure that empirically based best practices are developed and become common practice among schools, it is incumbent upon various professional and advocacy organizations to monitor and hold school districts (as well as other agencies) across the nation accountable. These organizations need to act as watchdog agencies monitoring the compliance of schools to ensure that children are kept out of harm's way. . . .

Conclusion

Due to the current risk of student injuries and the mortality rates associated with the use of physical restraint, immediate action is required to ensure that schools employing restraint do not jeopardize student safety. Based on the review of case law, legislation, and recommended procedures from both professional organizations and advocacy groups, there is a need for clear standards regarding the use of restraint procedures in schools, as well as mandatory training of staff before they use restraint. Improved and standardized record keeping and notification of administrators and parents of incidents in which restraint occurs are also important. Additional research is needed to define situations in which restraint is appropriate in schools, as well as its effectiveness in containing or preventing violent or destructive behavior. Unless these recommendations are heeded and action is taken, headlines will continue to appear across our nation describing these preventable fatalities.

Sandy K. Magee
and Janet Ellis

 **NO**

The Detrimental Effects of Physical Restraint as a Consequence for Inappropriate Classroom Behavior

Physical restraint is often used to manage severely disruptive classroom behavior. One form of physical restraint, called basket-hold time-out, involves confining the student in a chair or placing the student face down on the floor while restraining the student's arms. This form of physical restraint is used to protect the student or others or to punish problem behavior. Research findings on the basket-hold time-out indicate that it is effective in treating disruptive behavior.

Nevertheless, the use of physical restraint could be problematic if the function of problem behavior is not identified. Because of the close physical contact required to implement the basket-hold procedure, restraint could function as a positive reinforcer for problem behavior that is maintained by attention from others. Likewise, physical restraint may result in escape or avoidance of aversive events due to its incompatibility with most academic task requirements. The misapplication of procedures (i.e., focusing on procedural form rather than on its behavioral effects) has been evaluated with other common interventions, such as planned ignoring.

We hypothesized that the physical restraint used to manage 2 students' problem behavior in the classroom was contraindicated based on behavioral function. To test this hypothesis, we evaluated the effects of physical restraint as a consequence for problem behavior after results of typical functional analyses were inconclusive.

Method

Participants and Setting

Sid, a 13-year-old student who had been diagnosed with Down syndrome, engaged in physical aggression toward teachers and peers and sexual touching of female teachers. Paul, a 13-year-old student who had been diagnosed with mild mental retardation and cerebral palsy, used a wheelchair and engaged in

From *Journal of Applied Behavior Analysis*, vol. 34, no. 4, Winter 2001, pp. 501–504. Copyright © 2001 by Society for the Experimental Analysis of Behavior, Inc. Reprinted by permission. References omitted.

yelling, self-injury, and aggression toward teachers. All sessions were conducted at the participants' school in an unused classroom containing tables, chairs, desks, and materials necessary to conduct the experimental conditions.

Response Measurement and Reliability

Sid's target behaviors were defined as (a) *aggression:* hitting or kicking others, or throwing objects so that they made physical contact with others; and (b) *sexual touching:* touching others' buttocks or genital area. Paul's target behaviors were defined as (a) *yelling:* vocalizations above normal conversational volume; (b) *self-injury:* hitting his face with a closed fist or biting his hand; and (c) *aggression:* hitting, biting, or scratching others, or throwing objects so that they made physical contact with others. Data were collected using 10-s partial-interval recording. Interobserver agreement data were collected for 25% of sessions. Overall agreement averaged 92% for Sid and 80% for Paul.

Procedure

Functional analysis. Participants were exposed to four functional analysis conditions alternated in a multielement design, as described by Iwata, Dorsey, Slifer, Bauman, and Richman. Three to five daily 15-min sessions were conducted with each participant, 3 days per week. A different therapist conducted each condition. During the no-interaction condition, the student was in the room with a therapist who did not interact with him. During the attention condition, the therapist ignored the student but made statements describing the behavior following each occurrence of a target behavior (e.g., "You hit yourself," "You are yelling"). During play sessions, the therapist interacted continuously with the participant but withdrew attention for 30 s contingent on any target behavior. During the demand condition, the therapist delivered requests (e.g., "Write your name," "Count the dots") continuously for both subjects. With Sid, the therapist moved away and discontinued requests for 30 s contingent on occurrences of the target behavior. Paul was wheeled into a time-out area for 30 s following each target behavior.

Evaluation of physical restraint. Results of informal, naturalistic observations of each participant in the classroom prior to the functional analysis indicated that teachers used physical restraint several times each day following inappropriate behavior. Based on these observations, the effects of physical restraint (i.e., basket-hold time-out) on problem behavior were evaluated. The specific antecedents and consequences were analogous to those observed in the classroom. For Sid, the physical restraint condition was identical to the attention condition except that the therapist placed him face down on the floor and held his arms behind his back for 10 s contingent on target behavior. For Paul, procedures were identical to the demand condition except that following occurrences of the target behavior, the therapist folded his arms across his chest and held his wrists under his armpits for 10 s while he remained seated in his wheelchair. Physical restraint and play conditions were alternated in a multielement design.

Results and Discussion

Results of Sid's initial functional analysis [show] . . . problem behavior initially occurred in the attention and play conditions but decreased to zero across sessions. High levels of problem behavior occurred in the physical restraint condition. These findings suggested that physical restraint either maintained or evoked Sid's problem behavior.

For Paul, problem behavior occurred in both the attention and demand conditions but increased across sessions only in the demand conditions. These results suggested that escape from demands and possibly access to attention maintained Paul's problem behavior. High levels of problem behavior continued to occur in the demand condition when physical restraint was used. These results further suggested that Paul's problem behavior was maintained by escape from demands and that the use of physical restraint following occurrences of problem behavior was contraindicated because demands were briefly removed while restraint was applied. Based on these outcomes, physical restraint was discontinued in the classroom, and effective interventions involving differential reinforcement and extinction were identified for both students.

These findings highlight the importance of identifying and evaluating idiosyncratic events that may be functionally related to problem behavior, especially when initial assessment outcomes are unclear. For Sid, physical interaction rather than verbal attention was a positive reinforcer for problem behavior. Results for both participants also showed the detrimental effects of using physical restraint when this common classroom intervention is applied without regard for the function of problem behavior.

POSTSCRIPT

Is Student Restraint Ever Justifiable?

Physical restraint can certainly be used in some positive ways, but it remains controversial. Consider this small portion of a manuscript written by Wanda Mohr, Ph.D., RN; Theodore A. Petti, MD, MPH; and Brian Mohr, MD. The manuscript is entitled "Adverse Effects Associated with Physical Restraint" and was submitted to the Canadian Psychiatric Association.

> The practice of restraint puts both patients and staff at risk for injury and death. Moreover, restraints can be traumatic even when they do not result in injury and death. The 1998 *Hartford Courant* investigation noted that, between 1988 and 1998, 142 reported deaths in mental health settings were connected to the use of physical restraint. Those who died were disproportionately young children. The *Courant* observed that deaths occurred in all 50 states and that the statistics represented only reported documented deaths. This newspaper exposé, as well as a Sixty Minutes documentary of conditions in some psychiatric facilities, prompted a Congressional investigation that confirmed the risks inherent in the use of mechanical restraints.

The manuscript goes on to say that there is no true consensus regarding the causes of death and injury in relation to physical restraint in the research literature. In addition, the psychological literature does not comprehensively address the physiological responses to physical restraint, nor does it address the emotional arousal that can be compromising to a student in the instance of physical restraint. These authors certainly discuss the negative nature of physical restraint and imply that additional scientific information needs to be included in the research literature.

A final thought is this: If it is true that 142 deaths in mental health settings were connected to the use of physical restraint, what would the result have been in these cases if physical restraint had not been employed?

For more information, please refer to J. Cornwall, "Might Is Right? A Discussion of the Ethics and Practicalities of Control and Restraint in Education," *Emotional and Behavioural Difficulties* (vol. 5, no. 4, 2000, pp. 19–25), J.K. Mullen, "The Physical Restraint Controversy," *Reclaiming Children and Youth* (vol. 9, no. 2, 2000, pp. 92–94), American Academy of Child and Adolescent Psychiatry, *Policy Statement on the Prevention and Management of Aggressive Behavior in Psychiatric Institutions with Special Reference to Seclusion and Restraint* (American Academy of Child and Adolescent Psychiatry, 2000), R.J. Jones and G.T. Timbers, "Minimizing the Need for Physical Restraint and Seclusion in Residential Youth Care Through Skill-Based Treatment Programming," *Families in Society: The Journal of Contemporary Human Services* (vol. 84, no. 1, 2003, pp. 21–29), and D.M. Day, "Examining the Therapeutic Utility of Restraint and Seclusion of Children and Youth: The Role of Theory and Research in Practice,"*American Journal of Orthopsychiatry* (vol. 72, 2002, pp. 266–278).

Contributors to This Volume

EDITORS

ROBERT G. HARRINGTON, Ph.D., has been a full professor in the department of psychology and research in education at the University of Kansas for the past 25 years, training thousands of educators in classroom management, and he has also taught courses in behavior management for other major universities. Professor Harrington has served as president of the National Association of the Trainers of School Psychologists, and he has served three times as the president of the Association for Psychological and Educational Research in Kansas. One of his research interests is the impact of teacher stress on classroom management, and he is one of the developers of the Quality of Teacher Work Life Scale, which measures teacher stress. Professor Harrington is in demand as a keynote speaker for national conventions and for workshops on classroom management, student anger management, treatment of AD/HD, bully prevention, etc. In addition, he is very involved in parent education and has conducted many parent education workshops. For more information about workshop training, contact Psychoeducational Assessment Associates (PAA), (785) 841-3658.

LETICIA (TISH) A. HOLUB, Ph.D., completed her doctorate in school psychology at the University of Kansas and is a licensed child psychologist in the state of Kansas. Dr. Holub has worked in the public school setting in Kansas and Illinois for eleven years, serving students of all grade levels. Currently, Dr. Holub works as a school psychologist with USD 497 Lawrence, Kansas public schools, where she provides school consultative services to teachers and other professional staff working with students who are having behavior problems in the classroom. Dr. Holub has extensive experience with children of varying backgrounds, ethnicities, and disability types. In addition, Dr. Holub teaches courses in child and adolescent development at the University of Missouri–Kansas City, the University of Kansas, and Johnson County Community College (Overland Park, Kansas). She has worked within an elementary therapeutic classroom, and especially enjoys working with students with emotional and behavioral difficulties.

STAFF

Larry Loeppke	Managing Editor
Jill Peter	Senior Developmental Editor
Nichole Altman	Developmental Editor
Beth Kundert	Production Manager
Jane Mohr	Project Manager
Tara McDermott	Design Coordinator
Bonnie Coakley	Editorial Assistant
Lori Church	Permissions

AUTHORS

JALEEL ABDUL-ADIL, Ph.D., is an assistant professor of clinical psychology and associate director of the Disruptive Behavior Disorders Clinic in the department of psychiatry at the University of Illinois at Chicago. His primary research interests are children's mental health services research, childhood externalizing disorders, and community-based mental health.

K. ANGELEQUE AKIN-LITTLE, Ph.D., is an assistant professor of the School of Psychology at the University of the Pacific. Her research interests include applied behavior analysis, particularly the effects of extrinsic reinforcement on intrinsic motivation, professional issues, overscheduling, and systems change. She graduated from the University of Southern Mississippi.

AMY E. ASSEMANY, Ph.D., is a professor at the State University of New York at Albany. She is interested in the negative side effects of parent education programs.

MARC S. ATKINS, Ph.D., is a professor of psychology and director of psychology training in the department of psychiatry at the University of Illinois at Chicago. His primary research interests are children's mental services research, school-based mental health services, urban children and families, and childhood AD/HD and aggression.

KIRK A. BAILEY, Ph.D., is a professor at the Hamilton Fish Institute on School and Community Violence at George Washington University. He is interested in the legal implications of profiling students for violence.

KATHY BELAND is creative director for the Character Education Partnership and is the lead developer of Second Step: A Violence Prevention Curriculum (pre-K–grade 9). She is interested in student education about aggression and alternatives to anger.

SARA K. BESZTERCZEY is a graduate student in the doctoral program in clinical psychology at the University of Massachusetts at Boston.

SUSAN BLACK, Ph.D., is a contributing editor to *American School Board Journal*. She is an education research consultant, writes for several publications including *Scholastic Administrator*, and has contributed chapters to books on education.

DAVID A. BRENT, M.D., is currently academic chief of child and adolescent psychiatry at Western Psychiatric Institute and Clinic and is professor of psychiatry, pediatrics, and epidemiology at the University of Pittsburgh School of Medicine. He co-founded and now directs Services for Teens at Risk (STAR), a commonwealth of Pennsylvania-funded program for suicide prevention, education, or professionals, and the treatment of at-risk youth and their families. His work in the area of suicide has focused on the epidemiology of adolescent suicide, and he has helped identify the role of firearms, substance abuse, and affective disorders as risk factors for youth suicide.

DOUGLAS C. BREUNLIN, Ph.D., is a research professor at the Family Institute at Northwestern University. He is interested in school climate, strategies for personalizing the high school, and school violence prevention.

MICHELE BRIGHAM teaches high school special education and music at Albermarle County public schools in Charlottesville, Virginia.

SHANNON R. BRINKER is affiliated with the department of psychology at Bowling Green State University. She is interested in the social psychology of children's perceptions and their judgments about consequences for immoral behavior.

TARA L. BRYANT-EDWARDS is a professional counselor with Rape Victims Advocates. She is interested in conflict resolution and violent behavior.

GEORGE W. BUSH is the forty-third president of the United States of America. He was sworn into office in January 2001, reelected on November 2, 2004, and sworn in for a second term on January 20, 2005. Prior to his presidency, President Bush served for six years as the forty-sixth governor of Texas. He has signed into law a comprehensive educational reform called the No Child Left Behind Act of 2001, which calls for accountability, flexibility, local control, and more choices in education.

REGINA BUSSING is an associate professor and chief of the division of child and adolescent psychiatry, department of psychiatry, pediatrics, and health policy and epidemiology at the University of Florida. She is interested in teachers' attitudes and attributions toward students with disabilities.

ERIC CARBONE, Ph.D., is a professor in the department of teaching and learning at New York University. He is interested in teaching methods for students with disabilities.

SAM CHALTAIN is the coordinator of the Freedom Forum's First Amendment Schools Project in Arlington, Virginia. He is interested in the intersect between student rights and safe schools.

PAULA L. CHAPMAN, Ph.D., is a faculty member at Florida State University. She is interested in classroom issues related to young children.

ROCCO A. CIMMARUSTI is a research professor at the Family Institute at Northwestern University. He is interested in school climate, strategies for personalizing the high school, and school violence prevention.

MIKE CORDING is an educational consultant in Southport, England, who is interested in the theory and practice of classroom management.

JENNIFER COUZIN is a contributing author to *Science*. She is interested in side effects of children's antidepressants.

BENJAMIN DOWLING-SENDOR is an authority on school law and is an assistant appellate defender of North Carolina in Durham. He is interested in issues related to the enforcement of legal policies on student expression in schools.

TANYA L. ECKERT, Ph.D., is an associate professor in the department of psychology at Syracuse University. She is the associate editor of *School Psychology Review*. Her research interests include examining procedures for assessing academic and behavioral programs, developing classroom-based intervention, and measuring the acceptability of assessment and intervention procedures. She earned her Ph.D. from Lehigh University.

MAURICE J. ELIAS is a professor at Rutgers University and vice-chair of the leadership team of the Collaborative for Academic, Social, and Emotional Learning (CASEL).

DAVID ELKIND, Ph.D., is a professor emeritus at Tufts University in Medford, Massachusetts, and a prolific writer, researcher, and lecturer. He is perhaps best known for his popular books *The Hurried Child*, *All Grown Up and No Place to Go*, and *The Miseducation of Young Children*. Professor Elkind is past president of the National Association for the Education of Young Children. He currently is the co-host of the Lifetime television series, *Kids These Days*.

JANET ELLIS, Ph.D., received her doctorate from University of North Texas at Denton, where she is also a professor in the department of behavior analysis. Her research interests include applied behavior analysis and functional behavioral assessment.

RUTH ERVIN, Ph.D., is a professor at Western Michigan University. Her research interests include positive peer reporting to improve the social interactions of socially rejected students and social rejection in residential treatment settings.

STACY L. FRAZIER, Ph.D., is a visiting research assistant professor of psychology in psychiatry at the Institute of Juvenile Research in the department of psychiatry at the University of Illinois at Chicago. Her primary research interests are mental health services for children and families in poverty, school-based models for mental health services, and mental health benefits of after-school programs.

KARIN S. FREY, Ph.D., is director of research at the Committee for Children and associate research professor of education at the University of Washington. She is interested in the social psychology of changing adolescents' attitudes about aggression.

MONICA M. GARCIA, Ph.D., is a professor in the department of psychology at the University of Pittsburgh. She is interested in factors contributing to the development of conduct disorders in students.

FAYE A. GARY, Ph.D., is a distinguished service professor in the College of Nursing at the University of Florida.

LAUREL M. GARRICK DUHANEY, Ph.D., is an assistant professor in the department of educational studies at the State University of New York at New Paltz. Her research interest is in teaching violence prevention in a culturally sensitive manner.

CHARLES GO is a youth development advisor in Alameda, California. His research interest is on the effects of bully-proofing on the reduction of subsequent acts of delinquency.

SARA E. GOLDSTEIN is affiliated with the department of psychology at Bowling Green State University. She is interested in the development of moral reasoning in young children.

JENNIFER GORING is a research assistant at the Clinical and Research Program in Pediatric Psychopharmacology at Massachusetts General Hospital in Boston.

PATRICIA A. GRACZYK, Ph.D., is an assistant professor in the department of psychiatry at the University of Illinois at Chicago. Her primary research interests are children's mental health services research, school-based mental health, childhood anxiety and mood disorders, and children's social competence.

ROSS W. GREENE, Ph.D., is director of cognitive-behavioral psychology at the Clinical and Research Program in Pediatric Psychopharmacology at Massachusetts General Hospital in Boston and an associate professor of psychology in the department of psychiatry at Harvard Medical School. He is the co-director of the Center for Collaborative Problem-Solving, where he specializes in the treatment of explosive, inflexible, and easily frustrated children and adolescents and their families. He is a consultant at the Cambridge Hospital and the Somerville Hospital.

JUDY GROULX, Ph.D., is an associate professor in the department of educational foundations and administration in the School of Education at Texas Christian University. Her interests are in teacher preparation, especially in multicultural schools.

ROBERT G. HARRINGTON, Ph.D., is a professor in the department of psychology and research in education at the University of Kansas. His research interests are in the areas of behavior management of angry and defiant children and adolescents and related problems in home management. Professor Harrington is one of developers of the Quality of Teacher Work Life scale that is used to measure teacher stress related to classroom management. Professor Harrington is widely sought as a speaker for school district in-services on topics related to behavior management in the classroom.

KELLY HENDERSON, Ph.D., received her doctorate in special education at the University of Maryland in 1997 and is an educational research analyst at the U.S. Office of Special Education Programs (OSEP), where she works on OSEP's national studies and evaluations. Her primary research interests are special education policy, emotional, behavioral, and attention deficit disorders.

JOSHUA S. HETHERINGTON is a professional counselor with Community Family Services of Western Springs, Illinois, and is interested in training students and teachers in conflict-resolution strategies.

KIMBERLY HOAGWOOD, Ph.D., is director of research on child and adolescent services for the Office of Mental Health in the state of New York, and is professor of clinical psychology and psychiatry with the department of child psychiatry at Columbia University. Formerly she served as associate director of child and adolescent mental health research with the National Institute of Mental Health (NIMH), where she oversaw a broad range of scientific studies on child and adolescent mental health. Dr. Hoagwood has directed numerous research programs on children's clinical and educational services at NIMH, in Texas, and now New York. She earned her doctorate in school psychology in 1987 from the University of Maryland.

JENNIFER HOLLADAY is a program coordinator and survey developer for the journal *Teaching Tolerance*.

KEVIN JONES, Ph.D., is a professor at the University of Connecticut. His research includes increasing peer praise of socially rejected youth and interventions to improve cooperation and acceptance among adolescents.

TAI KATZENSTEIN is a graduate student in the doctoral program in clinical psychology at the University of California at Berkeley.

JAMES M. KAUFFMANN, Ph.D., is the Charles S. Robb Professor of Education, University of Virginia, Charlottesville. He is well known for his research and books on the topics of best practices in special education with special emphasis in the area of identification and treatment of students with behavioral disorders.

ALFIE KOHN is an author and lecturer. He is the author of eight books on education and human behavior including, *Punished by Rewards: The Trouble with Gold Stars, Incentive Plans, A's, Praise and other Bribes*; *The Schools Our Children Deserve*; and *What to Look for in a Classroom*.

TAWNYA KUMARAKULASINGAM, Ph.D., received her doctorate in school psychology from the University of Kansas in 2002. Currently, she is coordinator of school psychological services in the Scottsdale, Arizona schools. Her research interests are in the area of teacher stress and classroom management.

CHRISTINA E. LEON is a graduate assistant in the department of educational psychology, College of Education, at the University of Florida.

ELIZABETH A. LINNENBRINK, Ph.D., is an assistant professor of educational psychology in foundations of education at the University of Toledo. She has studied the effects of different motivational classroom contexts on student's emotional well-being, strategy use, and achievement and is interested in the interplay among motivation, affect, and cognition. She has applied this research to learning in cooperative groups in math and conceptual change in science understanding.

STEVEN G. LITTLE, Ph.D., is an associate professor at the University of the Pacific and is the departmental chair of the department of educational and school psychology. He has previously held academic positions in Alabama, Illinois, and New York. His research interests include teacher attributions for student behavior, applied behavior analysis, overscheduling of children and youth, and professional issues in school psychology. He received his Ph.D. in school psychology from Tulane University.

BENJAMIN J. LOVETT is a doctoral candidate in the school psychology program at Syracuse University.

JOHN W. MAAG, Ph.D., is a professor in the department of special education and communication disorders at the University of Nebraska–Lincoln. His research interests include parent education, managing child resistance, stress inoculation in children, and promoting children's social development in general education classrooms.

SANDY K. MAGEE, Ph.D., is a professor in the department of behavioral analysis at University of North Texas at Denton. She is interested in the detrimental effects of physical restraint as a consequence for inappropriate classroom behavior.

W. MICHAEL MARTIN is supervisor of the office of elementary education for the Loudon County (Virginia) public schools. He is interested in the application of zero-tolerance policies in the public schools.

KATHLEEN McGEE is a special education teacher at the high school level at Westerville (Ohio) public schools.

DAVID E. McINTOSH, Ph.D., is a professor at Ball State University. He is interested in behavioral parent training programs.

GALE M. MORRISON, Ph.D., is a professor in the graduate school of education at the University of California at Santa Barbara. She is interested in characteristics of students with disabilities who are recommended for expulsion from school, system indicators and expulsion, and student pathways through school discipline options.

SHELLEY MURDOCK is a community and youth development advisor in Pleasant Hill, California. Her research is on the cyclic relationship between bullying and victimization.

CHRISTINE E. NEDDENRIEP, Ph.D., is a professor at the University of Tennessee. Her research interests include bully prevention in the schools and development of prosocial skills in school-age children.

KENNETH PARK is a former research assistant at the Clinical and Research Program in Pediatric Psychopharmacology at Massachusetts General Hospital in Boston.

REECE L. PETERSON, Ph.D., is a professor at the University of Nebraska at Lincoln. He is interested in the management of severely disruptive student behavior in the public schools.

PAUL R. PINTRICH, Ph.D., (1953–2003), was a professor of education and psychology and chair of the combined program in education and psychology at the University of Michigan. Paul Pintrich published more than 120 articles and chapters and was co-author or co-editor of nine books, including the "Advance in Motivation and Achievement" series.

CHRISTINE A. READDICK, Ph.D., is an associate professor at Florida State University in the department of family and child sciences. Her research interests include young children's attributions about classroom management, as well as young children's perceptions of the larger world around them.

ROBERT REID, Ph.D., is an associate professor in the department of special education and communication disorders at the University of Nebraska, Lincoln.

HEATHER RINGEISEN, Ph.D., is chief of the child and adolescent services research program at the National Institute of Mental Health. This program directs and supports research on patterns of mental health service use, and the quality, organization, and financing of services for children with mental disorders; services provided in multiple sectors and settings, such as schools, primary care, child welfare, juvenile justice, and mental health; and the evaluation of innovative service-delivery models. Dr. Ringeisen received her Ph.D. in clinical child psychology from Auburn University in 1999.

SHERI L. ROBINSON, Ph.D., is a professor at the University of Texas at Austin. Her research interests include effects of positive statements made by peers on peer interactions, and social status of children in residential treatment settings.

JOSEPH B. RYAN, Ph.D., is a professor at the University of Nebraska at Lincoln. He is interested in issues related to physical restraint of students in school settings.

DANIEL S. SHAW is affiliated with the department of psychology at the University of Pittsburgh. He is interested in destructive sibling conflicts.

RUSSELL SKIBA, Ph.D., is a professor at Indiana University. He is interested in whether zero tolerance can lead to safe schools, comparative effects of prevention versus zero tolerance, race and gender bias in disciplinary policies, and disciplinary interventions in middle schools.

CHRISTOPHER H. SKINNER, Ph.D., is a professor at the University of Tennessee. His research interests include bullying, prevention of academic skill deficits, and interventions with interdependent group contingencies,

JEREMY SWINSON is a senior educational psychologist and honorary lecturer at Liverpool John Moores University. He is interested in issues in classroom management, especially assertive discipline.

CORNELL THOMAS, Ph.D., is an associate professor in the department of educational foundations and administration in the School of Education at Texas Christian University and special assistant to the chancellor for diversity and community. His interests are in the area of educational equity, urban education, and perceptual barriers to achieving in schools.

MARIE S. TISAK, Ph.D., is a professor in the department of psychology at Bowling Green State University. Her area of specialization is developmental psychology. Her research interests are in the areas of development of social cognition and social behavior, development of moral and social reasoning, reasoning about authority and peer relations, social reasoning among youth offenders, and development of aggressive behavior.

KATHLEEN VAIL, Ph.D., is an associate editor of the *American School Board Journal*. She is interested in the relationship between classroom management and parent education.

LEIHUA VAN SCHOIACK-EDSTROM is a research scientist at the Committee for Children. She is interested in relational and physical aggression in students.

HERBERT J. WALBERG, Ph.D., is research professor of education and psychology and university scholar at the University of Illinois at Chicago and a member of the CASEL leadership team.

MARGARET C. WANG (deceased 2000) was the director of the Mid-Atlantic Regional Educational Laboratory for Student Success and distinguished professor of education at Temple University.

DEBORAH E. WATKINS, Ph.D., is an assistant professor at York College of Pennsylvania in special education in the education department. Her area of expertise is working with prospective teachers on how to manage children with special needs who are behaviorally challenged. Her research interests include studying the interactions of children with AD/HD in peer collaborative groups.

ROGER P. WEISSBERG, Ph.D., is a professor of psychology and education at the University of Illinois at Chicago and executive director of CASEL.

KATHRYN R. WENTZEL, Ph.D., received her doctorate from Stanford University in 1987. She is a professor at the University of Maryland in the department of human development. Her research focuses on young adolescents' interpersonal relationships with parents, peers, and teachers and their motivation and social and academic adjustment to middle school.

JEANETTE WILLERT, Ph.D., is an assistant professor and coordinator of secondary education at Canisius College in Buffalo, New York. She is interested in issues related to the reinforcement of positive social habits to reduce school violence.

RICHARD WILLERT, Ph.D., has been a child and family therapist at Condrell Counseling Center in Orchard Park, New York. He is interested in factors related to the development of anger and violence in school-age students.

CYNTHIA WILSON GARVAN, Ph.D., is an assistant research professor in the department of statistics in the College of Medicine at the University of Florida.

EMILY B. WINSLOW is affiliated with the department of psychology at the University of Pittsburgh. She is interested in the development of aggressive behavior in students.

KIRSTEN E. YAGGI is affiliated with the department of psychology at the University of Pittsburgh. She is interested in conflicts between siblings.

JOSEPH E. ZINS, Ph.D., is a professor in the college of education at the University of Cincinnati and a member of the CASEL leadership team.

PERRY A. ZIRKEL, J.D., is Iacocca Professor of Education at Lehigh University. He is interested in educational law as it relates to the rights of students, teachers, and parents.